PEAK INJUSTICE

"I hope we've not reached Peak Dorling – we need Danny's wisdom and knowledge to help us root out injustice and work towards a better world."

Kate E. Pickett, University of York

"In this book, a world-class scholar of inequality convincingly makes the case that, despite everything, and not just perfunctorily, it's worth having hope."

Marcos González Hernando, UCL Social Research Institute and Universidad Diego Portales

"Danny Dorling embodies the conscience of the left in Britain, disappointed, angry but still hopeful. This book raises uneasy questions about prolonged social injustice. A new government should answer them."

Guy Standing FAcSS, SOAS University of London

PEAK INJUSTICE

Solving Britain's Inequality Crisis

Danny Dorling

First published in Great Britain in 2024 by

Policy Press, an imprint of
Bristol University Press
University of Bristol
1-9 Old Park Hill
Bristol
BS2 8BB
UK
t: +44 (0)117 374 6645
e: bup-info@bristol.ac.uk

Details of international sales and distribution partners are available at
policy.bristoluniversitypress.co.uk

British Library Cataloguing in Publication Data
A catalogue record for this book is available from the British Library

ISBN 978-1-4473-7261-5 paperback
ISBN 978-1-4473-7262-2 ePub
ISBN 978-1-4473-7263-9 ePdf

Cover design: Sarah-Louise Deazley
Front cover image: Sarah-Louise Deazley

Bristol University Press and Policy Press use environmentally responsible print partners.

FSC
www.fsc.org
MIX
Paper from responsible sources
FSC® C013604

Printed in and bound in Great Britain by CPI Group (UK) Ltd,
Croydon CR40 4YY

For Dawn Foster (1986–2021)
journalist, writer, and friend.

She said the things that others might have thought,
but were usually too afraid to say.

Dawn Foster Forever

Contents

List of figures and tables

Figures

Tables

Acknowledgements

I would like to thank Guy Standing, Karen Shook, Kate Pickett, Avner Offer, Lu Hiam, David Dorling, Alison Dorling, Roy Darke, George Davey Smith, and five very helpful anonymous referees for comment on the earlier chapters in this book. Chris Brazier and Louise Waters at *New Internationalist* kindly gave permission to reproduce a chapter from the magazine they edited. Martin Jordan, editor of *Public Sector Focus*, similarly did so for the chapters that first appeared as articles in that publication. I would also like to thank Alan Rusbridger of *Prospect Magazine* for permission to reproduce Chapter 1.8; Nikki Talebi of the University of Chicago Press for allowing me to include Chapter 3.1; Alice Spawls at the *London Review of Books* for letting me know I had permission to reproduce Chapters 3.2 and 5.6; Bhaskar Sunkara of *Tribune Magazine* similarly for Chapter 3.3; James Stephens of *Biteback* for Chapter 4.2; Matt Ward of *The Guardian* and *The Observer* for Chapter 4.4; and many unnamed workers at Sage and Elsevier who responded to my emails (they had to reply anonymously via automated systems). I am grateful to Martin Baxter for permission to reproduce Figure 1.5; the National Portrait Gallery for permission to produce Figure 1.15; *The Economist* for Figures 1.17 and 2.9; Alamy for Figure 2.12; Alasdair Rae for Figure 3.6; Oxford City Council for Figure 3.12; the BBC for Figure 5.12; Isabella Lill for Figure 6.7; and istock for Figure 6.13. And finally, Grace Carroll, Ellen Mitchell and Ginny Mills at Bristol University Press helped greatly both in putting all this together and in assisting me with cutting its length down from something that was originally far too long; Jo Morton copy edited the text and patiently and kindly managed the book's progress through production, and Marie Doherty typeset the book and prepared all of the tables and figures for publication. And, thank you – for reading.

Introduction: Britain's inequality crisis

Injustice concerns what is understood to be unfair. Among everything else that we now know is not fair, not just, is that a few have access to so much more of almost everything than the large majority of people, than the many. This injustice is felt especially acutely when inequalities are high and living standards are falling. No one doubts that the UK, and especially England, is in a deep inequality crisis. By 2024, child poverty had become more common in every region of England than in the whole of Northern Ireland or Scotland. It had recently risen by more in the UK – as a whole – than in all of the other countries around the world that were monitored by the United Nations (UN) in their Innocenti reports.[1] The latest of these reports, published in December 2023, was by far the most damning. It concentrated on children and the future. Collectively, we find the suggestion that we should continue to tolerate injustice, especially rising injustice, into the future – abhorrent.

We now know so much that we did not know until very recently. The average height of the UK's children is now falling, and (on average) has been for all children born in the UK since 2005 – for almost two decades! More babies and children of all ages and in all areas now die before reaching adulthood than died a few years ago, despite lower birth rates overall. More children in the UK are now going hungry than were just a few years ago. More schools are now unfit for children to be taught in because the roofs might fall in at any time. And yet all the leading

[1] For further detail on all the statements made in this opening paragraph, see Danny Dorling (2024) 'Visualising the 2020s UK cost-of-living crisis', *Social Policy & Administration*, 5 May, http://doi.org/10.1111/spol.13035

politicians in England, in the heart of the UK, continue to talk as if none of this is happening.

Despite the current crisis – the widespread bankruptcy of the country as a whole, the under-resourcing of the schools for the many, and the rising hunger of a group that is no longer small – we continue to persevere with – and, indeed, actively seek to preserve – an education system in which a very small proportion of our children are (privately) taught at great expense, as compared to what is spent on the large majority. The worse things get, the harder 7 per cent of parents try to segregate their children from others – partly because of how bad the outside world of the 93 per cent is becoming. By 2024, the UK spent more on private education, per capita, than any other country in the world.

Children, at least, are protected to some extent. Children are still almost always housed in temporary accommodation with their parents if they are made homeless.[2] Children have some recourse to the dwindling numbers of social workers assigned to protect them. It is worse for young adults, aged 18 and above, as the state offers them much less protection and imposes many more penalties on them if they do not behave exactly as expected in this unjust state. Even for better-off adults, living at home with their parents into middle age begins to look more and more like an inevitability – if there is any space, and if they get on at all with their parents in their increasingly overcrowded homes. But a few young adults are doing very well. Some of them own multiple properties. Britain has also never had as many spare empty bedrooms as it has today. Never have such a small group owned so much that is so often empty.

That is what an *inequality crisis* looks like. Not everyone is badly affected. A few prosper.

A tiny few even benefit from the desperation of others, such as from others' need to be able to live independently from their parents and, eventually, to be able to start a family, even if they cannot get a mortgage. Landlords, including young landlords, increased rents for their tenants by more in the year to March 2024

---

[2] It is only in London that we have a count of children living rough on the streets; see Danny Dorling (2024) *Seven children*, London: Hurst, p. 178.

than at any other time recorded in official statistics. It is the actions of the few people who today increase rents so quickly for so many others that clearly signal we are in an inequality crisis.

The old are doing well, you might think? But when we look carefully, we find that most older people in the UK are not doing well. In fact, they have been doing so badly that there are now fewer old people in the UK than were planned for. Life expectancy in Britain fell after 2014. It has been lower every year since then, except, briefly, in 2019. That moment was just before the COVID-19 pandemic arrived, which was shortly after Brexit was 'done'; and only a dozen years after the banking crisis had hit, and following a whole decade of post-banking-crisis austerity decimation.

What can you say? What can you do? How ridiculous it sounds to believe that it is even possible to think of solving Britain's inequality crisis, given that the UK almost certainly now has the highest levels of income inequality in all of Europe. Money lies at the heart of injustice, and income inequality is the inequality that matters most of all – because it is about what you have to live on – this year, this month, this week, today.

This book is about what we have to accept *before* we are able to start addressing the series of crises that afflict the countries of this disunited 'UK' state and which have led to a level of overall injustice that is both utterly intolerable and – possibly, hopefully – now at a peak. Eventually, inevitably, a peak is always reached. We cannot credibly claim that a situation is getting worse if we are not prepared to acknowledge those times when, overall, it is actually improving in some ways.

In early 2024, the world inequality database (WID) released estimates that suggested that the take of the top 1 per cent within the UK had been falling rapidly since around the autumn of 2020. The WID was set up and is maintained by a great many very dedicated social scientists, including Thomas Piketty. Other affluent states had not yet reported the same trend, but some may have done by the time you read these words. If the WID estimates turn out to be true, then people in the UK may well today be some of the first to be on the cusp of a great transformation.[3]

[3] See https://wid.world/country/united-kingdom/

The extent to which this might be possible, might be about to happen, is the central question of this book.

The text that follows is a curated collection of writings produced over the past six years (2018–24). Each of the six sections of this book covers a different theme – relating in turn to hope and politics, poverty, housing, education, health, and how change comes about. Each section is prefaced with a new essay, then continues with a series of writings presented in chronological order to build a short case in support of why we might now be at a peak of injustice in relation to the set of issues discussed.

Much of the content of each section consists of arguments that have been made recently elsewhere, written by the author, often with colleagues, but here edited and arranged to better fit together and to try to build towards a more coherent whole. There is a sense, throughout the accounts in this book, that while at times we often now come to believe 'it has got so bad it cannot possibly get worse, but it might', there is also evidence to argue that hope has not died, and growing evidence that a turn is occurring.

Peak Injustice begins with the question of hope, and a first section on politics. This is introduced with an essay titled 'How did you not see me?', based on the words used by the cyclist Keir Starmer hit, when Keir was driving his car in London in October 2020.

Sir Keir may be prime minister when you read these words or, if you are reading this many years from now, he may have been prime minister and have long since gone, his triumphs and failings etched into history. Or there may be some reason he never did become prime minister, or did not last long in the post.

We cannot know the future (though we often fool ourselves that we can), but we can at least look much more clearly at the past, and especially at the most recent past. Because of this, the first chapter in the first section of this book concerns the former Labour leader, Jeremy Corbyn, and how we might better look back on his time in that position – now that we have the benefit of a little hindsight – if we want to have any chance of improving our current state and not remaining at a peak of injustice.

The second section of this book concerns the most basic of social evils: destitution; but also its opposite, happiness. The third section deals with levelling-up, especially in relation to housing.

The fourth discusses education, and some of the eugenic beliefs of great inherent differences in ability – beliefs that remain in British society and help sustain such great injustice in this corner of Europe. Concerns over global population numbers and immigration are also touched on here.

In future, it will be hard to explain to our grandchildren that the Prime Minister of the day in the spring of 2024 really had stopping the 'small boats' as one of his five great priorities! Our grandchildren might ask: 'What kind of a small-minded person would think that?'. And we will have to explain to them who Rishi Sunak was.

The fifth section of *Peak Injustice* concerns public health, austerity, the crisis in the NHS, but not the pandemic. The pandemic is only mentioned briefly in concluding this book. It is too large a subject to adequately address in these pages. As yet we do not know how great its impact might be in the long term, or whether it may be one of the reasons why injustices in the UK may, possibly, be at a peak now.

Possibly it was the pandemic, on top of everything else, and the cost-of-living crisis that followed it (and which was partly caused by global supply chain issues associated with the pandemic), which was the straw that broke the camel's back of complacency in the UK.

The sixth and final section of this book returns to hope, the behaviour of the elite, and the possibilities for change. We cannot see the future. But we can influence it and choose not to accept particular scenarios as inevitable.

We live on a mountain of injustice in the UK today – stumbling around in the dark, we do not know if we have yet even reached the top, and often do not realise that we should be trying to get down, because we do not understand that this is not a good place to be. We are so unaware of how lost we have become and of how used to breathing the rarefied, oxygen-starved air up here that we often no longer think clearly. You cannot level mountains of inequality. You have to climb off them, to find a way down, and you do that when you are shattered.

At least we knew we were shattered by 2024. We now more desperately look out for signs of hope, such as those estimates of the income share of the UK's top 1 per cent falling, and we should now constantly ask whether we are at the start of the way down. We can learn from our past. We are not doomed to repeat it. This matters because after 1918, the last time when income and wealth inequalities fell in the UK, we took a very slow and tortuous route down from the peak. We did not get to the bottom of the mountain until 1974.

There were 56 years between 1918 and 1974. I am 56 years old as I write these words. It took the equivalent of an entire lifetime for a person of my age now for the UK last to reduce income and wealth inequalities to a minimum and then begin to open up so many other opportunities. These were opportunities that can only be truly opened up once you come down from the mountain – greater freedoms for people to be who they wish to be and to tackle many other forms of prejudice as well as the key eugenic hatred and contempt for the majority that prevails at peaks of income inequality among a few who consider themselves 'worthy winners' when injustice is at a peak.

Peak Injustice ends with a short conclusion concerning the mountain of pain we have created and proposes ten things an incoming government could do if led by people who care about the injustices documented in this book. However, what matters most – now – is accepting that where we are currently is a very bad place to be, and to understand that to continue to climb upwards would be foolhardy. As R.H. Tawney wrote in 1920 (two years after the last peak of inequality) of our political masters a century ago:

> they repeat, like parrots, the word 'Productivity', because that is the word that rises first in their minds; … When they are touched by social compunction, they can think of nothing more original than the diminution of poverty, because poverty, being the opposite of the riches which they value most, seems to them the most terrible of human afflictions.[4]

[4] R.H. Tawney (1920) *The acquisitive society*, New York: Harcourt, Brace and Company, Ch I, para 5; see: https://www.gutenberg.org/files/33741/33741-h/33741-h.htm

Injustice is about so much more than poverty. Economic growth is no salvation for inequality. There is no need for us to learn this lesson afresh about the preferred parroted response of so many British politicians to injustice. We are not the same people today, as we were then, in the 1920s. Our great grandparents had usually left school in their early teens. Jingoism was the order of the day. The Empire was at its height. All that is gone. This time we could, we should, and we must, find a better, faster, safer, route off the mountain of pain.

SECTION 1

The politics of hope

The inequality crisis: how did you not see me?

This book, *Peak Injustice*, covers both new ideas and also writing from the period 2018 through to the summer of 2024. These were lean years for Britain, but they had not followed seven good years, far from it. However, it is possible that during the six years I cover here a peak was passed, a peak where the very worst of the rise in injustice began to end and a new era became visible on the horizon. Not an era of sunlit uplands, but of the dawning realisation that what had been tolerated for so long was intolerable. However, we begin with the question of what is to come next and what you may miss if you are so blind that you cannot see clearly.

You cannot know the peak has passed until you have well and truly passed it. When you are at the peak, it simply feels like everything will continue to get worse. Although new possibilities for things to get better were opening up amid all the chaos of life in the UK in the six-year period this book considers, those possibilities were not as dramatic and arresting as the fear that things could carry on getting worse, prices could rise even higher, poverty deepen further, and our society become even more unjust each year than the year before. People do not choose to be victims of crumbling infrastructure and decimated services, or of weapons and of war (worldwide, disproportionately British-made): usually others choose that future for them. The injustice we were living with in 2024, in the UK and in many countries worldwide, was not of the vast majority of people's making.

Good news, in contrast to bad news, is quiet, often statistical, initially hardly noticed, and frequently ignored when it is found. Here is some good news: Tom Forth, an online commentator, wrote (on Twitter/X), 'Well there's your result. Travel to work areas in Great Britain with lower wages in 2015 saw higher average wage growth in mean full time wages (without bonuses) between 2015 and 2021. And as a result, … it's convincing that regional wage inequality thus measured went down.'[1] Forth was confirming the findings of a working paper, published in July 2023, that suggested that we might have very recently passed a peak, possibly the great peak, of regional inequalities in the UK,[2] although it is too early to be sure. Just as we cannot yet be sure of the world inequality database estimates for the declining take of the 1 per cent in the UK released in 2024.[3] What is important to remember is that the charting of injustice also includes looking out carefully for the routes towards justice; looking for all these signs and seeing if they might be mapping a way out. As Oscar Wilde once said:

> A map of the world that does not include Utopia is not worth even glancing at, for it leaves out the one country at which Humanity is always landing. And when Humanity lands there, it looks out, and, seeing a better country, sets sail. Progress is the realisation of Utopias.[4]

I am a cartographer, a maker of maps. I have made many, with the help of many others, and using a huge amount of data: world atlases, and numerous others, of Europe, but especially of the UK. I also draw maps with words, and I collect as much

---

1 Tom Forth (2023) 'A comment on "World Inequality Lab – Working Paper No. 2023/14"' (full reference in n. 2), 2 August, Twitter/X, https://twitter.com/thomasforth/status/1686522552963706882

2 Luis Bauluz, Paweł Bukowski, Mark Fransham, Annie Lee, Margarita López Forero, Filip Novokmet et al (2023) *Spatial wage inequality in North America and Western Europe: Changes between and within local labour markets 1975–2019*, Working Paper No. 2023/14, World Inequality Data Lab, July, https://wid.world/document/spatial-wage-inequality-in-north-america-and-western-europe-changes-between-and-within-local-labour-markets-1975-2019-world-inequality-lab-working-paper-2023-14/

3 See https://wid.world/country/united-kingdom/

4 Oscar Wilde (1891) 'The soul of man under socialism', *Fortnightly Review*, February 1891, appearing on p. 40 of the 1900 edition of the essay, which can be found here: https://www.gutenberg.org/ebooks/1017

evidence as I can to do that, from wherever I can. In early 2023 I noted, for the first time in my adult life, that the differences between social classes (below the top 1 per cent) as determined by income inequalities were now falling within the UK and had been doing so for a couple of years, but especially so in late 2022 and all of 2023.[5] House prices had also stopped rising by as much as wages, and so wealth inequalities were starting to fall; the future value of private pensions was now looking increasingly doubtful – which may be worrying to many, but reduces wealth inequalities and makes many of the better-off more interested in what their state pension might be. People with some wealth were beginning to find they suddenly had much less. Others were using up their savings rapidly. Although this was also very bad news for those with very little saved, wealth erosion is one way in which injustices fall. However, wealth taxation is far more efficient and less slow a process.

By 2023 the latest statistics, looked at in the round, began to suggest that it was not fanciful to believe that we had seen income inequality peak in 2018 and wealth inequality peak shortly afterwards. In early 2024 *The Times* reported that: 'Some major UK employers spend tens of millions on two or three executives alone. This inevitably means there is less available for their lower-earning colleagues.'[6] This gross economic inequality was not just as measured between individuals but included income and wealth inequality between areas. All this occurred despite Brexit, which increased inequality by reducing our rights, including our rights under employment law. Brexit finally took place in January 2020 after income inequalities had peaked, so a little too late for it to explain that peak. Various Brexit payoffs and bribes to constituents in Northern Ireland during those bitter years

[5] See Chapter 1.8 of this volume (and in full as: Danny Dorling (2023) 'Are things about to get better?', *Prospect Magazine*, 5 April (May issue), pp. 38–41, dannydorling.org/?page_id=9653).

[6] David Brenchley (2024) 'Are company bosses paid too much?', *The Times*, 11 January, https://www.thetimes.co.uk/article/ceo-salary-uk-vs-employee-ratio-fair-wages-z7n0xbr5x, quoting Luke Hildyard, and also published as Luke Hildyard (2024) 'Excessive executive pay has negative consequences for everyone', The High Pay Centre, 16 January, https://highpaycentre.org/excessive-executive-pay-has-negative-consequences-for-everyone/

2016–19 may have helped to reduce UK regional inequalities, as did the way the Westminster chaos stirred up the Scots to be more radical than they otherwise might have been.

Just as 'Brexit was done', the pandemic came, which briefly also *increased* inequality, with income for the bottom fifth *falling* most when it began, but as this was only temporary, that short-term widening of the gap was not enough to buck a possible longer-term trend that was only then just beginning to emerge. The pandemic was, in absolute terms, most deadly to the rich. Being old is the greatest risk factor by far for dying from COVID-19. As a group, the rich live the longest. In the UK, among the population aged over 90, more people who are rich and from higher social classes can be found than in any other demographic age group. Some 15 per cent of all men and 10 per cent of women of those ages (90+) in the UK died earlier than they would have done during the first three years of the pandemic directly from catching the new disease. It was a disaster, but not one that increased inequality between social classes. Initially, their deaths *appeared* to increase wealth inequality as their monies, homes and savings were passed to mostly already well-off children and a very short-lived housing boom ensued, the pandemic flight to the countryside being in part a flight to the homes of the recently deceased.

Inequality in wealth and income is only one aspect of injustice, and economic inequalities are only a part of inequality, albeit the most important part.[7] There are great health and housing injustices, and educational injustices, too, although it is the rest of the world's super-rich who more and more often now fill up Britain's most expensive schools, and that, in an odd way, reduces some of the home-grown divides.[8] How we treat others is at the core of injustice.

---

[7] Danny Dorling (2023) 'When we were young: inequality revisited, a commentary on Geoffrey Deverteuil's essay', *Dialogues in Urban Research*, 21 September, pp. 1–7, https://journals.sagepub.com/doi/10.1177/27541258231204002

[8] Richard Adams (2016) 'Third of students at many British boarding schools come from overseas: number of Russian students has trebled in the last decade but some schools are wary of reaching a tipping point', *The Guardian*,

So why write a book on peak injustice now?

The title for this book comes from a *Guardian* article published in 2017, 'We've hit peak injustice', in which Hugh Muir explained that:

> Revelations about the wealthy buying citizenships confirm a sorry truth: the migration door, closed to the poor, swings open to those with vast fortunes... In our regression from liberal aspiration to the brutal realities of Trump and Brexit, one of the nirvanas set aside has been the notion of a world without borders. 'America first,' says the president. 'Britain first and always,' chant the Brexiters. The majority demand is for migration curbs in principle, even if they are unlikely to be achieved in practice. The global village will be refashioned with barbed-wire fencing. And yet in this, as in most things, money talks.[9]

Brexit was a disaster,[10] but it was a disaster that occurred as we were staggering up the last steps towards the peak of many injustices. Six years after Hugh Muir's article, those who called for Brexit, and got it, would write about their friends in terms that were often less than glowing. Daniel Hannan, one of those friends, continued to repeat ridiculous depictions of supposedly Leftist governments, such as that of Douglas Carswell, the former Conservative and UKIP MP, who later emigrated to Mississippi, and complained that 'Leftist governments can reduce entitlements without being accused of murdering the poor... we shall be bickering about diversity and inclusion right up to the moment

---

1 September, https://www.theguardian.com/education/2016/sep/01/third-of-students-at-many-british-boarding-schools-come-from-overseas

9 Hugh Muir (2017) 'We've hit peak injustice: a world without borders, but only for the super-rich', *The Guardian*, 18 September, https://www.theguardian.com/commentisfree/2017/sep/18/peak-injustice-world-without-borders-super-rich-buying-citizenship-migration

10 Danny Dorling (2023) *Report: Brexit: a failed project in a failing state*, London: Friedrich Ebert Stiftung, 25 October, https://www.anothereurope.org/report-brexit-a-failed-project-in-a-failing-state/

when the final economic calamity overwhelms us.'[11] You may wonder why a former UKIP MP might find life in Mississippi so attractive, or shake your head in disbelief at the views of most of those who write about such things in *The Telegraph* newspaper, but I think these can all be viewed as signs, portents, that we are reaching the end of an era. We are moving from bickering about diversity and inclusion to demanding it: No Justice, No Peace. The days of people like Daniel and Douglas seeking to maintain injustices being taken seriously are starting to be numbered, and so increasingly they seek refuge overseas, or in the darkest corners of bile-filled, far-right online publications: they are not creatures that like the light when it is shone more brightly on them, their motivations and their sometimes unusual peccadilloes, prejudices and preoccupation with trying to be the prime producers of 'meaning'.

When, in 2023, Tory MP Danny Kruger argued for the introduction of compulsory one-year service for every citizen that entailed working (presumably for free) in local councils, he claimed, 'People are crying out to be summoned to duty', adding that: 'It is right for government to be involved in the production of meaning'.[12] The very same government that was going to add more meaning to the lives of people in Britain also presided over an unprecedented series of bankruptcies of local councils. Within days of Kruger's words being printed, Europe's largest local authority, Birmingham, went under, and everything that could be sold off would have to be. Local councillors would no longer have any power. Local democracy was in effect suspended. That was the real 'production of new meaning' that Kruger's party had achieved. More and more parts of the UK being run by diktat, sold off and further run down.

---

[11] Daniel Hannan (2023) 'Britain is now a poor nation. This is the number one issue we face – yet our leaders ignore it', *The Telegraph*, 22 July, https://www.telegraph.co.uk/news/2023/07/22/britain-is-now-a-poor-nation-this-is-our-number-one-issue/

[12] Will Lloyd (2023) 'Danny Kruger: "The moral condition of England is worse": The MP and former political secretary to Boris Johnson reflects on the Tories' decline', *New Statesman*, 30 August, https://12ft.io/proxy?q=https%3A%2F%2Fwww.newstatesman.com%2Fencounter%2F2023%2F08%2Fdanny-kruger-interview-tories-disunited-britain

It is not hard to paint this picture as worse than it was. It had already become so bad that few people would notice further exaggeration.[13] With a little double-counting, you could claim that as many as two million Britons were killed though the actions of the government that had been in power up to 2023, and even make comparisons with 'Joseph Stalin, Mao Zedong, Pol Pot, Augusto Pinochet, Adolf Hitler and Idi Amin'.[14] But this would be foolish, and as much of a distraction as calling for people to be 'summoned to do their duty'. The situation had become terrible, but the death toll (within the UK) has not been as high as two million – at least not yet. The UK government of 2019–24, with its three prime ministers, was not suffering from genocidal mania, nor were they cunning purveyors of an extreme form of banal evil. They were mostly, put most simply, incompetent fantasists, who believed that the economic models of how the world worked that they had been taught as teenagers had been right, and that such models still – somehow – held true. Prime Minister Rishi Sunak had previously published three books that each read like the A-level projects of an over-enthusiastic and somewhat pedestrian public schoolboy who had never been shown any alternative to the survival of the (so-called) fittest

---

13 The Labour Party had become just as divided as the Tories by 2023 and into 2024. Although they presented a more unified public face, they had become run by zealotry, paranoia, and a command-and-control style that backfired and looked weak. Even when this ensured an election victory on 4 July 2024, what was actually won? Voters in the 2023 Uxbridge and South Ruislip by-election explained to the BBC that the Labour Party 'don't offer anything new, exciting or different'. Labour Party members felt that they 'were just fodder' for a central party machine not interested in them: Yasmin Rufo (2023) 'Labour aren't offering anything new – Uxbridge voter', *BBC News*, 20 July, https://www.bbc.co.uk/news/live/uk-politics-66181315; Aditya Chakrabortty (2023) 'Uxbridge was not just an anti-green protest: it was the sour spirit of Brexit revived', *The Guardian*, 3 August, https://www.theguardian.com/commentisfree/2023/aug/03/uxbridge-brexit-tories-anti-green-labour-local

14 Prem Sikka (2023) 'How Tory government policy has led to more than 2 million Brits dying', *Left Foot Forward*, 1 September, https://leftfootforward.org/2023/09/how-tory-government-policy-has-led-to-more-than-2-million-brits-dying/

philosophy, while also believing that austerity is necessary for all but the likes of himself, and that spending on war is in some way good. In April 2024 Sunak committed a UK in the economic doldrums to increasing military spending to 2.5 per cent per year of GDP by the year 2030. However, few people took any notice of him at this point. Sadly, the Labour Party supremos of that month replied along the lines of 'Maybe, if the circumstances are right', rather than explaining that such behaviour would not help anyone but, on the contrary, would harm a great many in the world through the pain and suffering that military spending results in. The UK was at a potential peak of stupidity in the late spring of 2024.

Looking back over the past half-century, we could choose any one of a number of examples of people saying extreme things, and claim each as evidence that a peak of injustice had been reached. It would not have been. Attacks have been made on political parties for selling out their principles in every decade of the past 50 years.[15] No matter how much of a betrayal or provocation the latest government announcement may appear to be, why should we take any such claims today with anything other than a pinch of salt? Even as the articles and books began to be printed thick and fast suggesting that we really had got it all wrong by not fixing the roofs of our school and hospital buildings before they began to crumble, and the insulation and heating in our homes before the mould spread, let alone our broken society before it fractured, it began to become clear that we were no longer easily shocked.[16]

When the new government was formed in July 2024 no one had great expectations, despite the opportunities there were.

---

15 Josh Ryan-Collins (2023) 'In ditching a wealth tax, Labour is rejecting growth and embracing bad economics', *The Guardian*, 30 August, https://www.theguardian.com/commentisfree/2023/aug/30/wealth-tax-labour-economics-rachel-reeves

16 Harry Lambert (2023) 'Britain's great tax con: the UK's tax system entrenches inequality, stymies growth, and rewards a few at the expense of the many', *New Statesman*, 30 August, https://www.newstatesman.com/politics/economy/2023/08/britains-great-tax-con

Taxes in the UK now amount to 37 per cent of national income: 'the highest level seen in the UK since the 1940s'.[17] Yet that is less than almost any other country in Europe secures – apart from Ireland and Switzerland, where the tax take looks low because so much money today passes very lightly taxed through those economies (the UK could no longer even excel at financial chicanery). Meanwhile, despite these higher UK taxes, the roofs on a growing number of our school buildings were threatening to literally fall down on the heads of children, because the austerity government had not fixed them while the sun was shining, despite spending more on 'defence' than it had done for many decades and then promising in 2024 to increase such spending further. One right-wing Labour politician, talking about the war in Ukraine, tried to suggest that all these arms exports and military posturing were about 'desiring goodness for all mankind'.[18]

You might believe that there is no way we could have reached the peak of injustice when we were selling more of our weapons abroad, and as the chances of those weapons being used rose, as hunger increased at home, as more and more schools were shutting because they were unsafe, as once again more and more people were sleeping rough, and then, with an accelerating boost from the cost-of-living crisis, as the black mould spreading in increasing numbers of unheated homes made more people ill, sometimes fatally. Thus, when all this was occurring, and inflation remained high, we could clearly see that our situation could get still worse. Things would cost still more next year. So, you might well ask, *How could we be at a peak of injustice?* My answer is that we have been at such peaks before. Reducing injustice does not mean that all suddenly becomes fine. It means that more victories are being won than defeats are occurring. But life can, and usually

---

17 Isaac Delestre and Helen Miller (2023) *Tax and public finances: The fundamentals*, London: Institute for Fiscal Studies, 23 August, https://ifs.org.uk/publications/tax-and-public-finances-fundamentals

18 Tom Stevenson (2023) 'Disappearing ink: review of "*And Then What? Inside Stories of 21st-Century Diplomacy*" by Catherine Ashton', *The London Review of Books*, 45, 16, 10 August.

does, feel worse when you begin to come down from the peak of inequality, as it did in the UK in both the 1920s and the 1930s.

Globally, there are also more victories now than defeats. Extreme poverty is falling; but we do not know if we are at a peak of injustice worldwide. As Oxfam explained at the start of 2024 in regard to the global situation: 'Extreme poverty leapt up during COVID-19, and whilst it began to fall again, it is nowhere near its pre-crisis trend, and the impact of the global food and cost of living crisis is likely to have a further negative impact.'[19] Infant mortality is falling worldwide, while access to education, better housing and better healthcare are – on average – still rising. We cannot now claim that each passing year is worse than the one before, as we could do in 2020, and even more so in 2021. We could do so when the wealth of billionaires was skyrocketing; it is plateauing now. We could do so when tens of thousands were dying in natural disasters for want of basic infrastructure, warnings and concern. We can't say that now. The situation could worsen. Dystopian predictions abound. Wars begin, new genocides are committed. Despots get away scot-free. Corporations still rule the world. And yet most years are now better than the year before. Pandemics that kill many people are becoming less, not more, prevalent, despite our huge populations. Democracy is not collapsing worldwide. Greater rights for women continue to be won, with more victories each year than defeats. The 2022 overruling of (*Roe v Wade*) abortion rights in the US impacted upon only two per cent of the world's people, the women of the USA.

This brief introduction cannot summarise all the ways in which injustice may now be at a peak, and so this book aims, across its six sections, to take a closer look. The first, this one, concerns hope and politics; the second, poverty; the third, housing; the fourth, education; the fifth, health; the sixth, how change comes.

The first chapter of this section, 'On Jeremy Corbyn', explains how, more than four years after Labour's December 2019 general election defeat, it was clear that Corbyn's vision had not died –

---

[19] Oxfam (2024) *State of world's billionaires and global wealth inequality*, Report issued to coincide with the January meeting of the World Economic Forum in Davos, Chapter 1, 'Heads they win, tails you lose'.

and that what had been put in to try to replace it was floundering. As one well-placed commentator observed in 2017:

> For the first time in a generation, a significant layer of younger people re-engaged with politics and felt hope – the hope of someone speaking up for them on insecure work, low pay, poor-quality housing. That just maybe there was a prospect of a government that would stick up for them against the companies and landlords ripping them off.[20]

The temporary dashing of that dream might well have been part of the peak of injustice. Instead, Labour would go on to be led by a man who, in 2020, 'was running late for an appointment with his tailor' when he struck a cyclist. The cyclist was said by eyewitnesses to have been a food delivery rider for Deliveroo, who had to be taken to hospital.[21] The reporter suggested that the new Labour leader, Sir Keir Starmer, was performing a U-turn when he hit the cyclist, who had shouted at Starmer, 'How did you not see me?'.

Having begun with hope and the Labour Party, the remaining seven chapters in the book's first section concern: the Conservatives (and in particular Boris Johnson); the geography of Brexit; how and why we ended up in 2019 with the government we did; conservative politicians' obsession with growth; how the politics of the UK now compares with the politics of Sweden and Italy; why we should look back to 1922 for both parallels and inspiration; and how hope can be found.

So, where better to begin, and where better to turn to for hope, than to ask what happened to Jeremy Corbyn, why it happened, and with what long-term effect?

---

[20] Andrew Fisher (2022) 'Where's Labour's fervour? Can you imagine a crowd chanting "Oh, Keir Starmer"?', *The Guardian*, 14 December, https://www.theguardian.com/commentisfree/2022/dec/14/labour-keir-starmer-polls-jeremy-corbyn

[21] Simon MacMichael (2020) 'Sir Keir Starmer was "making U-turn" when he hit cyclist, says witness', *Road.cc*, 28 October, https://road.cc/content/news/witness-starmer-was-making-u-turn-when-he-hit-cyclist-278313

CHAPTER 1.1

On Jeremy Corbyn[1]

On a dismal night in December 2019, as I sat in a pub near London's Paddington Station watching the exit poll appear on the television screen, I thought Jeremy Corbyn had lost when Labour lost. I don't think that now.

Like 95 per cent of people born in Britain in 1949, Jeremy Corbyn doesn't have a university degree.[2] He did far better at school than the great majority of his generation, although this was not surprising as he was born with advantages. His mother was a maths teacher, his father an engineer; they had met in London in the 1930s at a rally to oppose the rise of fascism in Spain. Young Corbyn suffered the fate of a minor private school education, at a small and remote establishment where he saw first-hand how the English brought up those destined to rule an empire that no longer existed. He often found himself in a determined minority of one at his Shropshire school, speaking out against fox hunting, nuclear weapons and the Vietnam war.

In 1974, the 24-year-old Corbyn became an elected councillor in Haringey, North London. His early years provided an

---

1 This chapter is newly written but builds on Danny Dorling (2019) 'Why Corbyn's moral clarity could have propelled him to Number 10', Transforming Society blogpost, 13 November, https://www.transformingsociety.co.uk/2019/11/13/why-corbyns-moral-clarity-could-propel-him-to-number-10

2 The year after Jeremy Corbyn was born, 17,300 young people in the UK were awarded a university degree, or 2 per cent of those born 18 years earlier. By 1967, the figure had risen to 5 per cent: Paul Bolton (2012) 'Education: Historical statistics', *House of Commons Library*, 27 November, https://researchbriefings.files.parliament.uk/documents/SN04252/SN04252.pdf

education and set of experiences that are still unrivalled among modern British politicians.[3]

As an anti-apartheid activist and trade unionist, he came to the attention of Special Branch (part of the UK security services), who began to monitor his activities; they continued to do so for at least two decades. His close friend and fellow Labour MP Diane Abbott also had a file opened on her during that period, in the same 'subversive' filing cabinet.[4]

Jeremy Corbyn understood where those in power came from, what drove them, and the often clandestine tactics they used to win and to smear others. While travelling in Latin America in his early 20s, he had learnt how it was possible for the impoverished many to rise up against the wealthy and powerful few. After celebrating Allende's victory, he had then seen (from nearby) how the US had crushed Chile's democratically elected president in 1973 and imposed decades of murderous dictatorship on Chile so that it became America's testing ground for the new ruthless neo-liberalism. That phase only ended with the social explosion of 2019 in Chile and as yet we do not know what will replace it. Corbyn understood why politicians such as Margaret Thatcher, and the interests that backed them, were staunch supporters of racism and apartheid in South Africa and had worked so hard to prevent an uprising there.

In 1983 he stood as Labour's parliamentary candidate for the London constituency of Islington North, a seat that before the Second World War had almost always been Conservative. Not for the first time, members of the Labour Party moving to the political right propelled Jeremy Corbyn forward: his chances to

---

3 Unusually among his peers, he joined the Labour Party when he was still a child. At age 18 he worked for a local newspaper, and at age 19 he went to Jamaica with Voluntary Service Overseas and worked as a geography teacher. In 1969, aged 20, he travelled through Latin America, and at 21 celebrated Salvador Allende's party sweeping to power in Chile. At 22, he became an official for the National Union of Tailors and Garment Workers in London.

4 Hayley Dixon and Kate McCann (2017) 'Exclusive: Special Branch monitored Jeremy Corbyn for 20 years amid fears he was "undermining democracy"', *The Telegraph*, 6 June, https://web.archive.org/web/20170609215719/http://www.telegraph.co.uk/news/2017/06/06/exclusive-special-branch-monitored-jeremy-corbyn-20-years-amid/

stand were boosted when two potential rival candidates defected rightward from Labour to the newly formed Social Democratic Party (SDP). The SDP's 25.4 per cent share of the vote in the general election saw Labour lose 60 seats and helped to secure Thatcher an even larger majority than she had held in 1979. Corbyn, however, would win his seat, defeating the Conservative candidate David Coleman by 5,607 votes. Coleman went on to become a University of Oxford academic and the leading advisor of an anti-immigrant group, Migration Watch.

Corbyn's share of the Islington North vote rose at the next election, in 1987, from 40 per cent to 50 per cent, then to 57 per cent in 1992 and 69 per cent in 1997. It dropped to 62 per cent in 2001, and further to 51 per cent in 2005, with the Liberal Democrats polling second. But his vote share increased again to 55 per cent in 2010, 60 per cent in 2015 and 73 per cent in 2017, before falling slightly to 64 per cent in 2019. On 15 February 2023, Sir Keir Starmer declared that Corbyn, his predecessor as party leader, would not be permitted to stand as a Labour candidate at the next general election. He did so despite it being Labour policy for candidates to be chosen by the members of their local constituency party, and despite Sir Keir, in his leadership campaign, promising to support party democracy. In the event, and only after the July 2024 general election had been called, Jeremy Corbyn felt compelled to stand again to represent his constituents following a call from thousands of them for him to do so.

What had Corbyn done to be barred from standing for his own party? Had Sir Keir seen something in those Special Branch files when he was Director of Public Prosecutions for the Crown Prosecution Service that made him conclude that Corbyn was a threat to the nation? Or was Corbyn's ongoing support among so many Labour Party members a threat to Starmer?

The final chapter of the previous collection of essays I published (in 2018) was titled 'Why Corbyn's moral clarity could have propelled him to Number 10'.[5] It was an essay I wrote in May 2016, a year before the huge rise in the vote for both Corbyn in

---

[5] Danny Dorling (2018) *Peak inequality: Britain's ticking time bomb*, Bristol: Policy Press, pp. 383–92.

Islington North (to 73 per cent, 61.5 per cent more than the next candidate) and Labour nationally (to 40 per cent, only 2.3 per cent behind the Conservatives). In response to my essay, journalist Nick Cohen wrote in *The Spectator* a few days later: 'Corbyn defends the most grotesque anti-Semites: fantasists, who believed Jews eat Christian children, and were the diabolical power behind 9/11, the slave trade and every other catastrophe.'[6]

Something was eating Cohen up. What was it about Corbyn that so frightened and angered people with Cohen's views? At the time I didn't think the reason for their fear and anger was the allegations of anti-Semitism made against Corbyn, and often against Corbyn's supporters. I am even more certain now that this was not the case.[7]

Just like Jeremy Corbyn's leadership victory in 2015, the pronounced swing to Labour in the 2017 general election was unforeseen by the pundits. In the landmark postwar election of 1945, Labour's vote rose by just 9.7 per cent over 10 years; in 2017, it rose by 9.6 per cent in just two years. For those who enjoy electoral maths, the swing in 2017, when annualised, was two and a half times greater in its annualised magnitude than that which Clement Attlee secured at the end of the Second World War.

However, it was still not enough to put Jeremy Corbyn into 10 Downing Street. New Labour had polled so badly in the general elections of 2001, 2005, 2010 and 2015 that the

---

6 Note that *The Spectator*'s and Cohen's styling of 'anti-Semite'/'anti-Semitism' is used in this chapter. See: Nick Cohen (2016) 'The left's great illusion in praising Labour's "moral clarity" under Corbyn', *The Spectator*, 31 May, https://www.spectator.co.uk/article/the-left-s-great-illusion-in-praising-labour-s-moral-clarity-under-corbyn/

7 Views change over time. In August 2023 one commentator, looking at a list of signatories of a petition referring to Israel's 'regime of apartheid', supporting Palestinian rights and calling on US leaders to help stop the Israeli occupation, wrote: 'Interesting list. I personally know at least a dozen of the signers who would have considered this petition antisemitic hyperbole a decade ago. Not a criticism of them at all, rather a recognition of how dramatically the political ground has shifted.' The petition can be found here: https://sites.google.com/view/israel-elephant-in-the-room/home, and the comment here: https://twitter.com/Thrownpeas/status/1688345034398035968?s=20

huge increase in support for Labour that came with Corbyn's leadership did not result in enough votes overall, even though their 12,877,918 votes in 2017 were 3.5 million more than Ed Miliband secured in 2015, 4.3 million more than Gordon Brown won in 2010, and 3.3 million more than Tony Blair won in 2005.[8] But Corbyn's popularity *did* result in Prime Minister Theresa May losing her majority, and it *did* show what was possible. It also scared the living daylights out of many of those described by Cohen, in his *Spectator* piece, as 'the comfortable middle class'.

What I wrote in 2016 was that the UK was slowly changing into a multi-party political system; that grassroots fundraising through 'yes we can' campaigns worked; the message that was gaining credibility was that to win a campaign on the left, you needed an active, inspired membership willing to deliver leaflets and knock on doors in every constituency. And that Corbyn was seen by the majority of Labour voters, and many others (who chose that year to vote Labour for the first time in their lives), as an honest, modest and reluctant leader. He was a man who listened and could learn from his and his party's mistakes, he was not in awe of the United States, and many believed that he might – if the 2017 election produced the opportunity – be good at forming alliances, in contrast to Gordon Brown, who had so dismally failed to do so in 2010.[9]

Of course, Jeremy Corbyn has faults, although he may have fewer than most of us. His greatest fault – at least in the context of electoral politics – is his lack of Machiavellianism, despite being far from naïve. He understood many of the most devious, duplicitous and deceptive politicians of our times very well. From his vantage point on the far reaches of the Labour backbenches, he had seen these duds emerge over the decades, jostling for

[8] The UK electorate in 2005 was 44.25 million people compared to 46.80 in 2017, only 2.55 million more, but higher partly because more registered to vote. See: https://researchbriefings.files.parliament.uk/documents/RP05-33/RP05-33.pdf and https://commonslibrary.parliament.uk/research-briefings/cbp-7979/

[9] Danny Dorling (2016) 'The long read: Why Corbyn's moral clarity could propel him to Number 10', *Labour Hub*, 28 May, https://labourlist.org/2016/05/danny-dorling-why-corbyns-moral-clarity-could-propel-him-to-number-10/

position and indulging in showy battles with their opponents, often people they had been to school or university with. He had, in fact, met some of their kind at his school, and again in 1970s London politics, in the bitter 1980s, and in the 1990s' betrayal of Labour that New Labour represented. Corbyn was one of a tiny handful of parliamentary voices against the wars of the 2000s, and in the 2010s he watched as the UK's most extreme politicians since the 1930s took their party out of the Conservative political group in Europe. And he refused, point blank, to scheme or be unscrupulous himself. That was his weakest point.

When they came for Jeremy Corbyn, both from within the parliamentary Labour Party and beyond, they used what he thought was his greatest strength – his lifelong anti-racism. His opponents turned that on its head. Corbyn could have fought back. He could have played the man and not the ball. It would have been so easy. In April 2016 he could have deflected Nick Cohen's allegations by concentrating instead on the rumours then surrounding what the *Sunday Express* termed 'a mid-life crisis' in the then Chancellor George Osborne's personal life.[10] He could have sued Cohen and *The Spectator*. He could have mentioned Cohen's personal failings (now well documented on social media and beyond). He could have rounded on almost all those at the top of British public life and said what he knew of their greed and immorality, but he chose instead to offer a positive message of hope. He could have called in good lawyers and sued many others. Had he gone for the jugular, later, in May 2017, he might well have convinced a further 380,000 Conservative voters to vote Labour – which was all he needed for Labour to have garnered the most seats in that general election. But if he had done that, he would not have been the man who, as the darkest of dark horse candidates, had turned accepted wisdom on its head when he won the Labour Party leadership in September 2015, with 59.5 per cent of the vote. And in doing so, he inspired a mass movement whose impact will be felt for decades to come.

[10] Adam Helliker (2016) 'Mid-life crisis for Osborne?', *Sunday Express*, 16 April, https://web.archive.org/web/20170103025112/https:/www.express.co.uk/comment/columnists/adam-helliker/661726/George-Osbourne-Rosanna-davison-hacked-off-jeremy-paxman-basil-fawlty

The young are imprinted by their first political actions. They knew they were not alone, and they knew they were not voting for a bully.

What happened to those who tried to defend Corbyn? In April 2021, the Labour MP Lloyd Russell-Moyle was ostracised when he told Corbyn's supporters, 'I want to apologise from all of us but me in particular … if we have made you feel like you're alone, if we have not reached our arm around you enough in these tough times when you are being purged or set up with false allegations.' Russell-Moyle was swiftly silenced by being accused of anti-Semitism for saying these words.[11] On 29 May 2024, just a few days before it could have been confirmed that he would again stand for his constituency, Russell-Moyle was barred by the Labour Party from standing, along with Faiza Shaheen, in a move that was widely seen as vindictive and bullying.[12] The same tactics, or the threat of them, silenced almost all of the other Labour MPs who supported what Corbyn stood for. Then, 40 years after first being targeted by Special Branch, Diane Abbott also had the Labour whip removed.

There has always been anti-Semitism in the British Labour Party, although never as much as in the Conservative Party. Nevertheless, it was there from the start. In 1891 Keir Hardie, Labour's founding father, claimed that 'wherever rumours of war circulate and men's minds are distraught with fear of change and calamity, you may be sure that a hook-nosed Rothschild is at his games somewhere near the region of the disturbance'.[13] Beatrice and Sidney Webb, Fabian Society stalwarts and co-founders of the London School of Economics and Political Science, 'described Jews as a "constant influence for degradation" in their

---

[11] George Carden (2021) 'Anti-Semitism row: Lloyd Russell-Moyle facing complaint', *The Argus*, 12 October, https://www.theargus.co.uk/news/19640245.anti-semitism-row-lloyd-russell-moyle-facing-complaint/

[12] https://www.bbc.co.uk/news/articles/c5114q1x09eo; https://www.theguardian.com/commentisfree/article/2024/may/31/faiza-shaheen-labour-deselected-chingford-woodford-green-general-election

[13] Alan Johnson (2020) 'Corbyn is one man: Left-wing antisemitism is a tradition', *Fathom Journal*, October, https://fathomjournal.org/corbyn-is-one-man-left-wing-antisemitism-is-a-tradition/

1897 book *Industrial Democracy*', historian Ian Hernon noted.[14] In 1921, three years before he became prime minister, Labour leader Ramsay MacDonald wrote of 'the rich plutocratic Jew [whose] views upon life make one anti-Semitic'.[15] In the late 1940s, Ernest Bevin, a notorious anti-Semite, served as Labour's foreign secretary.[16]

It is not hard to compile a list such as this, although it is much easier to publish it when those on it are no longer alive. (You cannot libel the dead.) More importantly, it would be far easier to produce a list of anti-Semitic politicians on Britain's political right than on the left. Those on the right have never felt the need to be as careful with their words because they are far less scrutinised than those on the left, particularly those on the left who support Palestinian rights.

While sweeping assertions that Corbyn is anti-Semitic are still regularly aired by mainstream media, including the BBC, seemingly heedless of defamation law, anyone who aims to publicly question the charges of anti-Semitism made against Jeremy Corbyn needs a strong nerve.[17] If I were to use phrases such as 'the big lie' to describe the claims that the former Labour Party leader is anti-Semitic, I might well be accused of hinting that Adolf Hitler was correct when he used the phrase 'große Lüge'.[18] I would not be the first to be accused in this way.

And as a geographer, I cannot talk about land between a river and a sea without worrying about how my words might be interpreted, because some believe that the land of Israel is land that God promised the Jews in the Bible, the 'land between the

14 Robert Philpot (2020) 'Author says Labour always had anti-Semitic seam, but new leader could reboot it', *The Times of Israel*, 3 April, https://www.timesofisrael.com/author-says-labour-always-had-anti-semitic-seam-but-new-leader-could-reboot-it/

15 James Ramsay MacDonald (1922) *A socialist in Palestine*, London: Jewish Socialist Labour Confederation Poale-Zion, https://catalog.hathitrust.org/Record/007666298

16 Philpot (2020) (n. 14).

17 Asa Winstanley (2023) *Weaponising Anti-Semitism: how the Israel lobby brought down Jeremy Corbyn*, London/New York: OR Books

18 https://en.wikipedia.org/wiki/Big_lie

river (Jordan) and the (Mediterranean) sea'.[19] When, in private, I ask Corbyn detractors why this should be so, I am told, with a shrug of the shoulders, 'you will never understand'.[20]

I have also been told more than once that the phrase 'the many not the few' – a call to imagine an end to injustice that became associated with the Corbyn leadership – is a slur, and in some way anti-Semitic too. I reply that Percy Bysshe Shelley did not mean it as such when he ended his poem *The Masque of Anarchy* with 'Ye are many – they are few.' It really *was* about the Peterloo Massacre of 16 August 1819. It is not a reference to the 1987 play set in a fictional London court room in July 1967 about alleged choices that were made 'to risk the many in order to save the few'[21] in Hungary towards the end of the Second World War, or of some people both then and now feeling compelled 'to save the few out of the many'.[22] But you have to delve deep to see why 'the many not the few' might be considered a slur.

So, if it was not for this, why was Jeremy Corbyn hung out to dry? The answer, I think, was that he was popular, and his popularity was seen to grow during 2016 and into 2017 in ways that had never been expected by those who detested him. They thought he would be a one-term wonder.

Corbyn becoming elected Labour leader in 2015 was not the problem, it was the later swing of the general public towards him that frightened conservative interests, including those conservative interests within the Labour Party. And this was a fear that they felt through to their core.

---

[19] David Gardner (2013) *Between the river and the sea: Oslo at 20*, September, Oslo: Norwegian Peacebuilding Resource Centre, https://www.files.ethz.ch/isn/170282/Between%20the%20River%20and%20the%20Sea.pdf

[20] To understand more, start with Adam Johannes (2023) 'From the river to the sea: The true history of a famous slogan for Palestine', *Voice Wales*, 26 October, https://www.voice.wales/from-the-river-to-the-sea-the-true-history-of-a-famous-slogan-for-palestine/

[21] Jim Allen (1987) *Perdition*, London: Ithaca Press, p. 45. (Ideally, not a version with pages removed by the court, but an unredacted version of the original script of that play. The phrase 'many and the few' appears several times on the pages that were removed from it by the London courts.)

[22] Allen (1987) (n. 21), p. 63.

Today some especially well-informed commentators look back to what happened in Chile and see a parallel. It was not Allende being elected that was the catalyst for the coup, it was the growth in his popularity after that election which was seen as the terrible danger. That was when he had to be removed: 'The coup happened partly because the government's popularity, though never overwhelming, rose while it was in office. This rise convinced conservative interests that it would be re-elected, and would then take the patchy reforms of its first term much further.'[23] I believe the parallels are apposite. I wish that Corbyn had seen this coming, as he had been in South America at the time of Allende. Perhaps he knew it was inevitable that he too would be targeted and just hoped it would be by less violent means.

One evening in June 2016 I found myself standing on a fire engine on the edge of a crowd in Parliament Square. My overriding memory is wishing that Jeremy Corbyn, who was addressing the crowd, would be more terse. I was preventing the camera crews of Sky and the BBC from being jolted by overenthusiastic well-wishers trying to climb onto the Fire Brigade Union's fire truck. It was the evening when the first coup against Corbyn had been mounted in Parliament by some of the Labour MPs who had greeted his leadership first with incredulity and then with fury. The coup failed. The first 30 seconds of Corbyn's speech was remarkable; clear, concise and coruscating – but then he went on, adding detail and nuance, at length. The broadcasters, never inclined to show him at his most persuasive, chose something other than that first half-minute to feature on the evening news. I thought then that he should have been more cunning, more calculating, more sound-biting, more 'statesman-like' that night, although I don't think so now. I have changed my mind. He did not need to play their game. In the end, in the long game, he has won by not mimicking his opponents. If you doubt me, ask a young British person where they stand on Gaza and on the nature of what was occurring there in 2023 and 2024.

[23] Andy Beckett (2023) 'The 1973 coup against democratic socialism in Chile still matters – there, in Britain and beyond', *The Guardian*, 18 August, https://www.theguardian.com/commentisfree/2023/aug/18/1973-coup-chile-democratic-socialism-still-matters-britain

The rise in Corbyn's support in the 2017 general election was staggeringly high despite such bad press, and I now believe that he would have been eviscerated regardless of how he had performed, or even if Labour had emerged from the 2017 general election as the party with the most MPs.

I first met Jeremy Corbyn many decades ago in a room in Parliament. I mistook him for one of the mostly silent army of staff who arrange the chairs and tidy the rooms. He never told me who he was. On another occasion I met him briefly in a pub when he rushed in, bought everyone a round of drinks and left, without having a drink himself. Someone smiled, 'Oh, that's Jeremy.' Over the years I had many such encounters.

From 2015 onward, as the crowds around him grew bigger, I never asked for a selfie, although he would always oblige those who did. I only ever spoke to him briefly. The press painted him as thin-skinned and dim – he was the very opposite. I was pleased that it had been the Oxford East MP I had voted for, Andrew Smith, who had endorsed him, a few seconds before midnight on 15 June 2015, so that he could enter the race to be Labour leader.

A woman who cut my hair once in Oxford told me how Smith had employed her years before to iron his shirts for Parliament – just the front, as there was no need to iron the rest. Many Labour MPs are better people than you might believe, and only stuffed shirts when they need to be.

For decades before he became leader, Corbyn was seen as irrelevant to those enmeshed in the ambitions and machinations of the 'Mother of Parliaments', although not to his constituents, or to the left wing of Labour, or to the trade unions, or to the peace and community groups he has stood with for years, or in his support of supposedly 'lost causes' of justice ranging from South Africa to Ireland to Palestine and beyond. In the small and vicious Westminster village, he was just a random beardy lefty constituency MP. Not a threat. Not worth purging, even when he voted against the 2003 Iraq War.

He was put forward in 2015 as the left's choice for the Labour Party leadership ballot when the Socialist Campaign Group convinced him it was his turn. His nomination and victory would go on to overturn accepted wisdom, like that of a restaurant owner convinced no one would ever want a particular dish – and then, almost on a whim, puts it on the menu and discovers that very many people do want it, after all.

In addition to his being long dismissed and later hated by the Labour right, I suspect Corbyn has also long been taken for granted among the more ambitious and egotistical on the left of the Labour Party. When he became leader, some comrades from the past must have been wounded and jealous, especially as the remarkable enthusiasm for him grew around the country. Perhaps those comrades resented the outpouring of admiration and affection for someone they saw as too moral and dull. Even the way he dressed was critiqued – as if that was what mattered most.

And what about outside the Westminster bubble? While three generations of the people of Islington North have had the chance to get the measure of Corbyn, much of the rest of the country knows him only from how he has been portrayed by his detractors and the media, whose attacks intensified after Labour's unexpectedly strong performance in 2017. More than a few people, relying on the most right-wing media sources, believe he is some kind of terrorist. At best, they may know Corbyn from snippets of House of Commons footage in which he is a sober, critical and arguably pedantic voice against a backdrop of raucous booing, debating-society ad hominems and showy, scripted, unfunny, jokes.

Not by accident, it would seem, have mainstream media outlets rarely offered Corbyn neutral or even non-hostile interviewers, let alone sympathetic ones, or showed anything of his empathy and wit, or given him the opportunity to speak about his vision or his life. Nor, for some reason, have we seen him appear in the flattering standard features given to other senior political figures as a matter of course: no BBC Radio Four *Desert Island Discs* appearance; no fireside chats and panel shows for him; no features on light entertainment programmes. That would be too dangerous to allow.

Is it Corbyn's failing not to have learned how to foreground his personal warmth and humour via a well-crafted media persona? I have seen firsthand how misleading the public perceptions of political figures can be. I once sat at breakfast in a smart hotel next to a former Labour minister and his mistress. He was oblivious to everyone around him as he berated her ruthlessly for her failings, until she dropped her head and started to sob silently. In politics and in his post-government career, this man was regularly presented on TV and in political commentators' portraits as wise, jovial and kind; a salt-of-the-earth boy made good. In reality, he was a small, nasty bully.

To those who have heard or met Corbyn in person, rather than the mainstream media's filter, it is his compassion, moral rigour and consistency, at least as far as his policies are concerned, that resonate most. He is also extremely brave – in all the media discussion in the wake of the killings of Jo Cox and David Amess of the risks faced by elected politicians, it is rarely mentioned how many serious threats Corbyn received, and how much abuse he faced as leader and still does. In a terrorist attack outside Finsbury Park mosque in Islington North constituency in 2017, an elderly man, Makram Ali, was killed and more than a dozen others were injured. The far-right assailant, who drove his vehicle into a crowd, said at his trial that he had been aiming to kill Corbyn.[24]

Jeremy Corbyn did not win the 2017 general election, despite helping to inspire so many people to campaign for his party and increasing the vote so greatly for Labour, nor the 2019 general election, where despite gaining 10,295,907 votes, the Labour Party suffered what is almost always described as a 'historic defeat'. Posterity, however, will likely cast a much more positive light on the leadership of a man often described by his supporters as being 'on the right side of history'. And younger people who could not then vote because they were not yet aged 18 will count up the number of votes he won in 2019, compare it to those won by Blair and Brown, and ask why their parents and grandparents had been so easily fooled into not voting, or voting for the Conservatives and for Brexit. When you look back at political history, only a few are now celebrated.

---

[24] Wikipedia, https://en.wikipedia.org/wiki/2017_Finsbury_Park_attack

By sticking to his principles, Corbyn may have done something more important than becoming prime minister. In doing so, he helped further the process that Martin Luther King Jr described thus: 'The arc of the moral universe is long, but it bends toward justice.' He showed that it was possible to shift an apparently immovable political consensus, in a remarkably short time, by drawing on the power of decency, honesty and compassion – and hope. He is not the first political figure to have ever done so worldwide, but he is the first for many decades to have done so in Britain. He showed that a movement of over half a million people could rise up, making the Labour Party under his leadership the largest of any political party in Europe at the time. And his example continues to inspire those working for justice not only in the UK, but worldwide, from Ireland to Norway, from Chile to Brazil.

When I first wrote these words, in September 2023, Jeremy Corbyn had celebrated his 40th anniversary as MP for Islington North – and topped a YouGov poll as the UK's most popular politician (Figure 1.1).[25] By early 2024, Corbyn had become a European figurehead of calls for peace across the world and for an immediate ceasefire in Gaza.[26]

In the July 2024 general election Corbyn won his seat for the eleventh time. He was very close to becoming the longest-serving MP in the House of Commons and 'Father of the House'. Diane Abbott became 'Mother of the House'. The Labour government formed by Keir Starmer closely resembled John Major's 1992 Conservative administration in ideology. Labour had again become Tory. The Tories and Reform had become far- and extreme-right. We were at a peak of injustice.

---

[25] YouGov (2023) 'The most popular politicians & political figures (Q2 2023)'. See the archived webpage: https://web.archive.org/web/20230709064428/https://yougov.co.uk/ratings/politics/popularity/politicians-political-figures/all (and given by https://twitter.com/LeftieStats/status/1676321819006050307).

[26] Dave Burke (2024) 'Jeremy Corbyn joins South Africa delegation accusing Israel of genocide at The Hague', *The Mirror*, 11 January, https://www.mirror.co.uk/news/politics/jeremy-corbyn-joins-south-africa-31857624

Figure 1.1: Approval ratings for leading politicians in the UK, April–June 2023

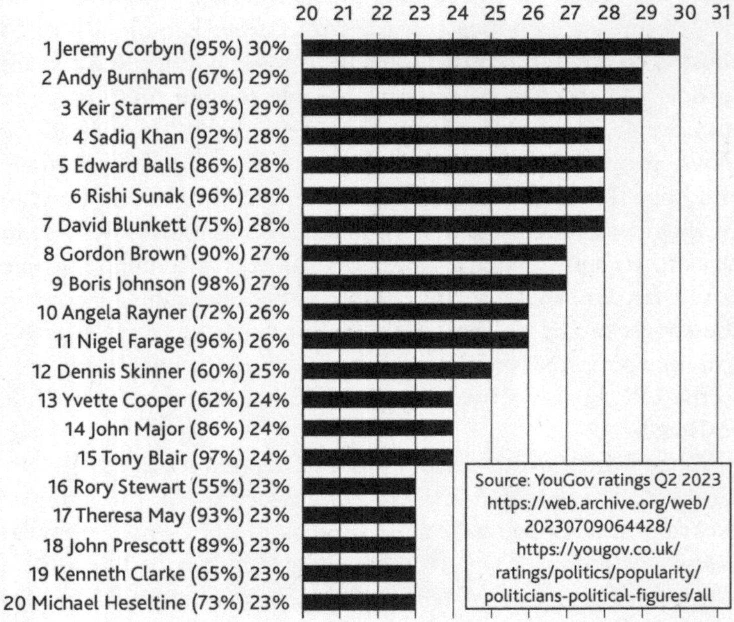

Note: The first percentage figure in each row (in parentheses) gives the percentage of respondents who recognised the politician's name. The second figure provides the main data point, the percentage of respondents who nominated them as their most popular politician.

Source: Drawn by author, inspired by https://twitter.com/LeftieStats/status/1676321819006050307

CHAPTER 1.2

Would you let Boris Johnson drive your daughter home?[1]

In the early hours of 19 July 1969, a few days before the first human stepped on the moon, a car swerved on a bridge in Chappaquiddick, Massachusetts. Ted Kennedy, the 37-year-old younger brother of the President of the United States of America, was at the wheel. The car plunged into the water. Kennedy managed to swim free. He left Mary Jo Kopechne, his passenger, in the vehicle. At some point, as it slowly submerged, she drowned. Kennedy notified the police of the accident ten hours later. Another man had recovered the vehicle and found Kopechne's body. She was a typist, a loyal political activist and a dedicated Democrat. She died just before her 29th birthday.

When pollster Lord Ashcroft posed the question 'Would you rather allow Jeremy Hunt or Boris Johnson to babysit your children?',[2] it was seen by some commentators as a joke, rather than a deft way to gauge perceptions of politicians' trustworthiness. The *Daily Telegraph* reported it as 'a curious little snippet from the weekend. According to a poll by Lord Ashcroft, only 10 per cent of voters would let Boris Johnson babysit their children.'[3] It was more than curious; some 52 per cent of all voters polled in

---

[1] Originally published in *Public Sector Focus*, August/September 2018, pp. 14–17.

[2] https://lordashcroftpolls.com/wp-content/uploads/2019/07/Conservative-Leadership-Survey-Results-Summary-July-2019-1.pdf

[3] Michael Deacon (2019) 'The gloom is gone. This was the boyish Boris of old', *The Telegraph*, 8 July, https://www.telegraph.co.uk/politics/2019/07/08/gloom-gone-boyish-boris-old/

the last week of June 2019 said they would not allow either of the two candidates vying for the leadership of the Conservative Party such access to their children.

When those surveyed in Lord Ashcroft's poll were broken down by party political preference, some 49 per cent of all Conservative voters, 59 per cent of Labour voters and 46 per cent of Liberal Democrats would not allow either candidate to babysit. Some 56 per cent of 'Leave' voters (who tend to be much older) would not allow either man to babysit; younger voters were even more averse to the idea. As many as 97 per cent of Labour 'Remain' voters said they would not allow Johnson to be their babysitter; even 80 per cent of his most loyal supporters – those who voted Conservative in the 2017 general election and Leave in the 2016 referendum – would not.

Lord Ashcroft also asked for voters' views on the Chappaquiddick question: 'Would you allow Boris Johnson to drive your daughter or the daughter of a friend home after a party?' Some 88 per cent of Conservative voters said no, as did 96 per cent of Labour voters and 98 per cent of Liberal Democrat voters (see Table 1 for the proportions who would select one of the two rather than the other, if they had to choose). Only 3 per cent of people who

Table 1: The voters' verdict: Question 11 in the Lord Ashcroft Poll of late June 2019 (%)

Who would you rather?:		**2017 GE vote**			**EU ref vote**	
% JEREMY HUNT/% BORIS JOHNSON	**ALL**	**Con**	**Lab**	**Lib Dem**	**Remain**	**Leave**
Allow to babysit your children	**32/10**	35/16	35/6	48/6	43/4	26/18
Have round for dinner	**19/38**	17/58	21/26	29/28	28/24	11/56
Trust with an important secret	**32/9**	35/15	34/5	47/3	42/3	26/17
Lend money to and expect to get it back	**35/10**	38/16	39/6	51/5	46/4	29/17
Allow to drive your daughter or the daughter of a friend home after a party	**40/8**	45/12	43/4	56/2	50/3	35/13

Source: Lord Ashcroft (KCMG PC) *Conservative leadership poll of July 2019*, https://lordashcroftpolls.com/wp-content/uploads/2019/07/Conservative-Leadership-Survey-Results-Summary-July-2019-1.pdf voted 'Remain' in the 2016 referendum would trust Johnson with that responsibility, and just 13 per cent of those who had voted 'Leave', including only 14 per cent of those who both voted 'Leave' in 2016 and Conservative in 2017. Only one in seven of the group of voters most in favour of Johnson being prime minister would trust him to do such a simple thing. We have been living in remarkable times.

Given the choice for leadership between Jeremy Hunt and Boris Johnson, I would have opted for Johnson. This is because I have monitored Hunt's actions as secretary of state for health. Life expectancy in Britain fell for the first time since the Second World War during his watch. Improvements made in life expectancy before 2014 slowed down markedly during Hunt's 2012–18 tenure as health minister. Hunt appeared more dangerous than Johnson.

I knew, and I believe Hunt knew, that the infant mortality rate in Britain rose from 3.6 babies dying per 1,000 born in England and Wales in 2014, to 3.7 in 2015, 3.8 in 2016 and 3.9 in 2017. I believe Hunt also knew that the Office for National Statistics said that each of these rises was statistically significant. I am sure he was not told that nowhere else in Europe was suffering such a health crisis. I cared; I'm not sure he did. I would have voted for Johnson, not because I think he cares, but because I am less sure that he doesn't. I would not trust Hunt with the lives of others. [Editorial note: Hunt later became chancellor of the Exchequer under Rishi Sunak's premiership and held that position during the years in which it became clear that poverty was killing more children.[4]]

UK voters' verdicts on the character of Jeremy Hunt were more sanguine than mine. As Table 1 shows, some 32 per cent in 2019 would trust Hunt with an important secret, whereas only 9 per cent would trust Johnson. Some 35 per cent, still a minority, would lend money to Hunt and expect to get it back, whereas only one in ten would expect Johnson to repay his debts. Then

---

4 Danny Dorling (2024) 'From the cradle to the grave: the abandonment of our social contract', *Byline Times*, 6 March, https://bylinetimes.com/2024/03/06/from-the-cradle-to-the-grave-the-abandonment-of-our-social-contract/

why did the Conservatives back Boris? The only clue is that a majority, 58 per cent, would have him round to dinner, whereas only 17 per cent of Conservatives would invite Hunt.

Lord Ashcroft's poll also revealed that the word voters most associated with Jeremy Hunt was 'smug'; with Boris Johnson it was 'arrogant' (see Table 2). A few of the British, and especially Conservative voters, have been brought up to quite like and admire people who are arrogant. It may have something to do with Britain's national legacy of arrogance. My friend Sally Tomlinson and I wrote about this in *Rule Britannia: Brexit and the End of Empire*. The book is largely about people being arrogant and smug, and speculation over when the British elite might finally become a little more normal and less arrogantly smug.

Lord Ashcroft's June 2019 poll also revealed that 91 per cent of Labour voters who had voted 'Remain' would prefer a government led by Jeremy Corbyn over one led by Boris Johnson, as would 56 per cent of the small minority of Labour voters who had voted 'Leave'.

In spring and early summer 2019 it was widely claimed that Labour was losing support to the (then) new Brexit Party (of

Table 2: The voters' verdict: Question 12 in the Lord Ashcroft Poll of late June 2019

Which three of the following words and phrases best describe JEREMY HUNT/BORIS JOHNSON

Determined / Weak / Down to earth / Out of touch / Principled / Indecisive / Up to the job / Out of his depth / Competent / Dishonest / Doesn't listen / Shares my values / Weird / Likeable / Ruthless / Fair / Stands up for Britain / On my side / Arrogant / Smug / Amusing / Dangerous / Tolerant / Human / Unreliable

Top 5 words

JEREMY HUNT	BORIS JOHNSON
Smug (23%)	Arrogant (26%)
Out of his depth (19%)	Dishonest (24%)
Competent (19%)	Dangerous (22%)
Out of touch (18%)	Unreliable (22%)
Arrogant (18%)	Amusing (21%)

Source: Lord Ashcroft (KCMG PC) *Conservative leadership poll of July 2019*, https://lordashcroftpolls.com/wp-content/uploads/2019/07/Conservative-Leadership-Survey-Results-Summary-July-2019-1.pdf

Nigel Farage). However, an earlier poll by Lord Ashcroft had revealed that fewer than one in seven of those who had voted Labour at the 2017 general election had voted for the Brexit Party in the May 2019 European elections. Furthermore, by May 2019 some 62 per cent of Brexit supporters were social class ABC1, as compared with 58 per cent of Labour voters. Brexit voters were (on average) posh in 2016 (59 per cent ABC1, with a 95 per cent confidence limit of 1 per cent) and were getting posher as a group by 2019. People who were social class C2, D or E were more likely to stop supporting Brexit between 2016 and 2019, or not to have switched their support towards it prior to the referendum.

Lord Ashcroft also carried out an exit poll of 10,280 UK voters in European Parliament elections on 23 and 24 May 2019. It revealed that some 22 per cent of previous Labour voters voted Liberal Democrat, 17 per cent Green, 4 per cent for the now-defunct Change UK Party, 2 per cent for UKIP (another of Nigel Farage's former platforms) and 1 per cent for the Conservatives. But in a general election, where the choice for the vast majority of voters is between the UK's two main parties, Labour and the Conservatives, and two potential prime ministers, most (I wrote before the election) will revert to that binary choice. The great unknown is, if the Brexit Party (recast as the 'Reform Party' by 2024, and possibly with yet another name by the time you read this) were to field candidates in a future general election, would it seriously erode the Conservative Party vote as it did in May 2019? Lord Ashcroft produced an especially colourful graphic to illustrate this.[5]

Finally, Lord Ashcroft's exit poll of late May 2019 revealed that the most popular political party in the UK was Labour, despite it having just lost ten seats at the European elections, its greatest-ever fall in support at any such an election. Contrary to popular understanding and most media messaging, Labour commanded more support in May 2019 among the population as a whole, and among every social class group other than those

[5] Michael Ashcroft (2019) 'My Euro-election post-vote poll: most Tory switchers say they will stay with their new party', *Lord Ashcroft Polls Blog*, 27 May, https://lordashcroftpolls.com/2019/05/my-euro-election-post-vote-poll-most-tory-switchers-say-they-will-stay-with-their-new-party/

with an occupation that classed them as C2, who preferred the Brexit Party by three percentage points, or AB, who preferred the Conservatives by two percentage points and the Liberals by a further two points above them (see Table 3).

Some 93 per cent of those who said they voted Labour in the European elections said they would do so in a future general election, as did 13 per cent of Liberal Democrat European voters, and 21 per cent of all those who had voted Green (but only 1 per cent of Conservatives). Labour was by far the most popular party among those who did not know if they were Leave or Remain, and among female voters; and it tied for most popular with the Conservative Party among male voters.

Labour, in May 2019, was the most popular among all voters younger than 55, and in the North East of England, the North West, Yorkshire and Humberside, in the West Midlands, and in London. In the South West of England, the Brexit Party was one

Table 3: Voter preferences, UK general election 2019, by party and social class

		Social grade			
	Total	**AB**	**C1**	**C2**	**DE**
Unweighted base	10,280	4,331	2,659	1,332	1,958
Weighted base	10,280	4,353	2,655	1,321	1,951
Q8. Which party do you think you are most likely to vote for at the next general election? (% shown below)					
Labour	21	19	20	21	26
Brexit Party	18	13	18	24	23
Conservative	18	21	17	17	13
Liberal Democrat	17	23	16	11	10
The Green Party	7	7	9	5	6
Change UK/ (Tiggers)	4	4	4	3	3
SNP	4	3	4	4	4
UKIP	3	2	3	4	5
Plaid Cymru	1	0	1	1	1
Another party	2	2	3	3	3
Prefer not to say	6	5	6	7	5

Source: Lord Ashcroft Polls, online fieldwork dates: 23–24 May 2019 percentage point ahead of Labour, two points ahead in the East Midlands, and level-pegging in Wales. Only in the South East of England were the Conservatives most popular in late May 2019, and then only just.

So, think – would you have let your daughter be driven home by Boris Johnson? If not, how would you (and everyone you know) have voted when you had the chance to get him out of the driving seat? [Editorial note: And, if Johnson was so very unpopular, how and why was his image improved in just a few months between May 2019 and December 2019? What was it that meant Johnson had to become the next UK prime minister? Why was the alternative to Johnson so frightening to those who decided what the media stories that year would be?]

At 11 am on Tuesday, 23 July, Boris Johnson was named leader of the Conservative Party, chosen by a two-thirds majority of party members who voted, some 92,153 people. Just 46,656 voted for Hunt. Turnout was 87.4 per cent, so total party membership at that time was 158,800 people, or fewer than 250 people per constituency. Before Johnson won the vote, ministers Philip Hammond, David Gauke, Rory Stewart, Alan Duncan and Anne Milton all resigned, along with Mohammed Amin, the chair of the Conservative Muslim Foundation and a party member of 36 years' standing, who compared Johnson to Hitler.[6] And that was all before lunch on the first day of Boris Johnson's premiership.

---

[6] Lottie Tiplady-Bishop (2019) 'BYE BYE BORIS: Who resigned over Boris Johnson becoming Prime minister? From Anne Milton to Sir Alan Duncan', *The Sun*, 27 July, https://www.thesun.co.uk/news/9565235/who-has-resigned-over-boris-johnson/

CHAPTER 1.3

The curve of inequality and the Brexit Way[1]

[Editorial note: This chapter was published as a blog before the general election of 2019 at a time when the polls still suggested the Conservatives might not secure an overall majority in the as-yet-to-be declared election, before Brexit had taken place, and before the pandemic began.]

In 2014 in the UK, the best-off 1 per cent took 15 times the average income, a share almost identical to what they took before the Second World War. In between those two dates they always took less – and in 1976, almost four times less (after tax). That was the year Britain was the most equal it has even been.

After 2014, the take of the top 1 per cent dipped slightly – but then began to rise again, to become as high in 2018 as it was in 2014. We are currently teetering on the edge of either the beginnings of a long downward curve towards the slow realisation of greater equality (as the gap between rich and poor begins to fall), or we are about to see inequality rise again to even greater heights. The curve has never flatlined. It either goes up or it goes down.

Politics is what matters most in this. Not the everyday politics of most general elections, which have made no difference at all to the long-term trend; but the underlying national politics. Between 1914 and 1976 income inequalities in the UK almost always fell – regardless of which party won power. Between 1976 and 2018 they almost always rose, again regardless of which party won power. By 2018 the 'bottom 90 per cent', the vast

[1] Originally published as an *LSE Brexit Blog*, 15 October 2019 (lightly edited).

majority of the population of Britain, were living on 67 per cent of average mean income. That was because the top 10 per cent, and especially the top 1 per cent, were taking so much more than in the decades before.

By 2018 the best-off 0.1 per cent took 67 times average earnings, a share so high that they had last achieved such excesses back in 1936 – apart from one single year, 2013, when their take was 7.2 per cent or 72 times average earnings, and in that year, the best-off 0.01 per cent took 130 times average earnings. By 2019, almost a third of UK adults with children under the age of 16 were food insecure.[2] The risk was greatest among the unemployed, those with long-term health conditions or disabilities, and those on the lowest household incomes. Between 2004 and 2016 food insecurity among the least well-off nearly doubled.[3] [Editorial note: It became very much worse later. By 2024 we were beginning to make comparisons with the 'hungry 1930s'.[4]]

We see wealth inequality still rising as more and more people go hungry in Britain, as homelessness rises and overall life expectancy begins to fall. Wealth inequality tends to lag behind the trend of income inequality, although that may not be the case when inequalities next begin to fall – if they fall. If UK house prices in the southeast continue to slump as was happening in September 2019 (Figure 1.2), wealth inequalities will drop even as income inequalities still, for a short time at least, teeter on a plateau.

In February 2019, the *Daily Telegraph* reported that income inequality in the UK was still growing, ten years after the great economic crash, because 'the richest grew their earnings but

[2] Rachel Loopstra, Aaron Reeves and Valerie Tarasuk (2019) 'The rise of hunger among low-income households: an analysis of the risks of food insecurity between 2004 and 2016 in a population-based study of UK adults', *Journal of Epidemiology and Community Health*, 73: 668–73, https://jech.bmj.com/content/73/7/668.abstract

[3] Loopstra et al (2019) (n. 2).

[4] https://www.theguardian.com/society/2024/mar/27/gordon-brown-calls-for-creation-of-poverty-fund-to-halt-slide-into-hungry-decade

Figure 1.2: Annual house price change by region in the UK, year to Q3 2019

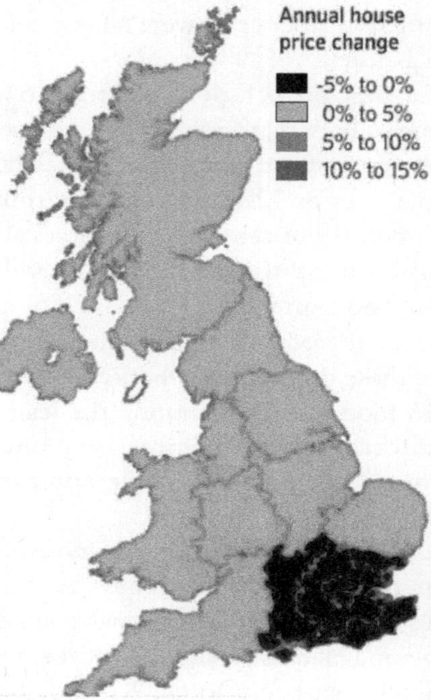

Source: Nationwide Building Society, press release, 30 September 2019.[5]

the poorest were faced with falling benefits'.[6] The newspaper explained to its typically well-heeled readers that median average household income after tax was stagnant at just £28,400, according to data for the financial year ending in 2018. That is just £77.80 a day to live on – to cover rent, food, clothing, bus

[5] The press release is no longer to be found on the web, but the image does appear here: Simon Lambert and Miriam Aldersley (2019) 'House prices fall in England for the first time in seven years as estate agents blame Brexit uncertainty and stamp duty rise', *The Daily Mail*, 30 March, https://www.dailymail.co.uk/news/article-6868135/House-prices-fall-England-time-seven-years.html

[6] Helen Chandler-Wilde (2019) 'Income inequality grew last year as poorest hit by benefits cut', *The Telegraph*, 26 February, https://www.telegraph.co.uk/business/2019/02/26/income-inequality-grew-last-year-poorest-hit-benefits-cut/

fares, gas and electricity bills, an internet access charge, a mobile phone, children's clothes, maybe a book or a birthday present occasionally. Fifty per cent of UK households – the homes of more than 50 per cent of the population, and of a much larger proportion of the UK's children than 50 per cent – had to manage on £77.80 a day, or less. (See Figure 1.3.)

In the latest financial year [Editorial note: before the pandemic began], the poorest fifth of households – those families surviving (or not) on £36.50 on average a day – have seen their incomes fall. In contrast, the richest fifth of households more recently saw their incomes rise as their earnings rose and as they reaped the rewards of very low rates of taxation. The Office for National Statistics reported that this was the second year in a row that income inequality as measured by household surveys had risen.

In March 2019 the Office for Budget Responsibility (OBR) explained that there were 31,000 people in the UK with incomes of a million pounds a year or more (giving them £3,000, £5,000 or even £10,000 a day to live on).[7] The OBR explained that this group accounted for 8 per cent of all PAYE (Pay As You Earn) income tax and national insurance receipts that the government had received in the financial year 2017–18. The average tax paid by each member of this 0.1 per cent of the population was £730,000 that year – which demonstrates that most of them were earning much more than a million pounds a year.

The most recent figures from the European Banking Authority reveal that the pay of bankers in the UK had begun to rise again so that now a record 3,567 were receiving more than €1 million a year, with the average yearly salary of UK bankers in this group being £1,700,000 (£4,660 a day).[8] This was nine times as many high-paid bankers as could be found in Germany, the next most 'banker-heavy' country in the EU. A decade after the 2008

---

7 Office of Budget Responsibility (2019) *Economic and fiscal outlook*, March, CP50, https://web.archive.org/web/20190324101319/https://cdn.obr.uk/March-2019_EFO_Web-Accessible.pdf

8 European Banking Authority (2019) *EBA report on high earners: Data as of end 2017*, Paris: EBA, 11 March, https://www.eba.europa.eu/sites/default/documents/files/documents/10180/2551996/239d027f-07ae-43f7-b161-3f458d443f3c/Report%20on%20High%20Earners%202017.pdf

Figure 1.3: Income inequality, 1910–2019, UK

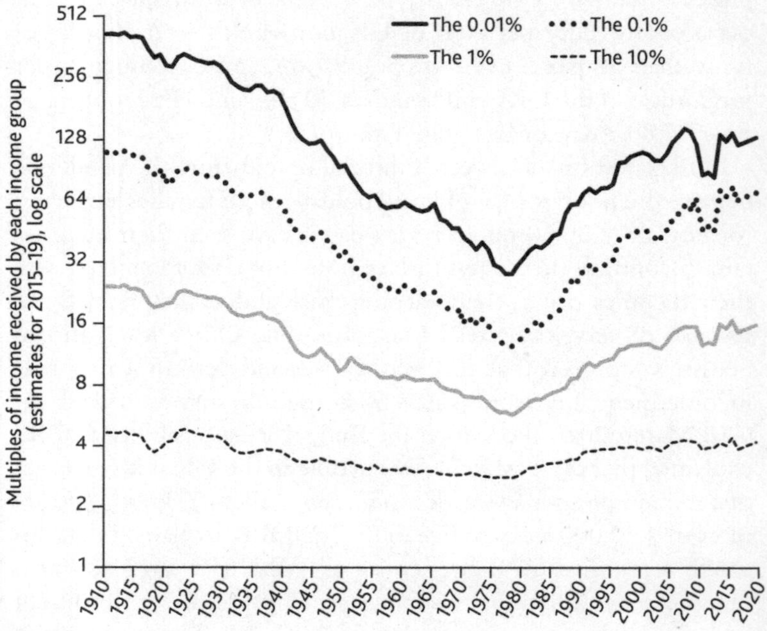

Note: The income inequality graph shown in this figure is derived from the following sources: A.B. Atkinson, 'The distribution of top incomes in the United Kingdom 1908–2000' in A.B. Atkinson and T. Piketty (eds), *Top incomes over the twentieth century. A contrast between continental European and English-speaking countries* (Oxford: Oxford University Press, 2007), ch 4 (in a series updated by the same author, and then updated by Tony Atkinson, Joe Hasell, Salvatore Morelli and Max Roser (2017) 'Economic inequality in the United Kingdom', *The Chartbook of Economic Inequality*, online resource and INET Oxford Working Paper no. 2017-10, May, https://www.chartbookofeconomicinequality.com/inequality-by-country/united-kingdom/); M. Brewer (2019) *What do we know and what should we do about inequality?* (London: Sage); with 2015–19 figures extrapolated from household data given in M. Shine and D. Webber (2019) *Using tax data to better capture top earners in household income inequality statistics*, London: ONS, 26 February. (Note that it is now complicated to construct and update because the UK government at that time did not encourage HMRC to release taxation data in a timely or useful fashion. See: Adam Corlett (2017) *Unequal results: Improving and reconciling the UK's household income statistics*, London: Resolution Foundation, December, https://www.resolutionfoundation.org/app/uploads/2017/12/Unequal-results.pdf)

Source: https://www.dannydorling.org/books/onepercent/Material.html

crash, three-quarters of all Europe's highest-paid bankers were still working and living in London, but the writing was on the wall – a change was coming.

At the same time as these figures were revealed, it was announced that 7,000 finance jobs could be lost from London in the very near future due to the Brexit mess.[9] The bankers were simply taking the money while they could, and once they did, many ran for it. In 2019 they knew the good times (for them at least) were likely to end very soon. We will probably see the fall in inequality begin at the top of the income and wealth scale, not at the bottom, and not until after life for the poorest in the UK has become even harder. This happened in the 1920s and 1930s and it may be what is just starting to happen now. It happens partly because rising wealth inequalities can never continue indefinitely.

In the year to October 2016, sales of individual properties within London 'worth' more than £10 million fell by 86 per cent;[10] and outside of London, the number of properties sold for such huge prices fell from ten in 2015 to none in 2016. In May 2017 it became clear that housing prices across London for all properties had begun to fall slightly.[11] In 2018 the London housing market fell faster.[12] In 2019 it is no longer polite to mention house prices at dinner parties in southeast England (see Figure 1.2). All postwar housing slumps have begun in London and spread outwards. In September 2019, the Nationwide Building Society reported that the average house in England had fallen in value, despite only the southeast and London showing falls. Prices in these areas were so very high that falls there have a significant effect on the national average – because wealth has become so unequally distributed across the UK. [Editorial note: By the spring of 2024 housing prices across the UK had slumped

9 Charles Riley and Ivana Kottasová (2019) '$1.3 trillion and 7,000 finance jobs are leaving Britain because of Brexit', *CNN Business*, 20 March, https://edition.cnn.com/2019/03/20/business/brexit-economy-bank-assets/index.html

10 Warren Lewis (2019) 'Super prime sales drop 86% according to new data', *Property Reporter*, 19 October, https://propertyreporter.co.uk/property/super-prime-sales-dr0p-86-according-to-new-data.html

11 Her Majesty's Land Registry (2017) *UK House Price Index (HPI) for June 2017*, London: HMLR, 15 August, https://www.gov.uk/government/news/uk-house-price-index-hpi-for-june-2017

12 Jonathan Prynn (2019) 'London house prices: property market fell for second year running in 2018', *The Evening Standard*, 4 January, https://www.standard.co.uk/homesandproperty/property-news/london-house-prices-property-market-fell-for-second-year-running-in-2018-a126856.html

in real terms and, when adjusted for either wages or inflation, were falling].

The overall fall in UK wealth inequality could have already begun. If you measure your wealth in dollars and you live and own property in the UK, you are already much worse off than you were in June 2016. But no one will have any sympathy for you in the most unequal state of all EU28 states. The map in Figure 1.4 shows a walking route through those counties where wealth may fall the most in absolute terms as the UK housing market currently adjusts to the Brexit mess. It is where the greatest number of people voted Leave.

Figure 1.4 shows a route past the homes of the majority of Leave voters, but a minority of the UK electorate. For every county shown on this map, there is a unique area of the UK outside of the south of England (as shown), where fewer people voted Leave despite there being a larger electorate able to vote in each comparator area. Because most people in the south of England live in the southeast, the majority of the map, by area, is of the southeast. Thus, across the majority of this map, house prices have already fallen, in some cases substantially. If the house price falls reported to have rippled out by autumn 2019 continue to do so, then very soon right across the south of England all

Figure 1.4: The Brexit Way, a walk around southern England mostly in Brexit-land

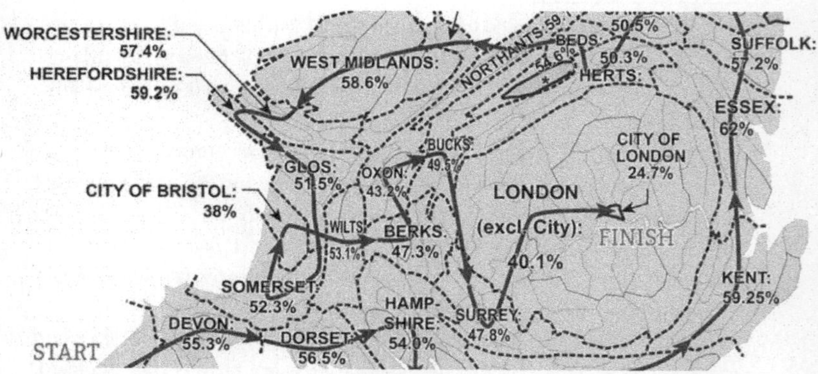

Note: Percentages denote how many people voted Leave of all who voted.

Source: Drawn by author with assistance from Ailsa Allen

housing will be falling in value.[13] [Editorial note: The falls did spread, then there was a brief rally at the height of the pandemic, and then the falls slowly and steadily continued – when measured in real terms.] That itself is not a bad outcome, unless the falls are very fast and show little sign of stopping. Then we are in uncharted economic waters.

[13] The third edition of Danny Dorling's *Inequality and the 1%* was published by Verso in September 2019 shortly after this article appeared. It contained all the references for the statistics given here, and a more nuanced argument about how rising inequality and its consequences may well have caused the vote for Leave to become so strong, most noticeably of all in the south of England. What it did not do was predict the coronavirus pandemic that would begin just a few months later, and how the very large number of deaths of mostly older people, predominantly homeowners, would result in the sale of their properties, which would be interpreted as a house price boom because they tended to own more expensive homes. The 'rush to the countryside' was only possible because of all those premature deaths in 2020 and 2021.

CHAPTER 1.4

So, how did we end up with this government?[1]

On 14 December 2019, the *Telegraph* newspaper reported:

> In a sign of the damage Mr Johnson's Tories have done to Labour, there are 24 constituencies that have voted Tory for the first time in decades. The new Conservative majorities in three of these constituencies is more than 20 percentage points: Dudley North (31.3 per cent), Bassetlaw (27.6 per cent) and Great Grimsby (22.2 per cent). All of these seats saw double-digit swings from Labour to the Tories. The seat with the longest history of backing Labour is Rother Valley, that had elected a Labour MP since Thomas Walter Grundy won the seat with 55 per cent of the vote in 1918 …[2]

So, what happened?

On 16 January, having analysed the polling data, Martin Baxter of Electoral Calculus published one of the first 'flow-of-the vote' diagrams of the 2019 general election (Figure 1.5). He divided voters into those who had voted Leave, Remain, or did not

[1] Originally published in *Public Sector Focus*, January/February 2020, pp. 14–17.

[2] Jamie Johnson, Izzy Lyons, and Ashley Kirk (2019) 'The 24 Labour heartland seats lost to the Tories for the first time in decades', *The Telegraph*, 14 December, https://www.telegraph.co.uk/politics/2019/12/13/stunning-tory-seat-victories-2019-general-election/

Figure 1.5: Migration of voters from 2017 to 2019, by 2016 referendum choice

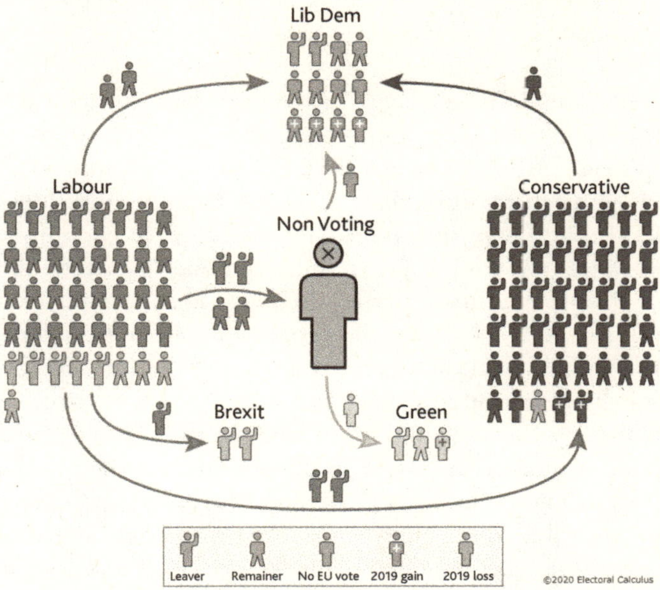

see colour version in plate section

Source: Martin Baxter (2020) 'Voter migration by party 2017–2019', *Electoral Calculus*, 16 January, https://web.archive.org/web/20200219124319/https://www.electoralcalculus.co.uk/pseph_transition2019.html

vote in the 2016 referendum. In his diagram, each stick person represents 300,000 voters. As he explained, the figures show that:

> Most but not all Conservative voters were Leave supporters, and the 43 Conservative voters were divided into 31 Leavers, 11 Remainers and one who didn't vote in the EU referendum. The 41 Labour supporters are divided into 26 Remainers, 12 Leavers and three who didn't vote (possibly because they were too young in 2016).... In terms of voter migration, the main story is that voters left Labour. Nine out of 41 voters left. They left for different reasons and went to different places, but they left. That partial collapse of the Labour vote is the most important fact of the 2019 election and explains why Labour did so badly.

> By comparison, the Conservatives were relatively stable and gained seats because Labour weakened. The largest group of Labour defectors were the four supporters who chose not to vote.[3]

Baxter's graphic is excellent. However, it had to simplify what happened by showing only net flows. In the election, some people who hadn't voted at all in 2017 would have voted Labour in 2019 and many more than 1,200,000 Labour voters (the four stick people shown in the diagram) would have chosen not to vote. While we tend to focus on the shifting size of the groups who vote for the main parties, in 2019, as in many elections, the largest group of all was the people who did not cast a ballot. Those who study elections tend to forget how uninteresting most people find elections; many devote little thought to their choice until the day. I drew Figure 1.6 to illustrate the results of the 2019 election in a different way to Baxter, by dividing the population of the UK into 66 groups of a million people and approximating how they each voted, choose not to vote, or could not vote, to the nearest million. The figure divides 66 into 11 equal-sized age groups, age-bands that contain six million people each.

What Figure 1.6 shows is that it was mainly older people who chose to vote Conservative in 2019, even more so than in 2017. The Labour vote was the most spread out by age, and the Liberal Democrat and Labour votes combined were equal to the Conservative vote. In practice that split the opposition very effectively. The disaggregation in this visualisation gives only a crude approximation for the smaller political parties, as they received so few votes that it is not possible to show the age range of their supporters. Instead, their solitary squares are placed against the age of many of their key supporters; and in such a way as to make the entire diagram square up correctly.

Just before the 2019 general election, two rival estimates were made of the likely outcome on 12 December. One, by Survation, relied on data collected between 16 November and 10 December

3 Martin Baxter (2020) 'Voter migration by party 2017–2019', *Electoral Calculus*, 16 January, https://web.archive.org/web/20200219124319/https://www.electoralcalculus.co.uk/pseph_transition2019.html

Figure 1.6: Disaggregation of the population of the UK in 2019, by age and vote

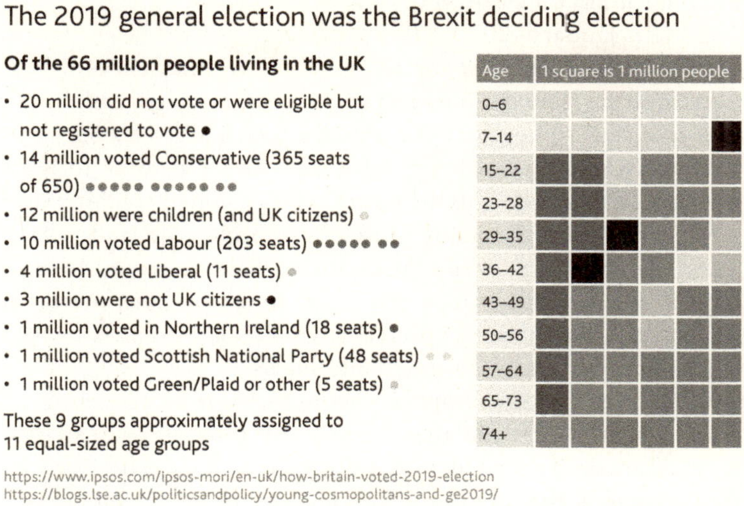

see colour version in plate section

Source: Drawn by the author as a simple summary of why age mattered so much to the outcome of the vote and the probability of not voting in 2019

from 42,138 respondents, and turned out to be closer to what actually happened. The second, by YouGov, polled a much larger group of people nearer to the date of the election and reported (with a great flourish), 'After much anticipation, YouGov's second and final MRP poll of the 2019 general election is here. The model which correctly called 93% of seats in 2017 currently shows that a small Conservative majority is likely. This is the final public polling YouGov will conduct before Thursday's vote.'[4] The result was not a small Conservative majority, but a large one.

---

[4] Adam McDonnell, Sam FitzPatrick, Abigail Axe-Browne, Matthew Smith, Chris Curtis and Tanya Abraham (2019) 'The key findings from our final MRP [multilevel regression with post-stratification] poll', *YouGov Report*, 10 December, https://yougov.co.uk/topics/politics/articles-reports/2019/12/10/key-findings-our-final-mrp-poll. The report continued: 'If the election were held now the Tories could win 339 seats (22 more than they took in 2017).' In fact the Conservatives won 365 seats in 2019, 26 more than predicted just days before the election was held.

Either voters had been lying to pollsters in ways they had not lied before, or a larger than usual number of voters changed, or made up, their mind on election day or the day before.

On 27 January 2020, *The Guardian*'s John Harris wrote that 'a lot of people on the left … [believe] that Labour's lost heartlands are synonymous with angry men, nostalgia and "social conservatism". They are not really like that at all.'[5] Of course, all six-word summaries are approximations – but if we were to assess the degree to which Labour voters who switched to abstention were more often nostalgic, angry (often also old and white) men who favoured social conservatism, then we would have to look at the data rather than relying so much on base anecdotal assumptions and the perceptions of a handful of journalists derived from their 'person in the street' interviews.

We tend to make assumptions about places from the names of their constituencies and their history. All four of the seats that most dramatically turned away from Labour (and were listed by the *Telegraph* at the start of this article) contain significant pockets of very low poverty. Figure 1.7 uses the very recent work of Alasdair Rae and Elvis Nyanzu to reveal that each of the four has at least three large neighbourhoods in the least-deprived quintile in all of England.

Figure 1.8 contrasts the four seats above with four others: the seat with the highest Labour vote in 2019 (85 per cent of voters in Walton in Liverpool); the seat with the highest Conservative vote (77 per cent in Castle Point in Essex); the seat where the Liberal Democrats did best, in Twickenham in London (56 per cent); and the seat where the Greens polled most, in Brighton Pavilion (57 per cent).[6]

The Liberal Democrats and the Greens now do best in some of the most affluent parts of the country. The Conservatives are

---

5 John Harris (2020) 'Labour is stuck in the last century. Its adversaries have seized the future', *The Guardian*, 27 January, https://www.theguardian.com/commentisfree/2020/jan/27/labour-party-leadership-keir-starmer-rebecca-long-bailey

6 Elise Uberoi, Carl Baker, Richard Cracknell, Grahame Allen, Nerys Roberts, Cassie Barton et al (2020) *General Election 2019: Results and analysis*, House of Commons Library, 28 January, https://researchbriefings.parliament.uk/ResearchBriefing/Summary/CBP-8749

Figure 1.7: Areas of high and low poverty in four significant seats in the 2019 general election

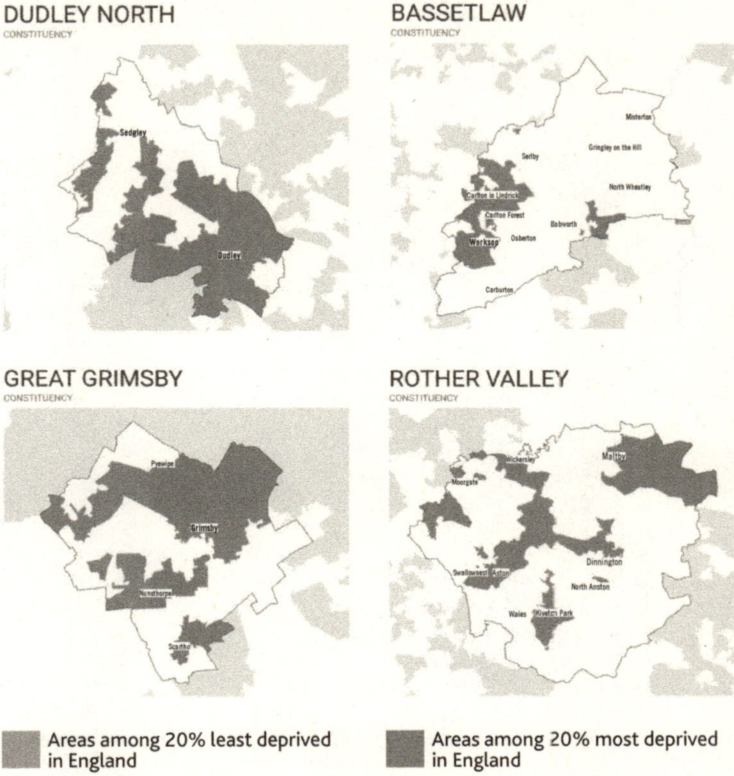

see colour version in plate section

Source: Alasdair Rae and Elvis Nyanzu (2019) *An English atlas of inequality: Technical report*, University of Sheffield, https://www.researchgate.net/publication/348298341_An_English_Atlas_of_Inequality. (Analysis by Elvis Nyanzu and Alasdair Rae, University of Sheffield. This work was funded by the Nuffield Foundation, www.nuffieldfoundation.org.)

no longer confined to the leafiest suburbs; but where they do best – such as in parts of Essex – those places are not too unlike the places where they have just (for one 2019 election at least) secured their new MPs in the North. These northern victories were predominantly in areas where people are older, and it may well be that in those areas it was mostly the nostalgic, angry men who favoured social conservatism who were most likely to vote for a party led by Boris Johnson (see Figure 1.9).

Figure 1.8: Areas where Labour, the Conservatives, the Liberal Democrats and the Greens do best

see colour version in plate section

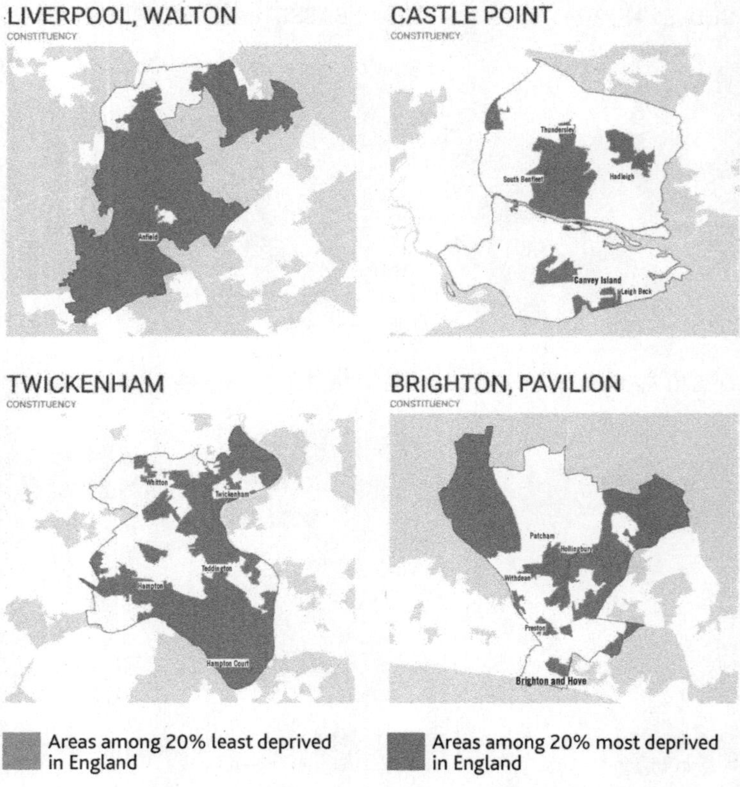

Source: Alasdair Rae and Elvis Nyanzu (2019) *An English atlas of inequality: Technical report*, University of Sheffield, https://www.researchgate.net/publication/348298341_An_English_Atlas_of_Inequality. (Analysis by Elvis Nyanzu and Alasdair Rae, University of Sheffield. This work was funded by the Nuffield Foundation, www.nuffieldfoundation.org.)

As to why Labour lost 1,200,000 voters to abstentions, understanding why so many people who had voted for a party led by Jeremy Corbyn in 2017 did not do the same in 2019 might take longer to determine. However, it is well worth remembering who thought they had most to lose from a Corbyn-led Labour victory – the best-off 5 per cent. It was the highest-income 5 per cent in the UK who were told that they would have to pay more tax, and who would have worried over paying the private school fees that almost all of them do pay (mostly with some difficulty). Almost none of that 5 per cent live in Essex or the north of England, but they have a disproportionate power to influence the views of the people who do.

On 28 January 2020 the House of Commons Library[7] produced the image in Figure 1.9. Tyne and Wear is still solidly red, Dorset still entirely blue. This is despite pockets of affluence on the banks of the Tyne and the significant poverty to be found in parts of Dorset. A 'red wall' can still be traced from East Yorkshire, through South Yorkshire, across Greater Manchester and Cheshire. But it now faces a solid blue wall stretching from Lincolnshire, through Nottinghamshire, Derbyshire, Staffordshire and Shropshire.

The 2019 general election was painted as the worst defeat for Labour in many years, and yet Corbyn's 32 per cent share of the vote was higher than the 30 per cent gained when the party was led by Ed Miliband in 2015, the 29 per cent won by Gordon Brown in 2010, the 31 per cent won by Neil Kinnock in 1987, the 27 per cent that Michael Foot secured in 1983, and the 31 per cent won by Arthur Henderson's Labour Party in 1931 and by Ramsay MacDonald's party in 1923. That 32 per cent is probably a solid base of support. It is less clear whether people in the blue squares in Figure 1.9 will think that the new Conservative government has improved their lives, and those of their children and grandchildren – and what will happen to the entire country and the one province of the UK that have both, in effect, already left mainstream UK politics some time ago: Scotland and Northern Ireland. Most people in those parts of the UK no longer vote for the three mainstream English political parties.

7 Carl Baker and Elise Uberoi (2019) *General Election 2019: The results*, House of Commons Library, https://commonslibrary.parliament.uk/general-election-2019-the-results-so-far/

Figure 1.9: The 2019 political map of the UK, drawn by the House of Commons

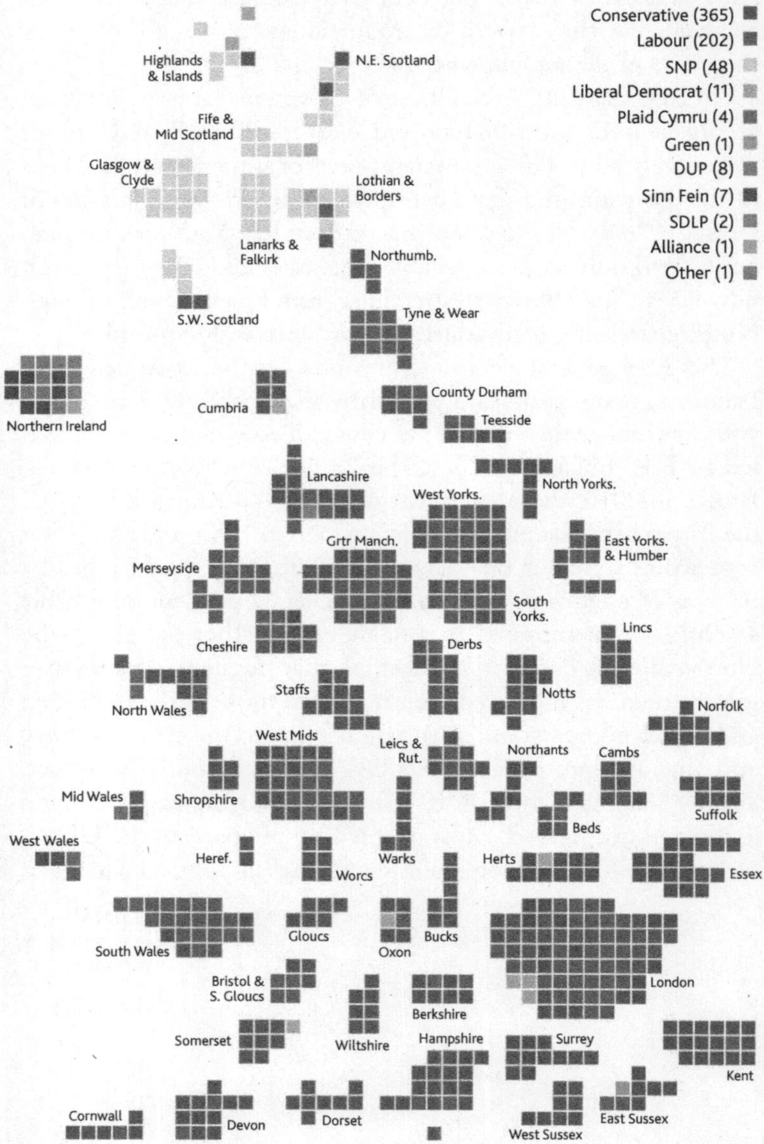

see colour version in plate section

Source: Elise Uberoi, Carl Baker, Richard Cracknell, Grahame Allen, Nerys Roberts, Cassie Barton et al (2020) *General Election 2019: Results and analysis*, House of Commons Library, 28 January, contains Parliamentary information licensed under the Open Parliament Licence v3.0. https://researchbriefings.parliament.uk/ResearchBriefing/Summary/CBP-8749

CHAPTER 1.5

Osborne, Johnson and Starmer: let them eat growth?[1]

Politics is about people, about our different views and our understandings about people – about what motivates them, why they behave in the way they do, and what will most help or hinder them. In the spring of 2016, I published a short book titled: *A better politics: How government can make us happier*, which is also free to read online.[2]

I argued that in our current era we have policies made by those who believe that poor people are lazy, and that this harms us all. The reality is we're all very much the same, driven by the same physiological and emotional needs. But we start at different points, and a few people are greedier and more selfish than others. When we live in a society as divided as the UK has become, more of us can become hardened and more indifferent to others' suffering.

The last six years have been a rollercoaster. David Cameron introduced his happiness index in 2016. The measures that contribute to that index were rising then. There was growing hope, despite the huge divisions caused by the Brexit referendum result. The proportion of people in the UK who said that life was worthwhile, that they were not too anxious, that their life

---

1 Originally published on the *Tribune MPs Blog* (the group Sir Keir Starmer belongs to), 29 September 2022 (lightly edited).

2 https://www.dannydorling.org/books/betterpolitics/

satisfaction and happiness was good, all climbed, peaking with the outcome and in the aftermath of the 2017 general election.[3]

However, all four of these measures worsened rapidly around the time of the 2019 general election. Two-thirds of the fall in happiness occurred between the third and fourth quarter of 2019, as did three-quarters of the rise in anxiety. The pandemic would make this worse, but the current [early 2020s] plunge to greater levels of despair began before it.[4] (See Figure 2.1, page 98.)

Politics is also about power and winning it. For the conservative establishment, maintaining, not reducing, inequalities is seen as essential. In the past it was almost exclusively under Conservative governments that inequalities in income were increased. They may be about to do so again. There is a fightback taking place, but as yet it is mainly confined to ad hoc protests, strikes, and proposals by a few think-tanks.[5]

We need a better politics than this, one which will require confronting the central deception about our current state and likely future.

On 7 July 2022, when Boris Johnson resigned, he said that if we stayed close to his chosen path then soon: '... we will be the most prosperous in Europe'.[6] We clearly would not. He ended his speech promising that 'even if things can sometimes seem dark now, our future together is golden'.[7] Liz Truss then took over

---

[3] Quarter Two, 2017: See Figure 6 in David Finch and Adam Tinson (2022) *The continuing impact of COVID-19 on health and inequalities*, London: The Health Foundation, 24 August, https://www.health.org.uk/publications/long-reads/the-continuing-impact-of-covid-19-on-health-and-inequalities

[4] See Figure 1 in ONS (2022) *Personal well-being in the UK, quarterly: April 2011 to September 2021*, Online: https://www.ons.gov.uk/people populationandcommunity/wellbeing/bulletins/personalwellbeingin theukquarterly/april2011toseptember2021

[5] New Economics Foundation (NEF) (2023) *Living income: A minimum income to ensure you can always afford life's essentials*, London: NEF, https://neweconomics.org/campaigns/living-income

[6] Boris Johnson (2022) Resignation speech, 7 July, https://www.youtube.com/watch?v=3h8Eha2MDwE

[7] [Editorial note: See the final paragraph of the Introduction to this book starting on page 6, and the words of R.H. Tawney, in that paragraph, who warned of such sunlit-upland thinking over a century ago, in 1920,

running the UK for a few weeks (Figure 1.10). Talk of sunlit uplands is wearing thin. The future now looks cold and cruel, not golden. There is no guarantee that the fuel bailout will avert actual shortages of gas this winter, and we already know that overall higher bills will cause rising hunger.[8]

Britain today competes with Bulgaria to be the most economically unequal country by income in Europe. Those surviving on the least in Britain now have living standards lower than their equivalents in some [Editorial note: now 'most'] parts

Figure 1.10: Liz Truss brought her plans to the Commons on Thursday

Source: Simon Dawson/No 10 Downing Street, licensed under the United Kingdom Open Government Licence v3.0, available from: https://commons.wikimedia.org/wiki/File:Liz_Truss_official_portrait_(cropped)2.jpg

when he talked of how politicians so often 'repeat, like parrots, the word "Productivity"'. He could have been writing in 2020. Sometimes we are very slow to learn.]

8 Torcuil Crichton (2022) 'How the Liz Truss energy price cap will work and how much households will save', *The Daily Record*, 8 September, https://www.dailyrecord.co.uk/news/politics/how-liz-truss-energy-price-27939413

of Eastern Europe.[9] Most of the poorest are in work, but work pays so badly that almost half of all UK adults are not taxpayers. The UK has low unemployment because people have to take any job they can. Often several jobs.

The UK has the lowest unemployment benefit for single people, in comparison to average wages, in all of Europe.[10] Other social security payments have continued to fall in generosity as a share of average wages. This fall continued even during the past 14 years when average wages also fell when compared to prices. The UK state pension remains among the lowest in Western Europe, despite being protected from rising inflation. The average UK pensioner saw their real-terms weekly income (after housing costs) rise by only £12 a week between 2010 and 2020, to £331 a week.[11] That is an extra £1.71 a day. Pensioners are the demographic group that did better than others in that decade. The reason why their income hardly rose at all, during the years when the state pension was protected by the 'triple lock' intended to ensure it did not lose value in real terms, was that the other social security payments that pensioners relied on were reduced in real terms. Those with disabilities have suffered particularly badly.

The current government's response is to tell people to work harder. In the first quarter of 2022 there were almost 50,000 sanctions issued to Universal Credit recipients for not trying hard enough to find work, almost three times the number

---

9 John Burn-Murdock (2022) 'Britain and the US are poor societies with some very rich people', *The Financial Times*, 16 September, https://www.ft.com/content/ef265420-45e8-497b-b308-c951baa68945

10 Olaf van Vliet and Koen Caminada (2012) 'Unemployment replacement rates dataset among 34 welfare states, 1971–2009: an update, extension and modification of the Scruggs' welfare state entitlements data set', *NEUJOBS Special Report No. 2*, Table 2, p. 7, https://papers.ssrn.com/sol3/papers.cfm?abstract_id=1991214 (also at https://www.researchgate.net/publication/228311401).

11 DWP (2021) *Pensioners' Incomes Series: Financial year 2019 to 2020*, London: Department for Work and Pensions, 25 March, https://www.gov.uk/government/statistics/pensioners-incomes-series-financial-year-2019-to2020/pensioners-incomes-series-financial-year-2019-to-2020

made in the last quarter before the pandemic began in early 2020. Sanctions are the removal of benefit payments – up to 100 per cent. This is most often for 'failure to attend or participate in a Work-Focused Interview'. Many of the people being sanctioned have indeed attended and participated in these interviews, but in the view of their 'work coach' have still not done sufficient work-search or other activities. This is how people are pushed into taking any work at all, no matter how bad it is. The researcher who released these figures explained: 'The latest reported rate of sanctioning would produce 593,000 sanctions on all benefits in a full year. This would be the highest number since 2014, and higher than in any year under the previous Labour government, as far back as statistics are available in their present form.'[12]

The average length that a sanction lasts is a month, but it can last much longer – deliberately causing severe immiseration. Conservatives have tried many different policies to preserve the high inequality they worked hard for and won. A large part of the reason they did not scrap Labour's minimum wage, and later rebranded it as the National Living Wage – a wage that many find that they cannot afford to live on – was to not have to address inequalities more widely. In 2022 the Trades Union Congress called for the minimum wage to be raised to £15 an hour from the then current rate of £9.50 for workers over 23 years old, £6.83 for those aged 18 to 20, and just £4.81 for 16- and 17-year-olds. These wages are far too low.

Labour needs to promise to raise social security support, at least to the more generous standards of most other European nations as compared to average incomes. It needs to agree to minimum wages rising and benefit sanctions being rapidly reduced. But it also needs policies that will curtail rising costs, otherwise no one will be better off. In September 2022 the Scottish government announced that 'emergency legislation will be introduced to bring in a freeze on rent increases and ban evictions in the private

---

[12] David Webster (2022) *Briefing: Benefit sanctions statistics*, Child Poverty Action Group, 24 August, https://cpag.org.uk/policy-and-campaigns/briefing/david-webster-university-glasgow-briefings-benefit-sanctions

and social rented sector in response to the cost of living'.[13] Policies such as these are needed across all of the rest of the UK.

How can Labour address the coming even-greater emergency and keep its promise to 'not spend day-to-day more than we tax'?[14] There is only one way, and that is to increase taxes on those who currently take the most. It is through higher taxes on incomes, but also sometimes on wealth, that other European countries ensure their societies are fairer, have higher long-term social mobility and lower poverty, and are not beginning to fall apart in the way that the UK is. You can be coy about it and pretend you will not do it, or you can choose to be honest – and also point out more trenchantly everything that is now falling apart around us. Labour need not increase the overall tax level by very much to bring public spending up to normal European levels; but it must alter the balance of who pays the most tax. Between 1979 and 1990, the basic rate of income tax was reduced from 33 per cent to 25 per cent, and the top rate from 83 per cent to 40 per cent. At the same time there were increases in both VAT, from 8 per cent to 15 per cent, and National Insurance. The overall tax level was 30 per cent in both 1978–79 and 1990–91.[15]

Taxation does not necessarily 'raise money'. What it does do is alter the distribution of which people can spend the most. If taxes are not increased when public spending is increased, then prices will rise faster, especially for services where the number of people providing that service is limited. Without raising taxes on the better-off, you do not redistribute consumption. Top-rate tax increases are also more effective than any cap on bankers' pay at

---

[13] Scottish Landlords Association (SLA) (2022) 'Immediate freeze on rent increases plus eviction ban', 6 September, https://scottishlandlords.com/news-and-campaigns/news/immediate-rent-freeze-and-eviction-ban/

[14] [Editorial note: As was hinted at many times, and as Shadow Chancellor Rachel Reeves implied in 2023: see Caroline Wheeler (2023) 'Labour will copy Tory tax and spending plans if elected', *The Sunday Times*, 9 July, https://www.thetimes.co.uk/article/no-more-tax-and-spend-labours-fiscal-plans-revealed-f7x7f5n5s.]

[15] Michael Jacobs (2022) 'Thatcherite mythology: eight Tory leadership candidates in search of an economic policy', *LSE British Politics and Policy Blogs*, 13 July, https://blogs.lse.ac.uk/politicsandpolicy/thatcher-tory-leadership-candidates/

reducing inequality, reducing unfairness, and reducing dangerous gambling by the financial sector.

People no longer believe the repeated promises that economic growth will be their salvation, because they have heard those promises far too many times. Boris Johnson's promise (as quoted previously) was almost identical to one given by George Osborne seven years earlier. It does not matter who makes these promises; they are simply not believable, not least because sustainable growth that benefits the majority never occurs in societies as unequal as the UK has become.

You can argue that in a more equal society growth is more sustained, because that is what happens in those countries that are more equal. You can argue that this growth tends to be in areas that are more beneficial to society, less polluting and less wasteful, because that is also the case. You can argue that if you do not address the emergency we are in, then we should not expect much growth in the future, especially not much green growth. But you cannot tell people to wait for growth, or that you will somehow increase growth without first addressing the emergency.

You can have long-term plans for a far better future. You can, if you wish, talk about how we could in time have a far less bureaucratic welfare state, and even of how universal basic incomes are becoming a possibility. However, none of that is believable if you do not have the strength of conviction to state publicly that you will address the immediate crises that so many people face, head on. Our future together may well not be golden, even with the best of policies. But it could soon be even worse than it is today. In the short term the pound is falling in value, stoking up even higher inflation; many people have exhausted the capacity of family and friends to help keep them afloat; debt levels are terrible; our health is being damaged, and not only our mental health – we are also rapidly falling down the ranks in terms of measures of physical health. Evictions are rising. Precarity is becoming the norm.

Call out the myth of sunlit uplands for what it is – a lie told by people who can afford to go on numerous holidays in the sun to people they hope will swallow the lie, or who can be convinced that the reason things are not getting better is because other people are not working hard enough. Don't offer the same lie, just a little more convincingly phrased. Instead, be honest: say that the current situation is terrible, worse than we have experienced in many decades. Tap into what so many people know to be true. Explain that the UK remains a very rich country, and that the very worst outcomes of current disastrous policy can be tackled immediately. Be clear that we have the resources to do that. Don't exaggerate. Be clear that in the longer term, recovery will take time because there is such a distance to go.

Currently Bulgaria is moving faster in that direction than Britain is. While inequality has been falling in Bulgaria, it is still rising in Britain. People on average wages will require pay rises this coming year that are higher than those of people earning twice average wages. All of these increases will actually be real-terms cuts in income. That might be somewhat more bearable if, at the very least, you know that the society you live in is becoming fairer.

During the 1920s and 1930s income inequalities in the UK fell during a series of crises not dissimilar to today. There was little celebration at the time, but had this not happened, then the great achievements of the late 1940s, 1950s and 1960s would have been far harder to secure. Today we have both the benefit of hindsight and the knowledge that other countries in Europe are currently achieving this.

Offer hope, honesty and fairness in response to a government that is promising only fairy tales. Don't dissemble. Instead, tell it as it is. And please don't rely too much on the promise of growth. People cannot eat growth.

CHAPTER 1.6

A tale of three elections: Sweden, Italy and England[1]

On 5 September 2022 Liz Truss was elected leader of the Conservative Party, and thereby prime minister, winning 81,326 votes, as compared to the 60,399 that Conservative Party members awarded to the former chancellor of the Exchequer, Rishi Sunak. On 11 September 2022 Sweden held a general election after which it appeared likely that Ulf Kristersson, the leader of the Moderate Party, would become prime minister, ousting a Social Democrat-led coalition. On 25 September 2022 the result of Italy's general election was that Giorgia Meloni, leader of the Brothers of Italy, would most likely become prime minister. Although they were all very different, these three events in the same month were said to be signs of a significant rightward shift across Europe – but arguably that is true of only one of the three, namely the UK results. If anything, events in the UK may have made the rest of Europe even more cautious about shifting to the right.

In the UK, Truss's election by Conservative members of parliament was a continuation of a series of chaotic events.[2] These included the British Conservative Party leaving the mainstream European Conservative block in 2014; David Cameron's Conservative government holding a referendum on EU membership in 2016; the UK becoming the second-most-

---

[1] Originally published in *Public Sector Focus*, September/October 2022, pp. 12–15 (lightly edited).

[2] See Chapter 1.5 in this volume, and the original at: https://tribunemps.org/let-them-eat-growth

unequal country in Europe by income in 2019 (Bulgaria was worse, but moving in the opposite direction); and the 'mini-budget' of 23 September 2022 that appeared designed to push the UK to the top of the European league table of inequality within months.[3]

The International Monetary Fund (IMF) warned the UK government that increasing inequality would further undermine its economy.[4] The UK had lurched to the far right of European politics; then out of the EU; then beyond what the IMF considered rational behaviour.

In contrast that month, in Sweden, 84 per cent of the adult population voted to choose the political parties that would govern them, and in effect who would be prime minister. The shifts in voting were small. The Social Democrats saw their vote share rise by 2.0 per cent, while there were rises of 3.0 per cent for the more right-wing Swedish Democrats and 0.7 per cent for the Greens. All other parties, including Ulf Kristersson's Moderate Party, experienced small falls.[5] Despite both parties gaining votes, the Social Democrats and Greens, who had formed the government in 2018, lost out because of the slightly larger rise in the Swedish Democrats' vote, which was just enough to allow it to form a majority coalition with minor parties. This was not a lurch to the right, but a tiny shift in comparison to what has occurred in the UK. Occasionally, the most extreme parts of some of the more right-wing Swedish parties advocate policies that are now common in the UK, for example on immigration. However, Sweden continues to be one of the most equal European countries, almost irrespective of which political parties are in power.

---

[3] Danny Dorling (2022) 'Growing inequality in the UK has implications for health', *British Medical Journal*, Opinion Piece, 2022;378:o2318, https://www.bmj.com/content/378/bmj.o2318

[4] Andrea Shalal (2022) 'IMF says UK fiscal measures will "likely increase inequality," urges rethink', *Reuters*, 27 September, https://www.reuters.com/world/uk/imf-says-uk-fiscal-measures-will-likely-increase-inequality-urges-rethink-2022-09-27/

[5] Wikipedia (2022) *2022 Swedish general election*, as accessed on 22 September 2022, https://en.wikipedia.org/wiki/2022_Swedish_general_election

In the Italian general election of 2022, the swings were far greater. Politics in Italy is far more volatile. After the UK, Italy is the next most unequal of the larger European countries. The only other European countries where income inequalities are higher than in Italy are Romania, Latvia, Lithuania and Bulgaria. These four Eastern European countries, alongside Italy and the UK, are now outliers in Europe.

The far-right Brothers of Italy saw their vote share rise by 22 per cent, the hard-to-define Five Star Movement's vote fell by 17 per cent, and the centre-left Democratic Party's vote rose by 0.3 per cent. The shifts occurred mainly because turnout fell dramatically to 64 per cent. Voters had become disillusioned with all the choices on offer.[6] The net effect was to make a right-wing coalition possible; but the Brothers of Italy hold only 119 of the 400 seats in the Italian parliament, less than one-third. They cannot govern without wider consensus. In contrast, in the UK, Truss became prime minister despite only gaining the support of a minority of MPs in the leadership battle (most backed Sunak), let alone the endorsement of any voters other than a tiny number of Conservative Party members.

The last UK prime minister who gained power when his party was voted into office and lost power when his party was voted out was Edward Heath (1970–74). For 22 years, no British prime minister has enjoyed approval ratings of even 40 per cent of the voting public for more than a few short months, almost always only just after they have won an election. See Figure 1.11, which originally appeared in *The Spectator* magazine, but which has been redrawn and updated here using publicly available data from a reputable pollster.[7] The long-term trend is downwards. Truss is expected to continue that trend, possibly taking it to an all-time low. [Editorial note: She did.[8] The figure has been redrawn to

[6] Wikipedia (2022) *2022 Italian general election*, as accessed on 29 September 2022, https://en.wikipedia.org/wiki/2022_Italian_general_election

[7] Michael Simmons (2022) 'Is Truss in trouble? New polling suggests she's unpopular, but it's not all gloom for her party', *The Spectator*, 22 September, https://www.spectator.co.uk/article/is-truss-in-trouble

[8] *The Guardian*, 'Liz Truss's poll ratings plummet lower than Boris Johnson's', 1 October; YouGov, 'Liz Truss is already less popular than Boris Johnson ever was', 5 October; *The Independent*, 'Liz Truss almost as unpopular as

Figure 1.11: Net satisfaction rating of British prime ministers, 1997–2024 (%)

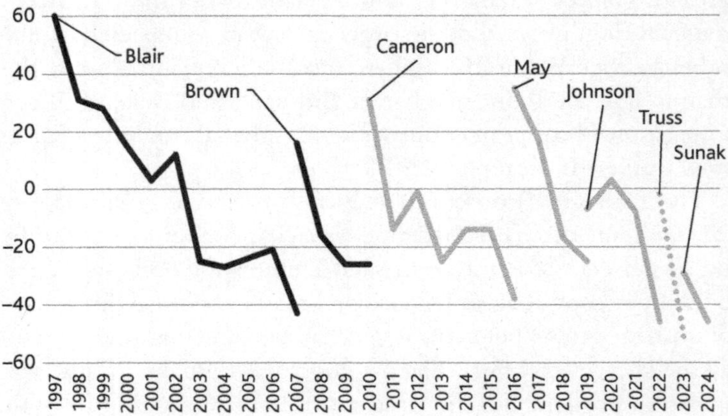

Note: Figure has been updated through to January 2024; ratings are for January of each year or the nearest month to that. Truss has a dotted line as her rating is shown from September 2022 through to October 2022, rather than for full years as for the rest.

Source: Drawn from data available at Ipsos MORI statistics, https://www.ipsos.com/en-uk/political-monitor-satisfaction-ratings-1997-present

include her and also to add Sunak who, as of January 2024, had not quite managed to become as unpopular as Truss had been, but was quickly heading in that direction. And, by April 2024, as I check these numbers, Sunak had succeeded in achieving a net approval rating of −59 per cent, a British historical record low, but he may still yet better his own record to become even less popular in what remains of the year.]

The September 2022 election in Sweden (in which five in every six adult Swedes participated) was reported by the BBC as 'Sweden election: How an ex neo-Nazi movement became kingmakers'[9]. But only one in every six of the Swedish electorate

Prince Andrew', 18 October; *New Statesman* 'Liz Truss has plumbed new depths, recording the lowest approval rating of any UK prime minister in history', 19 October; *Vogue*, 'Why was Liz Truss Prime Minister for just 44 days?', 20 October.

[9] Leo Sands (2022) 'Sweden election: How an ex neo-Nazi movement became kingmakers', *BBC News*, 15 September, https://www.bbc.co.uk/news/world-europe-62913356

voted for that party, and their leader was not considered a possibility for prime minister.

In Italy less than four in every six people eligible to vote did so. And again, just one in every six who could vote gave their vote to the party most talked about. It was most talked about because of its links to a fascist past. However, as fewer people voted overall in Italy, that party is now the largest party. In the UK two adults in every six in the electorate voted Conservative in 2019, but only one in every 600 people eligible to vote in general elections voted for Truss in 2022. The turnout in the 2019 UK general election had fallen to just 67 per cent, not that different from Italy in 2022. There was little comment in the British press on how some of the policies that Boris Johnson and then Liz Truss supported, such as proposing to forcibly fly some migrants to Rwanda, could be seen as echoes of past far-right fascist minority political parties in Britain. But the international money markets immediately saw Liz Truss's economic policies as far too extreme in other ways to be tolerable. Even the implied future cut in public spending to pay for the tax cuts for the very best-off was seen as a step too far by international bankers, because it would weaken the economy and make the UK a more dangerous place in which to invest.

The tax cuts proposed in the UK mini-budget of September 2022 were targeted almost exclusively at the very best-off. Although it appeared superficially that there would also be small gains for other groups, the immediate effect of proposing these tax cuts was to see the value of the pound plummet, increasing the costs of goods for everyone and so leaving only the best-off tenth expecting any possible net gain from the proposed tax cuts. For everyone else in the UK their incomes would fall after taxes and rising prices were taken into account. The chart shown in Figure 1.12 does not include the effects of rising prices and so much else that would have occurred between September 2022 and April 2023, had the implementation of this mini-budget been attempted.

These three different European elections in September 2022 resulted in three very different outcomes. In Sweden, very little at first appeared to change. There was no rise in financial instability or inequality as far as we can yet see. In Italy, talks began to ensure that the new government worked with its predecessor

Figure 1.12: IPPR estimates of the Truss/Kwarteng budget effects, had it been implemented

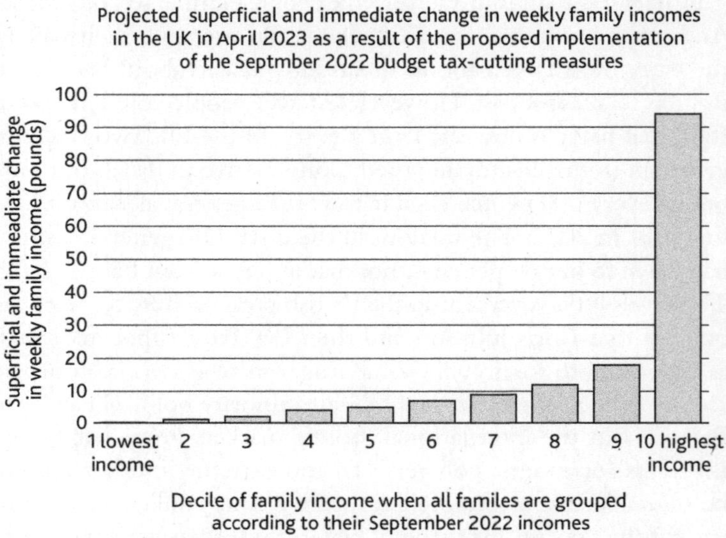

Source: Drawn from data generated by the IPPR tax-benefit model which includes the effects of the reduction in income tax basic rate, additional rate, dividend rates and the health and social care levy, as was reproduced widely in social media at the time, see: https://twitter.com/KumarAshwin/status/1573257087307612161/photo/1

to submit a draft budget to the European Commission in mid-October. The international markets did not react with horror to what had just occurred in Italy.[10] This was despite justifiable fears about the election's impact on human rights and much else that was precious.[11]

In the UK inflation rose, and the housing market looked to be in greater trouble with rapid price falls predicted. The Bank of England began the emergency buying up of government bonds

[10] Paul Kirby (2022) 'Italian elections: Meloni gets to work on picking right-wing government', *BBC News*, 27 September, https://www.bbc.co.uk/news/world-europe-63044973

[11] Alvise Armellini and Chiara Rodriquez (2022) '"Very real fears" for LGBT community after far-right win in Italy', *Reuters*, 27 September, https://www.reuters.com/world/europe/very-real-fears-lgbt-community-after-far-right-win-italy-2022-09-27/

to ensure pension funds were solvent in the short term. Homes and pensions are the main two ways in which wealth is held in the UK. Share prices also fell. Fuel and food prices rose. As I wrote these words in October 2022, I also wrote that I had no idea what else might have occurred between the last day of September 2022, and the month and year in which you read them. But it is clear that there was only one entirely disastrous election that took place in Europe in September 2022: the election of the new British prime minister. It reminded the world what occurs when a particularly extreme right-wing path is taken: chaos.

CHAPTER 1.7

What the UK in 1922 and in 2017 had in common[1]

You probably don't know about the 1922 general election in the United Kingdom. It was the 'breakthrough election'. The Conservatives under Andrew Bonar Law won; but Labour moved from fifth place in 1918 to third place and increased the number of seats they held from 57 in 1918 to 142 in 1922.

Labour was at this time led by John Robert Clynes (Figure 1.13). The son of poor Irish labourers, Clynes was a self-educated trade unionist who began his working life at the age of 10 in a Lancashire cotton mill. He was highly critical of government policy towards Ireland, and later opposed Ramsay MacDonald's support for austerity during the Depression years. Clynes was ousted by MacDonald as party leader within a month of the 1922 election. MacDonald would go on to form a National Government in 1931, with 473 Conservative MPs.

There was enormous division and strife within the Labour Party in the 1920s. These were years in which inequalities were actually falling in society, but very few people knew that they were. Income inequalities had peaked in 1918. They fell more between 1918 and 1938 than they would over the following 40 years.

Britain was changing rapidly in the 1920s. Hugh Dalton, who later became chancellor of the Exchequer, studied the beginning of the drop in income inequality while he was a student at the

---

[1] Originally published on *Labour Hub*, 21 February 2023, lightly edited here to add more detail on Clynes.

Figure 1.13: John Robert Clynes (1869–1949), leader of the Labour Party (1921–22)

Source: 1915–20 portrait, Library of Congress, Public Domain, https://www.loc.gov/item/2014709745/

London School of Economics. He was one of the few who measured what was happening.

Others wrote novels and plays where the backdrop was the fall in inequalities in the 1920s, but the two best remembered were not published until 1945. *Brideshead Revisited* and *An Inspector Calls* were both, in their very different ways, about unsustainable inequalities.

The 1922 election was not just notable for how well Labour did, but for it being the first election in many decades in which the geographical distribution of votes became more equal. In particular, the Conservatives lost more votes where they had been more popular in 1918. The graph accompanying this chapter shows the trend (see note within Figure 1.14).

From 1922 onwards, with just the smallest of blips in 1935, Conservative voters would become less and less geographically segregated in Britain. Irrespective of the ups and downs (in terms

Figure 1.14: Political polarisation, 1920–2017

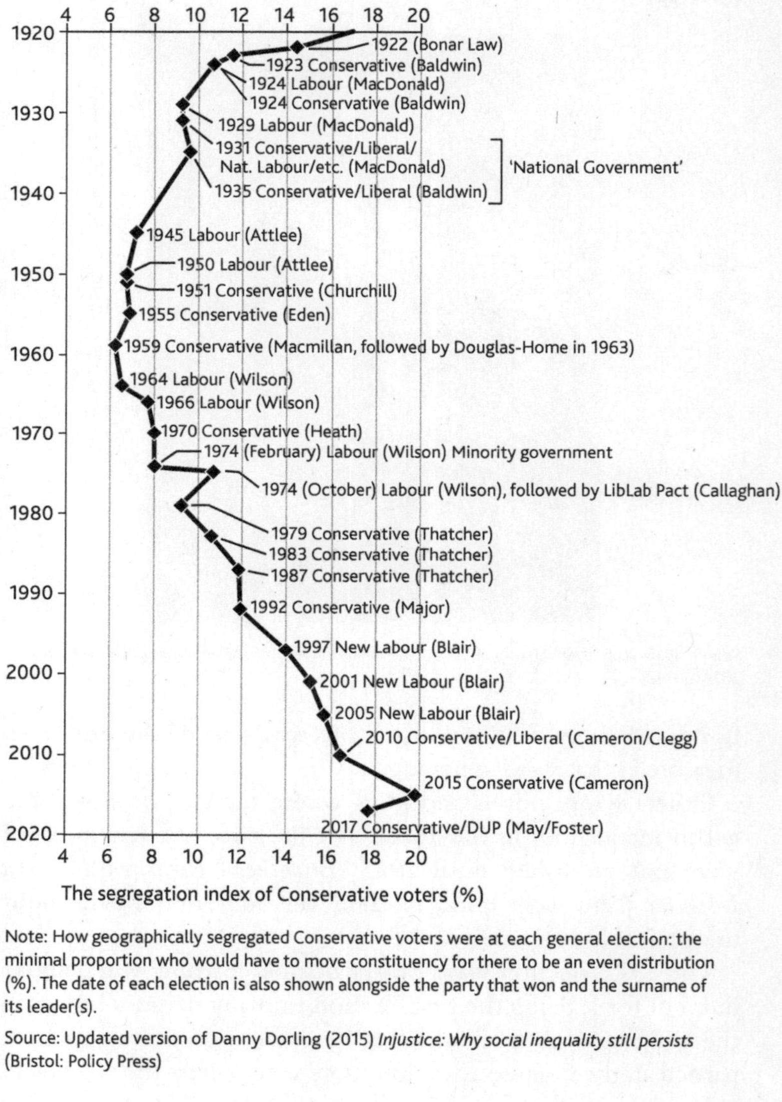

Note: How geographically segregated Conservative voters were at each general election: the minimal proportion who would have to move constituency for there to be an even distribution (%). The date of each election is also shown alongside the party that won and the surname of its leader(s).

Source: Updated version of Danny Dorling (2015) *Injustice: Why social inequality still persists* (Bristol: Policy Press)

of which party triumphed) at each subsequent election it became harder to predict how someone would vote simply by knowing which constituency they lived in. That trend continued onwards to 1959, and after that voter segregation hardly rose at all until the 1970s. However, after the election of Margaret Thatcher's government in 1979, the geographical segregation of voters across the UK rose at every successive election through to 2015.

None of this would be relevant today if it were not for one particularly uncanny contemporary parallel with the past. The first election after 1922 in which geographical segregation fell, and continued to fall thereafter, was that held in 2017. The 2017 election was remarkable not just for the damage done to Theresa May's majority, but because the tide had turned in the very long-term trend. It may be too early to say – but something quite remarkable began in 2017 and it appears to be continuing. For the first time in almost 100 years, geographical inequalities in voting between constituencies began to fall again.

In 2017, Labour picked up more votes in areas where it had had the least support in 2015, and fewer votes where it already piled them high. Although this might not be the best strategy to win elections, it was a sign of a shift. Voters in the south of England, in what had been solidly Conservative seats, began more often to vote Labour. Other voters, in seats where Labour had often taken support for granted, no longer voted Labour quite so enthusiastically.

In 2017 Labour increased its seat count to 262 (up 30), and its total vote to 12.9 million; but what was much less noticed was the shift in the geographical distribution of Labour and Conservative voters. That shift accelerated in 2019. Again, the shift was not much noticed. It was obscured by talk of a 'red wall' having been broken. Few people noticed that the Conservative share of the vote in all of southeast England fell between 2017 and 2019. The Tory share in London also fell in 2019. However, commentators were much more interested in the loss of 60 Labour seats. They rarely pointed out that the number of Labour votes falling to 10.3 million meant Labour still polled more votes in 2019 than it had done in 2005, 2010 or 2015. The fall in Labour voting was mainly due to lower turnout in 2019 than in 2017.

What parallels can we draw between 2017 and 1922? John Clynes was a very different MP and party leader to Jeremy Corbyn, not least because of the former's support for Britain's involvement in the First World War and the latter's lifelong campaigning for peace. Both, however, opposed the austerity of their times; both spoke vividly of the injustice of the immiseration of the many because of the enrichment of the few. Both were attacked from within their own party shortly after a seismic shift in voting patterns. Inequalities, if measured by the take of the top 1 per cent, were very high in both the 1920s and the first decades of the 21st century.

There are a few tentative signs that income and wealth inequalities are now falling, if only slightly. State pensions and many benefits have risen with inflation. This is certainly not enough, as inflation is higher for the poor, but it is a larger relative increase than most people in employment are receiving. Many pay deals now being struck, are progressive. Bosses offer higher increases for lower-paid workers in an attempt to shame unions into accepting an overall below-inflation deal. As I write, house prices have fallen for many months in comparison to wages and salaries. These falls are large when compared to inflation and may be the beginning of a redistribution of wealth.

I drew the graph shown as Figure 1.14 in 2006. I have been waiting a long time for the shift. I may be too optimistic. But when it last shifted in 1922, it was not because Labour came to power that year, but because inequalities had to fall. Steep social divides also began to fall, imperceptibly at first, under governments led by Conservatives who believed in the old ways, in hierarchy, and in people knowing their place. The divides fell while Labour were in disarray in the 1920s and 1930s, at war internally. People fought for the divides to fall, but they did so successfully without the need for particularly inspirational prime ministers.

CHAPTER 1.8

Are things about to get better?[1]

The gap between rich and poor is wider than it has been for a century. We think that change is impossible, but it may have already begun.

Two weeks before Christmas 1936, preparations for King Edward VIII's coronation the following May were abruptly abandoned. The King had abdicated, just 11 months after taking the throne. The plans had been for a low-key affair, without a procession through London the following day or a lavish dinner with dignitaries.[2] The country was in the depths of its worst depression since the Napoleonic wars.[3]

In 1929, seven years before he gave up the throne for 'the woman he loved', Edward, then Prince of Wales, had been photographed as he visited miners and their families in County Durham to see for himself their desperate living conditions in the wake of a huge fall in wages earlier that decade (see Figure 1.15).[4] Wages would not recover until 1931,[5] at which point the National

---

1 Originally published with a different title in *Prospect Magazine*, 5 April 2023, May issue, pp. 38–41. Lightly edited here to improve clarity and context.

2 https://en.wikipedia.org/wiki/Abandoned_coronation_of_Edward_VIII

3 Danny Dorling (2022) 'The trickle up of fear', *Public Sector Focus*, March/April, pp. 12–15, https://flickread.com/edition/html/index.php?pdf=62668d702a8e0#15

4 Note that the photograph was taken in 1929, not 1922, as implied here: https://www.alamy.com/stock-photo-prince-of-wales-later-king-edward-viii-visits-poor-miners-in-a-mining-76389345.html

5 Geoff Tilly (2018) '17-year wage squeeze the worst in two hundred years', *Trades Union Congress Blog*, 11 May, https://www.tuc.org.uk/blogs/17-year-wage-squeeze-worst-two-hundred-years

Government cut the benefits of insured workers by 10 per cent.[6] Inequality was high. The richest 1 per cent of people took home almost a quarter of all income in the country.

In 1936, the Labour Party was riven by division. The Conservative government could not find a way out of the economic morass. The Liberals were sinking, never to seriously resurface. Most of the Empire was still in British hands, but it was becoming clear that it would not last. When Edward VIII's brother succeeded him, the 12 May 1937 coronation of George VI and Elizabeth was criticised for costing three times as much as the 1911 coronation of George V and Mary, although the price was only 42 per cent higher when inflation was taken into account.[7]

But during the misery of these years, something remarkable happened. Edward's visit with the miners (Figure 1.15) coincided with the last time that either income or wealth inequality began to fall in the United Kingdom. In the aftermath of the First World War, income, and, later, wealth, inequities continued to tumble down. They did so for 50 years, through to 1973. Could we, a century on, be about to see something similar?

The coronation of Charles III and Camilla takes place on 6 May 2023, 86 years after that of George VI and Elizabeth. There are uncanny echoes of the past. Real wages have not yet recovered to the levels they reached in 2008 and aren't expected to do so for the foreseeable future. Fourteen years ago, in 2009, when *he* was Prince of Wales, Charles warned against capitalism and consumerism, saying that 'poverty, stress, ill health and social tensions cannot be ended by economic growth alone'. That year his son, William, slept rough for a night in London in solidarity with the homeless.[8]

---

6 The National Archives (2023) '1930s Depression and unemployment', *Archives for Everyone 2023–27 Website*, https://www.nationalarchives.gov.uk/cabinetpapers/alevelstudies/1930-depression.htm

7 Editorial (1937) 'Coronation costs', *The Advocate*, 21 April, https://trove.nla.gov.au/newspaper/article/68473040

8 Mark Memmott (2009) 'Prince William sleeps on London street to better understand plight of homeless', *National Public Radio Website*, 22 December, https://www.npr.org/sections/thetwo-way/2009/12/prince_william_homeless_street.html

Figure 1.15: Edward, then Prince of Wales, visits mining families in County Durham in 1929

Source: Illustrated London News Ltd/Mary Evans

In 1937, the best-off 0.1 per cent of people were receiving 66 times the national average income; the best-off 1 per cent, 17 times; and the best-off 10 per cent, four times (Figure 1.16). In 2019, the year before the COVID-19 pandemic hit – the latest year for which we have reliable figures – the best-off 0.1 per cent were receiving 70 times the national average income each year; the best-off 1 per cent, 16 times; and the best-off 10 per cent, four times.[9]

But, in contrast to today, by 1937 income inequalities were already falling, even if hardly anyone was aware that they were. By 2019, if you ignored the best-off 10 per cent of the population, you could just about claim that inequalities had fallen among the rest – a claim that almost every Conservative chancellor has made in almost every Budget speech of the past decade. But the share of the top 10 per cent remained stubbornly high, and actually rose

[9] This figure and its source data can be found here: https://www.dannydorling.org/books/onepercent/Material.html (and notes to Figure 1.3, page 48).

Figure 1.16: UK income inequality, 1910–2019

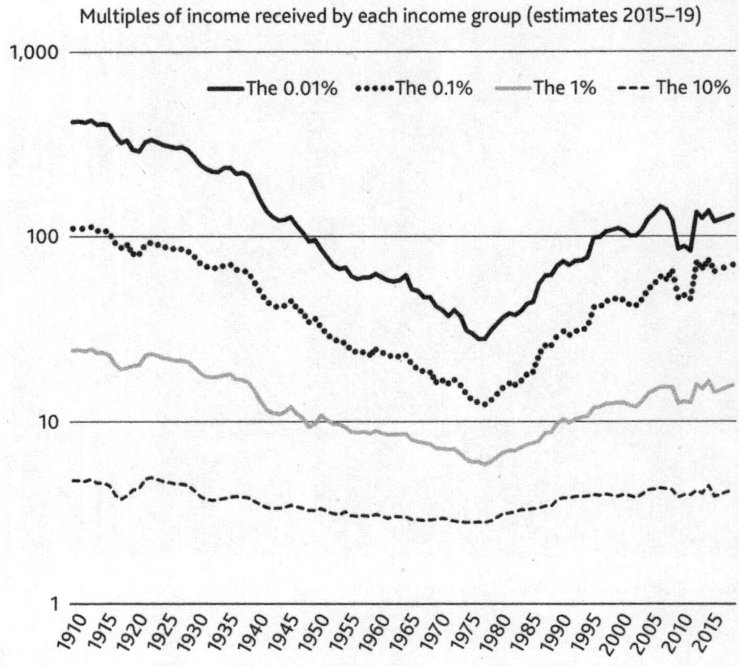

Source: Figure 0.1 from Danny Dorling (2019) *Inequality and the 1%*, 3rd edn. London: Verso, https://www.dannydorling.org/books/onepercent/Material.html

between 2010 and 2019. We were at 'peak income inequality' when the COVID-19 pandemic hit, and initially the new health crisis did little to dent it.

However, something began to change as we emerged from the worst of the pandemic years. We have started to see a rapid shift in the distribution of incomes – perhaps the first sign that we are at the beginning of a faster move towards equality than we have experienced in any year since the 1930s.

The most dramatic change has been in Scotland, where the Scottish Child Payment – given to any family in receipt of benefits, on top of other support – was raised to £25 a week for every child aged 16 or under. When Charles and Camilla holiday in Balmoral this summer [that is, summer 2023], they will do so in the only part of the kingdom where a poor family with three young children will be receiving £3,900 more in 2023 than in 2022, and so will be able to put food on the table. In the coldest months of the year, they may also be able to afford to heat their home, as long as they are extremely frugal. Scotland's first minister Nicola Sturgeon left office only when arguably the most important part of her work was done.

Consider, too, what has recently happened in pay negotiations across the United Kingdom. Pay agreements used to be simpler. For example, in 2010 the Communication Workers Union (CWU) struck a deal with BT worth 3 per cent a year for three years.[10] Everyone got 3 per cent, no matter what they earned. Now both bosses and unions are talking about more for the lower paid, less for the higher paid. And BT doesn't appear to be an outlier. Across almost every sector – including the more opaque private sector – we are seeing a strong trend towards more progressive deals, consisting of higher pay rises for lower-paid workers.

In contrast to the 2010 deal, in November 2022 the CWU negotiated a deal with BT in which the lowest-paid workers received an above-inflation 16 per cent pay rise, and the highest-paid a below-inflation 6 per cent rise.[11] Almost all private sector pay rises have been less than the rise in the state pension and less than the rise, in line with inflation, of benefits (although the actual inflation rate suffered by the poorest is higher than average). Roughly half of all private sector pay awards in early 2023 in the UK were below 5 per cent. Half were above that, but almost always below inflation.[12]

Adjustments in public sector pay appear to be even more progressive. Since 2010, junior civil service salaries have fallen in real terms by 12 per cent, but by 23 per cent at the most

[10] Julia Kollewe (2010) 'BT and union agree pay deal', *The Guardian*, 9 July, https://www.theguardian.com/business/2010/jul/09/bt-union-agree-pay-deal

[11] Michael Race (2022) 'BT and unions agree pay rise of up to 16% to stop more strikes', *BBC News*, 28 November, https://www.bbc.co.uk/news/business-63785421

[12] Zoe Wickens (2023) 'Half of private sector pay awards will give at least 5% raise in 2023', *Employee Benefits*, 3 February, https://employeebenefits.co.uk/half-of-private-sector-pay-awards-will-give-at-least-5-raise-in-2023/

senior level.[13] In March, workers in the biggest rail union, the RMT, voted for a pay deal that will give the highest paid among them a 9.4 per cent raise while the lowest paid will get 14 per cent more. This year, NHS employees were offered a deal that included a 3.5 per cent raise for the highest-paid staff, but over 9 per cent for the lowest paid. Under those terms, minimum pay rises in the health service would be £1,400 a year: a pay cut in real terms, but the cuts would be less for those who could least afford them. The unions rejected this offer in England. In Scotland, Unison and Unite have accepted an offer from the Scottish government of an average increase of 7.5 per cent for NHS workers. Again, those who are lower paid will receive more and those on higher wages, less. In Wales, unions accepted an offer that will increase staff costs by 7.5 per cent, but again it is progressive in the small print.[14]

The story is similar elsewhere. The offer made by councils in February 2023 to social workers in England and Wales was for a £1,925 rise for all, amounting to 3.9 per cent for the best paid but 6.4 per cent for the worst paid. The trade unions, which were calling for 12.7 per cent, rejected it.[15] In English schools outside of London, unions were offered a deal that involved increases of 8.9 per cent for early-career teachers, bringing their salaries up to £28,000 a year in their first year of teaching. Teachers at the top of the main scale and on the upper pay scale would receive only

---

13 Rhys Clyne (2023) 'Collapsing civil service pay undermines the government's ability to deliver', *Institute for Government*, 1 February, https://www.institute forgovernment.org.uk/comment/civil-service-pay-governments-ability-deliver

14 Alison Moore (2023) 'Department calls for affordable pay in 2023/24, but starts talks with nurses', *Healthcare Financial Management Association (HFMA)*, 22 February, https://www.hfma.org.uk/news/news-list/Article/department-calls-for-affordable-pay-in-2023-24-but-starts-talks-with-nurses

15 Mithran Samuel (2023) 'Council social workers offered "full and final" £1,925 pay rise for 2023–24', *Community Care Website*, 23 February, https://www.communitycare.co.uk/2023/02/23/council-social-workers-offered-full-and-final-1925-pay-rise-for-2023-24/

a 5 per cent rise, pushing their salaries to maximums of £38,810 and £43,685 respectively.[16]

Although all these pay offers are progressive, they are not very progressive. For example, in universities, the offer made in January 2023 ranged from a high of 8 per cent for the lowest-paid staff to 5 per cent for those on higher salaries. Under this deal, only staff earning less than £19,333 a year (barely above minimum wage) would receive the most generous 8 per cent rise, equivalent to an extra £1,547 a year. In contrast, the rise of 5 per cent would apply to members of staff currently receiving just over £31,000 or more a year, and they would take home upwards of an extra £1,570 a year. Someone paid twice that salary, almost £63,000, would receive twice as much in their increase: around an extra £3,140 a year. So even these pay offers still increase the gaps between university employees. A slightly more progressive offer would give all staff, no matter their income, the same bonus to take home: £2,000 more per year, for example, for high and low earners alike. The most progressive of all proposals would see pay cuts for the highest earners, and bigger rises for those at the bottom.

As yet these changes may not be enough to tip the scales towards a sustained fall in income inequalities of the kind that last began a century ago. Back then the incomes of the super-rich – the top 1 per cent of the top 1 per cent – had already been falling for 10 years. The modern super-rich suffered a blow to their incomes when corporate profits fell during the pandemic – in the period between 2021 and 2022 tax paid on corporate profits fell to 1.8 per cent of GDP, as compared with 2.9 per cent before the pandemic hit.[17] Some of that will be recovered, but expensive energy, higher wage costs for workers and the chancellor's announcement of an April 2023 corporation tax rate rise (from 19 per cent to 25 per cent) will mainly affect the very

---

[16] Callum Mason (2023) 'Has teacher pay in the UK risen with inflation, and how does it compare?', *Times Educational Supplement (TES) Magazine*, 1 February, https://www.tes.com/magazine/news/general/teacher-strike-has-teacher-pay-increased-inflation-and-how-does-it-compare-internationally

[17] Ian King (2023) 'Budget 2023: Corporation tax set to rise from 19% to 25% in April', *Sky News*, 6 March, https://news.sky.com/story/budget-2023-corporation-tax-set-to-rise-from-19-to-25-in-april-12827274

rich. Nonetheless, even if those with the most now begin to take more of a hit, there is unlikely to be much *Schadenfreude*. There was no joy a century ago when the rich were last squeezed. Every time we become more equal, there is usually a greater dose of increased misery along the way – often mostly simply from the fear of falling so as to become more like other people, a fear that is especially acute for those at the top.

Unions often point out how much real pay has fallen in recent decades. But in order to secure more progressive deals, they might be better off concentrating on how large other gaps have been allowed to grow. A head teacher of a large secondary school in the UK can be paid up to £101,126 a year; a police chief superintendent, £91,749; an army colonel, up to £104,671; the lowest-tier judge, £93,954;[18] and a long-serving NHS senior consultant can earn, as a basic salary, up to £119,133.[19] These may not seem unreasonable sums for people with such responsibilities, but in other European countries the pay of those in charge does not set them so far apart from the people they are in charge of. As Richard Wilkinson and Kate Pickett's landmark study *The Spirit Level*[20] demonstrated 15 years ago, societies work better when they are more equal.

People on higher pay in Britain often argue that they cannot get by without pay rises because of the costs of education and housing, which are higher in this country than across most of the rest of the continent. To a greater extent than in any other

---

[18] Other figures that differ slightly can be produced by taking different definitions of what a top job is. For example, on the high pay of most judges (the salary used here is for a low-tier judge – most judges are paid much more than £100,000 a year), see the salary scale listed in official government documents and consider why it is that judges, who, according to the Sutton Trust, are the most 'privileged' of all in terms of social background, are paid more than other people doing key roles, including senior government ministers: https://assets.publishing.service.gov.uk/government/uploads/system/uploads/attachment_data/file/1116006/judical-salary-schedule-2022-23.pdf

[19] Those other figures, such as those listed in the endnote above, and including a NHS senior consultant receiving £95,144 a year, are produced elsewhere: https://twitter.com/Max12to1/status/1570305201684332545

[20] Richard Wilkinson and Kate Pickett (2009) *The spirit level*, London: Allen Lane.

European state, they can easily point to people who are paid more: from university vice-chancellors to the several thousand London bankers who are paid over a million pounds a year and the chief executives of Britain's largest (FTSE 100) companies who, on average, take home around £4 million or £5 million, equivalent to a large lottery win, each year. They in turn can point to a handful of hedge fund managers, construction bosses and other unscrupulous individuals with annual incomes in the tens of millions. At the top of this spiral of excess can be found some of the more generous donors to the Conservative Party, a third of the UK's billionaires.[21]

Today, as in the 1920s, the arguments used to justify very high pay ring hollow. Luckless spokespeople defend high executive pay as 'benchmarked to the marketplace for equivalent roles', doubtless while feeling a little sick in their stomachs. In some sectors, leaders feel moved to take less: the most able university leaders began to take pay cuts of up to 20 per cent in 2020.[22] They are still a small minority, and those cuts mostly mean less university money is paid into government coffers through tax and

---

[21] In November 2019 it became clear that: 'Figures released by the Electoral Commission appear to back up what Jeremy Corbyn said at his manifesto launch – that the Conservative Party is the party of billionaires. Labour Party research has previously indicated that one in three of the UK's 151 billionaires donates to the Conservative Party': Joe Lo (2019) 'Billionaires give Tories over £2m since election called', *Left Foot Forward*, 21 November, https://leftfootforward.org/2019/11/billionaires-give-tories-over-2m-since-election-called/

[22] In 2020 university bosses mostly knew not to try and increase their take by the rate of inflation, but accepted a lowering of their pay. See: https://epigram.org.uk/2020/04/23/vice-chancellor-to-take-20-per-cent-pay-cut-amid-financial-concerns-over-covid-19/ and https://thetab.com/uk/nottingham/2020/04/30/exclusive-university-of-nottingham-vice-chancellor-to-take-pay-cut-47271, and https://www.edinburghnews.scotsman.com/education/university-edinburgh-principal-and-vice-chancellor-take-20-cent-pay-cut-due-coronavirus-2547206. The trend began as long ago as 2015, even before Brexit: https://www.cherwell.org/2015/01/16/oxstew-vicechancellor-takes-pay-cut/. Sadly by 2023 it did not appear this trend was being sustained and one remarkably sycophantic report stated that 'Every vice chancellor I have met in over a decade of working with universities has been impressive.' Which suggests its author

national insurance, but there could be more to come. Even *The Spectator* has suggested that some vice-chancellors could consider halving their salaries.[23]

There is growing evidence that something is tipping – not just in terms of wages and benefits, but in public attitudes and voting too. The 2017 election was the first since the 1970s where the Conservative vote did not become more geographically concentrated. In 2019 that trend accelerated – even as the Tories won a landslide majority, their vote fell in London and the southeast of England. And yet, just as our ancestors didn't notice the political twists and turns or the contractions in pay going on around them, these recent developments have not been widely commented on.[24] [Editorial note: 2024 was another shift in the same, new, direction.]

We frequently tell ourselves that the gaps between the richest and poorest aren't closing because those who argue for greater equality are naive fools who don't understand how to win elections. But a change in government might not be the only way to tip the scales of inequality.

Not a single election won between 1974 and 2019 resulted in any meaningful overall rise in income equality. For 50 years, the UK has become progressively more economically unequal, socially divided and politically polarised. Within that period there were some shifts. Income inequality between the medians of the top 20 per cent and bottom 20 per cent stopped rising around 1986. The Gini measure of inequality between all households hit a high in the mid-1990s and has remained on a plateau since. New Labour could not knock it off that plateau, not for a single year. The proportional pay of the top 1 per cent as a whole may have peaked before the financial crisis in 2008, but the wealthiest

---

met a remarkably small number of vice-chancellors; see: https://www.hepi.ac.uk/2023/08/31/new-report-discusses-the-scapegoating-of-vice-chancellors-pay-and-probes-the-question-of-how-to-fairly-set-the-rate-of-vice-chancellors-remuneration/

[23] Melanie McDonagh (2022) 'Can Oxford's new Vice-Chancellor fix the university?', *The Spectator*, 10 July, https://www.spectator.co.uk/article/can-oxford-s-new-vice-chancellor-fix-the-university/

[24] See Chapter 1.7 of this volume, and https://labourhub.org.uk/2023/02/21/what-did-the-elections-of-1922-and-2017-have-in-common/

among them kept on taking more, for years afterwards. The wealth of the richest 1,000 families in the UK rose steadily until 2020, when it faltered. Taken in the round, the gaps between us have been growing for half a century, in a way that other European countries did not allow. Instead, most became more equal; by 2019, only two countries in all of Europe – Bulgaria and Turkey – were more inequitable than the UK.

That could be about to change with the current wave of progressive and below-inflation pay offers. What would clinch it would be some self-control among the richest, or the threat of action if they show none. After the financial crash of 1929, the directors of most of the largest UK mortgage lenders took real-terms pay cuts for at least a decade.[25] The salaries of MPs, too, were temporarily reduced between 1931 and 1935 because of the economic crisis.[26] In part, they were fearful of revolution after seeing what had happened in Russia in 1917. But there was also, perhaps, a growing sense of social responsibility. It may seem unlikely that MPs would reduce their salaries again, but this year [2023] their pay rise will be only 2.9 per cent – a larger real-terms pay cut than almost all other public servants (but still an extra £2,440 a year).[27]

The ever-increasing trend in wealth inequality may also be starting to change. The wealthiest 10 per cent of households in the country have 43 per cent of the wealth; the bottom 50 per cent have just 9 per cent. The housing market, the second-largest source of wealth in the UK, was boosted during the pandemic but in the year to February 2023, prices fell in real terms. They could yet fall further: student loans are starting to take a bite out of the housing market as most young people go to university and 90 per cent leave with high loans to repay. Overall wealth

---

[25] Danny Dorling (2014) *All that is solid: How the great housing disaster defines our times, and what we can do about it*, London: Allen Lane, Figure 5, https://www.dannydorling.org/books/allthatissolid/Figures.html#4

[26] Richard Kelly (2009) 'Members' pay and allowances – a brief history', *House of Commons Library*, 21 May, https://researchbriefings.files.parliament.uk/documents/SN05075/SN05075.pdf

[27] Faye Brown (2023) 'MPs' pay to increase by 2.9% raising their salary to £86,584', *Sky News*, 9 February, https://news.sky.com/story/mps-pay-to-increase-by-2-9-raising-their-salary-to-86-584-12806962

is also falling, due to inflation. And the future values of private pensions, now the largest source of wealth, are also more in doubt today: many have caps that won't allow payments to rise in real terms (when inflation is above a certain level) in future. Far fewer people in Britain own stocks and shares than in the past, so there is no salvation even there. In 2022, the Resolution Foundation discovered that the top 10 per cent of people by income were now less likely to have savings equivalent to their monthly earnings than the bottom 10 per cent.

One hundred years ago, the last time that the UK saw the beginning of any fall in either income or wealth inequality, the country had been through one war and was heading for another. It is sometimes suggested that only a great catastrophe can truly turn the inequality tide, but the reasons why inequality last began to narrow are complex: while the First World War played a part in changing the course of inequality, during and after the Second World War, the established trend stuck. Today we are getting to test the catastrophe theory further.

The UK's political parties tend to move in concert, swinging as a group from right to left when inequalities fall, and vice versa as they rise. In recent years, the Conservatives have become one of the most right-wing major parties worldwide (Figure 1.17). Liz Truss's complaint that the left-wing 'powerful economic establishment' had thwarted her economic agenda was on the one hand laughable; on the other, she may have had a point. Some conditions and ideas become untenable. Moral sentiment does change over time, and no one, including the 'economic establishment', is immune. In the 1930s, the stockbroker and banker Oswald Falk wrote that John Maynard Keynes and his friends had helped change the moral sentiment of their times; but it was a far wider and more diffuse set of events that contributed to that shift.

The 2008 financial crash and the misguided austerity that followed it; Brexit; how Britain dealt with the pandemic; the global rise in prices in recent years: all these have combined to create a crisis not dissimilar to the one that we faced a century ago, when salaries at the top last rose by less than wages at the bottom. History makes no promises to repeat itself and it could be that what we are seeing now is a blip. But there are signs that it could be more than that.

Figure 1.17: Economic policies of almost all political parties in the world compared, left to right

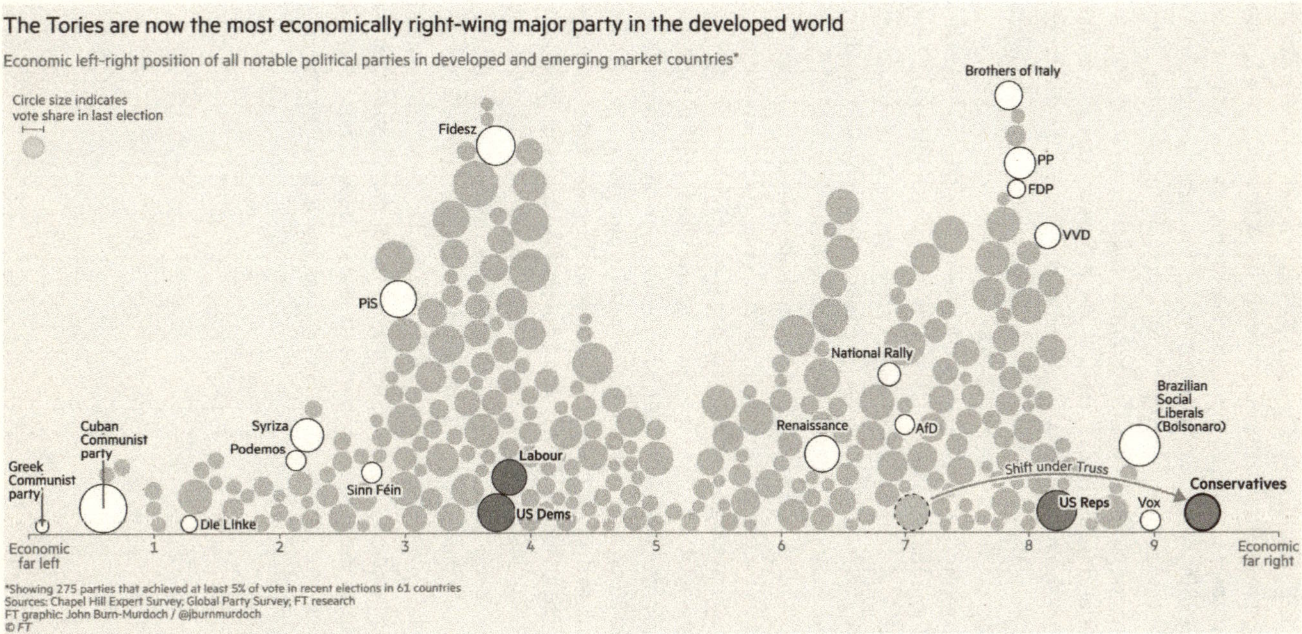

Note: Figure includes all the rich and mainstream world states.

Source: John Burn-Murdoch (2022) 'The Tories have become unmoored from the British people', *Financial Times*, 30 September. John Burn-Murdoch's graph: https://twitter.com/dannydorling/status/1575836071832604673?s=20

see colour version in plate section

The UK could revert to trend – we could become even more inequitable. Alternatively, we could be at the start of a long and at first painful process of gradually becoming more equal. The 1920s and 1930s were hardly good times for most people in Britain but, nevertheless, during those years of misery the inequality gap narrowed. By the 1940s it was possible to look back on the 1920s and publish plays such as *An Inspector Calls* and books such as *Brideshead Revisited* about how odd, how awful, the recent past had been. Will people in the 2040s be doing the same when they talk about Britain in the 2020s?

Between the year of King Charles's grandfather's coronation in 1937 and his mother's in 1953, the pay of the best-off 0.1 per cent in the UK halved from 66 times average incomes to 28 times. It fell as fast before and after the Second World War as during it. By the time of Queen Elizabeth's Silver Jubilee, in 1977, the take of the top 0.1 per cent had more than halved again, to 13 times average incomes. But then it suddenly increased threefold, to 42 times average incomes, by her Golden Jubilee in 2002. It had almost doubled again by the time she died, returning to a point slightly worse than it had been when her father became king.

If we are now on the downward slope once again, let's learn from history. No other country in Europe has made itself as unequal as we have. We don't have to do it again. We don't have to take so long to come down from this peak, and we don't have to try to become even more unequal again. All the many more equitable European countries that have monarchies have far more normal ones. Those without tend to be even more equitable still. Nowhere else in Europe goes in for such lavish coronations or allows income inequalities to rise so high. There is no innate flaw in the British that means we are forever doomed to be geographical oddities.

SECTION 2

Poverty, destitution and happiness

Anxiety, satisfaction, worth and happiness

Among countries in the rich world, those that tax more almost always have very little destitution, lower levels of poverty overall, and a much happier population as a result. Other than through the application of a flat-rate Value Added Tax (VAT), or other even more regressive taxes, government taxation rarely increases inequality. More normally, income taxation results in redistribution towards the poor. This is because taxes on income and wealth, unlike VAT, tend to be progressive. China, which is at least as economically unequal as the UK, now uses targeted luxury-item consumption taxation to increase equality and reduce polarisation. The Chinese do this now both across the country and within its capital city, Beijing.[1] In contrast to Beijing, socio-spatial inequalities in London have risen sharply in recent decades.[2]

Happiness levels are influenced by governments ensuring that taxation is fair, and hence by how economically equal countries are, much more than by anything else. It is sometimes suggested that people would be happier if they knew that a particular tax they were paying was going to be spent on a particular public good. However, attempts to hypothecate taxes usually fail, as does taxing a particular group that is not more affluent. This effectively is what happens to the UK's young people, 65 per cent of whom,

---

1 Including a progressive form of VAT which is regularly reviewed: Arendse Huld (2023) 'China's new draft VAT law – how is it different from previous tax regulations?', *China Briefing*, 11 September, https://www.china-briefing.com/news/china-value-added-tax-law-draft-legislation

2 Qiujie Shi and Danny Dorling (2020) 'Growing socio-spatial inequality in neo-liberal times? Comparing Beijing and London', *Applied Geography*, 115, 102139, ISSN0143-6228, https://doi.org/10.1016/j.apgeog.2019.102139

Figure 2.1: A worthwhile life, satisfaction, happiness and anxiety, UK, 2011–21

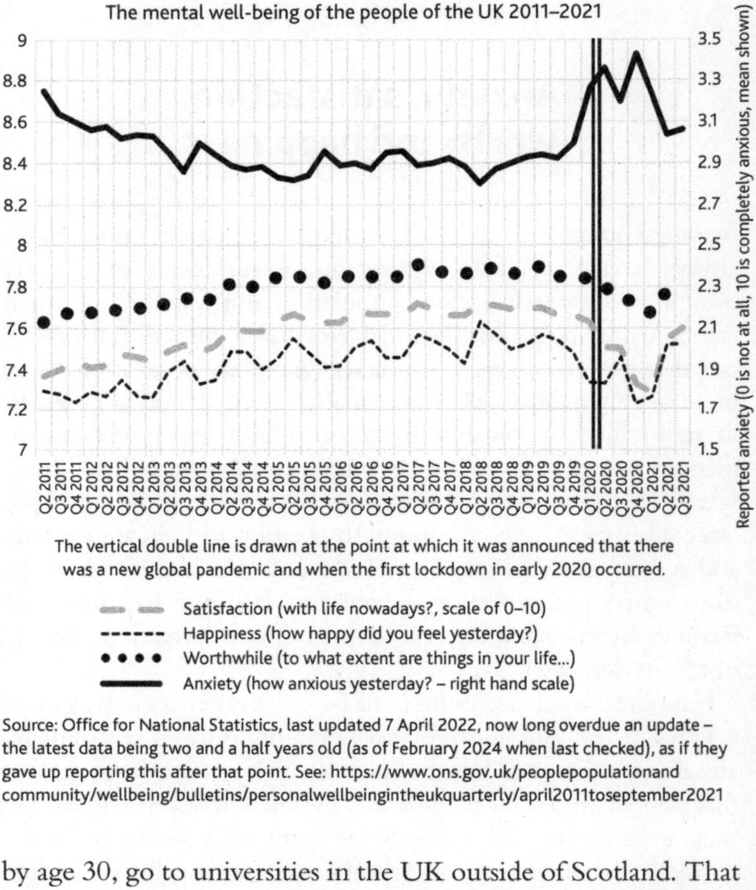

Source: Office for National Statistics, last updated 7 April 2022, now long overdue an update – the latest data being two and a half years old (as of February 2024 when last checked), as if they gave up reporting this after that point. See: https://www.ons.gov.uk/peoplepopulationandcommunity/wellbeing/bulletins/personalwellbeingintheukquarterly/april2011toseptember2021

by age 30, go to universities in the UK outside of Scotland. That group comprising a majority of young people in England are, in effect, taxed more to pay for their studies. They are told that this is not a graduate tax, but a deduction designed to repay their student loans (with interest). That, however, is as disingenuous as claiming that National Insurance contributions are what actually pays for the National Health Service, unemployment benefits and state pensions. Of course, the extra taxes that almost all university students are obliged to pay do not pay back their loans. If that were the case, there would not be an earnings threshold below which you do not have to make repayments.

Who spends their money most wisely? It is the very poorest, out of necessity, who do, followed by the state. As the graduate tax/loan fiasco illustrates, the state can at times be profligate. However, the least wise spenders are the richest among us, spending shockingly high amounts on fripperies (for instance, on horses, on wine and on postgraduate degree fees at elite universities). This is another reason to tax well and not to rely on philanthropy to address inequalities (Chapter 2.1).

Opting not to tax the rich, as British politicians chose to do more and more in the years from 1979 onwards, results in someone else having to pay – often through deteriorating standards of living. At first it was the very poorest – people in 'deprived inner cities' – who bore the brunt of the harms. Later it was 'middle England', and especially those living in the suburbs, where people suffered most (Chapter 2.2).

The Conservative government that came to power in 1979 didn't like to talk about poverty or even to ever use the word, because its leaders chose to see poverty as something that had ended in the UK shortly after the Second World War. The New Labour government that succeeded the Tories in 1997 preferred to talk about social exclusion rather than poverty, although it did try to claim that its policies would reduce child poverty. Whatever New Labour might have achieved – and that was very hard to determine because so much of the measurement was commissioned by self-interested government departments – was lost in 2010 when a Conservative–Liberal Democrat coalition came to power and introduced austerity, which resulted in rising destitution (Chapter 2.3). Most of the few good things New Labour introduced were very easy to cancel, or otherwise unwind. Happiness levels fell greatly with the banking crisis of 2008, rose a little after that, slowly, but then plunged again when Boris Johnson led the Conservative Party to another general election victory in 2019. His victory triggered a rise in anxiety far greater than the further rise that occurred when the COVID-19 pandemic arrived, or even that which followed when the second wave of that pandemic in the UK made it clear that the new disease was here to stay for some time (see Figure 2.1).

When destitution in Britain rose, so did deaths. First to rise, in 2012, were deaths among elderly women; not long afterwards, life expectancy for women over the age of 65 dropped. Soon there were more and more groups affected by austerity; and, after 2014, life expectancy fell across the whole of the UK for men as well as for women. Life expectancy dropped every year until 2019, when it only just managed to rise above the 2014 level for a very short time, in fact only for a few months, before the pandemic hit. All UK governments between 2010 and 2023 attempted – incorrectly – to blame influenza for these rises in mortality that occurred outside of the worst pandemic years (Chapter 2.4). However, as the introduction to this book explained, many inequalities began to fall slightly after 2018 in the UK, partly because it became unaffordable for them to rise further. It is very expensive to tolerate high inequality. The population of the US partly do so because that country, as a whole, is still so rich.

In the first few months of 2020, once the COVID-19 pandemic had hit, there was a short-lived but dramatic rise in inequality once again (Chapter 2.5). Since then, inequality has continued to fall in terms of both income and wealth, and those falls are accelerating as I write these words in the spring of 2024. Almost all wages fell in real terms in 2023, but the fall tended to be greater for those already better-paid. Wealth inequalities fell as housing values fell.

Even in the years when the UK was becoming more equal, people who had more wealth still frequently showed disdain for those who had less. Chapter 2.6 recounts a description by Peter Townsend as to how the distain of the affluent felt, even when seen at the much more muted level of 1950s Britain. That account contrasts greatly with attitudes in those countries that are most equal and where people are happiest and actually behave decently, with respect, to each other (Chapter 2.7). Increasingly, however, the large majority of adults in the UK now wish for a much fairer society than the one they have, and they also desire that respect much more today too (Chapter 2.8). When it was the prevailing view in the past, that respect was due, a small but significant number worked for and won just such a society: the UK in the decades immediately before the 1980s, where people who treated others with more genuine respect were more valued. A great part of respecting another human being is not expecting them to survive on much less money than you have.

By 2023, surveys were showing that a majority of adults in all groups of UK households, other than the very richest, thought that action now needed to be taken by the government to change the underlying ethos. The rate at which people were leaving key jobs in sectors such as further education had increased sharply. This was not only because pay in those sectors had fallen so significantly, but also because the work was becoming untenable (Chapter 2.9). People were taking more strike action to hold on to what they had won than they had for many years, although nothing like to the extent that had been required in the decade immediately after 1918 to reverse rising inequality (Chapter 2.10). However, history does not always repeat itself. Sometimes it is different, and occasionally it is very different.

It is possible that we might learn from our past this time. Poverty need not always be with us, and examples of where it can be reduced, even within the UK and even in the years leading up to 2024, are included in Chapter 2.8 in this section. Destitution is not our most obvious destination. Happiness, in the particular way it was measured to create Figure 2.1, did tend to rise each year in the UK until that fateful point where it appeared that a hard Brexit could not be avoided and the Corbyn promise was over, when, as the figure shows, happiness, and the idea of life being worthwhile, even satisfying, and anxieties low, plummeted rapidly across the nation with Johnson's elevation. Even the largest and most devastating pandemic since the influenza of 1918 appeared a minor event in the four nations' collective psyche as compared to that most unforeseen possibility slowly becoming a nightmare reality: Boris Johnson as prime minister – this was the nightmare in more people's minds than ever at the point that injustice in the UK peaked. Johnson doing well made the British public, in aggregate, sick, tired and unhappy.

Thankfully, the international patterns are quite clear, as shown in Chapter 2.7 in one of the simplest graphs in this book (Figure 2.13). There is a very straightforward way to becoming happier, which is intrinsic to our species, and that is to agree to be – or to fight to be, or to be forced through calamity to eventually be – more equal.

CHAPTER 2.1

Who spends more wisely: individuals or government?[1]

It is the poor who are the most careful spenders by far – because, of course, they have to be. If you believe in the efficiency of private consumption, you should aim for the poor to have more to spend, as they allocate money so much more wisely than the rich. Conversely, if a little more of the wealth and income of the rich were taxed and spent better by the state, we would all be better off.

In between individual choice and government diktat is the idea of a hypothecated tax, where people know where a part of the tax they pay is going. However, there is an argument that we should oppose hypothecation on the grounds that it frames the economy as a crude set of inputs and outputs.

The hypothecation of taxation implies that the economy works like a factory. In a cereal factory, if you increase the inputs of oats, wheat and sugar and ramp up the amount of cardboard you buy, more packages of cereal will probably come out of the other end of the production line. And in essence, the hypothecation model suggests that if you give the public power over the inputs, they will get more of what they want.

However, the factory model of taxation is misleading. It is just as misleading as to suggest that the economics of a whole country

1 Originally published in three parts in *The Common Vision Blog Series*, 4 and 6 October 2018, and 24 January 2019, and combined here and adapted to link to later work on student loans and a graduate tax. See: Danny Dorling (2019) 'Who spends more wisely: individuals or government?', Common Vision Blog (The Responsible Tax Lab), 24 January, https://www.dannydorling.org/?page_id=7095

is no different from a household's economy. The household – or 'handbag' – model of economics[2] suggests that if a country's politicians are frugal, and spend less, it will prosper. This model was used to defend the introduction of student loans in the late 1990s, and then raising tuition fees to the highest in the world in the 2010s by suggesting that fees are a fair form of graduate taxation (see Chapters 4.2 and 4.3). University fees are not fair. Neither are student loans, as lower-paid graduates end up 'paying back' by far the most.

There is, of course, some truth in all models. The handbag model of economics is an analogy that will at times appear to be pertinent. For instance, at some point it will not be possible for the United States to carry on spending vastly more money than it raises in taxes every year, increasing its national debt to astronomical levels.[3] However, the reason is not because the US economy is like a family's household budget. For a state, which is made up of many millions of households, money does not play the same role as the money you might have in your handbag. A country's current account does not determine what its people are able to spend at the shops on that day. The factory model of taxation, like the handbag model of economics, is initially attractive because it reduces a process to something you might think you understand well, even though most people have never been in a factory and most of us run our household economics on debt. I have a mortgage, even at my age, but no one calls me profligate because of it.

Consider healthcare. The factory model of healthcare implies that the more you spend on healthcare, the better your health will be. I am not saying that the opposite is the case – just that the way the economy works is not as direct a process as simply putting more in to get more out.

---

2 Most closely associated with Margaret Thatcher, the first person to call herself a 'handbag economist': Anthony James (2015) *Orwell's faded lion: The moral atmosphere of Britain 1945–2015*, Exeter: Imprint Academic Press.

3 Reaching $14,344,566,636,826.26 on 15 June 2011. See Thomas Friedman and Michael Mandelbaum (2012) *That used to be us: What went wrong with America and how it can come back*, London: Little Brown.

The US is, again, a useful example for this: far more is spent on healthcare in the US, per head, than in any other country in the world. As much is spent from the country's public purse on schemes like Medicare and Medicaid as is spent privately, and yet the results are not good. On closer inspection it turns out not to be health spending that best predicts health outcomes in the separate states of the US and other affluent countries of the world, but the influence of factors such as historical levels of economic inequality, especially income inequality (Figure 2.2).

Of course, you have to weigh multiple factors at once when considering tax. Health spending does matter in health outcomes, but many other factors also contribute – for example, housing policies that ensure that doctors and nurses can afford to live near their patients. Affordable housing is necessary so that most of the taxes spent on healthcare do not simply end up being wasted on the higher salaries that healthcare staff will otherwise need mainly to pay the rent to private landlords or to finance mortgages for the purchase of overpriced homes from an older generation who will be cash-rich but health-poor.

The same applies to education policy. Again, it is not just the amount that is spent on education that determines the education levels of the population as a whole. When societies are more mixed, children end up better educated. By contrast, in England, especially as inequalities grew, high tuition fees and loans for undergraduate degrees were introduced that allow loan terms and interest rates to change or the loan books to be sold off completely outside of students' control. If a university graduate goes on to earn more than a very low wage in future, and they also have taken out a loan to pay to study for a master's degree, they will be taxed an extra 15 per cent a year on all their income over that very low amount.[4] Should master's degrees be only for the rich?

[4] The Student Loan Company tells those borrowing for a master's degree that 'You'll repay 6% of your income over the Postgraduate Loan threshold (£21,000 a year) and 9% of your income over the lowest threshold for any other plan types you have.' Depending on what plan you are on, this is either until you are aged 65, or after 30 years, or upon death (but your relatives have 'to let SLC [Student Loans Company] know that the person has died

Figure 2.2 Take of the 1 per cent in 1983 and later versus life expectancy in 2015, in 19 countries and all US states

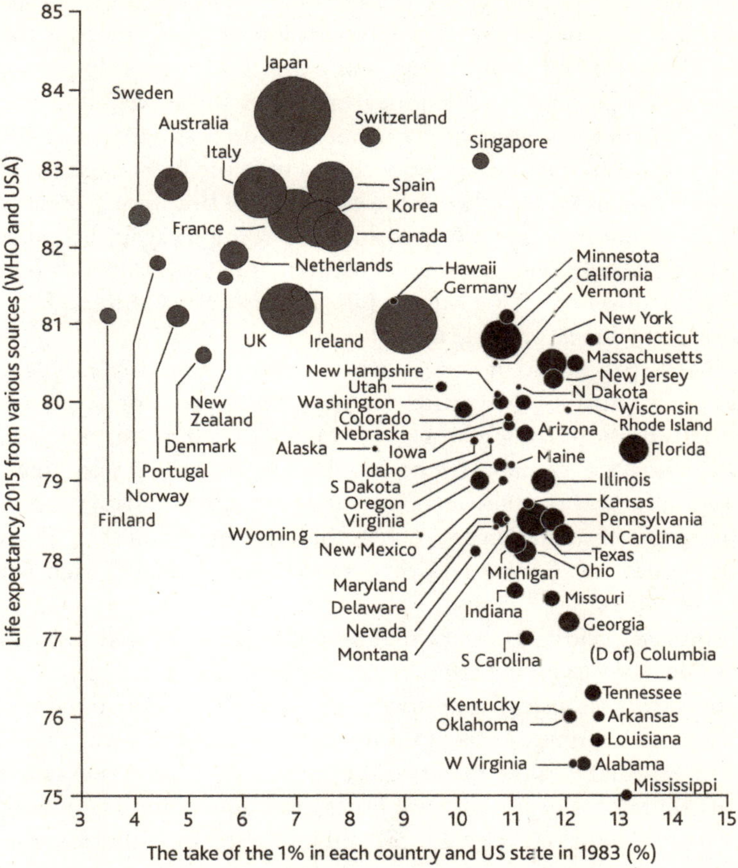

Source: World Wealth and Income database accessed December 2016 and life expectancy data from the 'Measure of America' and the World Health Organization (as of January 2017)

Source: Danny Dorling (2017) *Do we need economic inequality?*, Cambridge: Polity; see interactive figure at http://www.dannydorling.org/books/economicinequality/figures-and-tables/figure-5-2.html

---

and provide evidence (for example an original death certificate), as well as the person's Customer Reference Number)', or you go abroad to a country with no tax agreements with the UK and disappear from the UK system forever, or in the increasingly unlikely event that you actually pay the monies off. See: https://www.gov.uk/repaying-your-student-loan/what-you-pay

Social policy is not like a cereal factory. All the inputs go in and all the outputs come out, but they are mixed up in the middle in ways that we are still learning about. This lends itself to an argument against the hypothecation of taxes, which is too heavily reductive about inputs and outputs. However, life is not always simple, and crude politics sometimes works well, thus one case where the argument for hypothecation is stronger is in the introduction of new taxes, as occurred with the quasi-taxation of student loans in the UK outside of Scotland. But having uprated higher education spending in this way, doing so again becomes untenable, and the outcome increasingly unfair. [Editorial note: By the summer of 2024 many UK universities were thought to be on the brink of bankruptcy.]

Most people do not perceive the taxes they currently pay as unreasonable. Nevertheless, new taxes are almost always briefly unpopular when a government first introduces them, and they are often imagined as having only bad outcomes. Typically, however, the fears subside and taxpayers adapt (except for obviously unfair taxes, such as the UK's brief poll tax). Taxes are good, but fairer taxes that redistribute from the rich are better still.

Indeed, evidence shows that affluent countries that tax at a higher rate have far better social outcomes in terms of health, education, housing, pollution, transport use and happiness levels. In contrast, affluent countries that tax at a lower rate – and especially ones that tax the rich less – have the worst health and educational outcomes, the most inefficient and insecure housing systems, the highest rate of pollution per head, worse public transport provision and higher levels of antidepressant use. All of these factors are, of course, interrelated, but a government generally helps its people by taxing more, as long as it spends the money wisely, which usually means little hypothecation and no graduate taxes or loans (see Figure 2.3).

In England, I would support the introduction of a hypothecated land value tax to be spent on health and social care. This would free up general tax revenues to be better targeted on education, welfare, housing and much else in the UK that is in urgent need of attention. A land value tax would replace council tax and

Figure 2.3: State spending as a proportion of GDP, 12 rich countries, 2002–20 (%)

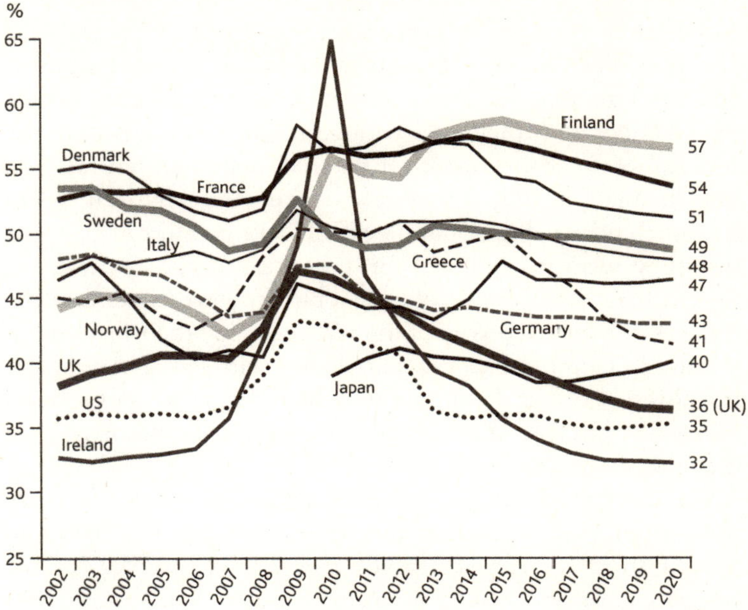

Source: The 2010, 2012 and 2015 IMF database, projections after 2014. (Naturally the projections did not predict the COVID-19 pandemic in 2020, when all countries saw spending rise in a similar way to when the banking crisis hit them all in 2008.) Figure from Danny Dorling (2016) *A better politics*, London: London Publishing Company (open access version available here: http://www.dannydorling.org/books/betterpolitics/). It only contains two key figures; this is the second one.

business rates, and the tax would enhance intergenerational equity, as it would be levied mostly on older people.[5]

A land value tax could replace inefficient wealth taxes with the promise that all the monies initially raised would be spent on enhancing health and social care – issues that matter most to older people, who also happen to be the largest owners of the most land. As taxes are tapered in when they are initially raised,

[5] Explained in more detail in the transcript of a talk given at the Government Economic Service and Social Research Annual Training Conference, 200 Aldersgate, St Paul's, London, 21 September 2018: 'You may see now (and the UK) as normal – but that badly colours how you think', http://www.dannydorling.org/?p=6820

and as the need for extra health and social care funding is now acute, this promise could be made binding for at least a decade.

Inevitably, the revenues collected from hypothecated taxes reduce over time, and become less 'ring-fenced'. This is what occurred with National Insurance payments, which have now become a general tax. But at the point of introduction, people would know what they were voting for when they voted for the political party that proposed a specific, hypothecated tax. On implementation, only a very few of the extremely rich would feel much financial pain, but they could take comfort in knowing that they were being taxed for a very good cause – not just to enhance the health of older people but also to increase the chances of babies across all of the UK surviving their first year of life and to help more elderly people live with less fear and pain. It is this sort of social contract on which the tax system is based in the first place, so if hypothecation helps make this case, then it could be effective.

Will 2019 see an end to austerity? [Editorial note: This piece was written that year, when none of us knew what 2020 would bring.] In 2018, the chancellor announced that the 'era of austerity is finally coming to an end', nearly four months *after* Theresa May said she would be willing to break her stance against tax increases in order to fund her pledge for an annual £20 billion for the NHS by 2023. Shadow chancellor John McDonnell reacted with disbelief to the Conservatives' declaration – Labour had just made a call for £108 billion in additional public spending to address the damages done by a decade of austerity. Less than a fifth of that could not even begin to address the scale of the job so urgently needed. [Editorial note: In the event, the health service was grossly underfunded when the pandemic hit. It was the oldest who died most often, disproportionately those who might have been taxed more in earlier years, but for whom there were few ventilators when they needed them, four times fewer per head, gasping for breath, than in Germany.]

Politicians who are opposed to spending on public services often choose to treat the public with disdain, telling them that they 'cannot spend what they do not tax' and implying that if they were to tax more there would be less 'growth'. The debate at present often lacks any analysis or recognition of what is best spent publicly and what is best spent privately – for example, in terms of who is best placed to make spending choices on social care in old age, or whether student fees should be paid by the state, via a graduate tax, or through loans taken out by students whose parents are not wealthy enough to pay their fees upfront for them.

In general, the state is a far more efficient provider of infrastructure than, say, private toll road entrepreneurs or those who would wish to privatise all public parks. It is especially the case that when goods are infrequently purchased, buyers can be easily duped, or at the very least disadvantaged. No one would want to become an informed consumer of heart surgery through the repeat purchase of bypass operations. It follows that healthcare is best funded by the state. Similarly, no one should wish to repeat so many years at school that they become an expert in selecting educational providers. As for housing, extensive international research has demonstrated that any country that does not have a mixed model of state and private housing provision will be likely to have a serious homelessness problem.[6]

In short, for items that you buy often – and where the consequences of making a mistake are not dire – the private market can be most efficient. But even for transport, countries that rely too much on private cars suffer from the greatest congestion, pollution and obesity, as well as the inefficiencies of longer traffic jams and the effects of the huge personal debts required to purchase yet more cars (see Figure 2.4).

---

6 Danny Dorling (2015) 'Review: *A World of Homeowners – American Power and the Politics of Housing Aid* (by Nancy Kwak)', *Times Higher Education*, 29 October, https://www.dannydorling.org/?page_id=4921

Figure 2.4: Proportion of people walking or cycling as their main means of travel

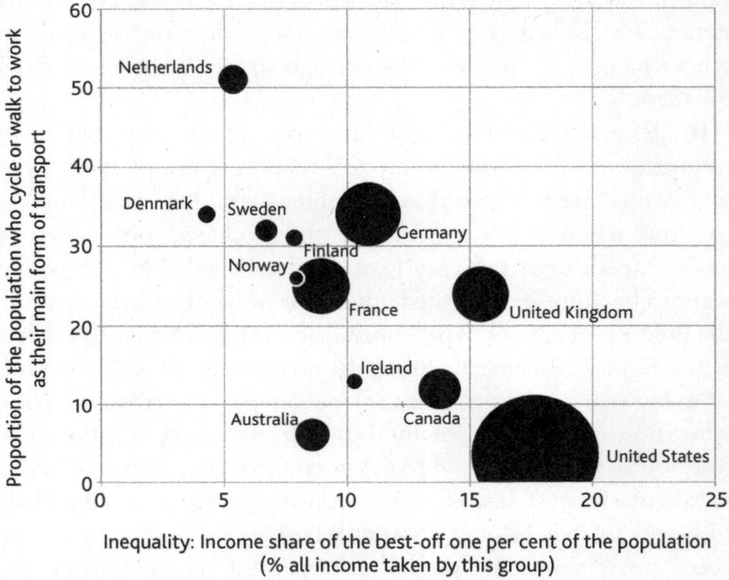

Note: Each circle is a country drawn in proportion to its population. Japan could be added here, strengthening the relationship, but this graph was originally drawn before that data was found.

Source: Danny Dorling (2015) 'The mother of underlying causes – economic ranking and health inequality', *Social Science & Medicine*, 128, 327–30, https://www.dannydorling.org/?page_id=4350, relying in turn on: Ralph Buehler and John Pucher (2012) 'Walking and cycling in Western Europe and the United States: Trends, policies, and lessons', *TR News* 280, May/June, https://onlinepubs.trb.org/onlinepubs/trnews/trnews280westerneurope.pdf

CHAPTER 2.2

Dying quietly: English suburbs and the stiff upper lip[1]

The English suburbs are dying. Years of austerity have slowly changed the landscape, and suburban poverty is now common. Since 2014 life expectancy has been falling across most of England, especially in the suburbs. Now infant mortality rates are also rising year on year, unlike anywhere else in Europe. In hindsight it is not surprising that the majority of suburban English people voted for Brexit, most noticeably in the Home Counties. Middle England is angry. No more fortitude in the face of adversity and the hiding of emotions. The stiff upper lip has slipped. Change is in the air.

The new suburbs

Mustn't grumble. Mustn't make a fuss. Cuts to services like Meals on Wheels, social worker visits, day centres, bus routes, post offices and many other suburban staples have hastened the exit of the elderly. In old age it is in the suburbs, far away from their children (if they had children), that people in England are much more frequently living and dying alone.[2]

---

1 Adapted from the start of an article first published in *The Political Quarterly*, 90, 1, pp. 32–44, 26 September 2018. The original keywords of this article were: 'Old-England', 'Dying', 'Empire-song', 'Dignified', 'Civilised', and 'Suburbs'.

2 [Editorial note: See Hiam, L., Estrin-Serlui, T., Dorling, D., McKee, M. and Minton, J. (2023) 'A deathly silence: why has the number of people found decomposed in England and Wales been rising?', *Journal of the Royal Society of Medicine*, 21 November, doi:10.1177/01410768231209001]

Margaret Thatcher's claim that there is no such thing as society, just families and their children, rings both true and hollow in the suburbs. The suburbs have become places in which the elderly who have not quite made it into the best-off echelons reside; not rich enough to decamp to idyllic villages, to private healthcare and eventually an exclusive retirement complex. Those who did well, but not exceptionally well, face an isolated suburban old age. Their grown-up children live in another suburb, far away, or have not yet escaped the city and are renting – still waiting for the inheritance, their ticket to suburbia.

The centres of cities are increasingly reserved for the young, the successful and those who can afford to avoid long commutes. A few select villages are where the very affluent go to as the places they choose to age – in the idyllic cottage in the country, and those other enclaves that have now been geographically reserved for England's upper-middle class, and for the children they now have so very late in their lives to grow up in. This includes streets in Kensington and Chelsea where every child attends a private school, where most adults only ever use private healthcare, and where it is normal not to have a mortgage but to have purchased the home with cash, or simply inherited it. The most successful of the English hop right over the suburbs, leaping from Notting Hill mews house to Oxfordshire cottage; from dinner parties to country suppers.

England accommodated its loss of empire by accepting rising economic inequality at home. After the 1970s the country as a whole became poorer when compared to the rest of the world, and to most of Europe, but in the 1980s, 1990s and noughties those at the top took a greater and greater share of the pie each year. As they did so, they were taking more and more from the poor and from suburban middle England, from the places where the majority lived, the places that saw progress stall.

Loft conversions in the city and barn conversions in the countryside contrast with steady decline in those suburban places that, in the 1930s to 1970s, embodied the ideal of a good life and a happy future. The suburbs were supposed to be safe places, where life's winners went. Suburban schools were 'good', suburban jobs were plentiful – and well paid. Suburban doctors were not overworked; hospitals were accessible, and always there for you when you needed them. Until the money began to run out and the waiting lists began to grow.

The money began to run out in the late 1970s. After that, there was less and less building of new suburbs. Home building in the UK had fallen from a peak of 400,000 new units a year in the 1960s, to 200,000 a year by the 1980s – after which it never recovered. It slumped even further after the 2008 crash.

As of August 2018, fewer than 200,000 homes were being built a year despite huge pent-up need for more housing in the most overcrowded places.[3] There was little complaint from the suburbs, where house prices rose and homeowners believed they were becoming richer. Meanwhile, the real riches were being made by those who could lend the huge sums to aspiring homeowners, or who could buy properties in cash and then rent them out. Older homeowners were not 'doing well'. In early 2018 England and Wales saw the worst rise in mortality since the Second World War (see Figure 2.5).

The suburbs are now more and more often the destination not of winners, but of those who have only just avoided becoming losers. And those who have lost out are starting to move in too. This is beginning to swing suburbs in the south of England towards Labour.[4] Landlords buy up suburban semis and rent them out to families who no longer qualify for a mortgage. In the poorest suburbs, unrelated immigrants live two or three to a room. But that is only in the suburbs of successful cities, the ones where the population is still rising. The suburbs that are faring worst are those in which the new private landlords who buy up property have no interest other than financial gain, and where today few immigrants arrive.

Suburban Conservative-voting England, where the fewest immigrants arrive, is where UKIP did best in various votes before 2017. We try to pretend it is the poor council estates, the East Coast and 'the North' where recent dissatisfaction was

---

3 Anonymous (2018) 'House building in England', *Full Fact*, 22 March 2018, https://fullfact.org/economy/house-building-england/

4 Ian Warren (2018) 'Watch out, Tories. Your southern strongholds are turning red', *The Guardian*, 9 May, https://www.theguardian.com/commentisfree/2018/may/09/tories-southern-red-south-england-london

Figure 2.5: The rise in mortality in England and Wales in the first 16 weeks of 2018

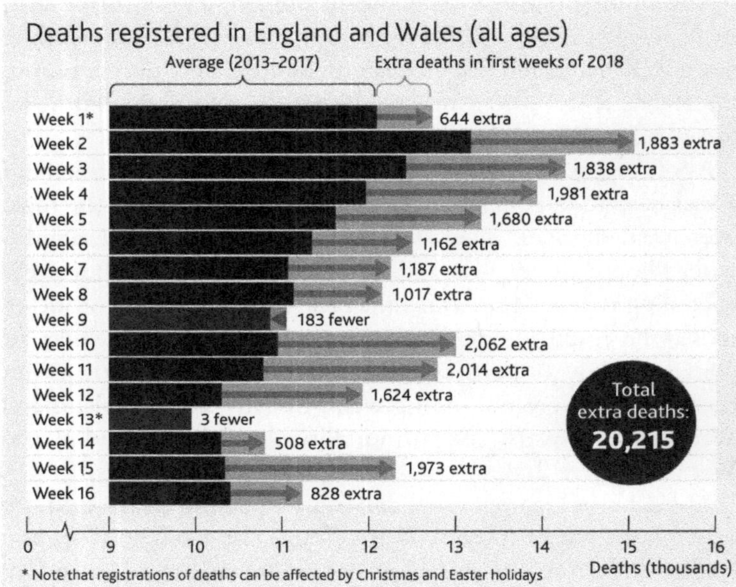

Source: Lu Hiam and Danny Dorling (2018) 'Rise in mortality in England and Wales in the first sixteen weeks of 2018: rapid response', *British Medical Journal*, 9 May, https://www.bmj.com/content/360/bmj.k1090/rr-8

greatest; but that is not where the sense of loss was strongest. Council estates lost their pride in the 1980s, when most of the homes that could be sold off under Thatcher's right-to-buy policy ended up in the hands of private landlords. The north of England had been repeatedly battered during the 1990s when the end of deindustrialisation ushered in an era of low-wage work, or none at all. It took until the 2000s for the suburbs and the south to begin to decline, for homeownership to begin to fall, as the 1 per cent took more and more. The 1 per cent are the winners today, and the 1 per cent don't live in the suburbs. They have homes in the city centre and the countryside – often both.

In 1997, the UK's best-off 1 per cent took 12.1 per cent of all income. This was more than twice what they took in Sweden, the Netherlands and Denmark. It was more than their take in any other European country. New Labour allowed the take of the 1 per cent to rise even higher, to 15.4 per cent, by 2007. That extra 3.3 per cent of national income was, in effect, almost entirely taken from the suburbs, and is still taken from them each and every year.[5] In other European countries, where the 1 per cent take less, the poor do much better – but it is the suburbs that most benefit from greater economic equality.

When the 1 per cent take so much there is not enough left for the rest. Compared to Scandinavian norms, the best-rewarded 1 per cent of people in the UK take enough extra *to fund a second national health service*. The groups just below them also take more than in any other European country, desperately attempting to keep up with the 1 per cent above them, often just to be able to afford a modest home in the city away from outlying suburbs. The income of the 1 per cent is not recycled outside of the city and the countryside. It creates opulence in a very few places, and jobs that are mostly for servants – although in the early 21st century, unlike in the late 19th and early 20th centuries, they generally aren't called servants and they don't live in.

The suburbs first rose up in England as working in service disappeared. Servants used to live in the large homes of the extremely rich. They were not allowed to have homes of their own and could not have afforded to rent, even if they had been allowed to move out. Today's rise in people working in service may be subtle, but it is substantial. It results in a rise in the number of people at the very bottom of the labour market. It is a rise that has hollowed out jobs in the middle. From school teachers in southern cities to labourers in the north, it means a rise in people who cannot afford to get by and cannot afford to start a family – just like the live-in servants of a century or more ago.

The suffering of the suburbs

The suburbs have an iconic place in the identity of England and Wales. In south Wales, the outer rim of homes on the edge of the valleys were the least desired and first to be demolished when

5 D. Dorling (2018) 'Peak inequality', *New Statesman*, 14 July, https://www.newstatesman.com/politics/uk/2018/07/peak-inequality

industry (especially the coal mines) declined. Scotland's great cities still have more in common with mainland Europeans' love of living in the city. It was mostly the English who wanted to live so far apart, and then only some of England's middle class. But a century ago, who would not have wanted to live away from the grime and soot of London, Birmingham and Manchester?

For decades the suburbs flourished. Landed wealth declined as inheritance tax was increased. Stately homes were handed to the National Trust, not out of altruism but because their owners could not pay the taxes or afford their upkeep anymore. All this as England became more equal in many other ways. London townhouses were divided up into flats. More and more suburbs were built as the slums were flattened, when the UK's growing population won the right to be treated with just a little decency. Population growth slowed as people had fewer children in the suburbs. For the first time ever, most children got their own bedroom, one they did not have to share with a sibling. The heyday of such never-before-seen affluence was the 1970s.

At first, when inequalities rose in the 1980s, the southern English suburbs appeared to do well. Thatcher's government not only rewarded the best-off 1 per cent but also a large group of those below that group, who overwhelmingly lived in the suburbs. Rotting bay windows were replaced. Double garages were built, and spare bedrooms were added, in attics and over the garages. But that was then, and it was mostly only in the southeast of England.

In the 1990s many inner-city homes and tower blocks in the north of England, in Scotland and in Wales were demolished. At the end of the decade, Northern Ireland experienced a mini housing boom when the Troubles ended and in the wake of strong economic growth in the Republic. But it turned out to be short-lived. House prices diverged rapidly between the southeast of England and the rest of the UK. And slowly, steadily the southeast began to become 'unaffordable'.

Between the censuses of 2001 and 2011 the number of people who had to resort to private renting in the UK doubled. The increases were greatest in the southeast and especially within London. This was portrayed as a 'buy-to-let revolution', but it was led not by small investors but by landlords who owned multiple properties. And all the while, living standards in the UK, especially in England, were falling in relation to those in the rest of Europe, as illustrated most dramatically by England's changing ranking in neonatal (first 28 days) mortality rates from 1990 to 2015 (Figure 2.6).

The decline in living standards was felt most acutely in the suburbs. From slowing improvements in infant mortality, through to declining school budgets, low-waged work for the majority,

Figure 2.6: Neonatal mortality rates, EU countries, 1990–2015

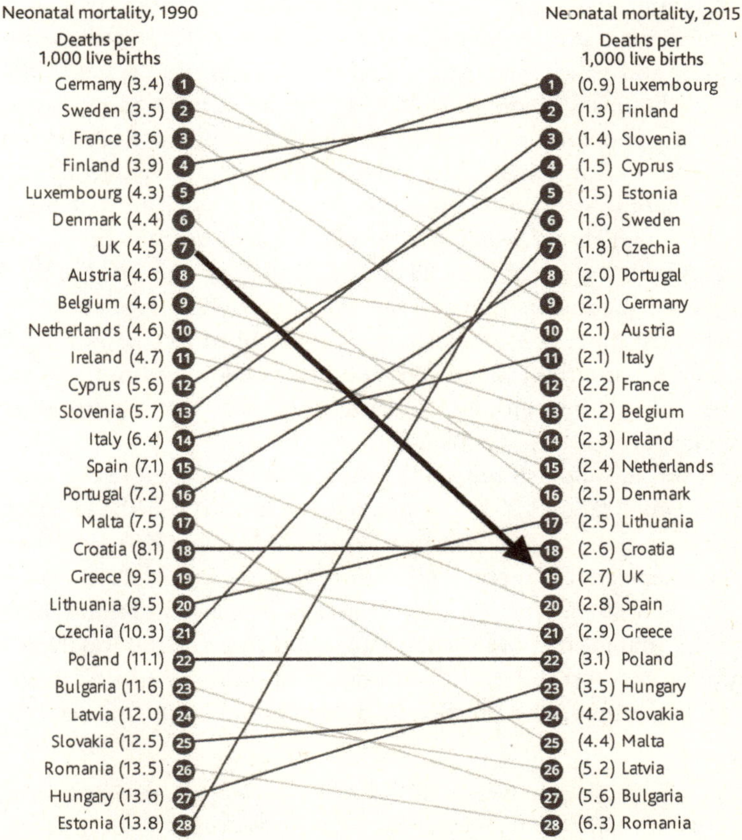

Source: ONS (2017) 'UK drops in European child mortality rankings', *ONS Child Health Web Report*, 13 October, https://www.ons.gov.uk/peoplepopulationandcommunity/healthandsocialcare/childhealth/articles/ukdropsineuropeanchildmortalityrankings/2017-10-13

the introduction of student loans and a rise in precarious jobs awaiting graduates, and then the highest rents in Europe, the problems of the English were no longer concentrated in the inner cities. The houses in the suburbs might in theory be worth a great deal, but many of their inhabitants had nowhere they could move to that would allow them to cash in on their apparent windfall, at least not near their existing friends, neighbours and a local hospital.

Since 2008 it has been the suburbs that have suffered most in relative terms. Poverty rose faster in outer London than in inner London. People who could not afford to live in London, Oxford or Brighton, or the more salubrious parts of York, Bristol or Exeter were mostly living in the suburbs of average towns and cities, and slowly seeing the opportunities around where they lived diminish. These included opportunities for well-rewarded work, opportunities for their children to attend a well-funded school without many pupils with more than average needs, opportunities to go to university without incurring that huge debt – namely by being able to pay the fees upfront instead of taking out a student loan. Half of all young women in England now go to university, but only the very richest avoid student debt. Just 8 per cent of all students didn't need to take out loans when I wrote this article. They are often children from the same families that buy property in cash – and who see mortgages as things for the 'little people'.

It was in southern England's suburbs that poverty rose the most between 2001 and 2011. So gradual and hidden was the rise that without a census it could not be seen.[6] People didn't grumble, they kept a stiff upper lip, at least through 2012, 2013, 2014 and even 2015. The suburbs are where loneliness became most concentrated. It is here where more and more of the foodbanks are located and the gas bills are not paid on time. At first it was just in the inner city that people did badly, but by 2018 it became

[6] Danny Dorling and Bethan Thomas (2016) *People and places: A 21st-century atlas of the UK*, Bristol: Policy Press, https://www.dannydorling.org/books/peopleandplaces/ [Editorial note: This trend then accelerated – slides 70 to 83 on this webpage: https://www.dannydorling.org/books/shatterednation/slides_all.html]

apparent that right across the UK life expectancy had peaked in 2014 and had declined since then. Most of that decline had to occur in the suburbs because the majority of people in the UK live in towns and cities, not in the inner city.[7]

Despite their recent woes, the suburbs are where most people are still holding on to the dream that if only they work hard enough they will be fine: they will own their home, and one day they will sell that home for a small fortune and retire to a warmer, friendlier country. But who will buy the 1930s semis in 2030? Will you sell up to a landlord when you leave suburbia? And how much will suburbia then really be worth? What is it becoming? And which warmer, friendlier country on the European mainland will take these folk, who are no longer European citizens, in the future? It is probably too late for most older British people now, but not necessarily for the young.

When, in 2016 and early 2017, young adults in Britain looked at what was increasingly on offer, they began to baulk at the unfairness of it all. Large numbers of them had not voted in the 2015 general election; Labour had not offered them much of an alternative back then. Not in 2015. Almost as many young adults did not vote in the referendum of 2016, for either side. Again, what was there to vote for? But come June 2017 their votes did stack up: against the landlords, against student fees, and against the decay of the suburbs that was increasingly looking like their fate.

The architecture of wealth extraction

> The architecture of wealth extraction is a cancer on this planet. It continually corrupts our governments, poisons the natural environment, and pits us against each other in a 'race to the bottom' that has only one logical outcome – the wholesale destruction of

---

[7] ONS (2018) *Changing trends in mortality: An international comparison: 2000 to 2016*, ONS, 7 August, https://www.ons.gov.uk/peoplepopulationandcommunity/birthsdeathsandmarriages/lifeexpectancies/articles/changingtrendsinmortalityaninternationalcomparison/2000to2016

> life-giving capacities for the only home planet we'll ever have.[8]

It is easy to become despondent. 'Progressives' – you the reader are likely to call yourself one, or be so labelled by others – are especially good at despondency, not least because they see the madness of carrying on as we are. In contrast, those few who are in favour of high inequality tend to be very optimistic about their own prospects and say the future will be fine; the planet will sort itself out. If the suburbs are slowly dying, with homeowners being replaced by renters, stability giving way to precarity, then that will become 'creative destruction' – or so they claim. Progressives are relegated to carping from the sidelines.

Joe Brewer's consultancy is based in the northern suburbs of Seattle. His words, quoted earlier, were written a few months before the votes that ushered in Brexit in the UK and Donald Trump in the US. Both were suburban-driven votes. It was the places where people who were often less physically fit, older, somewhat whiter and slightly better-off lived that swung both referendum and election on either side of the Atlantic. Elsewhere, in most of the affluent world, where the race to the bottom is better held back than in the UK or US, the suburbs continue to prosper and innovate.

Figure 2.7 shows how the suburbs voted to 'Leave' in 2016: even in London – and around the edge of Liverpool, which Stuart Wilks-Heeg explains is different[9] – the suburbs voted to leave the European Union.

If you want a modern-day definition of suburb in England it could be: 'That part of the end of your town or city where the majority of people quietly, desperately and angrily voted to leave the EU because they felt on the edge.' Look carefully at the map in Figure 2.7 – can you see the suburbs? Look around Bristol,

---

8 Joe Brewer (2016) 'The global architecture of wealth extraction', *The Land is Ours* website, 12 April, http://tlio.org.uk/the-global-architecture-of-wealth-extraction-by-joe-brewer/

9 Stuart Wilks-Heeg (2018) 'Safe Labour suburbia? The changing politics of the Merseyside suburbs', *The Political Quarterly*, 90, 1, pp. 53–63, https://onlinelibrary.wiley.com/doi/10.1111/1467-923X.12528

Figure 2.7: The human geography of the EU referendum vote, 2016

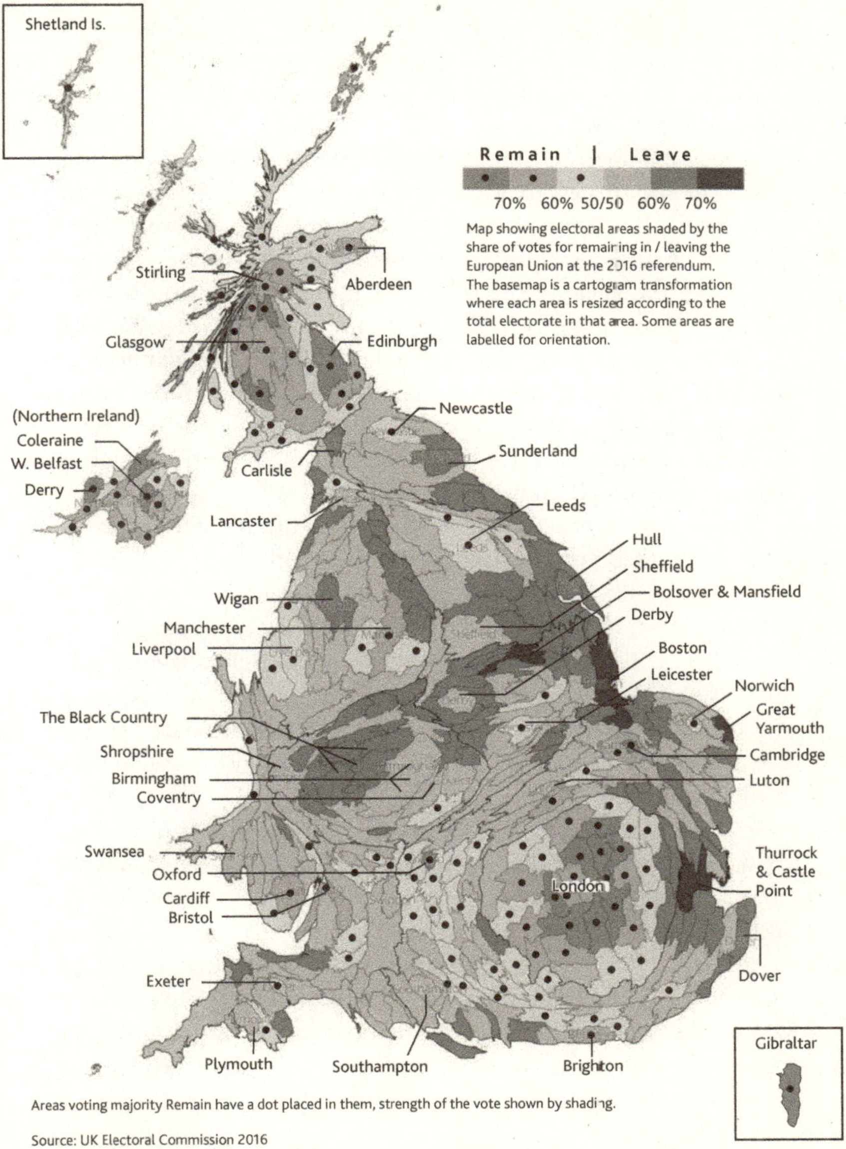

Source: Drawn by Benjamin Hennig and reproduced with his permission.

around Brighton, go a little further out from Cambridge than you might normally, and there you will find suburbia beginning, where the areas turn a paler shade and lose their dots: 'weak majority leave'. It was the suburbs that won Brexit. Just look at the map and forget your preconceived prejudices. The map shows the pattern.

As David Gilbert, Claire Dwyer and Nazneen Ahmed explain,[10] it is in the suburbs where Leave and Remain most often met, with Leave being in the majority in further-out suburbs and outermost suburbs (the places we once referred to as countryside – but are not now). However, if the map in Figure 2.7 does not convince you, then look at a graph (Figure 2.8) drawn by Daniel Watts. It shows that only the very most privileged areas of England voted solidly for Remain. The 10 per cent of England with the lowest rates of deprivation were the only places to solidly vote Remain. These are urban areas, not suburban, and many are in the more affluent and gentrified parts of London.

Figure 2.8 shows that it was middle England – suburban England – that voted most strongly for Brexit. It was in the middle four bars, representing areas in average constituencies in England, that the largest number and highest overall proportions voted Leave. The poorest three tenths and the richest three tenths were more likely to vote Remain. Some academics who have written on this issue appear to hate looking at this data because it was so often people living near where they lived, where they could afford to live, who voted Leave.

Political analysts produced sophisticated regression models to try to show it was the disaffected 'white working class', wallowing in racism and an identity crisis, that voted Leave – but it wasn't. Instead it was the successful boss of a small firm of electricians living next door to you (dear reader) in middle Britain, in the other half of your 1930s semi – you know the one – the one who wonders what the hell you are paid to do all day as you go off to lecture on 'political economy', and how you pull off that scam.

---

[10] David Gilbert, Claire Dwyer and Nazneen Ahmed (2018) 'Ethnic and religious diversity in the politics of suburban London, *The Political Quarterly*, 90, 1, pp. 72–80, https://onlinelibrary.wiley.com/doi/10.1111/1467-923X.12578

Figure 2.8: Decile of deprivation and the 2016 EU referendum, England

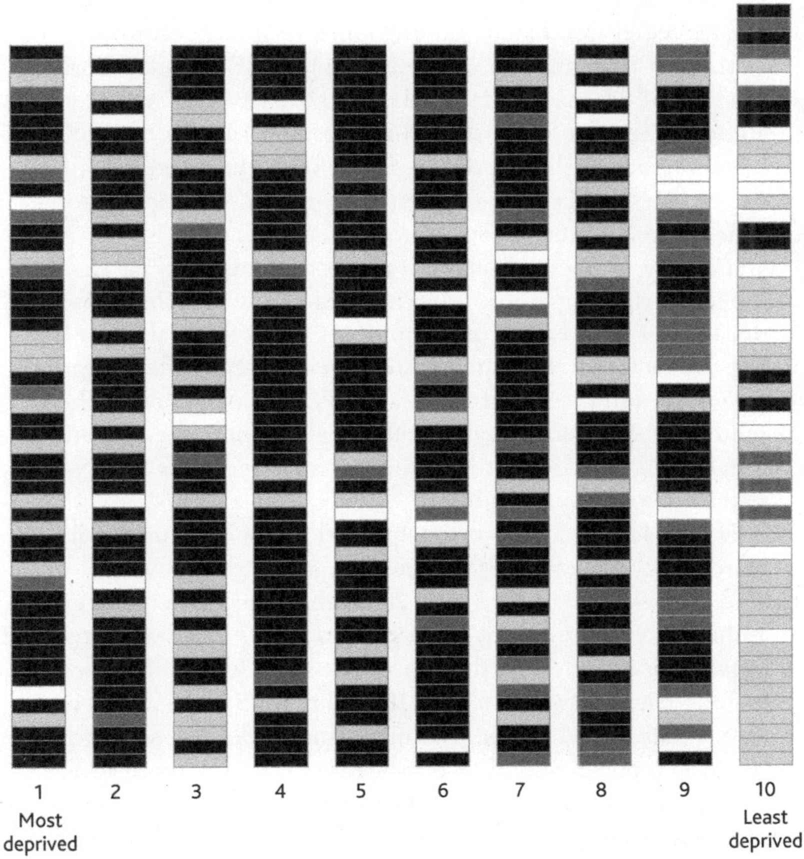

Note: This chart displays all 533 Parliamentary Constituencies in England divided into deciles by their position on the index of multiple deprivation, as listed by Parliament in 2015. The 1st decile are the most deprived constituencies, the 10th the least. There are three extra constituencies in the final decile as 533 doesn't divide perfectly into 10. The shadings represent how they voted in the 2016 EU referendum: light greys for Remain and dark greys for Leave. As this is based on a projection and not complete results, constituencies where the winning side won with 53% of the vote or less are given a slighly lighter version of the relevant shade.

Source: Drawn by Daniel Watts, reproduced with permission

Figure 2.8 shows that the very poorest three tenths of constituencies in England voted disproportionately for Remain. There is far more grey in the three bars to the left than there is in the columns in the centre of the chart. So much more valuable than a 1970s-style linear regression analysis or a 1980s logistic regression, Figure 2.8 uses Chris Hanretty's estimates.[11] It explains what Figure 2.7 is all about. Middle England, suburbia, the bulk of the middle class and the South have not been having a good time of it lately, and when offered a chance to vote for 'anything but this', they did so. In contrast, the poorest third of the country, who had not been having a good time for some time, were less jumpy.

It is easy to become sceptical about the possibility of change for the better, but if we cross the ocean to where the quote at the start of this section of this chapter came from, there is still hope to be found. In Seattle there is progress. And often progress is measured in the simplest of ways: in 2016, a 20-mile-an-hour residential speed limit was agreed for all of the city's residential streets, and arterial routes in the downtown Seattle area were restricted to 25 miles an hour.

Seattle's leaders aim to prevent all serious traffic injuries within the city by the year 2030. There were 130 serious injuries from road crashes there in 2015, and 20 deaths on its roads.[12] But even as this most progressive of American cities tries to make life more liveable for its residents, there is a sense that, overall, the clock is turning back. Progress in the UK and the US has – at the very least – stalled, and the innovations being made now seem to be too little too late. Suburbs can be denser, safer and more alive, as they are in much of Europe and Japan, or they can remain spaced out, suspicious and selfish.

The English and American suburbs are quietly dying. They were once places of success; now they are places of social and political retreat where people dream of being great again. Both the UK and the US are now political unions in economic and financial decline. Economic inequalities in both unions are

[11] Chris Hanretty (2017) 'Areal interpolation and the UK's referendum on EU membership', *Journal of Elections, Public Opinion and Parties*, 27, 4, pp. 466–83.

[12] Mike Lindblom (2016) 'Seattle may drop speed limits to 25 mph on arterials, 20 mph in neighbourhoods', *The Seattle Times*, 13 September, http://www.seattletimes.com/seattle-news/transportation/city-could-reduce-downtown-residential-speed-limits/

reaching new postwar maxima, with the suburbs the latest victims. People in the suburbs are beginning to experience real income falls too. The US vote for Trump was highest in those suburbs in which the inhabitants' health was declining most quickly. It was there, *The Economist*[13] suggested, that Trump won his presidency (Figure 2.9).

Figure 2.9: Local health outcomes predict Trumpward swings, 19 November 2016

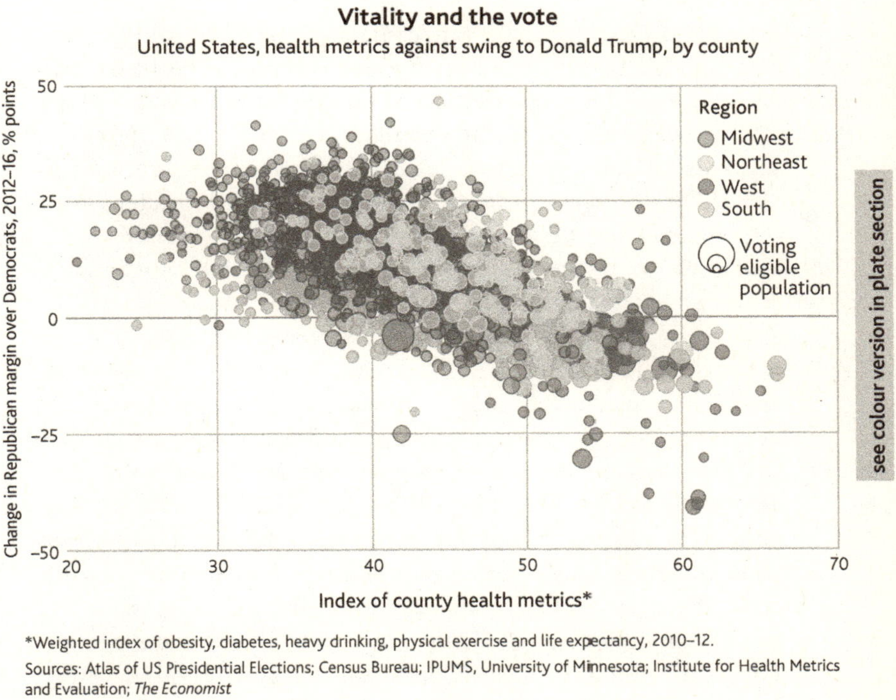

Source: *The Economist* (2016) 'The Presidential Election: Illness as an indicator, Local health outcomes predict Trumpward swings', *The Economist Magazine*, New York Edition, 19 November, http://www.economist.com/news/united-states/21710265-local-health-outcomes-predict-trumpward-swings-illness-indicator

[13] This figure also appears as Figure 5.6 in Danny Dorling (2017) *The equality effect*, Oxford: New Internationalist, p. 187.

CHAPTER 2.3

The wreckers who tore British society apart[1]

As a child I used to make sandcastles whenever I could get to a beach, which was usually once every summer. The beach was most often Whitesands Bay, on St David's Head in Wales. It is a very good beach for making castles. The sand is just about the right texture and there is a cleanish stream. During summers in the 1970s, hundreds of families would camp in the valley above the beach. They still do today. Each morning the children would run down to the sea. And there, cleaned by the tide, was a newly flattened beach upon which to build new sandcastles.

It takes a certain degree of competence to make a good sandcastle. To make a great sandcastle, however, requires much more than that. It requires teamwork. No single child working on their own can make a series of sandcastles on a beach that people stop and stare at in wonder and say: 'How were they ever made to look like that?' Often a few adults, secretly wishing they were still children, will have played a part (it helps to have some bigger spades). But for the best results, to build a sand sculpture of countless small castles and outbuildings, with the stream winding through them – and to do it all before the tide comes in – requires great cooperation with many other young builders and the spreading of competence as children learn from each other.

Very occasionally on the beach there was a child who did not like to share, or a small group of such children egging each other on, and they would wait until no one was looking and then

---

1 Original published in *Fabian Review*, Spring 2019, Vol. 131, No. 1, pp. 21–3.

knock the sandcastles down. I never understood their motivation; why they felt the need to destroy, why they hated what so many others had made by working well together. In just a few minutes, a handful could destroy what it had taken so many others to build up over many hours. Smirking and for some odd reason satisfied, the wreckers would leave a wasteland behind.

As I grew up and watched the Conservatives tear down so much of Britain's industry, so much of its welfare state, and so much solidarity, I was often reminded of the look on the faces of those odd, aberrant, angry, antisocial children. It was hard to work out what might drive someone to take apart what others have so carefully built up in a society and replace it with nothing but a wasteland. What pleasure could you get from doing that? Then I began to realise that they thought they were actually making something through their destruction. They were showing that cooperation was folly. And they were convincing themselves that they were more powerful and more successful, and destined to have their own way.

The Tories have a reputation for competence, for being 'safe hands', and they have kept this reputation in spite of the chaos we can see all around us today. So, while the U-turns, the bungled general election in 2017 and the mishandling of Brexit might suggest incompetence, attempts to portray the Conservatives as incompetent are folly because they ignore the party's undeniable success. Britain's Conservatives are the most successful right-of-centre party in Europe, not just for having been in power so many times and for so long, but for having successfully pursued the most right-wing agenda of any mainstream European party. During the 1980s and 1990s they succeeded in changing hearts and minds. Their aim was to transform the UK from being one of the most equitable countries in all of the continent in the 1970s, to the country which now consistently tops the OECD league table for income inequality in Europe. A league table shift of such great magnitude does not happen by accident. For a time, the Conservatives succeeded in deflecting Labour away from seeing issues such as inequality as so crucial. Only a decade or so ago the huge disparity between the super-wealthy and the rest was characterised by key Labour figures as: 'not a great problem, so long as the rich pay their taxes'.

On education too, the Conservatives have been remarkably successful in shifting the parameters of the debate. Essentially, their policies promote division, competition and fear in place of the norms of cooperation and coordination of provision seen elsewhere in Europe. In no other European country is so much money spent to give an unfair advantage to such a small number of children as the money spent on private schools in the UK. In every area of social life Conservatives promote evaluative voluntary individualist logic as the alternative to generous omnipresent ordered delivery. On their watch, preschool education became a private business opportunity; state schools were progressively underfunded and selection at age 16 was introduced via academies.

They have continued to prioritise grammar schools because each grammar school creates so many losers for every winner. Their ideology is that only a few can win, and most people deserve to be losers; Tories seem to be especially fond of grammar schools because the 11-plus exam is based on the idea that future winners can be identified in early childhood through a test. They repeatedly decimated further education and have turned higher education into a marketplace with loans for the many and free entry for the few. Those few who now go to university essentially for free are mostly Conservatives' own children, who will emerge with no student debt thanks to affluent parents paying their fees upfront.

On housing, the Conservatives have determinedly destroyed much of our social provision through right-to-buy, stock transfers and cuts to funding. One in four children in England now lives in a home from which they can be evicted with just two months' notice on the whim of a private landlord. Conservatives fix the housing market, constantly intervening to prop it up. Chancellor George Osborne's 'help-to-buy' schemes now leave future governments with the most enormous financial liability should house prices fall by more than 5 per cent (a relatively mild scenario, given that Mark Carney, governor of the Bank of England, has said that falls of 30 per cent could be possible). Those schemes were introduced to mask what was happening to the majority who could never get a mortgage to buy a home. Osborne's measure of success was house prices. The higher they were, the better he thought he was doing.

On health, Conservatives succeeded in moving the UK from being one of the highest ranked in the world for health outcomes in the 1960s and 1970s to one of the worst countries in Europe. The UK used to have one of the very best rates of child health in the world. By 1990, following 11 years of Tory underfunding, six countries in Europe had lower neonatal mortality rates than the UK, but that was just the start of the decline. By 2015 the UK ranked 19th for neonatal mortality across Europe.[2] Most recently the situation has become far worse, as infant mortality in the UK has risen year after year from 2015 onwards. Nowhere else in Europe has it risen. Similarly, but for separate reasons, overall life expectancy across the UK peaked in 2014 and has fallen since. Again, nowhere else in Europe has a record of decline as bad as this. And again, such an extreme record does not happen by chance. It requires a huge amount of work to shift a country from being so successful in terms of comparative health outcomes, to so unsuccessful over such a short space of time. The Conservatives are indeed competent – at making life much worse for most people.

How should Labour respond? How do you respond to wreckers who have such a different view of what is right and fair and decent? Labour has responded on education by offering a National Education Service, which is laudable, but which has echoes of the 1940s in its title, implying that Whitehall operating benignly from above will somehow create a situation in which your child – and since the 1980s it has been all about 'you and your family' – will prosper. If it's all about *you* and if *you* don't have children, or if you have the money to live in a good catchment area, or send your children to private school, then evaluative voluntary individualist logic tells you to vote Tory. In fact, for your children to get ahead, you need to have less money spent on the education of the 'competitor' children or grandchildren. In recent decades, a very large minority of the British population have been taught not to share well. Because of this it is perhaps not surprising that in 2019, around 40 per cent of adults have still been saying in

2 See Figure 2.6 on page 117, this volume, and also https://www.ons.gov.uk/peoplepopulationandcommunity/healthandsocialcare/childhealth/articles/ukdropsineuropeanchildmortalityrankings/2017-10-13

opinion poll after opinion poll that they are happy to lend their support to the Conservatives.

In the face of Tory individualist logic, Labour needs to be far bolder. Working with Michael Davies I recently wrote a paper for the Progressive Economy Forum titled *Jubilee 2022: Writing off the student debt*.[3] In it we explained why it was both right and practical for Labour to include a promise in the next election manifesto to cancel the vast majority of outstanding university student debt for all those students who went to university in 2012 or thereafter. The policy makes good economic sense as well as being fair. And, in a country where half of all young women now go to university, and where people have been encouraged to think more and more individualistically, it also makes brilliant political sense. Almost everyone who went to university in 2012, 2013, 2014, 2015, 2016, 2017 and 2018, and those who will go in 2019, 2020 and 2021 (and those thinking of going in future, and their families) would have an obvious extra incentive to vote Labour at the next general election – as would their parents and grandparents – but only if Labour promises to cancel most of the outstanding unfair debt.

We don't just need to unravel the recent errors made by Conservatives. That is just a first step to make a promise that if you vote Labour it will be as if the introduction of £9,000-a-year university tuition fees by David Cameron and Nick Clegg never happened. Labour also needs to offer something so much more enticing than a 'national service'. I have many ideas, but so do you, and so do many others. You don't build a good set of sandcastles on the beach alone; and you always have to be wary of those who would try to destroy what you have made. *Jubilee 2022: Writing off the student debt* is a small castle that I built recently with Michael and the help of a few other experts on student finance, and I'm quite proud of it. Would you like to make a castle to go next to it? Perhaps suggest a better pre school policy or housing policy, to add to the beautiful landscape of all the proposals that are already being suggested?

---

3 See: https://progressiveeconomyforum.com/jubilee-2022-writing-off-the-student-debt/

On housing, Labour has to stop being polite. Conservative policies are taking a huge toll in human lives. In early 2019, Roger Pepworth, the head teacher of what had been Marston Middle School in Oxford in the 1980s, wrote after the death of a former pupil who had most recently slept rough on the streets of Oxford: 'I do not have solutions. I only know that the dreams that Sharron, a lovely child, had until her death, have perished in the wreckage of an austerity programme that has literally killed her and her like.'[4]

Sharron's death will not be forgotten in Oxford for a long time to come. Decades ago the Conservatives dismantled the social provision that, had it still been in place, could have helped Sharron when she was a young girl in the 1980s. The Tories ensured later that when Sharron most needed help as an adult, it was not there. Millions live in fear of how they will pay the rent or cope with their mortgage payments. Millions more live with the misguided belief that the homes they own are worth a fortune now and will fund a luxury retirement for them (as long as they keep voting Conservative). But top Tories don't have mortgages. They buy and sell in cash and have property around the world – and they dupe other people into voting for their party. Top Tories care not one jot that homelessness rises when they are in power.

In the UK today, even just within London, we still have more bedrooms within residential homes than there are people who need a bed. We have not built enough where the need is great enough; but the fastest way in which we will better house ourselves in future is to repeat what we did for the whole period from 1921 to 1981; for those 60 years, each year, we better used

4 Roger Pepworth (2019) 'Harsh reality of life and death on the street below dreaming spires', Letters, *The Guardian*, 3 February, https://www.theguardian.com/society/2019/feb/03/harsh-reality-of-life-and-death-on-the-street-below-dreaming-spires [Editorial note: That same link will also take you to a letter by Councillor Linda Smith, then the Deputy Leader of Oxford City Council and board member for leisure and housing, which advocated more of an evaluative voluntary individualist logic approach for those who are homeless 'to successfully rebuild their lives', but with 'drug, alcohol and mental health support'. However, in Oxford, no amount of drugs or alcohol misuse support could create the bedrooms that were no longer there for people like Sharron.]

the stock we had than the year before. We built more, but more importantly each year we shared better. Growing income *equality* meant that the rich did not buy second homes so often. People increasingly moved into housing of the size their families needed; and a third of all housing was allocated on the basis of need, not greed. History will repeat, but the mechanism will be different in future.

On Whitesands Bay each summer, new and different sandcastles are being built with each new tide. The solution for our future will not be a return to the 1970s. That tide went out long ago, and many tides have come in since to wash the solutions of those days away. Just like the social policy of the past, new castles are made of sand, and they always melt into the sea – eventually. You just have to keep on building more. The better health system of the future will not simply be a return to what we had before the 2012 Privatisation Act. To be better, it has to be different.

For the past four decades, there have been more social wreckers on the policy beach than social builders, but that time has ended, and evaluative voluntary individualist logic (evil) has had its day. The alternative of generous omnipresent ordered delivery is becoming more obviously and urgently viable again. Well-ordered, for everyone, delivered in time, to where there is most need, and generous, not skimping. Achieving this will mean more investment, but it will also mean more ideas and above all more cooperation. For too long a party with a reputation for competence has been trusted with our social fabric and services. Those politicians who, as teenagers, joined the Conservative Party in the late 1970s and 1980s did so because they admired Thatcher's policy of wrecking – of so-called 'creative destruction'. They are, and were, very competent, but only at breaking things. Don't ever trust them again.

CHAPTER 2.4

Austerity, not influenza, caused the UK's health to deteriorate[1]

Prior to the COVID-19 pandemic, England and Wales had seen stalling life expectancy, rising infant mortality rates, increasing middle-aged mortality (including so-called 'deaths of despair'), and tightening restrictions on access to healthcare.[2] Spikes in age-standardised mortality rates (ASMR) have been attributed by many to influenza, though the evidence does not support this.

As we enter winter 2020 with a health and social care service that has endured a decade of insufficient funding, a population whose health has been worsened by austerity, and now a pandemic, it is time to stop claiming that influenza was the cause of excess mortality and cancelled elective surgeries in previous winters.[3] Figure 2.10 is taken from data in the Office for National Statistics (ONS) excess winter mortality data for England and Wales 2015–16. This shows weekly deaths from all causes, alongside influenza-like illness (ILI), from Public Health Wales and Royal College of General Practitioners consultations per 100,000 population in England and Wales from 1993 to 2016. Since 2011, ILI has not

---

1 With Lucinda Hiam and Martin McKee, originally published in *Journal of Epidemiology and Community Health*, 2021, 75: p. 312, http://dx.doi.org/10.1136/jech-2020-215556

2 Lucinda Hiam, Danny Dorling and Martin McKee (2020) 'Things fall apart: The British health crisis 2010–2020', *British Medical Bulletin*, 133(1): pp. 4–15, doi: 10.1093/bmb/ldz041 [published Online First: 29 March 2020].

3 Office for National Statistics (2019) *Excess winter mortality in England and Wales 2019*, 27 November 2019, https://www.ons.gov.uk/peoplepopulationandcommunity/birthsdeathsandmarriages/deaths/datasets/excesswintermortalityinenglandandwalesreferencetables (accessed 14 August 2020).

exceeded weekly mortality peaks. Notably, in 2015–16 when the biggest year-on-year increase in deaths for almost 50 years was seen,[4] ILI rates were not unusually high.

It is often claimed that we cannot prove that austerity has resulted in higher-than-expected mortality. We may disagree in each of our assessments as to how damaging austerity has been. However, what matters now is that as we head into winter 2020, after an incredibly challenging year for the four nations of the UK not only in terms of the pandemic, but also unemployment, housing precarity, hunger, poverty and the huge impact on mental health, we must accept the role austerity has played in the nation's deteriorating health, and not repeat past mistakes in blaming 'influenza'.

Figure 2.10: Weekly mortality and influenza-like illnesses, England and Wales, 1999–2016

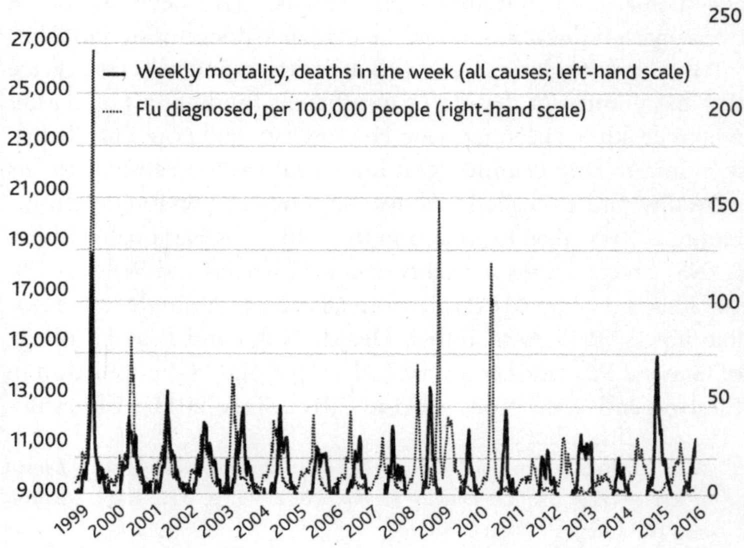

Source: Office for National Statistics (ONS) excess winter mortality data for England and Wales 2015 to 2016, https://www.ons.gov.uk/peoplepopulationandcommunity/birthsdeathsandmarriages/deaths/datasets/excesswintermortalityinenglandandwalesreferencetables

4 Office for National Statistics (2016) *Spike in number of deaths in 2015 driven by increased mortality in over 75s*, 7 April, https://www.ons.gov.uk/news/news/spikeinnumberofdeathsin2015drivenbyincreasedmortalityinover75s (accessed 7 May 2016).

CHAPTER 2.5

The income shock of 2020: a jolt in the fall after peak inequality[1]

The COVID-19 pandemic had an almost immediate and massive detrimental economic effect on the lives of the already worst-off in the UK. Both younger adults in precarious employment and, disproportionately, people of black and minority ethnicity, were more likely to have to borrow money to get by. However, the most significant factor in determining who was most badly hit economically was whether a person lived in a household that was rich, average or poor.

A study published in January 2021 spelt out in detail what had occurred, using figures of income adjusted for the size of each household and the number of children in it, after taxes and including benefits.[2] It showed that the average income of people living in the poorest fifth of households (lowest quintile) in the UK fell from £287 a week in February 2020 to £228 a week by May 2020. This fall, of over 20 per cent, was larger than for any other quintile group and resulted in a huge and sudden widening of the gap between the best-off and worst-off quintiles, which has probably not narrowed since then.

In contrast to people in the poorest fifth of households, the best-off fifth received £765 a week on average in May 2020.

---

1 Originally published with a shorter title in *Public Sector Focus*, March/April 2021, pp. 18–19.

2 Table 4 and supplementary material from: Thomas Crossley, Paul Fisher and Hamish Low (2021) 'The heterogeneous and regressive consequences of COVID-19: Evidence from high quality panel data', *Journal of Public Economics*, 193, January, 104334, https://www.sciencedirect.com/science/article/pii/S0047272720301985?via%3Dihub

However, the best-off had still seen an *average* fall of 11 per cent in their income since February. Although this was only half the percentage fall of the poorest households, it will often still have felt like a great fall to them.

Each income quintile became less well off, but the gap between the haves and have-nots widened, and this widening occurred despite a slight increase in welfare benefits for the poorest. The same study that revealed this sudden increase in the already wide gulf between the best- and worst-off also showed which groups were particularly acutely affected (see Figure 2.11).

Within the poorest quintile of the population, roughly 13 million people, the quarter that fared worst had lost 60 per cent or more of their income in these two months. That meant that 3.3 million people in UK households lost at least £172 a week. In contrast, the best-off quarter of the already best-off quintile had seen their income *rise* by 8 per cent or more; at least £69 more a week for the most economically fortunate 3.3 million people in the UK. The pandemic's few economic winners were almost all people who were already very well off.

At the most extreme, a tiny number became dramatically richer in 2020 by winning government contracts that had not been put out to tender. The BBC reported that, among many other scandals, 'The government has also been accused of favouring firms with political connections to the Conservative Party with a "high-priority lane".'[3] However, most winners will have just been already well-off people who were able to take advantage of the crisis. What matters is that it was only a few people, from among the best-off fifth, who were best placed to do this.

Other inequalities may have narrowed as the class gap widened. Men earned 9 per cent more than women in February 2020, but that gap fell to only 5 per cent by May as more men saw bigger pay cuts, due in part to more of them being furloughed. In February, people of black and minority ethnicity were, on average, 27 per cent worse off than their white peers – but that gap had also fallen, to 25 per cent, by May 2020.

---

3 BBC (2021) 'Timeline: Covid contracts and accusations of "chumocracy"', *BBC News*, 15 March, https://www.bbc.co.uk/news/uk-56319927

Figure 2.11: The amount of money people had to live on in the UK in May 2020

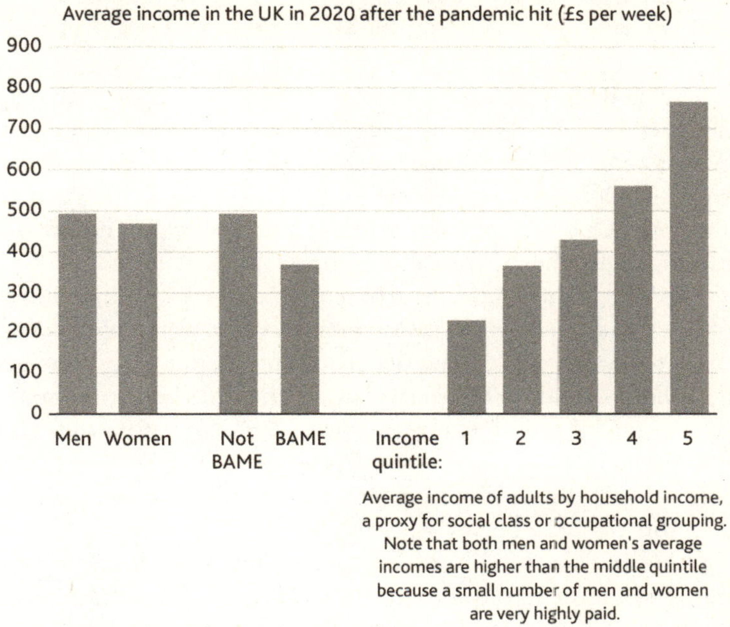

Source: Drawn by author based on data from: Thomas Crossley, Paul Fisher and Hamish Low (2021) 'The heterogeneous and regressive consequences of COVID-19: Evidence from high quality panel data', *Journal of Public Economics*, 193, January, 104334, https://www.sciencedirect.com/science/article/pii/S0047272720301985?via%3Dihub

Thus, by May 2020 there was a 5 per cent gap between the incomes of men and women in the UK and a 25 per cent gap between white and BAME groups, and the sizes of these gaps were slowly and only slightly changing over time. However, and in great contrast, the income gap between the lowest income fifth and the highest income fifth by household, again by May 2020, was much higher: 235 per cent, up from 200 per cent in February. This is the social class gap: it is enormous, and grew at this point far faster than any other income gap.

Your fortunes depend most on your social class, and what kind of job you have, if you have one. Whether you are male or female has an impact, but it is small compared to the impact of class, and it shrank as the crisis unfolded, despite the fact that women are more likely to be in jobs that are low paid or, if they are a single parent of a young child, not working outside the home. In May 2020 men in the UK were receiving £490 a week on average and women £467; two months earlier those numbers had been £573 and £526 respectively.

The gender pay gap narrowed while the social class gap widened because more men could be sacked or furloughed on 80 per cent of their normal pay. This was slightly less likely for women because more women were doing work that had to continue. One very obvious example was working in health and care services, where women dominate.

The same pattern seen for women was also seen for individuals of black and minority ethnicity: their incomes were lower before the crisis began, fell during the crisis, but did not fall as much as for others. By May 2020 social class was 9.4 times more important than ethnicity in influencing income (235/25); before the crisis that difference had been nearer 7.4 times (200/37). Part of the reason was that people of black or minority ethnicity, like women, are more likely to be key workers.

None of this should be very surprising. Within any ethnic minority group, just as among women, there is huge variation in incomes – whereas within occupation groups or social classes there is much less variation in income. However, what was unexpected was that the crisis saw the income gaps between men and women and ethnic groups narrow even as income gaps widened overall.

Despite the overall narrowing of gender inequalities, lone parents – the great majority of whom are women – were especially badly hit. Their average household income was similar to the poorest quintile group. Most lone parents are in this income group, but they are often poorer than the group as a whole. Four out of ten lone parents had to rely on gifts or loans from relatives at this time; and one in eight on a foodbank (compared to one in 12 for the poorest quintile).

Some 82 per cent of the adults who went to foodbanks in April or May 2020 were women. Among couples it was almost always the woman who went to the foodbank. Some 85 per cent of people who went to foodbanks were white, a fraction less than the 90 per cent of adults in the UK who are. Two-thirds of foodbank users were in the very poorest quintile of income. Virtually none were from the best-off 40 per cent of households.

CHAPTER 2.6

The roundabout: class hate in England[1]

One story I often remember is a seemingly quite mundane one. It was first told by the sociologist Peter Townsend in his book *The Social Minority*[2]. Townsend was born into poverty in 1928 in Middlesbrough, and died in 2009 much better off, but still unsatisfied with what had been achieved in building a fairer Britain. He had done many things in his life to work towards that goal, including, with others, setting up the Child Poverty Action Group.

Townsend's story featured a visit to a fair in 1958, when he was 30. There was a wrought-iron roundabout that parents could pay a penny for their children to sit on. The roundabout was pushed round by hand, hour after hour, by a man who used his brute strength to propel it. A young girl on the roundabout became upset and her parents demanded that the man help the child off the ride. The man rushed to help, but suffered a terrible blow to his back when the roundabout hit him as he passed the child to her parents. Rather than thank the man, the child's parents were indifferent to his suffering. Instead, Townsend heard them talk about how their daughter was special, was sensitive, and how terrible it was that she had been upset by the fairground

1 Originally published as chapter 7 in Phil Wrigglesworth et al (eds), *Left cultures: A lexicon of stories past and present* (see https://leftcultures.com/pages/about). If you are interested in Peter Townsend's story of the roundabout, I say more about it here: Danny Dorling (2011) 'Underclass, overclass, ruling class, supernova class', in Alan Walker, Adrian Sinfield and Carol Walker (eds) *Fighting poverty, inequality and injustice*, Bristol: Policy Press, ch 8, which is open access at: http://www.dannydorling.org/?page_id=2446

2 Peter Townsend (1973) *The social minority*, London: Allen Lane, p. 22.

Figure 2.12: 1950s, girl on a carousel ride at a fairground, England, UK

Source: Reproduced by permission from Alamy

ride. They simply did not see the man pushing the roundabout as being enough like them to care about.

Why does this story stay with me, and why did Townsend think it was worth telling? After all, it's just everyday nastiness; just one instance of callousness and indifference among millions. That, I think, is the point. All the time, all around us, there are people who simply don't care about others. In polite society they disguise their feelings, but those feelings are occasionally revealed when they are flustered. I'd like Townsend's story to be better known. It is about the moment when you suddenly realise that some people among you simply do not give a damn – and that this indifference is why it can be so hard to bring about positive change.

Today we still don't really know how many people feel like this; people who do not see others as being as human as them. We don't know what it is that alters that proportion and how it can be increased or decreased in any society. But we do know that some hearts and minds are far harder to win over than others.

CHAPTER 2.7

Why Finland is still the happiest country in the world[1]

Finland has been the happiest country on earth for the past six years, according to the World Happiness Survey.[2] This survey relies on the Cantril ladder life evaluation question:

> Please imagine a ladder with steps numbered from zero at the bottom to 10 at the top. The top of the ladder represents the best possible life for you and the bottom of the ladder represents the worst possible life for you. On which step of the ladder would you say you personally feel you stand at this time?[3]

Finland comes out on top, followed by Denmark and Iceland. Just why Finns are happier than others comes down to a number of factors including lower income inequality (and most importantly, the difference between the highest paid and the lowest paid), high social support, freedom to make decisions, and low levels of corruption.

Figure 2.13 shows all 44 countries for which there is both happiness data and income inequality data, each as a coloured

---

1 Originally published in *The Conversation*, 5 April 2023.

2 Helliwell, J.F., Layard, R., Sachs, J.D., Aknin, L.B., De Neve, J.-E. and Wang, S. (eds) (2023) *World Happiness Report 2023* (11th edn), Sustainable Development Solutions Network, https://worldhappiness.report/ed/2023/

3 Gallup (2023) 'Understanding How Gallup uses the cantril scale', *Gallup News*, https://news.gallup.com/poll/122453/understanding-gallup-uses-cantril-scale.aspx

dot. The vertical scale shows average happiness, the horizontal scale income inequality.

The measure of income inequality used here is the Gini coefficient[4] of income inequality, as reported by the Office for Economic Co-operation and Development (OECD).[5] It is the highest rate recorded in each country in any year after 2010 up to the most recent year for which there is data. The graph shows the close relationship between these two measures. In general, when income inequality is larger, money matters more and people are less happy.[6]

Finland also has other attributes that may help people feel happier. It has a highly decentralised publicly funded healthcare system and only a very small private healthcare sector.[7] This is far more effective and efficient than alternatives used in some other countries. Public transport is reliable and affordable,[8] and Helsinki's airport is ranked as the best in northern Europe.[9] There is a Finnish proverb that seems relevant: '*Onnellisuus on se paikka puuttuvaisuuden ja yltäkylläisyyden välillä*', or 'Happiness is a place between too little and too much'.

---

4 Named after Corrado Gini (23 May 1884–13 March 1965), https://en.wikipedia.org/wiki/Corrado_Gini

5 OECD (2023) *Income inequality*, Paris: OECD, https://data.oecd.org/inequality/income-inequality.htm

6 Shigehiro Oishi, Youngjae Cha, Asuka Komiya and Hiroshi Ono (2022) 'Money and happiness: the income–happiness correlation is higher when income inequality is higher', *PNAS Nexus*, 1, 5, November, pgac224, https://academic.oup.com/pnasnexus/article/1/5/pgac224/6754154

7 Statistics Finland (2018) *Finland among the best in the world*, 5 December, https://www.stat.fi/tup/satavuotias-suomi/suomi-maailman-karjessa_en.html

8 Adam Greenfield (2014) 'Helsinki's ambitious plan to make car ownership pointless in 10 years', *The Guardian*, 10 July, https://www.theguardian.com/cities/2014/jul/10/helsinki-shared-public-transport-plan-car-ownership-pointless

9 Finavia (2022) Helsinki Airport receives an esteemed airport industry award: Best Airport in Northern Europe, *Helsinki Times*, 17 June, https://www.helsinkitimes.fi/finland/finland-news/domestic/21756-helsinki-airport-receives-an-esteemed-airport-industry-award-best-airport-in-northern-europe.html

Figure 2.13: Average levels of happiness and inequality for all countries with data, 2023

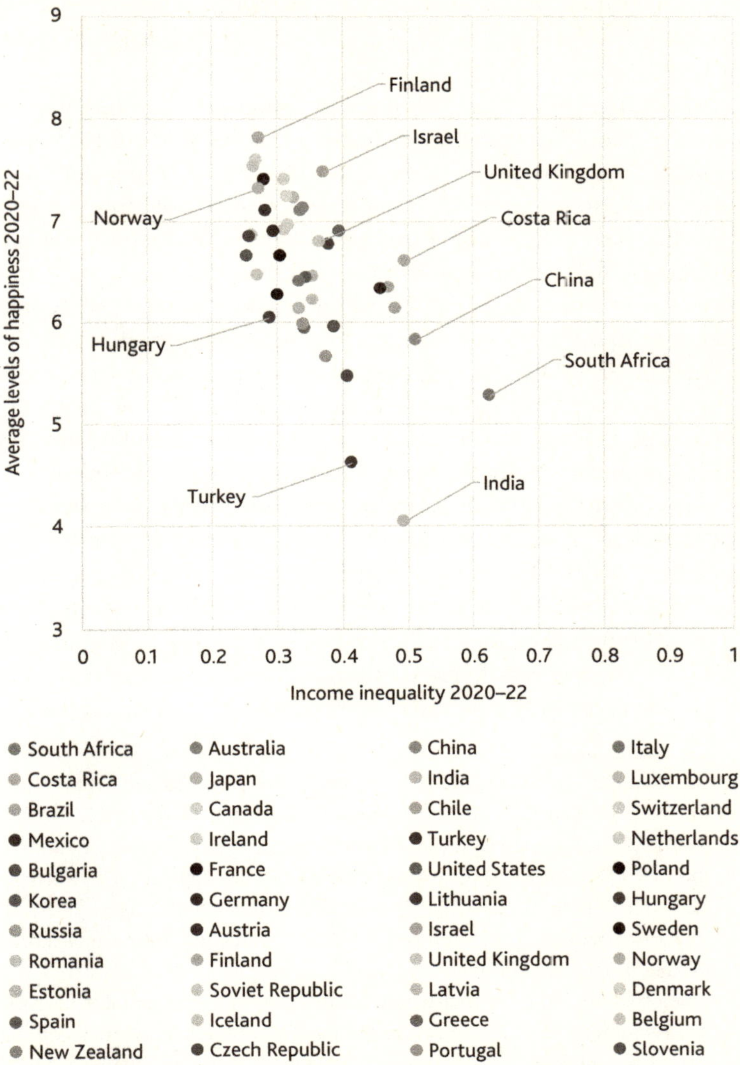

see colour version in plate section

Source: Figure 2.1 in 'Ranking of Happiness based on a three-year-average 2020–2022', in John Helliwell, Haifang Huang, Max Norton, Leonard Goff and Shun Wang (2023) 'World happiness, trust and social connections in times of crisis', in *World Happiness Report 2023* (11th edn), Sustainable Development Solutions Network, ch 2, https://worldhappiness.report/ed/2023/world-happiness-trust-and-social-connections-in-times-of-crisis/#ranking-of-happiness-2020-2022. Based on data from the World Happiness Survey and OECD income inequality statistics.

How Finland compares

Finland, Norway and Hungary report similar levels of income inequality, yet people in Finland are, on average, happier. Why is this?

According to the World Inequality Database, the highest-paid tenth of people in Finland take home a third of all income (33 per cent).[10] The equivalent group in the UK takes 36 per cent and in the US, 46 per cent. These differences may not appear great, but they have a huge effect on overall happiness because in more unequal countries so much less is left for everyone else – and the rich become more fearful. When a small number of people become so much richer, this reaction may be inevitable.

In 2021, a sociologist suggested that by having more reasonable expectations, people in Nordic countries appeared to be happier.[11] However, that cannot explain the difference between Finland and Norway on the happiness scale (see Chapter 6.5, on Finland).

All kinds of explanations are possible, including slight nuances of language as well as culture.[12] There is even the question of whether this global survey is beginning to introduce its own bias, as Finns now know why they are being asked the question (they moved even further ahead of Denmark in the most recent survey).

However, it is very likely that Finland having a more equitable education system,[13] where you are likely to get a good education

---

[10] *World Inequality Database 2023*: Income inequality, Finland, 1980–2019 (https://wid.world/country/finland/), the USA (https://wid.world/country/usa/) and the UK: (https://wid.world/country/united-kingdom/).

[11] Jukka Savolainen (2021) 'The grim secret of Nordic happiness: it's not hygge, the welfare state or drinking. It's reasonable expectations', *Slate*, 28 April, https://slate.com/news-and-politics/2021/04/finland-happiness-lagom-hygge.html

[12] Tomi Visakko and Eero Voutilainen (2020) 'Language and happiness: Cultural epistemologies and ideological conflicts in Finnish online discourses on the causes of happiness', *Language and Communication*, 71, pp. 39–54, https://doi.org/10.1016/j.langcom.2019.12.003, https://helda.helsinki.fi/bitstream/handle/10138/338664/Language_and_Happiness_MANUSCRIPT_REVISED.pdf?sequence=1

[13] Countries are ranked in order of between-school variation: see OECD PISA 2009 database, Table II.5.1, http://dx.doi.org/10.1787/888932343627;

no matter what school you attend, as well as a fairer school policy than Norway (almost all Finns go to their nearest school), might actually matter too. Also significant are its better housing policy with a wide variety of social housing (see Chapter 3.6) and lower homelessness,[14] and a health service with waiting times that are the envy of the world – sometimes only a matter of days, even during the height of the pandemic.

Finland ranks first, second or third in more than 100 global measures of economic and social success – better than Norway.[15] And it has less money than Norway overall (and hardly any oil). You could excuse the Finns a little *omahyväisyys*, or smugness.

Why does Hungary do so badly despite the income gap between its people being hardly any wider than in Finland and Norway? One could argue that this is to do with its divided politics. In 2022, a report published by the European Parliament and approved by a large majority of MEPs stated that 'Hungary can no longer be considered a full democracy'.[16]

Freedom matters greatly to people, as does freedom from fear, and that could explain why Turkey[17] and India[18] have lower

---

OECD (2013) 'Does it matter which school a student attends?', *PISA in Focus*, No. 27, OECD Publishing, Paris, https://doi.org/10.1787/5k4818hwp89v-en, reproduced in https://www.dannydorling.org/finntopia/figures_files/page0-1016-full.html

14 Ella Hancock (2022) 'Helsinki is still leading the way in ending homelessness – but how are they doing it?', *World Habitat*, 6 October, https://world-habitat.org/news/our-blog/helsinki-is-still-leading-the-way-in-ending-homelessness-but-how-are-they-doing-it/

15 https://www.dannydorling.org/finntopia/contents_files/Finland.pdf

16 Press Release (2022) 'MEPs: Hungary can no longer be considered a full democracy', *European Parliament News*, 15 September, https://www.europarl.europa.eu/news/en/press-room/20220909IPR40137/meps-hungary-can-no-longer-be-considered-a-full-democracy

17 Servet Yanatma (2018) 'Polarisation, misinformation and fear: insights into Turkish media', *Digital News Report 2018 – Turkey Supplementary Report*, Oxford: Reuters Institute for the Study of Journalism, https://reutersinstitute.politics.ox.ac.uk/news/polarisation-misinformation-and-fear-insights-turkish-media

18 Aakash Hassan and Hannah Ellis-Petersen (2023) 'Bulldozer politics: Modi's demolition drive fuels Muslims' fears in Kashmir', *The Guardian*, 19 March,

levels of happiness than their levels of economic inequality might predict.

In contrast, South Africa[19] and China[20] are a little happier than their levels of inequality would suggest. South Africa became a democracy in 1994 shortly after Nelson Mandela was freed,[21] and many people will remember the years of apartheid that preceded it. People in China are not as fearful as they are often portrayed in the West.[22]

Inequality is a factor

Most countries exhibit happiness levels that are quite predictable from their inequality levels. The UK is right in the middle of what you would expect for one of Europe's most economically unequal countries.

Figure 2.13 also shows that (nearly as unequal) Israel is a little happier than it ought to be – although it is not clear that the sample taken there included all groups living in that state.

---

https://www.theguardian.com/world/2023/mar/19/bulldozer-politics-modi-demolition-drive-fuels-muslims-fears-in-kashmir

19 Ashleigh Nefdt (2023) 'South Africa is happier than ever, against all odds – 2023 World Happiness Report', *Good Things Guy Website*, 26 March, https://www.goodthingsguy.com/lifestyle/south-africa-is-happier-than-ever-against-all-odds-2023-world-happiness-report/

20 Huang Lanlan and Zhang Yue (2023) 'Chinese people are the happiest in the world, Ipsos survey shows', *Global Times*, 29 March, https://www.globaltimes.cn/page/202303/1288231.shtml

21 The Special A.K.A. (1984) Nelson Mandela (Music Video), https://www.youtube.com/watch?v=AgcTvoWjZJU [Editorial note: Not all was bad about the University of Oxford in 1984, although many things were. It was the year in which the Bullingdon Club 'partied' most obnoxiously of all, but it was also the year when, in defiance of them and their 'hang Nelson Mandela' T-shirts, 'the students union (JCR) at Wadham College, Oxford, passed a motion to end every college "bop" (dance) with the song. That tradition continues to this day.' https://en.wikipedia.org/wiki/Free_Nelson_Mandela].

22 Chinese General Social Survey (CGSS) launched in 2003, http://cgss.ruc.edu.cn/English/Home.htm

Moreover, that sample was taken in 2022, before the country's recent widespread protests.[23]

The other outlier in the graph is Costa Rica, where the president said in 2019:

> Seventy years ago, Costa Rica did away with the army. This allows for many things. Eight per cent of our GDP is invested in education because we don't have to spend on the army. So our strength is human talent, human wellbeing.[24]

What can you do if you want your country to be happier? The most important thing is to elect governments that will ensure the country becomes more equal by income.[25] After that, ensuring your social services – school, housing and healthcare – are efficient and equitable matters most. And finally, consider your degree of freedom, whether you are actually including everyone in your surveys, and how fearful your population is.

---

23 Reuters (2023) 'Israeli government's judicial overhaul plan and reaction', *Reuters*, 27 March, https://www.reuters.com/world/middle-east/israeli-governments-judicial-overhaul-plan-reaction-2023-03-27/

24 Josephine Moulds (2019) 'Costa Rica is one of the world's happiest countries. Here's what it does differently', *World Economic Forum*, 31 January, https://www.weforum.org/agenda/2019/01/sun-sea-and-stable-democracy-what-s-the-secret-to-costa-rica-s-success/

25 David Mac Dougall (2023) 'Everything you need to know about Finland's general election', *Euro News*, 27 March, https://www.euronews.com/2023/03/27/everything-you-need-to-know-about-finlands-general-election

CHAPTER 2.8

Most people in the UK now share Robert Owen's views[1]

From 1798 to 1822 Britain suffered its longest-ever fall in wages and a huge drop in living conditions, in the wake of prolonged wars in Europe and the early effects of new technology and industrialisation. This 24-year-long record will be broken only if real wages do not recover to 2008 levels until after 2032. That is very possible – but it can be averted. Figure 2.14 was drawn in early 2022 when it was estimated that the real pay crisis would end in 2027, but then pay fell further as compared to prices.

Prolonged cost-of-living crises, coupled with high inequality, have often brought about profound change. In 1817, after almost two decades of suffering across the UK, a Welsh businessman, Robert Owen, turned to what was then called socialism. On 12 March he wrote to the chair of the House of Commons committee discussing the Poor Laws, outlining a 'New View of Society'.

Owen appealed to the new capitalists' self-interests. He argued that life in Britain would be better organised along communal lines, with communities the size of the model village of New Lanark in Scotland, where he had become manager of the cotton mill in 1800. Over the years he had come to understand that if they carried on as they were, it would end in disaster. He saw industrialisation leading to mass poverty and stunted children,

[1] Article originally published in *Public Sector Focus* 2020, March/April, pp. 10–13, but Figure 2.14 has been added to this version to illustrate the depth of the current falls in real wages.

Figure 2.14: The worst squeeze on pay for over 200 years

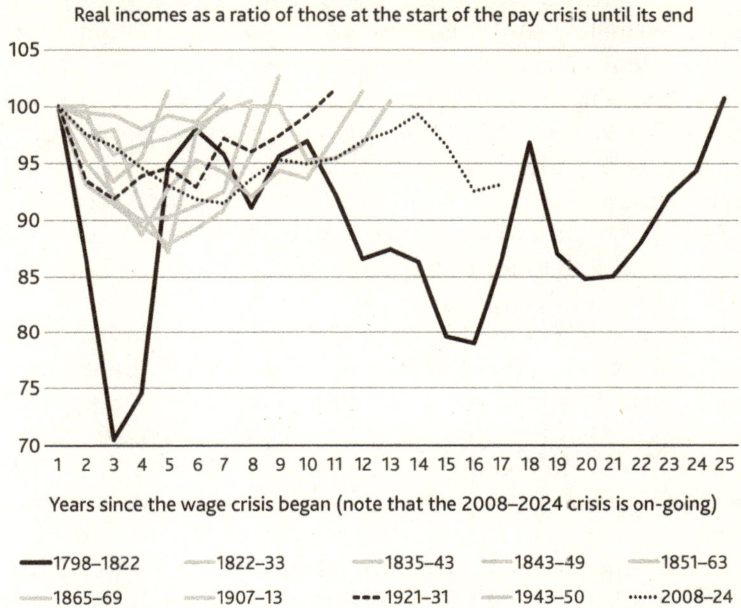

Source: Figure 2 in Danny Dorling (2022) 'The trickle up of fear', *Public Sector Focus*, March/April, pp. 12–15, https://flickread.com/edition/html/index.php?pdf=62668d702a8e0#15. Based on Bank of England, Trades Union Congress and ONS analysis of UK pay crises, 1798–2027, all collated by Geoff Tily, Senior Economist at the TUC, and kindly passed to the author.

to appalling housing conditions and very often deteriorating standards of living within the heart of empire.

Cotton planted and picked by enslaved people had become more expensive to import into Britain after American plantation owners won their independence. British mill owners tried to minimise their losses by making workers toil harder for less reward. As life expectancy continued to drop, they argued for small government and low taxes.

Owen suggested that education should be provided by the community, beginning with free childcare for all from the age of three. Communities would work together, aided by government, to ensure that standards of living rose and that life could be enjoyed rather than endured. Ideas like Owen's spread, but it took time for them to be enacted. The Poor Law he opposed was not abolished until 1948.

From 1921 to 1931 Britain suffered its next-longest fall in wages. There had been a general strike, then a banking crash and mass unemployment. Inequality was again at an all-time high. Most colonies had followed the United States into independence. British rule in most of Ireland ended in 1921 with the signing of the Anglo-Irish Treaty. The UK was becoming poorer again. Inequality, however, began to fall, and the rich were being taxed more than they ever had been before. Greater changes then came in the 1940s and 1960s in a form that Robert Owen might well have recognised as mirroring many of his ideas – including the establishment of playgroups.

Britain suffered its next longest fall in wages nearly eight decades later, from the 2008 financial crash onwards. In Scotland, new Child Payments were introduced and in November 2022 they were increased to £25 per week per child aged 16 and below for all children living in families in receipt of Universal Credit or other state benefits. Universal Credit was yet another new Poor Law. The new Scottish payments were more akin to a Basic Income, but not yet a universal one, and only for children.

Although the Scottish Child Payments were entirely affordable, other elements of Scotland's ambitions to be a better country – free university education, a high-quality health service, and good, affordable housing for all – were not fully achievable because of existing funding arrangements with Westminster and limits on how much taxation Scotland was allowed to raise.[2] By 2020 it became obvious it would soon become untenable for Scotland to remain in the Union if its people also wanted to live fairer lives. The British Labour Party no longer appeared to offer a route towards that. Between 2015 and 2019 it could be argued otherwise, although the financial architecture was never properly addressed by that party when in opposition, even in those years.[3]

---

[2] Jim Cuthbert (2019) 'The Barnett formula as we knew it is dead. Here's what that means for Scotland …', *The National*, 15 August, https://www.thenational.scot/news/17837412.barnett-formula-knew-dead-means-scotland/

[3] Jim Cuthbert (2020) 'Review of the fiscal settlement must be transparent to avoid Whitehall tricks', *The Source*, 17 August, https://sourcenews.scot/jim-cuthbert-review-of-the-fiscal-settlement-must-be-transparent-to-avoid-whitehall-tricks/

But what of Owen's dream of quality childcare and preschool education? In 2023 it was revealed that the average hourly pay for people looking after children in UK nurseries was only £7.42.[4] That is much lower than the minimum wage – and it is hard not to see sexism at the heart of it, because almost all early-years workers are women. Many are classed as apprentices and so can be paid lower than the national minimum wage.

In April 2023 the minimum wage was £10.42. It was only £10.18 for 21–22-year-olds; £7.49 for 18–20-year-olds; and just £5.28 for 16–17-year-olds. The national minimum wage for apprentices was even less: £4.81 per hour. Should you wish to compare this to what you were paid when you were young, that apprentice's wage is the equivalent of receiving the following hourly pay in the past:

2010: £3.40	1980: £1.22	1950: 18p
2000: £2.76	1970: 38p	1940: 11p
1990: £2.12	1960: 26p	1930: 9p

A few weeks later, the Fairness Foundation reported that when polled (Figure 2.15), more than four in five people in the UK agreed that the government should fund minimum levels of provision for social care (84 per cent); for good quality childcare and preschool education (84 per cent); and ensure cheap public transport (81 per cent). More than seven in ten agreed that government should provide enough funding to ensure basic decent provision in relation to social or rented housing (77 per cent) and to lifelong learning (71 per cent); and more than three in five agreed that the government should provide a minimum income (64 per cent); and also that people who lose their job should be paid a percentage of their income by the state to help them get back to work (62 per cent).[5]

[4] Will Snell (2023) 'Eight in 10 Britons think early years workers' pay is too low', *The Fairness Foundation*, 12 March, https://fairnessfoundation.com/critical-days

[5] Will Snell (2023) 'Britons want a bigger role for the state in delivering a social contract', *The Fairness Foundation*, 3 April, https://fairnessfoundation.com/role-of-gov

Figure 2.15: Fairness Foundation survey of 2,052 people in the UK: 22–23 March 2023

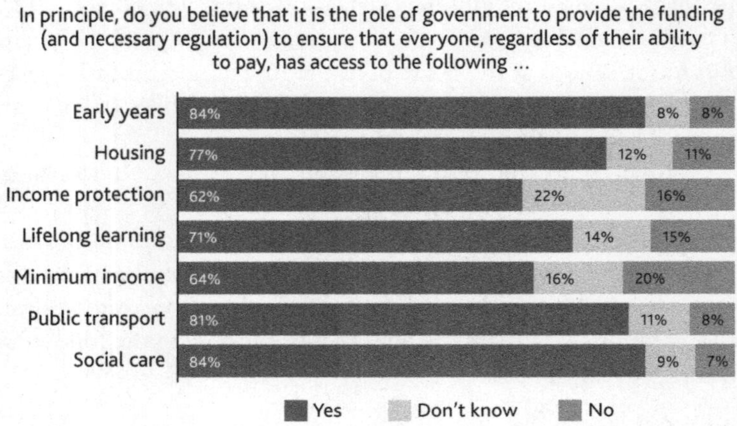

Source: Will Snell (2023) 'Britons want a bigger role for the state in delivering a social contract', *The Fairness Foundation*, 3 April, https://fairnessfoundation.com/role-of-gov

In their press release, the Fairness Foundation explained that the rise in public agreement with these stances began long before 2023. That shift could also be seen among many who were themselves well off. The foundation cited the 2021 book *What We Owe Each Other: A New Social Contract* by economist Dame Minouche Shafik, director of the London School of Economics and Political Science (LSE) and a former deputy governor of the Bank of England, as an example of how such beliefs were becoming much more widespread.[6]

This trend is accelerating. In 2023 Daniel Chandler, an economist and philosopher based at LSE, published a book titled *Free and Equal: What Would a Fair Society Look Like?*[7]. Andy Haldane, former chief economist of the Bank of England, greeted its publication as 'energising and timely'. David Miliband, who had once been Britain's foreign secretary, called it 'clear, brave and compelling'. Rowan Williams, the former Archbishop of

---

6 See https://www.penguin.co.uk/books/441227/what-we-owe-each-other-by-shafik-minouche/9781529112795

7 See https://www.penguin.co.uk/books/316077/free-and-equal-by-chandler-daniel/9780141991948

Canterbury, said it was 'exceptional'. Stephen Fry, author, actor and 'national treasure', summarised *Free and Equal* as 'timely, wise, authoritative and clear'. Dame Minouche Shafik urged people to 'Read *Free and Equal* and feel hopeful about the future.'

What was in Chandler's book that had so excited these luminaries? Is it possible that some of them did not read all the way through? In the second half of his book, he writes approvingly of how Belgium limits the amount any individual can donate to a political party to €500 per year. He suggests that it should be a little less than that, with the state matching personal donations or even exceeding them.

Chandler also writes in supportive terms about Universal Basic Income. He suggests that there is no evidence of economic detriment from very high taxes, although he is unsure of whether tax rates of over 75 per cent on incomes of over $500,000 a year might encourage tax avoidance. He sees inheritance taxes for billionaires of 80 to 90 per cent as a first priority and shows that – combined with decent income taxes on capital – 'a seemingly low annual wealth tax of 1–2 per cent could see some people paying most if not all of their capital income on taxes' (p. 238).

Why were so many of Britain's great and good drawn to these suggestions, people who had previously not advocated such policies? The answer might be that they were simply fitting in better with the views of the rest of society. Our times are changing rapidly.[8] Chandler says his ideas are not socialist. But socialism has many meanings. At its heart it means to be social. In 1858, Robert Owen said on his deathbed: 'My life was not useless; I gave important truths to the world, and it was only for want of understanding that they were disregarded. I have been ahead of my time.'[9]

8 Danny Dorling (2023) 'Are things about to get better?', *Prospect Magazine*, May, pp. 38-41. [Editorial note: This article is reproduced as Chapter 1.8 in this volume.]

9 https://en.wikiquote.org/wiki/Robert_Owen

CHAPTER 2.9

A majority of people think the government does too little[1]

In the Carnegie UK Trust report *The long shadow of the cost of living emergency*,[2] authors Hannah Paylor and Amy Baker revealed that by early 2023 one in six people were less able to exercise, two in six less able to afford a healthy diet, and three in every six much less able to partake in the norms of society than just a year ago. Eating out with friends or family was no longer an option for many. The cinema had become unaffordable to half of society.

At the extremes, a growing number of people talked of being 'freezing cold to the point of feeling ill … [too] scared to turn on the heating'. Corroborating the Carnegie findings, the Resolution Foundation's *2023 UK Living Standards Report* showed that the majority of children with two siblings in the UK went hungry at least once a week.[3]

As I write in mid-2023, even the well-off have been affected. More than a fifth of people in families with a household income of £70,000 or more say they find it hard to maintain a healthy diet as the cost of food, rent or a mortgage, fuel and many other essentials soars.

---

1 Originally published by the Carnegie UK Trust, 23 May 2023, in response to this report: Hannah Paylor and Amy Baker (2023) *The long shadow of the cost of living emergency*, Carnegie UK, 27 April, https://www.carnegieuktrust.org.uk/publications/the-long-shadow-of-the-cost-of-living-emergency/

2 Paylor and Baker (2023) (n. 1).

3 Mike Brewer, Emily Fry and Lalitha Try (2023) *The Living Standards Outlook 2023*, The Resolution Foundation, 9 January, https://www.resolutionfoundation.org/publications/the-living-standards-outlook-2023/

There is no sign of prices falling, just the hope that soon they will not rise much higher. More people are becoming physically ill. Anxiety has risen. Increasing numbers of adults say they feel they can barely afford to exist.

Two thirds of parents say they are less able to participate in leisure activities in 2023 than in 2022, which will include taking their children on an annual holiday. Even before the cost-of-living crisis began, more than a third of British families no longer had an annual holiday because they could not afford one. This has been the case for at least 20 years, as the government's annual Household Below Average Incomes[4] report regularly reveals in a story that is now such old news that it is hardly ever reported.[5]

Almost no one believes that is acceptable, however, and a majority of all adults in all families earning less than the top 1 per cent believe that 'the government is offering too little support to help people through the rise in cost of living' (Figure 2.16). Only in the very richest of families, with household incomes of over £150,000, are a majority of people satisfied with levels of state support for those in need. However, even two people in every five of this group are now sympathetic to the need for action.[6]

The consensus is now so strong that it is likely that the government will act to go further than it has done to date.

[Editorial note: What the YouGov survey carried out for Carnegie UK did not delve into was the views of those adults (a minority among all households apart from the richest, where they were in the majority) who thought that current government

4 Department for Work and Pensions (DWP) (2023) *Households below average income (HBAI) statistics*, DWP, 23 March, https://www.gov.uk/government/collections/households-below-average-income-hbai--2

5 Danny Dorling (2018) *Which children in Britain will have no holiday this summer?*, University of Oxford; Oxplore, https://www.dannydorling.org/?p=6732 Originally posted on Oxford University's 'Explore' Webpages (Oxplore): as 'Close to home: what does poverty in the UK look like?', https://oxplore.org/question-detail/can-we-end-poverty#2055

6 YouGov/Carnegie UK Survey Results, sample size: 2,366 adults in UK, fieldwork: 3–6 February 2023, https://docs.cdn.yougov.com/3i7w1ajgm8/CarnegieUK_UK_Results_230203_W.pdf

Figure 2.16: A majority of people with incomes of £150,000+ don't worry much about others

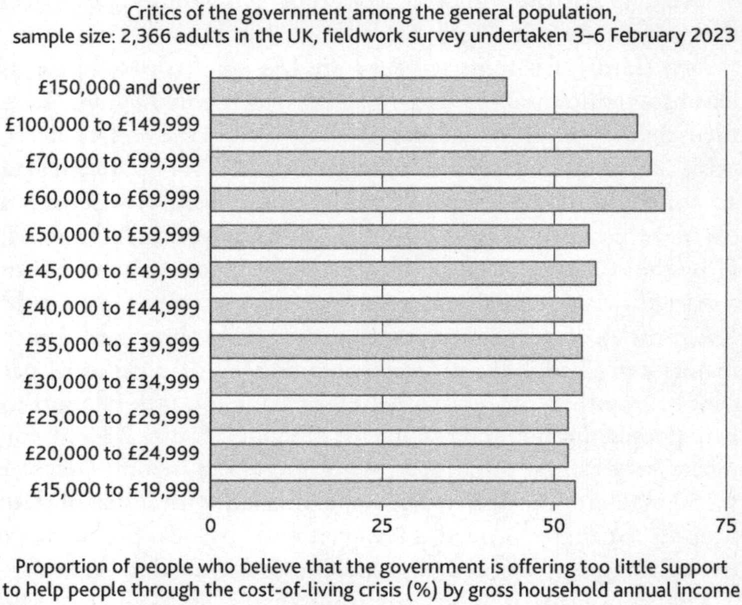

Note: The income shown is gross household income.

Source: Redrawn from data and from a graph produced by Hannah Paylor based on data collected by YouGov, in a survey commissioned by Carnegie UK.[7]

support was adequate. Around the same time as the Carnegie survey (3–6 February 2023), YouGov undertook a larger survey from 24 January to 10 February 2023. It suggested that 75 per cent of people thought that those on benefits should not be able to have a holiday in the UK, 59 per cent thought they should not be able to afford a basic laptop computer, 43 per cent thought a home internet connection was not warranted for the likes of them, 37 per cent thought they should not be able to afford haircuts (since they could cut their own hair), 26 per cent thought there was no need for this group to be able to afford food that allowed them and their children to eat a balanced and

[7] Hannah.Paylor@CarnegieUK.org or simply go to the link in n. 6 to get the data.

healthy diet, and 24 per cent did not believe they should be able to pay their electricity, gas or water bills.[8] It is very likely that some people were confused over what they were being asked and whether the question being asked was 'ought this to be attainable?' or 'is it attainable?' – the word 'should' in YouGov's question is very ambiguous. (The question can be interpreted in different ways. By contrast, the question YouGov asked for Carnegie UK was clearer: 'To your knowledge, do you think that the Government are currently offering too much, too little or about the right amount of support to help people through the rise in the cost of living?'). Nevertheless, there are clearly many bitter and heartless people out there – although thankfully always in a minority except in the very richest households. Some people are made more bitter and heartless the longer they live in an unequal society, and the more unequal it becomes.]

8 Fintan Smith (2023) 'What should living standards look like for people on benefits, minimum wage, and average earnings?' *YouGov*, 2 August, https://yougov.co.uk/topics/society/articles-reports/2023/08/02/what-should-living-standards-look-people-benefits-

CHAPTER 2.10

The crises combine: austerity, the cost of living, jobs and pay[1]

The UK government may be taxing people, other than the very well-off, more than it has in many decades, but that does not mean it is spending more on public services in real terms, or even living up to what it has previously promised to spend.

In April 2023 it was quietly announced that Rishi Sunak's government had halved the funding it had pledged to give to support the social care workforce. In December 2021, when Sunak had been chancellor for almost two years, a promise had been made to invest 'at least £500m over the next three years' into social care. This was part of the White Paper on adult social care reform. Fifteen months later, in April 2023, that promise was cut to £250 million.

The learning disability charity Mencap reacted angrily, labelling the U-turn an 'insult' and explaining that 'the plan had now been diluted beyond recognition'.[2] There are currently 165,000 too few care workers in place and now there is little hope this will be remedied.

One consequence of previous cuts to social care spending in the UK had been a rise in mortality, starting in 2012, among many at-risk groups, especially the frailest and most elderly. When the promise was broken, the charity Age UK explained that funding

---

1 Originally published in *Public Sector Focus*, May/June 2023, pp. 10–13.

2 Adam Forrest (2023) 'Tory ministers accused of "insult" to social care as workforce reform funding halved', *The Independent*, 4 April, https://www.independent.co.uk/news/uk/politics/social-care-funding-tories-sunak-b2313677.html

was no longer even 'remotely enough'. The King's Fund health think-tank was also damning in its assessment. The Trades Union Congress called the U-turn 'slashing'. The GMB union, which represents many care workers, called it 'disgraceful'.

Earlier in the spring of 2023, the Institute for Fiscal Studies (IFS) had highlighted a dire situation in another state sector, further education, which employs 50,000 teachers. The IFS noted that by 2023, the median pay for a school teacher had fallen to £41,500 a year, but for a further education college teacher it was now only £34,500. In real terms, between 2010–11 and 2022–23, the median salary for a school teacher had been cut by 14 per cent, but the median salary for a college teacher had been slashed by 18 per cent (Figure 2.17).

As a result of worsening conditions and declining pay, some 16 per cent of all further education college teachers leave the profession each year. This compares with 10 per cent of school teachers, 10–11 per cent across most NHS occupations and

Figure 2.17: Cumulative real-terms pay changes for FE staff relative to 2010–11, 2007–23

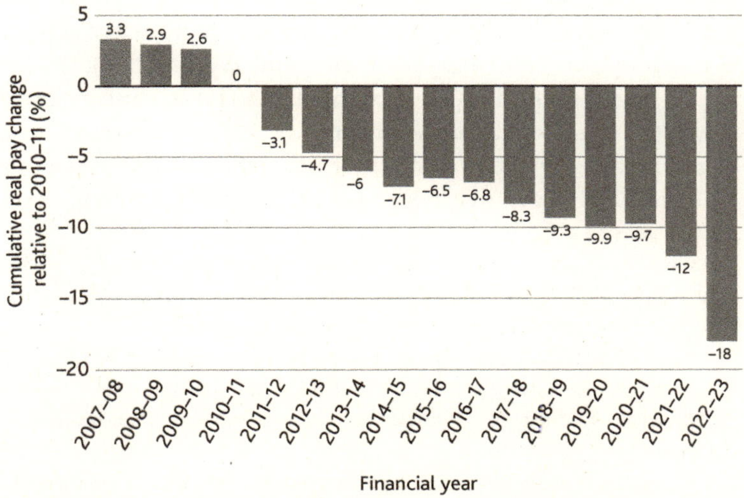

Source: Luke Sibieta and Imran Tahir (2023) *What has happened to college teacher pay in England?*, Institute for Fiscal Studies, 30 March, Figure 2, https://ifs.org.uk/publications/what-has-happened-college-teacher-pay-england

7–8 per cent in the civil service.[3] The cut in real-terms pay was far worse in 2023 than in any preceding year, and possibly any year since further education began. In the 1970s pay tended to increase above inflation. How had we got into this state? What is to be done?

On 29 November 2022 the ONS, in effect, nationalised the further education college sector by reclassifying it in the public accounts. Overnight, further education colleges were made public bodies, no longer private. Suddenly those who run them can no longer be paid more than £150,000 a year unless colleges seek express permission from government.[4] The government immediately declared that 'Following the reclassification, colleges and their subsidiaries are now part of central government.'[5] One implication was that no one in the sector could be paid more than the prime minister. Those further education bosses who had been setting the salaries of college teachers so low now had to look at their own pay. This is a start, but there is so far to go.

These are just two parts of a British public sector that has, as a whole, been decimated many times over now. All of this is part of a much longer process. It began in the 1970s when the fight to protect jobs and the public sector more widely was lost. The public sector and decent progressive taxation had been won in the 1920s and 1930s through a huge amount of collective action, not least by people striking for their rights (Figure 2.18).

The strikes of the 1920s contributed to a rise in equality, both at the time and especially afterwards. The wave of strikes that began in the 1970s dwindled after the defeat of the miners in 1984–85. The wave that began in 2022 is still extremely small

---

[3] Luke Sibieta and Imran Tahir (2023) '*What has happened to college teacher pay in England?*, Institute for Fiscal Studies, 30 March, https://ifs.org.uk/publications/what-has-happened-college-teacher-pay-england

[4] Julian Gravatt (2023) 'Are universities really at risk of ending up in the public sector?', *Higher Education Policy Institute* (HEPI), 21 March, https://www.hepi.ac.uk/2023/03/21/are-universities-really-at-risk-of-ending-up-in-the-public-sector/

[5] Department for Education (2023) *Further education reclassification: Government response*, Policy Paper, 29 November, https://www.gov.uk/government/publications/further-education-reclassification/further-education-reclassification-government-response

Figure 2.18: Numbers of days lost per year due to strikes in Britain, 1892–2022

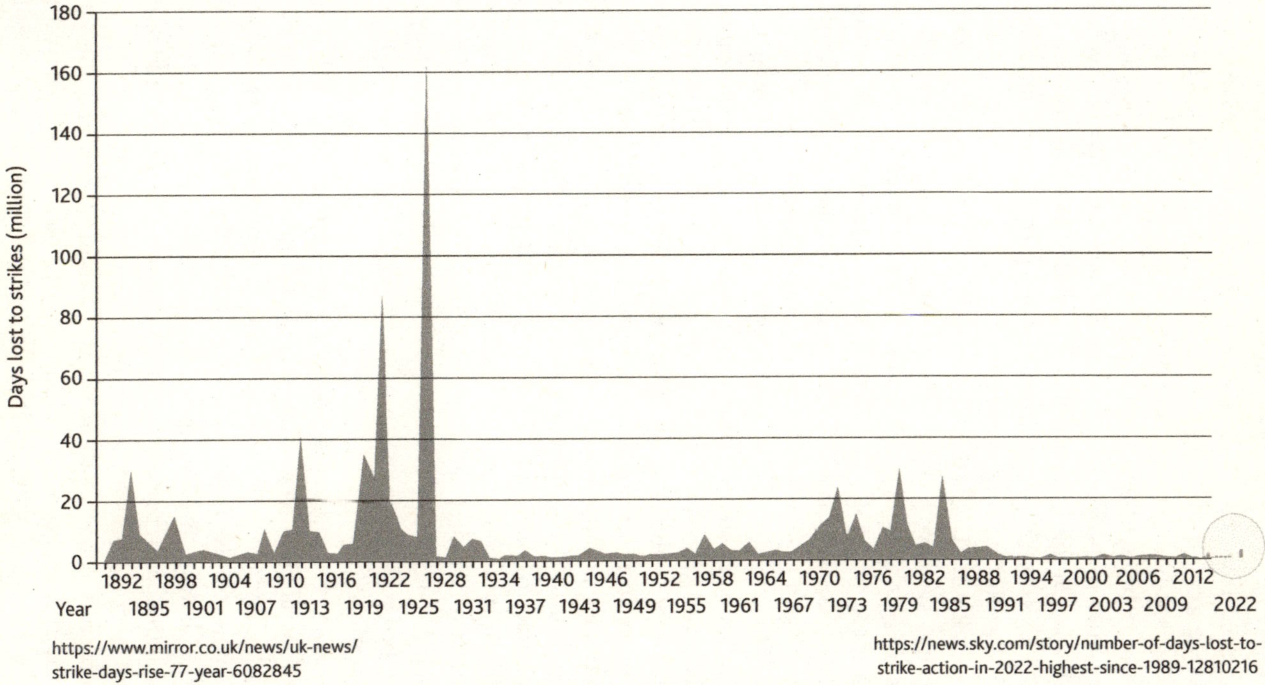

Source: Recent sources from the *Mirror* newspaper and *Sky News* are shown within the figure. They both in turn relied for the long term historical series on ONS (2015) The history of strikes in the UK, 21 September, https://www.ons.gov.uk/employmentandlabourmarket/peopleinwork/employmentandemployeetypes/articles/thehistoryofstrikesintheuk/2015-09-21 and has to be highlighted even to be visible in this historical series (Figure 2.18). This is despite the workforce being far larger today and the graph not being corrected for that population growth.

We are still living in a land that was poisoned by Thatcherism. We were brought low by a doctrine of 'me-first' selfishness that continues to hobble effective action against injustice. We were torn apart in the 1980s as inequality soared to levels not seen since the 1920s. We have not recovered any ground at all. High levels of inequality are now embedded.

Socially, the UK is more starkly divided than any other state in Europe. We have a multi-tier education system, a two-tier health system (private and state), and a chasm between those who rent and those who own their home. Living standards will continue to fall even as the rate of inflation falls, because prices will still be rising faster than wages for some time to come.

Politically, the UK is riven with divisions that reflect our underlying economic and social severing. The resentment is rising, and many attempts are being made to stop that resentment becoming more focused by trying to direct people's attention to worrying instead about migration ('Small Boats') or road safety and pollution measures (clean air zones and low traffic neighbourhoods). Brexit and the culture wars are still being exploited by charlatans. They have fertile ground to till as social division results in ever-shorter fuses, and a loss of patience and tolerance. We desperately need a more cohesive society with a much higher degree of trust between people and – eventually – a renewed sense of common purpose. The UK is such a long way from this.

Not everything can be blamed on Thatcherism. Labour and the Liberal Democrats must take part of the blame, especially in England, where there has been such an enormous failure to think differently. New Labour offered a methadone alternative to the Tories' heroin. It alleviated a few of the symptoms, but we are back hooked on the true opiates again now. You cannot kick the habit by just watering down the product.

Jeremy Corbyn's vision for the Labour Party, and the aims of the mass movement behind his leadership, were viewed by many as an impossibility. However, all the Corbyn project really offered, in terms of economic policy at least, was a bit more tax-and-spend. The hostility with which it was greeted revealed how salted Britain's earth has become. Even modest redistributive proposals, of a kind commonplace across Europe, were ruled out of bounds with Labour's general election loss in 2019. In 2023, however, the renationalisation of further education and much else, from railways to housing associations, is being forced on us, or at the very least has become a topic for consideration, as the privatisation experiment of 1980–2020 crashes and burns.

There is no shortage of policy solutions to our current problems – green deals, wealth taxes, common ownership of utilities and public services, and a growing co-operative and employee-owned business sector – but these are hard to introduce and sustain while UK politics remains as poisonous, and shifted so far to the right, as it is now.

Proportional representation, a constitutional overhaul and limits on individuals funding political parties are the building blocks we require to achieve high levels of progressive taxation and more.[6] They seem beyond reach at the moment, but to construct anything you first have to visualise and articulate it, so let's at least do that with energy and hope. The alternative is no care in our old age, no teachers for our children at college, and almost no decency left in public life.

As the crises combine and continued austerity mixes with a cost-of-living nightmare, as public sector jobs are lost and pay in real terms is cut, there are nevertheless some signs of hope: nationalisation returning and progressive pay deals becoming the

6 [Editorial note: As Chapter 2.9 mentioned, and as appeared in the original version of this chapter, in 2023 Daniel Chandler explained in his book *Free and equal* (endorsed by Vince Cable, Angus Deaton, Stephen Fry, Andy Haldane, David Miliband, Jesse Norman, Amartya Sen, Dame Minouche Shafik, Thomas Piketty, Rowan Williams and Linda Yueh) that an entire overhaul of our electoral system, introducing proportional representation, strict controls on any individual person funding political parties more than any another, and very high levels of progressive taxation would be needed, but I am not sure that all those who endorsed the book read it right through to Chandler's conclusions at the end, before they wrote their words of praise. Although maybe many of them did.]

norm.[7] Even so, the sunlit uplands seem so far away that it is easy to give up hope. Perhaps the UK running out of money (to buy enough imports) will make us realise that the sunlit uplands are further away than they have been for many a decade, and this is what it will take for change to come? Will the bad times have to run their course for us all to understand just how wrong the ideas that got us here were?

---

7 Danny Dorling (2023) 'Are things about to get better?', *Prospect Magazine*, 5 April, May issue, pp. 38–41, https://www.prospectmagazine.co.uk/essays/have-we-reached-peak-inequality and at https://www.dannydorling.org/?page_id=9653

SECTION 3

Levelling across housing

We will finish what we started

On 13 August 2018, the Ministry of Housing, Communities and Local Government set a goal of 'halving rough sleeping by 2022 and ending it by 2027'. On 5 September 2022, just four years later and under the same political party, that strategy was abandoned and the policy paper officially withdrawn.[1] The ministers who had set the 2018 strategy almost certainly had little intention of achieving it, beyond, perhaps, preferring that the constituents who voted them into office – those in the places which back then saw the highest levels of Conservative voting – would not see people sleeping on the streets of their neighbourhoods, or when they went shopping in the nearby smaller city.

A new strategy, 'Ending Rough Sleeping for Good', was announced in 2022. It included a laughable claim to have made great achievements. Here is what someone had the gall to write and the others who put their names to it said at that time (see Figure 3.6):

> We also recognise that a societal problem as long-standing and entrenched as rough sleeping demands *long-term solutions*. Over the last few years, we've gone much *further and faster* in *reducing rough sleeping* than many thought possible. With this bold, new Strategy, *empowered partners* on the ground *ready to deliver*, and a broad coalition of government departments *wholly*

[1] Ministry of Housing, Communities and Local Government (2018) 'The rough sleeping strategy: The rough sleeping strategy sets out the government's vision for halving rough sleeping by 2022 and ending it by 2027', Policy paper, 13 August, https://www.gov.uk/government/publications/the-rough-sleeping-strategy

> *committed* to the task ahead, we will *finish what we started* and, together, we will *end rough sleeping for good.*[2]

The minister who announced the strategy, Greg Clark, had been in office for just three weeks when he unveiled it.

Greg Clark was reshuffled within a week of the new strategy being announced. That move had nothing to do with the strategy – which did not matter at all to him or his bosses. He was reshuffled because a new prime minister was playing power games. His replacement as Secretary of State for Levelling Up was Simon Clarke, who remained in office for just over six weeks (and then, 15 months later, in January 2024, Simon had a brief period of fame when he called for the man who had promoted him, Rishi Sunak, to resign).[3]

Over the past decade, junior ministerial posts with specific responsibility for housing have had among the highest rates of turnover of all government positions. Housing is the lowest of government priorities. The Minister for Rough Sleeping and Housing at the time of the new strategy, Eddie Hughes, was sacked within a few days of its publication, to be replaced – after the post was left vacant for two weeks – by Andrew Stephenson, but with the words 'Rough Sleeping' removed from his ministerial title. Another barely known backbencher took over from him as junior minister at the end of October 2022. After just five weeks, Felicity Buchan, a former JP Morgan Chase banker, former managing director of the debt capital markets division of the Bank of America, and an alumna of Christ Church, University of Oxford, replaced Stephenson and has now kept the role through to May 2024 – for well over a year. But she has done little with it

---

2 Emphasis added. Source: Greg Clark (2022) *Housing and Communities, Ending Rough Sleeping for Good*, Command Paper 713, London: Department for Levelling Up, Housing and Communities, September, https://assets.publishing.service.gov.uk/government/uploads/system/uploads/attachment_data/file/1102408/20220903_Ending_rough_sleeping_for_good.pdf

3 Aletha Adu (2024) 'Simon Clarke advised to lie down by Tory MP after calling for Sunak to quit', *The Guardian*, 24 January, https://www.theguardian.com/politics/2024/jan/24/simon-clarke-tory-backlash-after-calling-rishi-sunak-resign

that could be seen as a success or achievement. She has admitted that rising rough sleeping concerns her,[4] and in March 2024 she refused permission to build more homes.[5]

Previous housing ministers may not have cared much for the post but they managed at least to control the growth of rough sleeping in England and occasionally to reduce it. You have to look to Scotland to see where rough sleeping has been most effectively tackled in the UK (Figure 3.1), or to Finland to see that it can be almost entirely eradicated as an issue, should a people decide to do that (Chapter 3.6).

Figure 3.1: Sleeping rough in Scotland and seeking assistance, April 2002 to March 2020

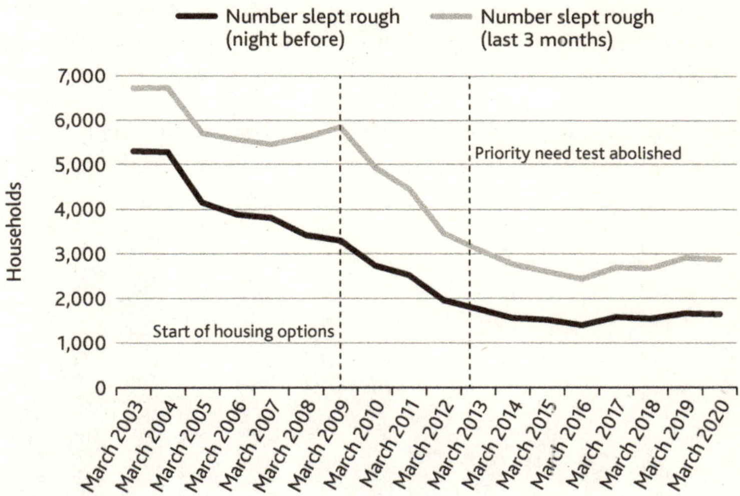

Note: Households applying for homelessness support which included a household member having slept rough, April 2002 to March 2020.

Source: Tom Capon (2021) 'Rough sleeping in the UK: 2002 to 2021', Office for National Statistics (ONS), 10 June, https://www.ons.gov.uk/peoplepopulationandcommunity/housing/articles/roughsleepingintheuk/2002to2021

---

4 Felicity Buchan (2023) 'Rise in rough sleeping is a "great concern". But we're still aiming to end it for good', *The Big Issue*, 4 September, https://www.bigissue.com/opinion/rough-sleeping-rises-homelessness-minister-felicity-buchan/

5 See: https://www.planningresource.co.uk/article/1865557/minister-refuses-1400-green-belt-homes-inspector-justified-local-plan-delay

In contrast to Scotland, the record of housing ministers in England has been abysmal. Their incompetence stretches from deliberate actions intended to keep house prices high, to their ignoring the growth of black mould. At the extremes of housing failure, the number of people sleeping rough doubled in the first six years of the Coalition government (2010–16; see Figure 3.2). That number only appeared to fall in 2018 because the very poor weather on the autumn night when the annual count was taken made it difficult to find where people were sleeping. It is likely that autumn 2019 count was affected by similar issues, because the numbers of people in England claiming relief duty (as they were statutorily entitled to) actually rose between quarter 3 of 2018 and quarter 3 of 2019.[6] The fall in 2020 was entirely due to the pandemic and the 'Everybody In' strategy, which was enacted not because ministers cared, but because they were afraid that the rough sleeping population would become a well, or hotbed, of

Figure 3.2: Sleeping rough in England as counted on a single night in autumn, 2010–20

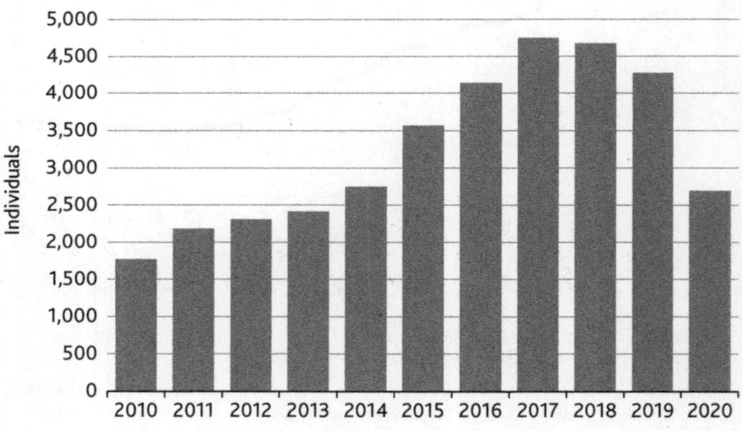

Source: Ministry of Housing, Communities and Local Government (MHCLG) annual survey data, as reported in official statistical publications by Tom Capon (2021) 'Rough sleeping in the UK: 2002 to 2021', ONS, 10 June, https://www.ons.gov.uk/peoplepopulationandcommunity/housing/articles/roughsleepingintheuk/2002to2021

[6] See Figure 7 in: Ministry of Housing, Communities and Local Government (MHCLG) annual survey data, as reported in official statistical publications by Tom Capon (2021) 'Rough sleeping in the UK: 2002 to 2021', ONS,

continued infection. In almost every way in which it was possible to test them morally, the English housing minsters appeared to take the most selfish route – to try to increase their own and their supporters' housing wealth and to help others as little as possible.

One image, taken in 2017, encapsulates this selfishness and incompetence: Figure 3.3.

How can I be hopeful that the UK may have reached peak injustice when it is run by such incompetent and selfish people? Why have hope when the most basic things in life, such as access to safe housing, are so clearly such a low priority for our governments, and when the statistics about how many people are so poorly housed are now so dire?

I have hope because I believe that the party is over for these politicians. In 2023 they were in office but not really in power. Something similar occurred in Ireland following the banking crash of 2008, which was even more extreme there than in the UK, at least in part because Irish ministers followed the UK's financial advice.

Chapter 3.1 in this section is a response to an article by social psychologist Séamus Power in which he quotes an influential member of the Irish government remarking, in December 2016, on a former government minister's suggestion that those in power had simply partied:

> You get in trouble if you say it. But that's not true. [whispers] It's bullshit. *Everyone partied. People mightn't have bought fancy houses*, but I don't know anyone who didn't *upgrade their car*, who didn't *buy art, or a sculpture, or something to upgrade their life*. But you can't say that – you just can't say it.[7]

One reason to have hope is that it is now very hard to imagine the UK's situation becoming any worse than it already is, because

---

10 June, https://www.ons.gov.uk/peoplepopulationandcommunity/housing/articles/roughsleepingintheuk/2002to2021

7 Séamus Power (2018) 'The Deprivation–Protest Paradox: How the perception of unfair economic inequality leads to civic unrest', *Current Anthropology*, 59, 6, 765–74, December, p. 767 (emphasis added).

Figure 3.3: Grenfell Tower, Notting Dale, Kensington during the 14 June 2017 fire

see colour version in plate section

Source: Photograph taken by Natalie Oxford, reproduced from Wikimedia Commons, the free media repository, Creative Commons Attribution 4.0, https://commons.wikimedia.org/wiki/File:Grenfell_Tower_fire.jpg

fewer and fewer people now benefit. But the few who still did by 2015 rarely mixed with those who did not even if they lived very close by (Figure 3.4)

Felicity Buchan lives in an area of London where one in 29 people are homeless. She is a member of the Chelsea Arts Club. And, as I write in May 2024, she is (remarkably, given the usual turnover rate) still Parliamentary Under-secretary of State for Housing and Homelessness, the minister responsible for understanding why so many people are sleeping rough, or living

Figure 3.4: Neighbourhoods in Kensington coloured by their poverty rate, 2015

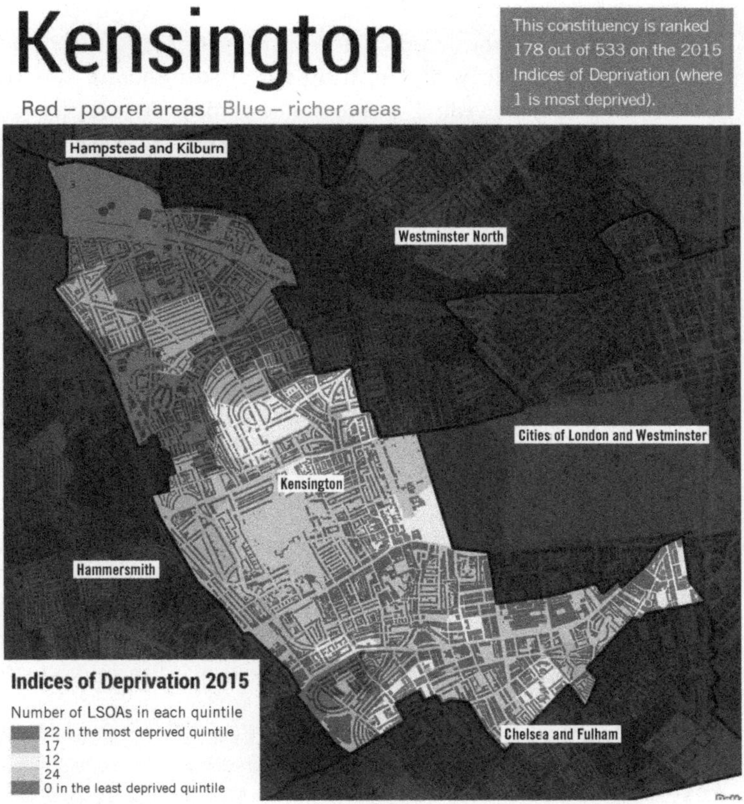

see colour version in plate section

Source: Map drawn by Alasdair Rae on 11 June 2017, three days before the fire, reproduced with permission: https://x.com/undertheraedar/status/873948896401215493

in accommodation that is very insecure, temporary, inadequate, or unfit for humans to inhabit. However, despite the housing minister's interests in the finer things in life, including art, her register of interests does not mention what art she buys or whether she owns sculptures.[8] Homelessness in her London parliamentary constituency of Kensington has risen while she has been an MP, not just street homelessness, but also people having to sofa-surf, or being housed by the council in temporary accommodation. The majority of those being housed in temporary accommodation are children. As documented previously in this chapter, Felicity's reaction to reports of rising rough sleeping is to report that she is 'concerned'. She does this at the same time as refusing planning permissions to build new much-needed homes very near London.[9]

Good housing is about much more than trying to clear the streets of roofless adults and putting them somewhere out of sight. It is about providing homes of a quality at least fit for human habitation. Scotland now has a far better record of doing so than England. Its record used to be worse (Figure 3.5). When Felicity Buchan was an undergraduate at Christ Church in the early 1990s, it is unlikely she would have known she was sleeping in the Oxford electoral ward with by far the highest premature mortality rate in the city at that time. University students lived entirely separate, although not entirely safe, lives. She may well have known all about the death of one student in a room in Christ Church a few years earlier,[10] but not about what was occurring directly outside her college's walls.

---

[8] Felicity Buchan does not have to pay the £623 annual membership fee of the Chelsea Arts Club as, according to her register of interests as an MP, the club gifts her that: https://members.parliament.uk/member/4821/registeredinterests

[9] See: https://www.theplanner.co.uk/2024/03/18/recovered-appeal-housing-minister-refuses-1400-home-scheme

[10] Neil Tweedie (2023) 'What a waste of gilded lives: The heroin death of heiress Olivia Channon 32 years ago stunned Britain. So what happened to the other players in this sordid drama?', *Daily Mail*, 5 July, https://www.dailymail.co.uk/femail/article-5424867/Olivia-Channons-friends-32-years-drugs-death.html

Figure 3.5: The child in the window: health and housing, a lasting relationship

Note: This photograph was taken by Mary Shaw in the Glasgow constituency of Shettleston, shortly after it was reported to have had the highest premature standardised mortality ratios in Britain, in the period 1996–98. 'Leaking soil pipes have caused the dark patches visible on the walls. Although most of the windows are boarded up, two of the flats are still occupied. These flats were built in the early 1950s and are due for demolition; much of the rest of the street has already been demolished.'

Source: Mary Shaw (2001) 'Health and housing: a lasting relationship', *Journal of Epidemiology and Community Health*; 55, p. 291, https://jech.bmj.com/content/55/5/291

Deaths of students were and are very rare in Oxford. It is locals who are much more likely to die young, most often due to lack of housing. In the early 1990s the main cause of death of people in Oxford aged under 65 was sleeping rough. Many of them would have been of a similar age to Buchan when they died within a few metres of where she would have been sleeping. The situation in Oxford has not improved. More local people, who were children in Oxford and have returned as young or middle-aged adults, die sleeping rough or in halfway houses now.[11] On 25 February 2019, the BBC reported that Blackburn had the highest death rate, by area, among people who were homeless, followed closely by Oxford, and then Camden.[12] In the neighbourhoods represented by Felicity Buchan in Parliament, homelessness is just as bad as it was before the pandemic, but it has recently become even worse in other parts of the capital (see Editorial note at the end of Chapter 3.2). However, Kensington, like so much of Britain, is so socially divided that it is possible to live there and not be aware of what life elsewhere in that borough entails.

There are many ways the wider crisis in housing can be addressed, and they could be applied very quickly. They do not require building many new homes (Chapter 3.3). Sadly, current government ministers give no sign they even imagine these actions to be possible. The UK spends less public money than any other affluent country in Europe on goods such as securing housing (Chapter 3.4). The UK has spent the most money propping up house prices, which has led to the current fall in the value of private homes being even sharper (Chapter 3.5). Almost every other country in Europe does far better, some almost unbelievably so, at addressing homelessness (Chapter 3.6). The UK has been extraordinarily badly governed in recent years (Chapter 3.7). If Labour come to power, they should be very wary of emulating the Tories (Chapter 3.8).

So why be optimistic? There are many reasons given in this book, but for now I will leave you with Figure 3.6. Can you imagine any other set of government ministers more incapable than the eight whose pictures adorned the inside pages of the 2022 homelessness strategy?

The recently released homelessness figures for 2023 (see Figure 3.7) highlight the scale of the UK's failure to date.

---

11 Nicola Brimblecombe, Danny Dorling and Mark Green (2019) 'Who still dies young in a rich city? Revisiting the case of Oxford', *The Geographical Journal*, 12 November.

12 Danny Dorling (2022) 'Houses, not homelessness', *European Journal of Homelessness*, 15, 3, pp. 87–97, p. 90, https://www.dannydorling.org/?page_id=8876

Figure 3.6: Signatories to the Joint Ministerial Foreword to Command Paper 713

see colour version in plate section

Source: Greg Clark (2022) *Housing and Communities, Ending Rough Sleeping for Good*, Command Paper 713, London: Department for Levelling Up, Housing and Communities, September, https://assets.publishing.service.gov.uk/government/uploads/system/uploads/attachment_data/file/1102408/20220903_Ending_rough_sleeping_for_good.pdf

Figure 3.7: Proportion experiencing homeless per 10,000 people, 2023 or latest year

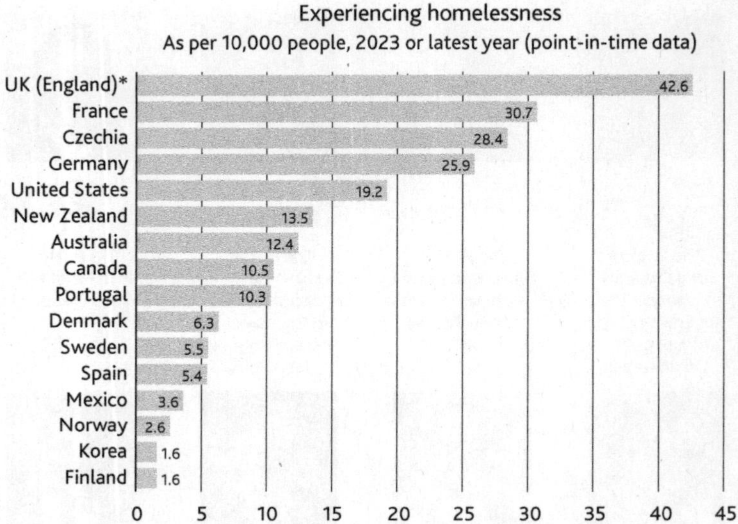

Note: People experiencing homelessness (PIT data) who are living rough or staying in emergency accommodation (ETHOS Light 1, 2, 3), as reported by governments. *Data for the United Kingdom (England) refer to the number of households experiencing homelessness per 10,000 households for ETHOS Light 2 and 3; data also include people enumerated in the Rough Sleeping Snapshot (ETHOS 1).

Source: OECD Affordable Housing Database, HC3.1 People experiencing homelessness

CHAPTER 3.1

When everyone you know buys art[1]

People protest when they can take no more, but also when there is a glimmer of hope: when it becomes obvious that although there is enough to go around, all boats are not being lifted. People protest when they find out just how much is being squandered and how little the elite know – or care.

Writing about Ireland, social psychologist Séamus Power[2] quoted Alexis de Tocqueville (1856), who had pointed out that it was 'in those parts of France where there had been most improvement that popular discontent ran highest'. The French Revolution occurred when and where it did within France not only because there was great suffering and poor harvests, but also because the squandering of great and growing riches had become so clear to so many.

Ireland is not about to have a revolution, but it suffered by far the greatest financial crash of all affluent nations in 2008. Figure 3.8 shows how in many countries public expenditure rose because banks were being bailed out, but in Ireland the bailouts were greater, as were the subsequent cuts to public expenditure.

In the US, protest erupted in the 1960s when it became clear that a large proportion of the population were not being listened

---

1 Adapted from: 'Ireland: When everyone you know buys art, or a sculpture, to upgrade their life: a commentary on "The Deprivation-Protest Paradox: how the perception of unfair economic inequality leads to civic unrest" by Séamus A. Power', *Current Anthropology*, 59, 6, pp. 777–8, December 2018.

2 Séamus Power (2018) 'The Deprivation-Protest Paradox: How the perception of unfair economic inequality leads to civic unrest', *Current Anthropology*, 59, 6, pp. 765–74, December.

Figure 3.8: State spending as a proportion of GDP, 12 rich countries 2002–20 (%)

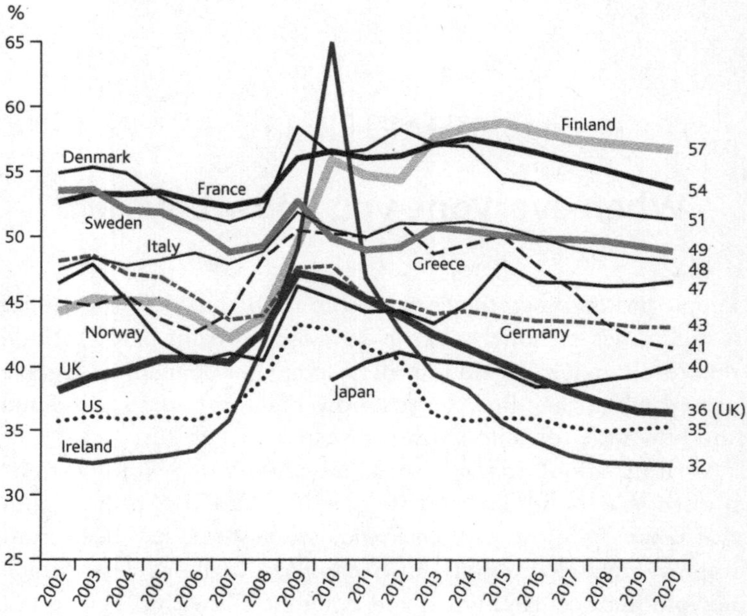

Source: The 2010, 2012 and 2015 IMF database, projections after 2014. (Naturally the projections did not predict the COVID-19 pandemic in 2020, when all countries saw spending rise in a similar way to when the banking crisis hit them all in 2008.) Figure from Danny Dorling (2016) *A better politics*, London: London Publishing Company (open access version available here: http://www.dannydorling.org/books/betterpolitics/). It only contains two key figures; this is the second one.

to. They were simply unheard; not even ignored but unknown. Speaking three years after the 1965 riots/uprising in Watts, a predominantly Black neighbourhood in Los Angeles, Martin Luther King Jr told an audience at Grosse Pointe High School in Michigan:

> It is not enough for me to stand before you tonight and condemn riots. It would be morally irresponsible for me to do that without, at the same time, condemning the contingent, intolerable conditions that exist in our society. These conditions are the things that cause individuals to feel that they have no other alternative than to engage in violent rebellions to get attention.

> And I must say tonight that a riot is the language of the unheard.

In England, the 2011 riots in the wake of the police killing of Mark Duggan, a Black man, were mainly confined to London. They were not riots over austerity but, nevertheless, their geography revealed economic inequality to be key. It was where there was most to be looted, where the riches and ignorance of the very affluent were flaunted most, that rioting was most common.[3]

Figure 3.9 shows that more rioters lived in a ring of boroughs outside central London than did so in entire English regions

Figure 3.9: England, sized by the numbers of people accused of riot in 2011

Defendants brought before the courts for offences relating to the public disorder between 6th and 9th August 2011

By region of the defendant's origin • Total number of court cases: 3,103

Key map showing land area of English regions and London boroughs

Cartograms showing the regions/boroughs resized according to the number of defendants resident in each area of origin

* A total of 169 court cases have not been allocated to individual regions: these cases have been redistributed equally over all regions without any cases in the source data as marked in the reference map

Source: Ben Hennig (2014) 'The cartography of riots', *Worldmapper Blog*, 14 August, http://london.worldmapper.org/the-cartography-of-riots/ (note: original is in colour)

---

[3] Danny Dorling and Carl Lee (2014) 'Inequality constitutes a particular place', in David Pritchard and Francis Pakes (eds) *Riot, unrest and protest on the global stage*, Basingstoke: Palgrave Macmillan, chapter 7, pp. 115–31.

located far away from the capital and the shopping malls of the rich.[4]

Séamus Power suggests that: 'In the Irish context, people accepted austerity because they believed by doing so the entire economy would benefit.'[5] However, emigration from Ireland rose rapidly: hardly an example of accepting austerity.

On 30 September 2008, a 'bank deposit guarantee' was introduced that made people wonder why it was needed. Within days the crash had begun – most probably just after 10 pm on 2 October 2008, when the chief executive of the Financial Regulator of Ireland appeared on Irish television news. As Michael Lewis so eloquently explained, three years after these events, quoting Colm McCarthy, the reaction of the Irish public to that man's appearance on TV was: 'They saw him and said, Who the fuck was that??? Is that the fucking guy who is in charge of the money??? That's when everyone panicked.'[6]

Analysis of large-scale survey data taken each year in Ireland between 2004 and 2014 recently revealed that life satisfaction reached its lowest level in 2010, driven by the despair of those who were worst off. Social trust fell and in 2010: 'belonging to the lowest income quartile … had a significant negative impact on life satisfaction. This is in marked contrast to 2008, where the income stratification of life satisfaction was completely due to subjective economic hardship.'[7] In other words, by 2010, the poorest in Ireland had come to realise that they were disadvantaged as a group, whereas just two years earlier their answers to survey questions did not reveal that knowledge.

Only analysis of survey data taken from across a whole country can tell you when the overall mood changes. Anecdotes, such as Colm McCarthy's quoted earlier, help identify plausible trigger

[4] Danny Dorling (2014) 'Mapping the August 2011 riots', *The New Statesman*, 5 August, https://www.newstatesman.com/voices/2014/08/danny-dorling-mapping-august-2011-riots

[5] Power (2018) (n. 2), p. 765.

[6] Michael Lewis (2011) *Boomerang: The meltdown tour*, London: Allen Lane, p. 98.

[7] Mikko Weckroth, Teemu Kemppainen and Danny Dorling (2017) 'Income-based social stratification of life satisfaction in Ireland between 2004 and 2014', *Irish Journal of Sociology*, 25, 2, pp. 128–49.

points. Anecdotes also identify the ignorance of the elite, like the rich Irish woman quoted by Power who said that prior to the crash she did not know anyone 'who didn't buy art, or a sculpture, or something to upgrade their life'. Power suggests that when the crash came, the rich lost the most. He says: 'in objective terms their relative loss is greater'.

But in objective terms, who really lost the most? Is it the person who has to sleep in a car because they can no longer pay the rent on their old home? Or the person whose home is now worth a few hundred thousand euros less, but they still live in it and own it?

By 2015 the situation in Ireland had become much worse, as Figure 3.10 reveals. The public spending cuts being made then were a political choice, they were not inevitable. However, the official measure of GDP also began to rise, but with little benefit to the government or people of Ireland. It rose because one of

Figure 3.10: Ireland: public expenditure as a proportion (%) of GDP, 2001–22

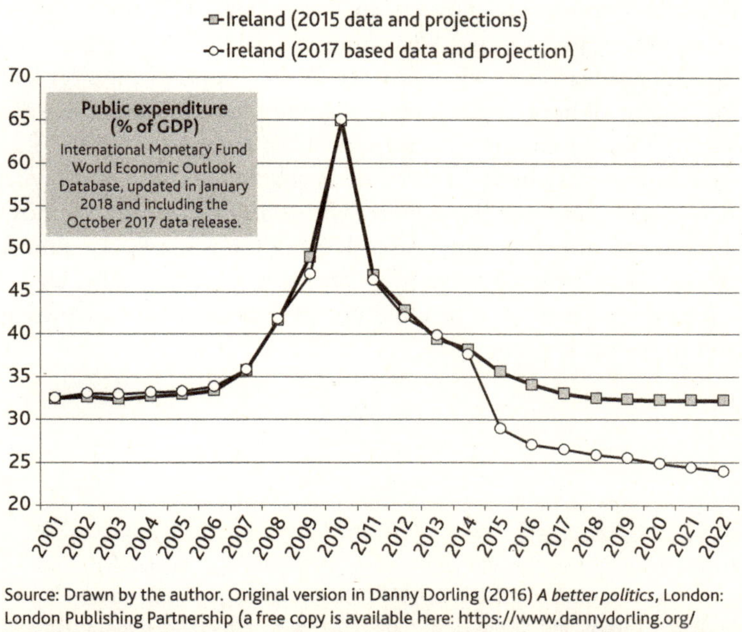

Source: Drawn by the author. Original version in Danny Dorling (2016) *A better politics*, London: London Publishing Partnership (a free copy is available here: https://www.dannydorling.org/books/betterpolitics/), and subsequently revised with updated data from the IMF in January 2018 (sources in figure, and originally found at: http://www.imf.org/external/pubs/ft/weo/2015/02/weodata/index.aspx).

the government's responses to the banking crisis in Ireland was to offer low tax incentives to overseas firms to base their European headquarters there. Tax takes did not rise much as a result, but as GDP did, public expenditure as a proportion of GDP began to be artificially deflated. Almost everyone, who could, stopped buying art; but there was still something very odd occurring in the Emerald Isle.

[Editorial note: In 1998 the United Nations had reported:

> Ireland has the second highest concentration of poor people in the western world … The report focuses on the gap between rich and poor which is remarkably wide in comparison to most other industrialised countries. According to the report more than one in seven people in Ireland are living in poverty. Only the United States is worse.[8]

In 2023 it was stated: 'More than 89,000 children [1 in 13] were living in "consistent" poverty in Ireland in 2022, up by more than 40% in just a year.'[9] That report continued to explain that the Central Statistics Office in Ireland 'also found that almost half (43.5%) of all households with one adult with children under the age of 18 are living in deprivation. That compares to 17.7% in two-parent households.' Thus, one in six children in Ireland with two parents, and half those living with only one parent, are now poor at any one time, and one in 13 children is now poor almost all the time, with all these proportions now rising. The UK is worse than this as far as its child poverty statistics are concerned; and in so much more.]

8 Joe Little (1998) 'Ireland and poverty 1998', RTÉ, 9 September, https://www.rte.ie/archives/2023/0909/1401274-warning-to-tackle-poverty/

9 Ann Murphy and David Kent (2023) 'More than 89,000 children living in "consistent" poverty in 2022', *The Irish Examiner*, 23 February, https://www.irishexaminer.com/news/arid-41077982.html

CHAPTER 3.2

Short cuts on homelessness[1]

Today, one person in every 200 in England and Wales is homeless – either sleeping rough or living in temporary accommodation.[2] In London the proportion is even higher: one in 53. In Kensington and Chelsea, it's one in 29.[3] In that borough alone, 5,263 people are homeless. They are mostly not the same people as the homeless who were there last year. Most of those will have moved on to another area; some will still be homeless, some will have found housing of some kind, and some will be dead.

The number of homeless people started to increase around 2010 with the implementation of austerity. Between 2010 and 2011 the numbers living in temporary housing or on the street doubled in seven London boroughs.[4] This pattern wasn't confined to London: nationally, homelessness doubled and doubled and

---

1 First published as 'Short cuts (homelessness)' in *London Review of Books*, 20 December 2018, 40, 24, p. 14, https://www.lrb.co.uk/the-paper/v40/n24, and also here: https://www.lrb.co.uk/the-paper/v40/n24/danny-dorling/short-cuts

2 Patrick Butler (2018) 'At least 320,000 homeless people in Britain, says Shelter', *The Guardian*, 22 November, https://www.theguardian.com/society/2018/nov/22/at-least-320000-homeless-people-in-britain-says-shelter

3 Lucy Dyer (2018) 'Homeless levels in London's richest borough branded "shocking"', *South West Londoner*, 30 November, https://www.swlondoner.co.uk/news/30112018-homeless-levels-in-londons-richest-borough-branded-shocking-by-charity-boss

4 Shelter (2012) 'Homelessness figures up 18%', Press release, 8 March: 'In seven London boroughs the number of homeless households more than doubled over twelve months, with the biggest rise in Hounslow at 245%'

doubled again. You could argue that the census form should start to ask: 'Have you ever been homeless, and, if so, when and for how long?' It is not a question that has been put before. But census questions do change over time. The last time people were asked if they had hot running water in their home was in 1971.

We expect progress, but we don't always get it. Many children spent last Christmas in a single room with a microwave in a B&B.[5] In the first quarter of this year, 123,130 children in England were living in temporary accommodation. That figure has been rising every year for a decade; it's up nearly 80 per cent since 2011. Ten years ago, in January 2009, it was so low that housing charities were focusing instead on children living in overcrowded conditions.[6]

In the 12 months to October, 449 homeless people died on the streets or in temporary accommodation, the highest proportion in January.[7] A fifth were women; the gender of a tenth of the bodies could not immediately be determined. The annual number of homeless deaths has risen at least tenfold in the past five years, far more quickly than the increase in rough sleeping.

Why did homelessness rise so quickly after 2010? The problem is not a shortage of housing. The 2011 Census confirmed that there are enough houses in the UK, and that there are more bedrooms in these houses than ever before. Even in London, there are more bedrooms in houses and flats than there are people to sleep in them. There are, for the first time, enough bedrooms for everyone in the UK to have their own.

---

https://web.archive.org/web/20130604035601/http://england.shelter.org.uk/news/previous_years/2012/march_2012/homelessness_up_18

5 Shelter (2017) '128,000 children in Britain will be homeless on Christmas day', Press release, 6 December, https://england.shelter.org.uk/media/press_releases/articles/128,000_children_in_britain_will_be_homeless_on_christmas_day

6 Shelter, 'Overcrowding figures up', Press release, 29 January 2009, https://england.shelter.org.uk/news/previous_years/2009/january_2009

7 Patrick Greenfield, Sarah Marsh and Maeve McClenaghan (2018) 'At least 440 homeless people died in UK in past year, study shows', *The Guardian*, 8 October, https://www.theguardian.com/society/2018/oct/08/homeless-people-die-uk-2017

Since 1981 housing in England and Wales has been increasingly unevenly shared out. For the 60 years between the censuses of 1921 and 1981, as well as new housing being built each decade, the housing stock was better distributed at the end of each decade than at its start. In every census fewer homes were found to be empty or underoccupied or overcrowded than in the one before. A rising proportion of the housing stock was allocated on the basis of need. Families were offered council houses with a suitable number of rooms. In the private market, as incomes became more and more equitable, behaviour changed. People were more likely to buy homes closer to the size they needed, instead of much larger ones. Meanwhile, the inefficient private rental sector shrank.

We know that 1981 was a turning point because of work done by Rebecca Tunstall of the University of York. She found that around this time the number of empty rooms in privately owned homes started to rise rapidly. As income inequality widened, more rich people purchased holiday houses and city pads, making it harder for locals to afford homes. After Margaret Thatcher implemented her 'Right-to-Buy' policy in the 1980s, public housing stock – especially of more desirable properties – decreased, and so fewer homes were allocated on the basis of need, since councils owned fewer properties and weren't allowed to build more. A maisonette that would once have been home to a family of four became the property of a single 'yuppie'; between the early 1970s and today, the proportion of one-person households has risen from 17 per cent to 28 per cent.

The situation worsened in the 1990s, but the steepest increase in wasted housing space came during the New Labour years, between the censuses of 2001 and 2011. By 2011 the richest tenth of households in England and Wales had five times as many rooms in their homes, per person, as the poorest tenth. There was no longer any slack in the housing system. A much larger proportion of the few homes coming onto the market in the years after the 2008 crash were being bought by private landlords. Rent rose to whatever level the market could take. Homelessness duly began to rise in 2010.

One of the first pieces of legislation the coalition government passed when it came to power in 2010 was a Bill amending Empty

Dwelling Management Orders. The New Labour government had introduced these to enable local councils to take possession of disused properties and make them habitable. Any property that had been empty for six months could have an order applied to it. The scheme had been introduced in 2006 when homeless rates were low and had helped them stay that way. Only a hundred or so orders were made while Labour was in power, but landlords knew they existed and made sure that their properties weren't left empty. The coalition extended the length of time a landlord could leave a property empty in England from six months to two years. The next year only 17 homes had orders applied to them and many thousands of properties were left empty.[8] By 2015, some 600,000 properties in England were empty, but continued to make money as house prices rose. There has been a huge increase in evictions at the end of tenancies, the result of relentless rent increases. A quarter of all children in England live in properties owned by a private landlord, and their families have on average just two months secure tenancy. Their parents are paying more per square metre to be housed than any other group. Tenancies coming to an end are the main driver of the increase in street homelessness.

When he was housing minister, Brandon Lewis, now Conservative Party chairman, said that the compulsory purchase of disused property was 'an ineffective and unpopular policy of the last administration, which undermined civil liberties and which simply didn't work'. Lewis held the job until July 2016, when he was replaced by Gavin Barwell. Less than a year later Barwell was replaced by Alok Sharma. After less than seven months, Sharma was replaced by Dominic Raab. Raab lasted six months before giving way to Kit Malthouse. In 2004, as deputy leader of Westminster Council, Malthouse had introduced the policy of using police officers to help street cleaners hose down areas where homeless people slept.[9] In December 2017, the Public Accounts

---

[8] Hilary Osborne (2015) 'Powers to bring empty houses into use "ignored"', *The Guardian*, 11 February, https://www.theguardian.com/money/2015/feb/11/powers-empty-houses-ignored-empty-dwelling-management

[9] Rachel Wearmouth (2018) 'New Housing Minister Kit Malthouse admitted making homeless people's lives "uncomfortable"', *The Huffington Post*,

Committee announced that as many as 9,100 people were sleeping rough on any one night in England. 'The Department for Communities and Local Government's attitude to reducing homelessness has been unacceptably complacent,' it said. 'The limited action that it has taken has lacked the urgency that is so badly needed and its "light touch" approach to working with the local authorities tackling homelessness has clearly failed.'[10]

What is to be done? A few schemes are being piloted, often poor copies of ones that have worked elsewhere, for example in Finland, where homelessness is low and falling. But the dominant narrative in this country tells of the perceived failures of those who become street homeless: their alcohol dependency, substance misuse and 'high/complex needs'. I saw my first dead body when I was a child, walking to the pantomime in Oxford in the early 1980s. My father told me that the man was sleeping, but he wasn't. I remember us staying with the body and how long it took for the ambulance to arrive. They were in no rush. I remember that we were late for the show. I couldn't see the man's face – only his coat and hair.

[Editorial note: Three years after this article was written, by December 2021, and after the 'Everyone In' policy on homelessness introduced during the worst years of the pandemic, the rate of homelessness in Kensington and Chelsea was the very same as that reported in this article in 2018: 1 in 29. However, some things had changed. Of the 170,000 people who were homeless in London in 2021, children were now the majority. In response, 'A Government spokesperson said it had committed more than £2 billion in funding over the next three years (2022–2024) and claimed that tackling homelessness was an "absolute

9 July (updated 11 July), https://www.huffingtonpost.co.uk/entry/new-housing-minister-kitmalthouse-operated-callous-policy-to-make-life-more-uncomfortable-for-rough-sleepers_uk_5b43895fe4b07aea7542aa1a

10 Public Accounts Committee (2017) 'Government's complacent attitude has failed homeless, 78,000 households are homeless', House of Commons Select Committee Report, 20 December, http://www.parliament.uk/business/committees/committees-a-z/commonsselect/public-accounts-committee/news-parliament-2017/homelesshouseholds-report-published-17-19/

priority".'[11] Two years later, the number of homeless people in London was even higher still, having risen by 17,000 in one year. At the start of the new school year in 2023, one child in every classroom in London schools was living in emergency accommodation.[12] The London press began to feature more pictures of homeless camps. Most people who die homeless are young, some are very young.[13] By summer 2024, the situation was worsening rapidly yet again.]

[11] ITV News (2021) 'Almost 90,000 children among "rising tide" of London homeless', *ITV London*, 9 December, https://www.itv.com/news/london/2021-12-09/almost-90000-children-among-rising-tide-of-london-homeless

[12] Adriana Elgueta and Aurelia Foster (2023) 'One in 50 Londoners homeless and in emergency homes – London Councils', *BBC News*, 3 August, https://www.bbc.co.uk/news/uk-england-london-66387577

[13] See: 'About the Dying Homeless Project', https://museumofhomelessness.org/dhp

CHAPTER 3.3

How to solve the housing crisis[1]

'I'll build houses for your children!' said the man with the microphone at the front of the packed hall. No one had really been able to see the slides he had shown, but the images were colourful from a distance. They were artists' drawings of the proposed new development: images suggesting that it would not greatly affect the view from the city and would be built below the 'ridge line'. It would all be constructed to the highest of environmental standards, he said. 'We have to build for the next generation,' he explained. 'Any questions?' I put my hand up. Eventually I was chosen. 'My children will not be able to afford your houses,' I said. 'Is that why you will not say how much they will cost?' He looked at me partly in pity, partly in annoyance. Some of the audience laughed as they knew I was a professor in the city, and they realised that the property developer was assuming I was poor.

But it was true. The housing he was planning to build would not be for any of our children, not even mine. He wasn't going to tell us the price. He knew that he planned to sell these new-build homes to whomever would give him the most money. He knew that this would not be anyone in the room, let alone any of their children. But he needed to try to minimise our complaints for when he sought planning permission. He had to be able to say that he had consulted the 'local community'. Even he did not realise that inequalities had risen so high that the

[1] First published in *Tribune Magazine*, 23 July 2019, pp. 75–9, https://tribunemag.co.uk/issue/summer-2019 and at https://tribunemag.co.uk/2019/08/chests-of-gold-and-silver

children of a university professor would not be able to afford to live in the city they had grown up in. Not unless they had some huge inheritance.

In the more affluent parts of the UK, money is made from building large, detached homes for people who commute to another city, or who simply buy one as an investment. The big money cannot be made out of the little people. It cannot even be made out of the average or even those much better off anymore. Income inequalities have risen decade after decade, wealth inequalities have reached astronomical levels, and almost all the 'spare' money is now held by the extremely well-off. The extremely well-off have become 'the market'.

The man standing at the front slicked back his hair. Most of the objections he had heard in the hall had been from elderly and better-off people complaining that his development might spoil their views. This was what he wanted. He wanted to present himself as the champion of the underdog, the provider of homes for the young. It soon became apparent that who exactly would get those homes and at what price was none of our business – that was for 'the market' to decide. What he had to do was to ensure he was allowed to play in that market. He had to get permission to build. He was a property speculator, and this was what he did best. He looked rather pleased with himself.

Learning to love taxation

How do you stop speculation? How do you ensure that homes are built for the people who need them? How do you make sure that the homes that exist are well-occupied? That particular planning meeting was mostly populated by well-off elderly people who, when not attending meetings such as these, rattle around in what was once a large family's house, watching the value of 'their' property rise and objecting to any development nearby that might damage their accrued wealth.

These wealthy older people only partly want to protect their wealth for themselves and their cruise holidays. They are also worried about their children and grandchildren and want to pass on as much as they can when they die. They see it as in their interests to do whatever they can to both maximise the price of their own homes and minimise the taxation their children might have to pay on what they inherit. They have been taught that being selfish is good and tax is bad. This is, after all, the generation that saw a prime minister pronounce that 'there is no such thing as society', fight a political war over that premise, and win. But the truth is the very opposite. Taxation is a social good – and it is our most powerful tool to solve the housing crisis. Short of a command-and-control economy, it has only ever been through effective taxation that cities have been well planned. Taxation preserves choice but deters speculation. Should your motive be to build to amass great profits, but you know that such profits might be properly taxed, you will not bother to build and someone else with far better motives than you will build in your place.

Where homes are well taxed, people try to fit into them efficiently. The more people living in a home, the more there are to share the paying of the local property tax. And where a local property tax is made progressive, where it rises continuously (and preferably exponentially) with the value of the property, there is an incentive not to live in the most expensive property you can.

One factor that matters greatly is how property tax assessments are determined and how that process is influenced politically. An efficient system is one that ensures that the tax is actually being applied to the true value of the land and property upon it. One useful way to ensure this is for the state to have the power to compulsorily purchase property at the value it has been assessed for taxation. This gives owners an incentive to declare that their property is worth more and to volunteer to pay more property tax.

New property taxes are introduced from time to time and show what is possible. Since 2013 in Ireland, the national property tax has been 0.18 per cent of a property's value per year. Thus, on a property worth €300,000, the owner has to pay €540 a year in addition to all other taxes. However, for properties valued at over €1 million, the rate is 0.25 per cent a year on any value over that million. This means that someone living in a property worth €1.3 million would pay €3,040 a year. Someone on a low income in an expensive property that they own outright would have no problem paying this tax, if they secured a small mortgage on it – a mortgage that could be repaid when the home is sold.

The new rates in Ireland are quite low and 90 per cent of properties are worth less than €300,000, so most Irish residents pay only €90 to €495 a year. There is clearly a great deal of scope to raise these taxes if a government wants to get property prices and speculation under control. Prices are currently rising rapidly in Dublin, not least because of Brexit. However, a further slight increase to property taxes would soon soften that rise. Wealth taxes such as this are also progressive because they reduce inequalities in the future, meaning that the rich inherit less through the taxation's effect in dampening prices.

In New Hampshire in the US, property taxes range from 0.21 per cent to 0.41 per cent a year, as a proportion of the value of the home and according to the county it is in. Critics argue that these 'high' taxes mean a big and inefficient government. In reality, Americans have very little opportunity to get to know what a big government actually is. All of the US has small government: in general, taxes are lower than in almost any other affluent country, and public services are generally poor as a result. This especially harms education, and Americans are generally at the bottom of international league tables of ability in mathematics (Figure 3.11). In almost all other affluent nations in the world,

Figure 3.11: Economic inequality and the maths ability of young adults up to age 24, 2012

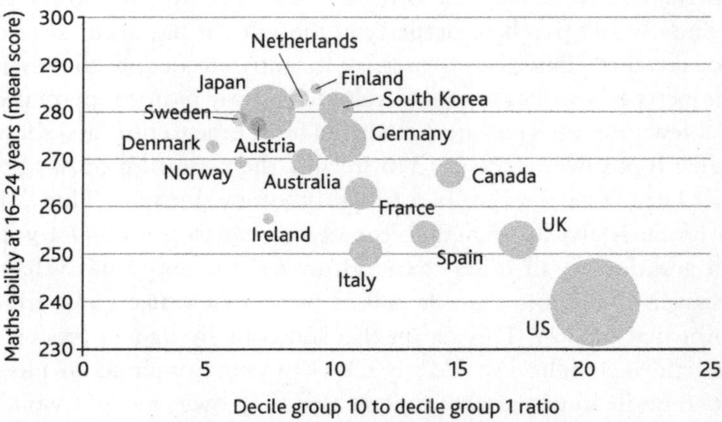

Source: Danny Dorling (2017) *The equality effect: Improving life for everyone*, Oxford: New Internationalist, Figure 4.14, https://dannydorling.org/books/equalityeffect/material/

schools are not funded by local property taxes: they are funded nationally, so that poor areas do not get poorly funded schools.

In the Netherlands, one of the countries with the most numerate populations in the world (see Figure 3.11), property is taxed at around 0.1 per cent to 0.3 per cent a year. Second and subsequent homes, however, are assumed to have an annual yield of about 4 per cent. This is taxed at 30 per cent a year, meaning each second home property in the country incurs a total tax of about 1.2 per cent of its value of per year. In the Netherlands, children become numerate, the old live longer and land is efficiently used. You don't leave a second home empty when you have to pay such a tax on it.

In the US, the popular narrative is that taxation and freedom are opposites. In reality, taxation *is* freedom, because it is taken from everyone. It is the very opposite of theft. Theft is about individual loss and a criminal act. Taxation is everyone's gain. When property and land is well taxed, its value does not rise and rise with speculation; homes instead become affordable and local schools and hospitals are well funded. No one loses out because the affluent are still able to live in the same kind of apartments as they do elsewhere; the apartments just cost less to buy in the first place.

In contrast, where property is not well taxed it tends to rise exponentially in value. The property in some regions and some parts of cities becomes worth much more than in other parts. Before you know it, walls are being built around more affluent estates, to separate the children from the poorer end of the road from those at the richer end. At the extreme these walls can be eight feet high and topped with metal spikes sharp enough to kill a child. Figure 3.12 shows just such a wall was built in 1934 in my home town of Oxford.

Without taxation of property, social divides increase, walls begin to be built ever higher and the fear of others grows. Determining what level of taxation is best and how it can best be collected is not easy, but you can tell from the social outcome when you are getting it right. Taxation is a tool to find freedom, improve housing, enhance education and ensure good health.

When people begin to see their freedom to choose increase; when most know they might really be able to choose where to

Figure 3.12: One of the two Cutteslowe walls dividing streets in Oxford from 1934 to 1959

Source: 'One of the Cutteslowe Walls, between Wolsey and Carlton Roads, taken before demolition, in March 1959', see: https://heritagesearch.oxfordshire.gov.uk/images/POX0108730

live in the city; when there is a greater mix of people and housing along a road, and also within almost all neighbourhoods; then you know something is working well.

If you want to see the greatest housing success in the world, then travel to Japan and see how Tokyo works, or smaller cities like Kyoto. In Japan, the annual property tax is about 1.4 per cent of the value of property. Over and above that, there is a municipal tax of around 0.3 per cent. Furthermore, to quote the local press, 'empty land is taxed at a higher rate than land that has a residential structure on it, just as land designated for agriculture is taxed at a higher rate if it is not being used to grow something'.[2] Societies with lower income inequalities and better property taxes tend to

[2] Masako Tsubuku and Philip Brasor (2012) 'The rise and fall of property taxes', *The Japan Times*, 3 January, https://www.japantimes.co.jp/community/2012/01/03/how-tos/the-rise-and-fall-of-property-taxes/

almost always be better housed, better educated and have better health than those that do not.

In the UK, one of the most unequal countries in the rich world, people are at a loss as to how to solve the housing crisis. 'Section 106' agreements are now used to build the bulk of any so-called affordable housing, which is only done at the whim of property owners and developers. Taxation is still seen as a social bad, profit as good, and there is a 'this is as good as it gets' attitude to what might be possible. In Canada, both Toronto and Vancouver now levy 15 per cent taxes on foreign buyers to start to address speculation by overseas investors. As yet London shows no signs of even considering such a move.

The UK government says it can't introduce a property tax like Ireland's that covers all property, because they have not quite got around to registering all properties in Britain. This is particularly the case for those that have not changed hands for a few hundred years or more. It is always easy to come up with such excuses. The Irish suddenly taxed all their property when the economic crises of 2008–09 forced them to. They created a register of all property in Ireland in little over a year. Google Earth has many uses!

The housing pendulum

Property taxation is not only good for the less well-off, and for society as a whole. It is also a mechanism for protecting the affluent from folly. Land and property speculation both inevitably end in disaster. Many people find this impossible to believe, and that is part of the reason why prices can rise so high.

'Surely central London will always be one of the most desirable places on the planet?' they say. They forget what central London was like in the 1980s. They also forget that it is a major financial city in a country that is now in relative economic decline. They forget that in the early 1990s, the prices of homes almost halved in central Tokyo in just a few years. But, most importantly, they forget the stories from the beginning of capitalism. Our current way of living began in Amsterdam in the 16th century, and that city provides the most serious warning of what happens when speculation is not controlled.

Today the Dutch live in a country with one of the lowest rates of income inequality. Life expectancy is high and rising. People are well housed and a majority of the population walks and cycles to work. How was this achieved in the cradle of capitalism? One answer is that the Dutch have had far longer to learn from their earlier mistakes, especially those mistakes that concerned property.

In Amsterdam there was euphoria in the early 1700s. The power that Spain had held over South America for over 200 years had been waning. Some Dutch merchants began to invest in companies designed to exploit the new power vacuum and profit from increased trade with the Americas. All went well for a few decades. Amsterdam was already an incredibly rich city, and it began to teeter towards dizzying new heights of affluence.

The United Provinces (with Amsterdam at their centre) had seen the founding of the Dutch East India Company a century before, in 1602. Within decades, that private company had come to dominate trade with New Guinea, Borneo, Sumatra and Java. The Dutch had colonies in the Caribbean, in Brazil and in what is still known as Manhattan. Manhattan was an American development that was commissioned by the Dutch East India Company after the *Halve Maen* sailed from Amsterdam and dropped anchor in a convenient harbour in 1609. It only became part of a larger 'New York' when the English took it by force in 1664. But the English didn't really own it for long. Four years later the Dutch stadtholder William III, Prince of Orange invaded England in what came to be called the Glorious Revolution. The Dutch were far more important in the pasts of both the US and the UK than is commonly recognised.

At the start of the 18th century, Amsterdam was on top of the world. But then, around 1738, there was a sudden loss of confidence and a financial crisis ensued. House prices in the Herengracht, one of Amsterdam's most expensive streets, peaked that year and subsequently fell by a third in real terms by 1751. The market rallied a little to a new peak in 1778 '… and then not again for 250 years [from 1738 to 1988]', according to Neil Monnery's 2011 book *Safe as Houses*: 'The middle of the eighteenth century marked the beginning of a period of plodding decline that would continue for the next two centuries.' After being at the top of the world, the fall can take a very long time.

Housing prices can fall, and have fallen for more than 200 years in the very centre of Amsterdam. Think about that. That will happen again in other parts of the world, especially the parts that are today most overheated. The end result need not be disaster – in this case, it resulted in the most densely populated large country in Europe, relying on planning and taxation to bring about some of the highest levels of freedom experienced anywhere on the planet. Freedom is what equality and justice brings.

★

Back in Oxford, the man with the slicked-back hair was wrapping up the meeting in the community hall. He was about to go on to get permission from the local planners to develop what would soon be some of the most expensive homes to ever be built on the edge of the city where I live and work, where I grew up, where my parents were young adults and where my grandfather once lived, and where my children will never be able to settle down unless everything changes. He had the audience where he wanted them, opposing his housing not because it would be unaffordable, but because they were NIMBYs.[3] Someone asked him what all the rush was about. Why, after all these centuries, did his firm of property developers, and the Oxford college that owned the fields on the edge of the city, want to build now?

'Corbyn,' he muttered and then looked embarrassed, as if he had let something slip that he should not have. A few months earlier, the shadow housing minister John Healey had announced:

> We will build for those who need it, including the very poorest and most vulnerable, with a big boost to new social rented homes. We will also build Labour's new affordable homes for those in work on ordinary incomes who are priced out of the housing market and being failed by housing policy.

[3] [Editorial note: NIMBY is the acronym for Not In My Back Yard – an American phrase for someone who refuses to agree to necessary facilities being located near to them.]

Two months prior to that, the Labour Party had said how it would get the land for these new homes. News reports used negative framing in articles like this one, which was subtitled 'Party proposes raid …', to explain that:

> Labour is considering forcing landowners to give up sites for a fraction of their current price in an effort to slash the cost of council house building. The proposal has been drawn up by Healey and would see a Jeremy Corbyn-led government change the law so landowners would have to sell sites to the state at knockdown prices. Landowners currently sell at a price that factors in the dramatic increase in value when planning consent is granted. It means a hectare of agricultural land worth around £20,000 can sell for closer to £2 million if it is zoned for housing.[4]

A Labour government would take the land, pay just £20,000 an acre, and build the homes.

The man needed to build now, because after another election it might well be too late for him to make his profit. Rather than a few large, detached houses being built on those fields on the edge of Oxford, the space could be used for social housing. To his mind this was the worst kind of housing of all – good-quality social housing with views into the city; housing that meant that, given a choice between renting securely and having a mortgage, you might actually choose to rent.

Housing that would help housing prices fall.

Housing that was a home.

Sometimes the pendulum swings.

---

[4] Robert Booth (2018) 'Labour plans to make landowners sell to state for fraction of value: party proposes raid on private land to cut cost of building new council houses', *The Guardian*, 1 February, https://www.theguardian.com/politics/2018/feb/01/labour-plans-landowners-sell-state-fraction-value

CHAPTER 3.4

Public spending in the UK and Europe[1]

For many years the UK, and almost all other states in the world, have been reporting the amount they spend on public services, and what they expect to spend in future, to the International Monetary Fund (IMF). The three graphs in this article report those figures, first for the UK alone, then for the UK and the four other most populous European countries, and finally for another ten affluent Western European countries. This is to provide a much wider comparison. But first consider the UK alone, illustrated in Figure 3.13.

Over time public spending in the UK appears to have been rising, and this is true. But it is only true more recently because of two great economic shocks: the banking crisis of 2008 and the pandemic of 2020. Bailing out the banks, increasing and servicing public borrowing, and paying for a huge 'moon-shot' track-and-trace system all count as public spending, as well as furlough payments and so much more. Public spending includes the NHS, state education, state pensions and local government, but also the armed forces and many other outgoings often not thought of as public spending. For example, the rise in the early 2000s in the graph shown here was due in part to military spending to pay for the UK's involvement in the Iraq war.

Public spending in the great recession of the early 1980s rose as unemployment grew and peaked at three million people out of work. Most had to rely almost entirely on state benefits. Spending then fell for the rest of the 1980s as the Conservative

---

1 Originally published as 'Public spending in the UK, and elsewhere in Europe, 1980–2026', *Public Sector Focus*, May/June 2021, pp. 16–19.

Figure 3.13: Public spending in the UK as a share of GDP (%), 1980–2019, projected to 2026

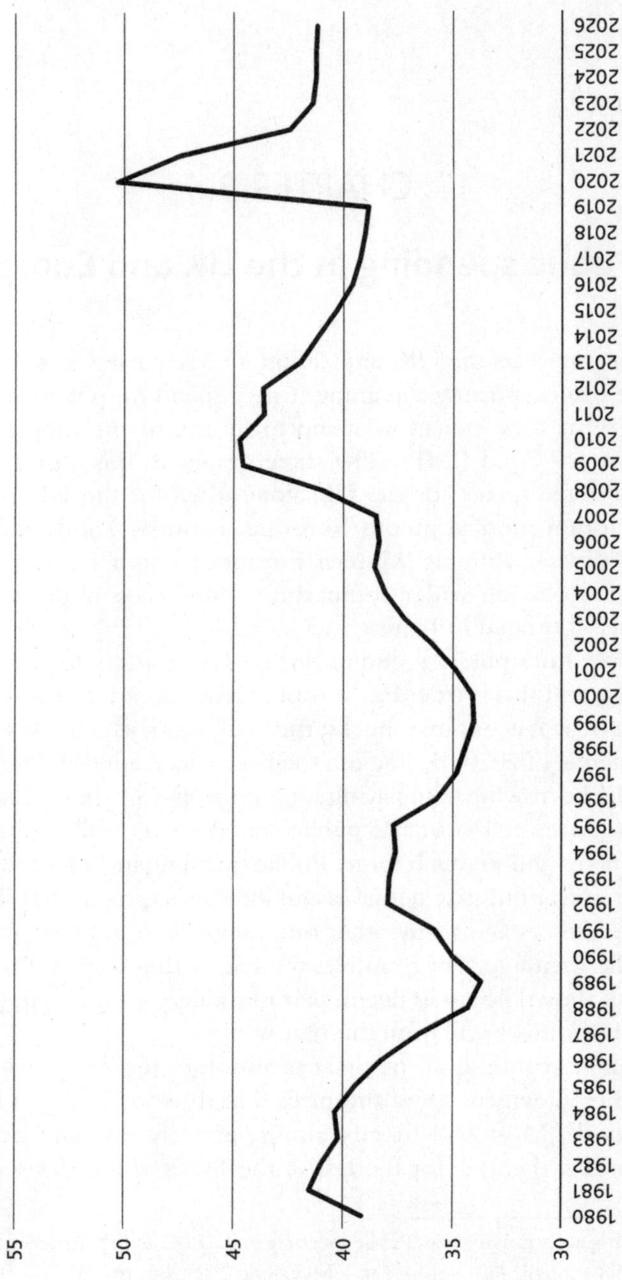

Source: International Monetary Fund, World Economic Outlook Database, April 2021, variable GGX_NGDP: General government total expenditure as a proportion of GDP

government made cut after cut to health and education spending and tried to privatise as much as it could. Public spending rose in the early 1990s when there was another, smaller recession, and again a rise in unemployment. It then rose during the New Labour years partly as spending on health was improved, but also because of war. However, it was cut extremely deeply after 2010 by the coalition and then Conservative governments, who claimed that there was no alternative to deep austerity – until the pandemic hit.

UK public spending is now forecast to be cut to its lowest level yet in the years to come; and to only remain above 40 per cent by 2026 because of public spending on servicing the increase in public debt. Once that part is taken into account, austerity in the UK will be as great as before the pandemic – according to the figures the government submitted to the IMF – but is now to be enacted in a much shorter timeframe: with a cut of more than six percentage points of UK GDP planned for the three years between 2021 and 2024. In contrast, the cut that took place over ten years from 2009 to 2019 was less than six percentage points *in total.*

What of the rest of Europe? First, consider the other four largest European economies. Apart from when Spain was still emerging from the Franco dictatorship, all four have always chosen to spend a higher proportion of their GDP for the public good: on education, housing, health, pensions, welfare and so on (if not quite as much on their militaries). The second graph, Figure 3.14, shows how the UK's track record looks in comparison – it is the most miserly and is set to remain so.

There was a period in the mid- to late 2000s, and especially when Gordon Brown was chancellor (and then became prime minister), when public spending in the UK was almost as high as Spain's. In 2019 the Labour Party manifesto made spending promises that would have increased public spending to just below German levels, had all those promises been honoured by the end of five years in government. In the event, the Conservative government elected in 2019 was forced to increase public spending levels in the UK to far above the amount Germany had been spending in 2019; but not on things such as improving funding for British state schools to German state school funding see colour version in plate section

Figure 3.14: Public spending in the five most populous European countries as share of GDP (%), 1980–2019, projected to 2026

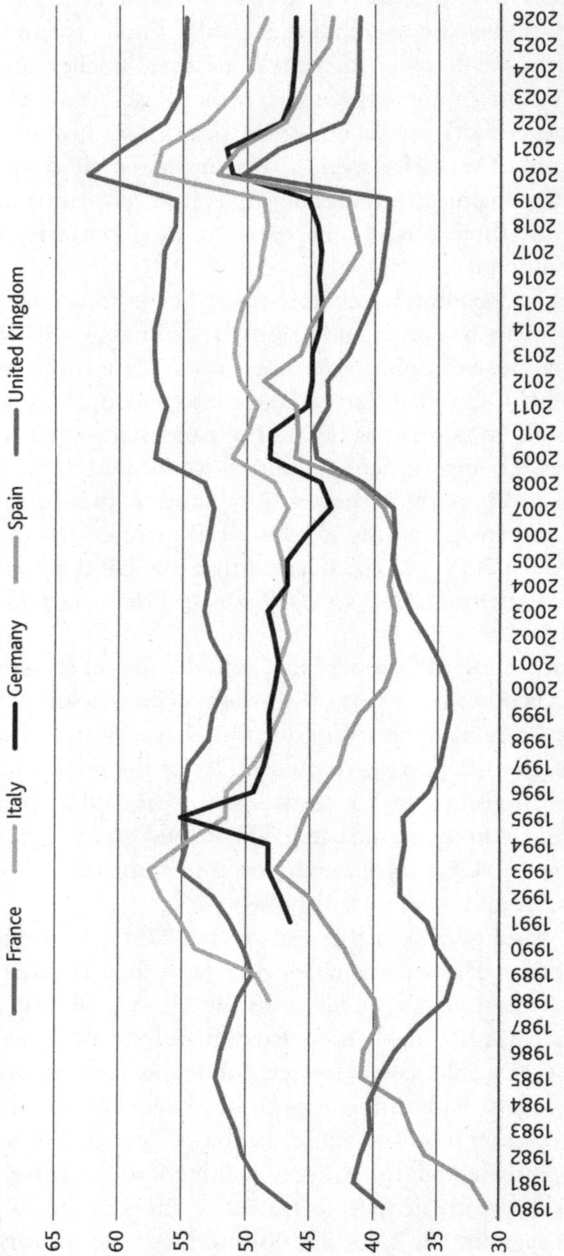

Note: The UK spends more on its armed forces than the other large nations of Europe, and only France also has nuclear weapons, so actually useful public spending is lower than shown.

Source: International Monetary Fund, World Economic Outlook Database, April 2021, variable GGX_NGDP: General government total expenditure as a proportion of GDP

levels, or funding the normal activity of the NHS at the level of German public health spending (where roughly a billion more euros are spent each week). Note how all the large European countries increased their public spending as a share of GDP by a remarkably similar amount in 2020; but how they all project slightly different falling trajectories in the projection up to 2026, with the UK sloping steepest downwards.

Note that Switzerland is not included in the comparison because it has an unusually high GDP-to-public spending ratio due to some global companies being nominally based there, or their profit repatriated there. Its public spending on health is amongst the very highest in Europe and yet its overall public spending as a proportion of GDP looks low. There are similar issues in the cases of Ireland, Luxembourg and San Marino.

Finally, is the UK still an outlier when smaller European countries are also included? Figure 3.15 adds another ten European countries, also drawn from more affluent Western Europe but not including some of the smallest countries in this region. It is again clear from this graph that the UK has been an outlier in Europe for many decades. Public spending in the UK has been so low for so long that it is only comparable to Spain's after the Franco era when it was just returning to democracy; and to public spending in Greece, but again only as it was becoming a democratic country following the military dictatorship of 1967–74. In some of its features the UK has behaved economically like a state that has been largely ruled for the past 50 years by a kind of non-democratic junta that sees public spending on services as something to be suppressed.

Figure 3.15 shows that France is not an outlier: Belgium and Finland spend just as much. Italy's spending is now similar to that of Norway, Denmark, Austria, Sweden and Greece. What this graph also shows is that Germany is, nowadays, a little miserly, though similar to the Netherlands. And Spain, which in most years spends a little less on its public services than Germany, is not dissimilar to its neighbour Portugal. All larger affluent countries in Western Europe have been, and will be, spending relatively more on the common good than the UK.

Public spending levels tend to track taxation. Internationally, those states that tax less, spend less. The majority of the

Figure 3.15: Public spending in 14 affluent European countries as share of GDP (%), 1980–2019, projected to 2026

see colour version in plate section

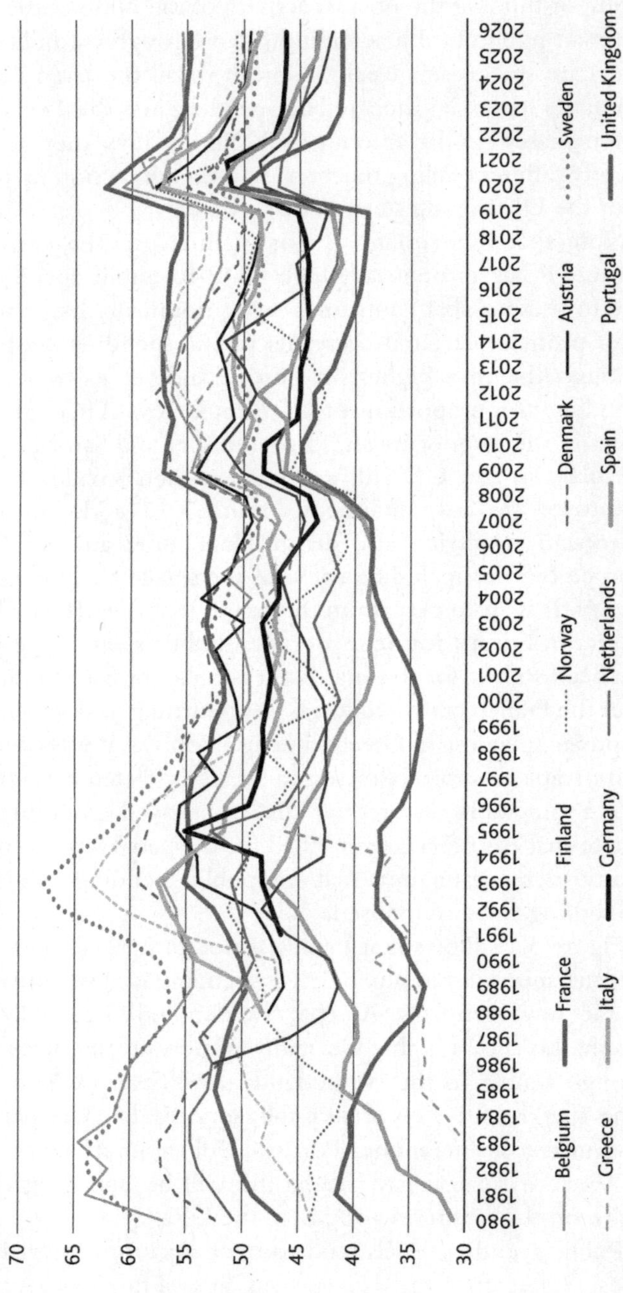

population have poorer-quality healthcare, schools and housing. Their universities, railways and water supplies are more often privatised. And their citizens suffer by being less well educated, living with poorer health, and being looked down on more often by those in control. Until the UK is a more democratic state with, for instance, a voting system with proportional representation that truly reflects the will of the people, it is likely that it will remain at the foot of these graphs. However, as the transition to a fuller and more just democracy has eventually happened for every other state shown in Figure 3.15, it might well be too pessimistic to think that it will never happen in the UK, and in all its regions.

CHAPTER 3.5

House prices: welcoming a crash[1]

British governments don't deliberately do things that negatively affect house prices. Instead, the booms that they have bolstered have usually inflated prices. We tend not to think about the long-term problems this creates. But we should reflect on it, because government actions that push prices higher make instability – and falls – more likely in the long term.

The British public today believes that house price falls are very unlikely. The last time there was a sustained drop in house prices over a period of as long as four years was after September 1989. That is such a long time ago that few people remember it. Indeed, few adults today know that the average UK house price did not return to its autumn 1989 level until 1998[2] – almost nine years later!

The superficial reason for the fall in house prices after 1989 was 'overheating' in the UK, accelerated by a rush among some homebuyers to purchase property before a particular form of tax relief for couples (MIRAS) was withdrawn by the government.[3] It was a very British house price crash. In contrast to 1989, the falls that came with the global financial crisis of 2008 are today better known and remembered.

---

1 Originally published as 'House prices: should we welcome a crash?', *UK in a Changing Europe*, 24 July 2021, https://ukandeu.ac.uk/house-prices-crash/

2 https://www.nationwide.co.uk/house-price-index/#xtab:regional-quarterly-series-all-properties-data-available-from-1973-onwards

3 https://en.wikipedia.org/wiki/Mortgage_interest_relief_at_source accessed 21 August 2023.

Figure 1.5: Migration of voters from 2017 to 2019, by 2016 referendum choice

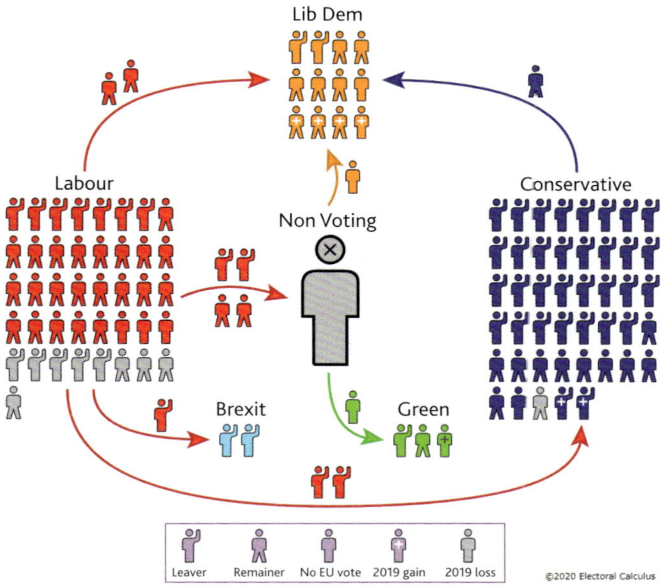

Source: Martin Baxter (2020) 'Voter migration by party 2017–2019', *Electoral Calculus*, 16 January, https://web.archive.org/web/20200219124319/https://www.electoralcalculus.co.uk/pseph_transition2019.html

Figure 1.6: Disaggregation of the population of the UK in 2019, by age and vote

The 2019 general election was the Brexit deciding election

Of the 66 million people living in the UK

- 20 million did not vote or were eligible but not registered to vote ●
- 14 million voted Conservative (365 seats of 650) ●●●●● ●●●●● ●●
- 12 million were children (and UK citizens) ●
- 10 million voted Labour (203 seats) ●●●●● ●●
- 4 million voted Liberal (11 seats) ●
- 3 million were not UK citizens ●
- 1 million voted in Northern Ireland (18 seats) ●
- 1 million voted Scottish National Party (48 seats) ● ●
- 1 million voted Green/Plaid or other (5 seats) ●

These 9 groups approximately assigned to 11 equal-sized age groups

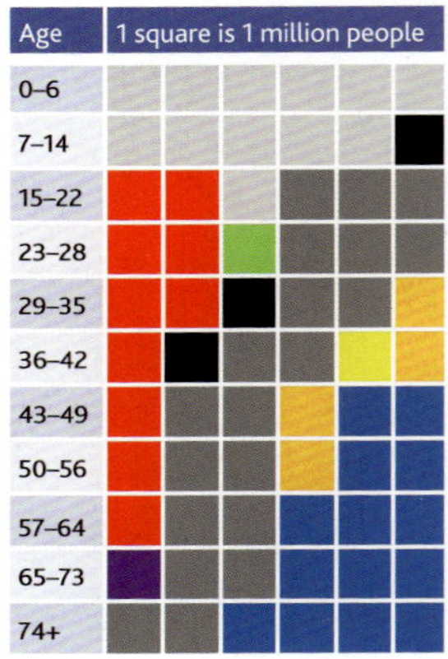

https://www.ipsos.com/ipsos-mori/en-uk/how-britain-voted-2019-election
https://blogs.lse.ac.uk/politicsandpolicy/young-cosmopolitans-and-ge2019/

Source: Drawn by the author as a simple summary of why age mattered so much to the outcome of the vote and the probability of not voting in 2019

Figure 1.7: Areas of high and low poverty in four significant seats in the 2019 general election

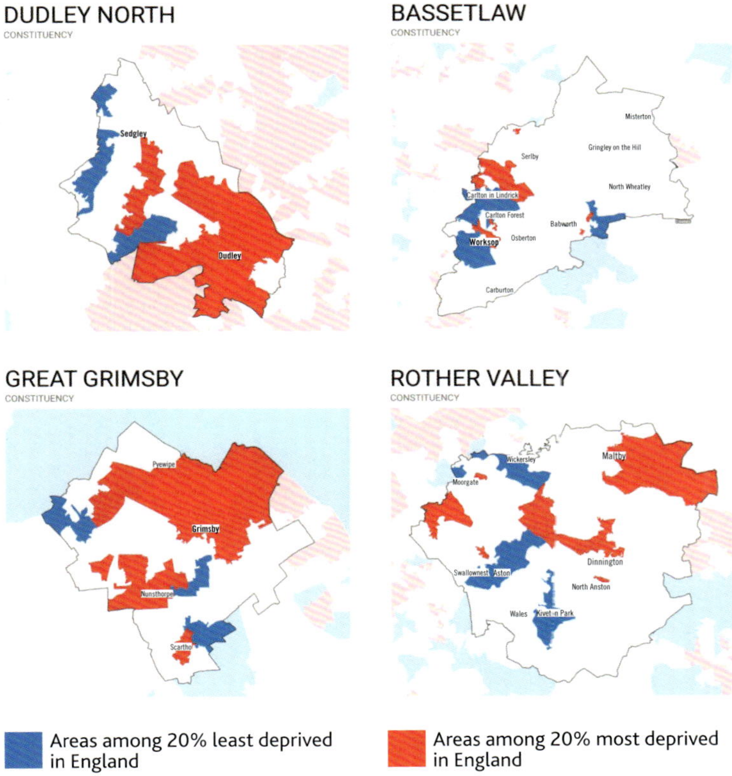

Source: Alasdair Rae and Elvis Nyanzu (2019) *An English atlas of inequality: Technical report*, University of Sheffield, https://www.researchgate.net/publication/348298341_An_English_Atlas_of_Inequality. (Analysis by Elvis Nyanzu and Alasdair Rae, University of Sheffield. This work was funded by the Nuffield Foundation, www.nuffieldfoundation.org.)

Figure 1.8: Areas where Labour, the Conservatives, the Liberal Democrats and the Greens do best

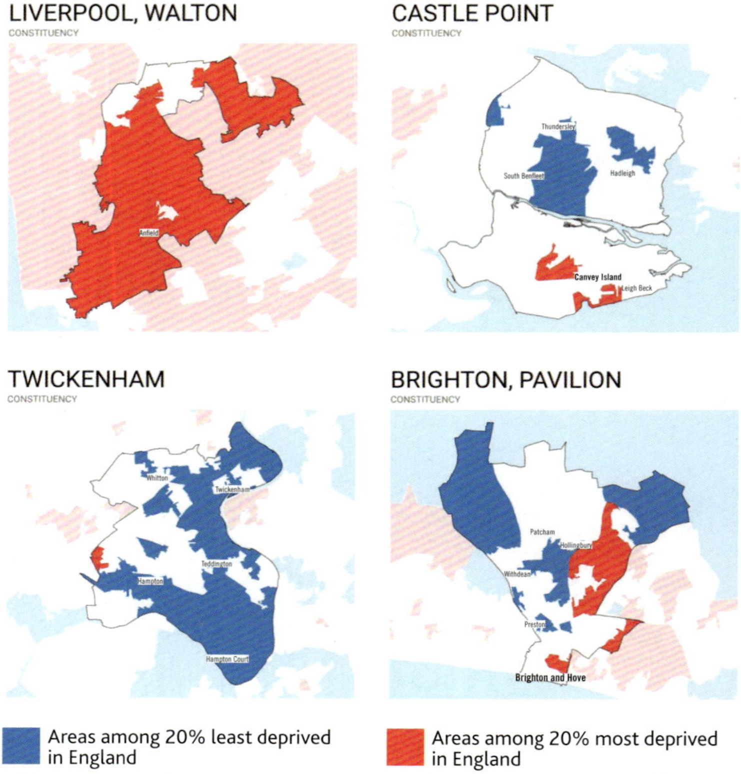

Source: Alasdair Rae and Elvis Nyanzu (2019) *An English atlas of inequality: Technical report*, University of Sheffield, https://www.researchgate.net/publication/348298341_An_English_Atlas_of_Inequality. (Analysis by Elvis Nyanzu and Alasdair Rae, University of Sheffield. This work was funded by the Nuffield Foundation, www.nuffieldfoundation.org.)

Figure 1.9: The new political map of the UK, drawn by the House of Commons

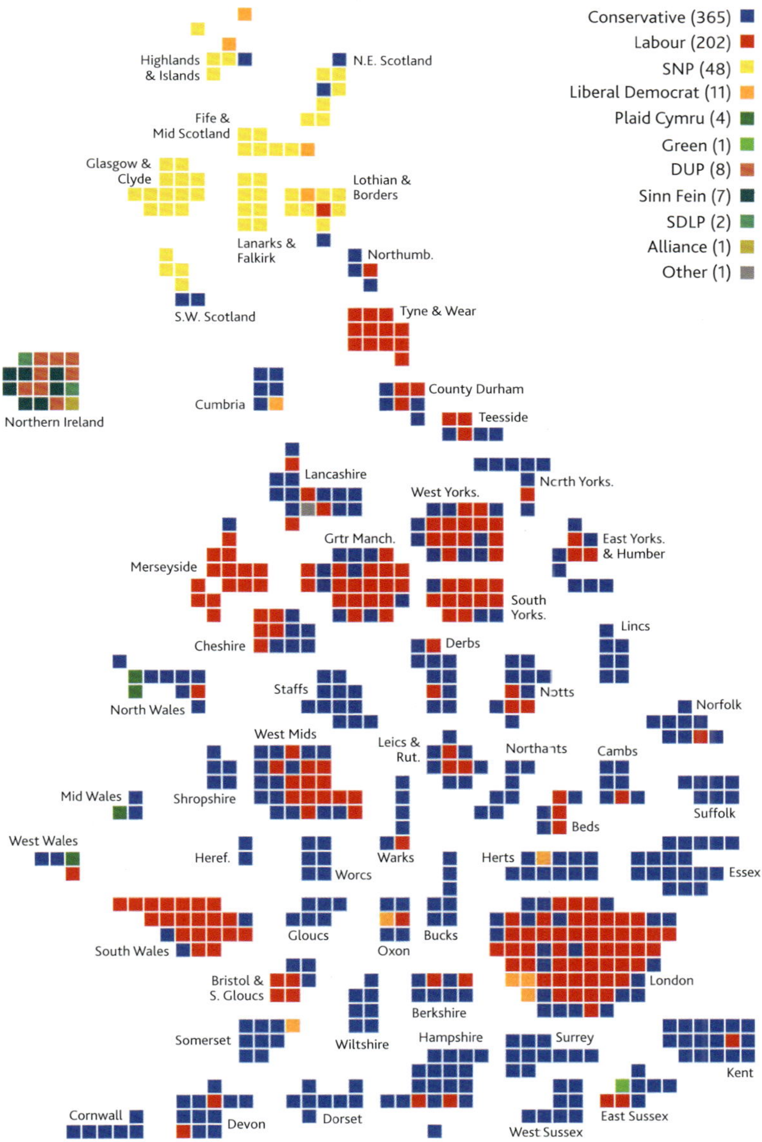

Source: Elise Uberoi, Carl Baker, Richard Cracknell, Grahame Allen, Nerys Roberts, Cassie Barton et al (2020) *General Election 2019: Results and analysis*, House of Commons Library, 28 January, contains Parliamentary information licensed under the Open Parliament Licence v3.0. https://researchbriefings.parliament.uk/ResearchBriefing/Summary/CBP-8749

Figure 1.17: Economic policies of almost all political parties in the world compared, left to right

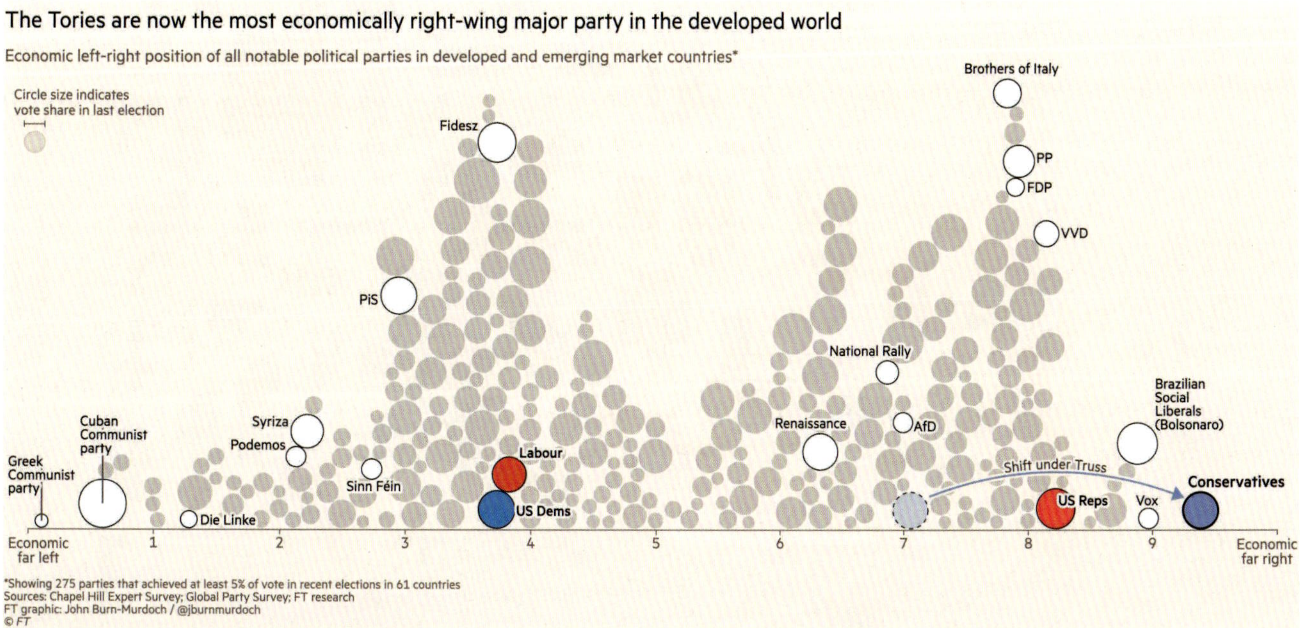

Note: Figure includes all the rich and mainstream world states.

Source: John Burn-Murdoch (2022) 'The Tories have become unmoored from the British people', *Financial Times*, 30 September. John Burn-Murdoch's graph: https://twitter.com/dannydorling/status/1575836071832604673?s=20

Figure 2.9: Local health outcomes predict Trumpward swings, 19 November 2016

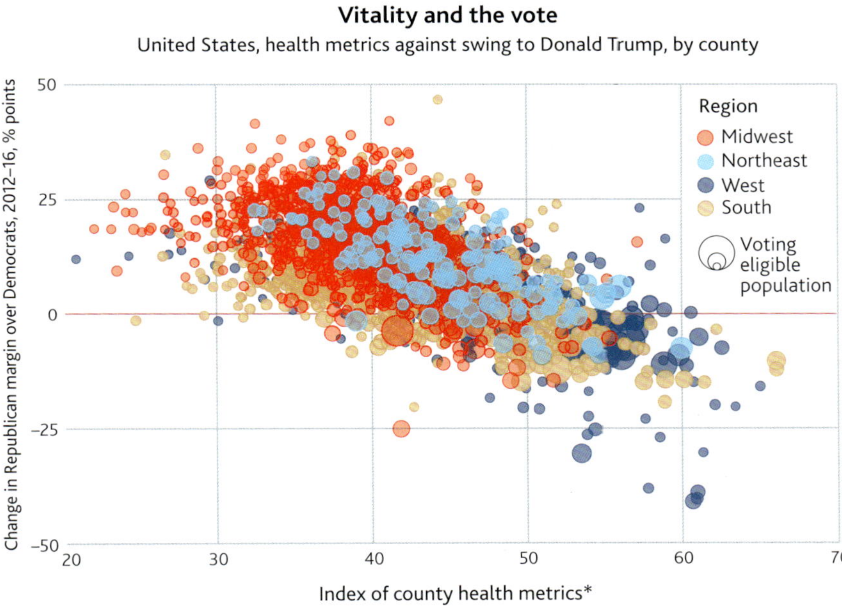

*Weighted index of obesity, diabetes, heavy drinking, physical exercise and life expectancy, 2010–12.

Sources: Atlas of US Presidential Elections; Census Bureau; IPUMS, University of Minnesota; Institute for Health Metrics and Evaluation; *The Economist*

Source: *The Economist* (2016) 'The Presidential Election: Illness as an indicator, Local health outcomes predict Trumpward swings', *The Economist Magazine*, New York Edition, 19 November, http://www.economist.com/news/united-states/21710265-local-health-outcomes-predict-trumpward-swings-illness-indicator

Figure 2.13: Average levels of happiness and inequality for all countries with data, 2023

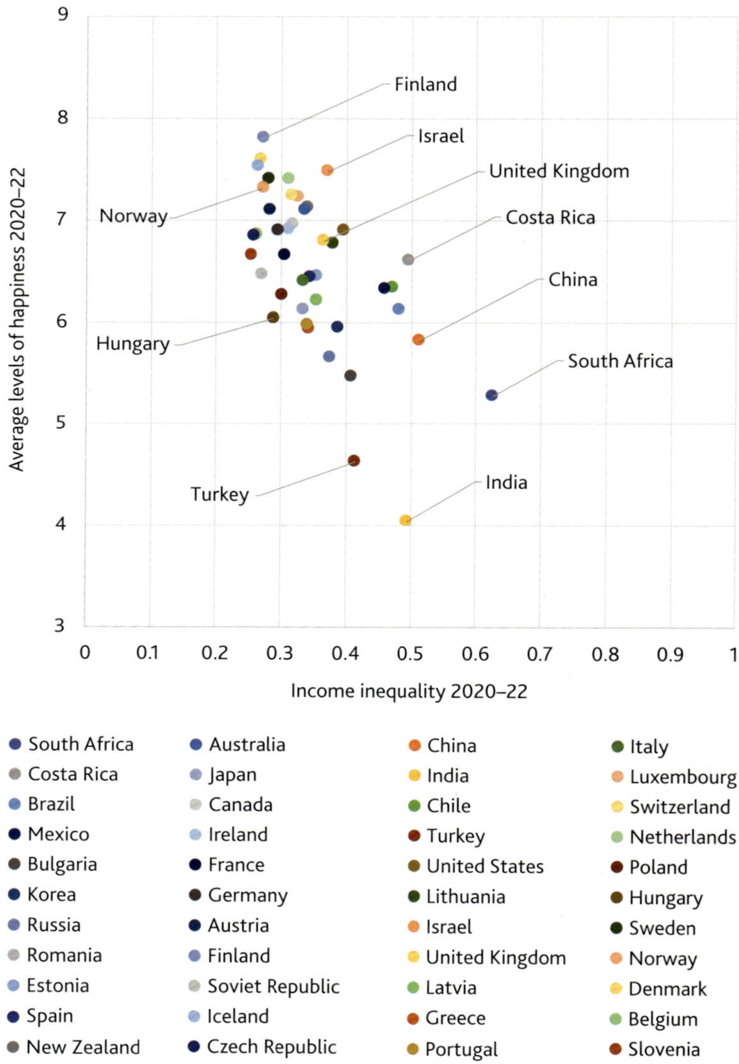

Source: Figure 2.1 in 'Ranking of Happiness based on a three-year-average 2020–2022', in John Helliwell, Haifang Huang, Max Norton, Leonard Goff and Shun Wang (2023) 'World happiness, trust and social connections in times of crisis', in *World Happiness Report 2023* (11th edn), Sustainable Development Solutions Network, ch 2, https://worldhappiness.report/ed/2023/world-happiness-trust-and-social-connections-in-times-of-crisis/#ranking-of-happiness-2020-2022. Based on data from the World Happiness Survey and OECD income inequality statistics.

Figure 3.3: Grenfell Tower, Notting Dale, Kensington during the 14 June 2017 fire

Source: Photograph taken by Natalie Oxford, reproduced from Wikimedia Commons, the free media repository, Creative Commons Attribution 4.0, https://commons.wikimedia.org/wiki/File:Grenfell_Tower_fire.jpg

Figure 3.4: Neighbourhoods in Kensington coloured by their poverty rate, 2015

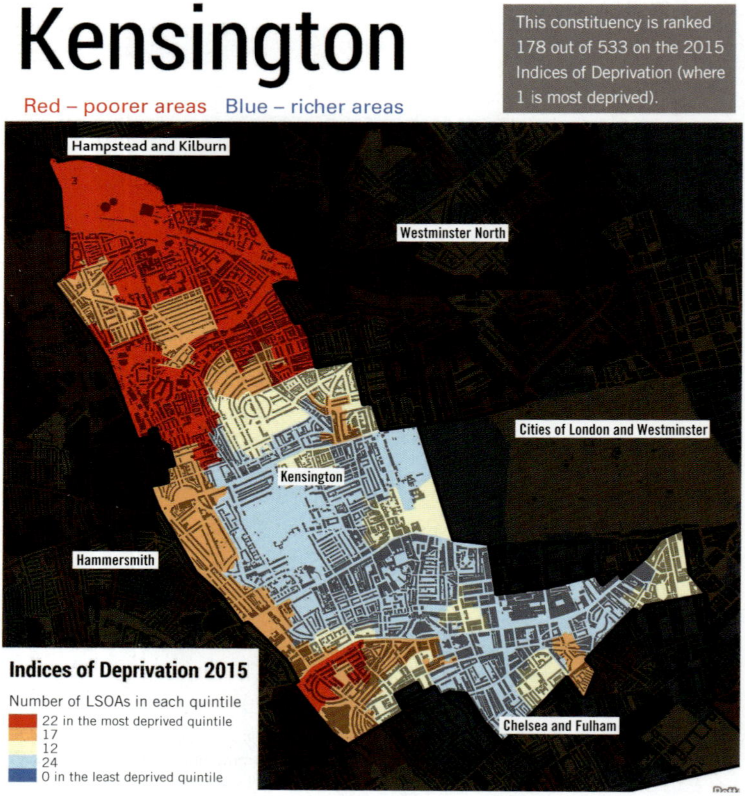

Source: Map drawn by Alasdair Rae on 11 June 2017, three days before the fire, reproduced with permission: https://x.com/undertheraedar/status/873948896401215493

Figure 3.6: Signatories to the Joint Ministerial Foreword to Command Paper 713

Source: Greg Clark (2022) *Housing and Communities, Ending Rough Sleeping for Good*, Command Paper 713, London: Department for Levelling Up, Housing and Communities, September, https://assets.publishing.service.gov.uk/government/uploads/system/uploads/attachment_data/file/1102408/20220903_Ending_rough_sleeping_for_good.pdf

Figure 3.14: Public spending in the five most populous European countries as share of GDP (%), 1980–2019, projected to 2026

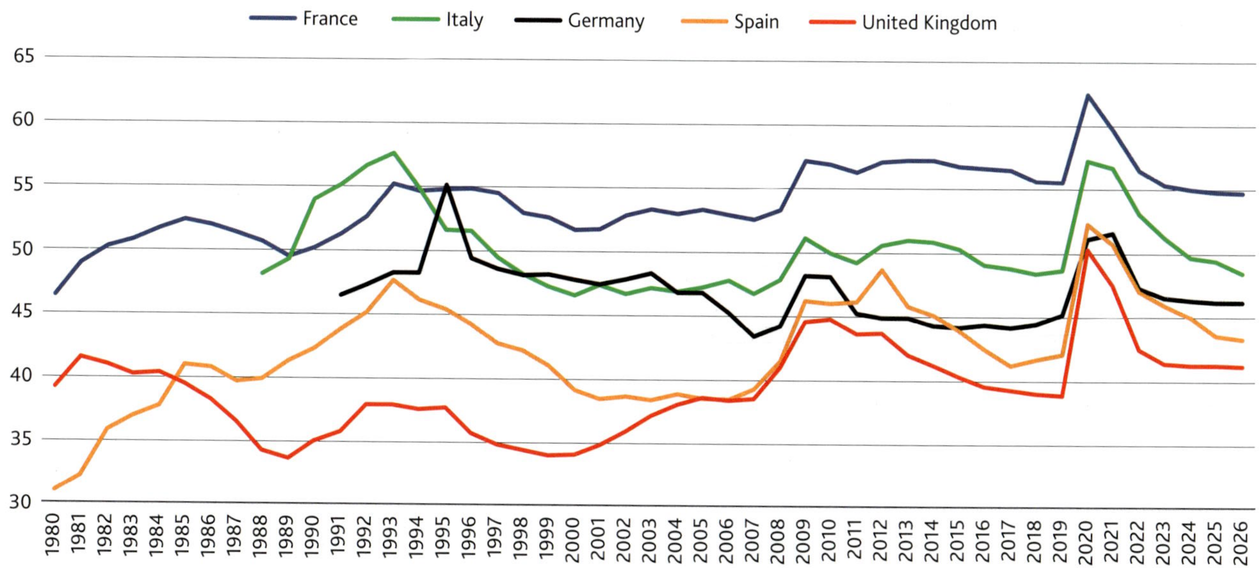

Note: The UK spends more on its armed forces than the other large nations of Europe, and only France also has nuclear weapons, so actually useful public spending is lower than shown.

Source: International Monetary Fund, World Economic Outlook Database, April 2021, variable GGX_NGDP: General government total expenditure as a proportion of GDP

Figure 3.15: Public spending in 14 affluent European countries as share of GDP (%), 1980–2019, projected to 2026

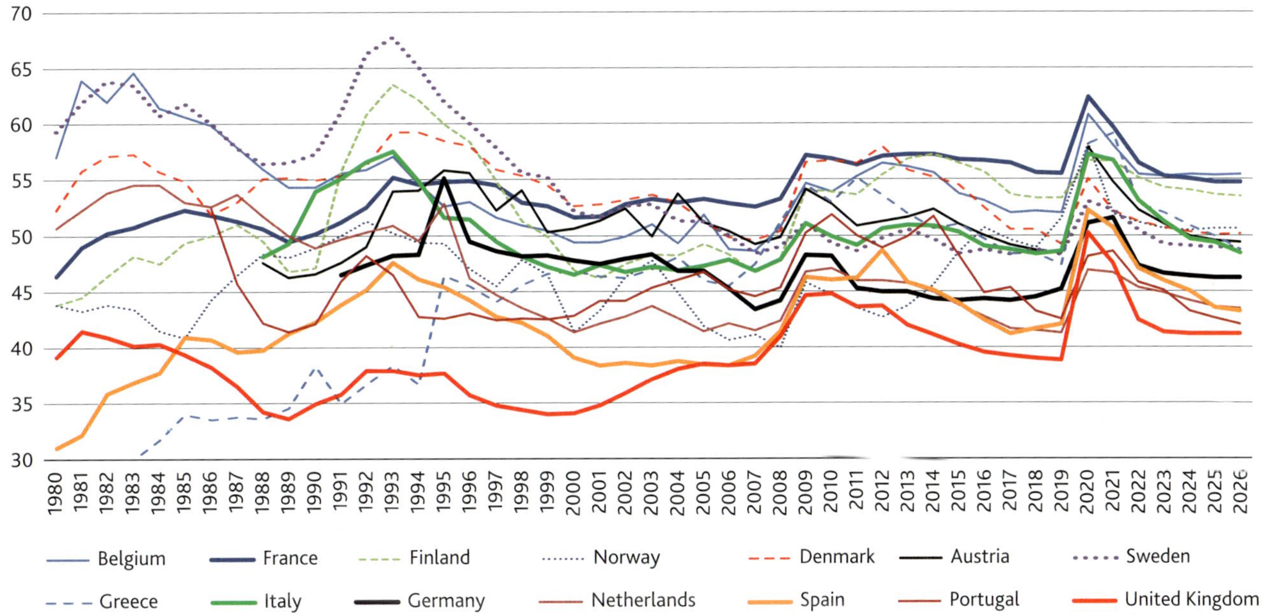

Figure 3.19: The ranking of rich countries by their levels of income inequality in 2022

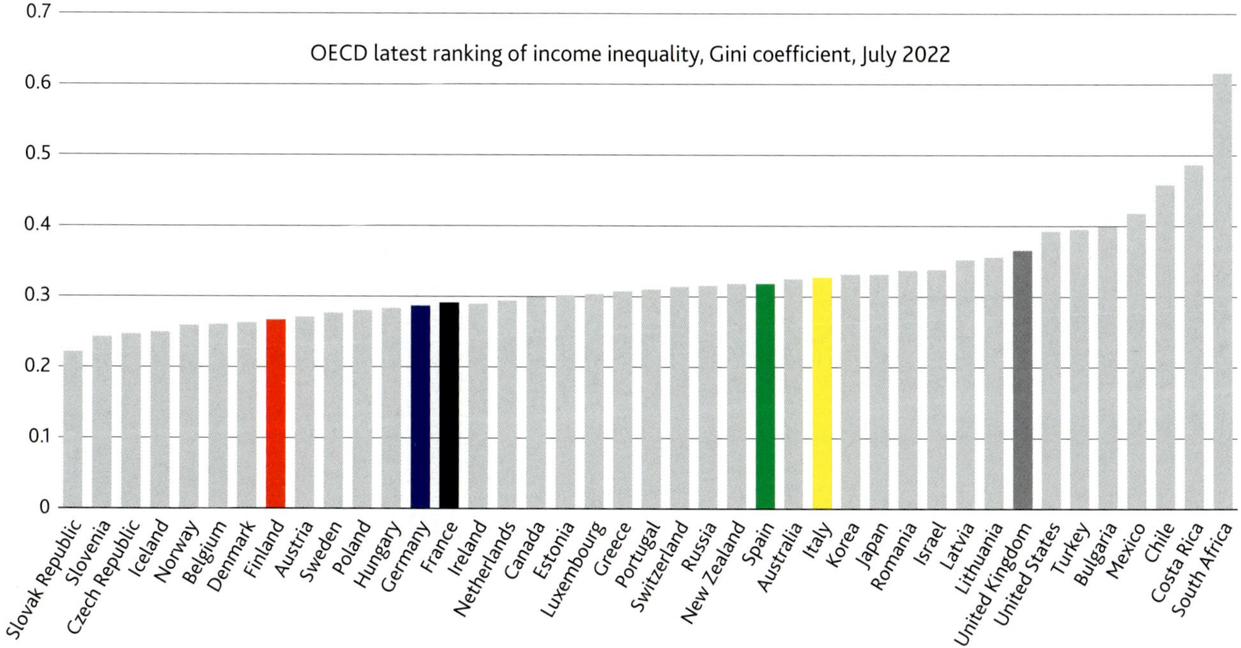

Source: OECD income inequality database, https://data.oecd.org/inequality/income-inequality.htm

Figure 4.4: Banner of the East Bradford Socialist Sunday School, Fred Liles 1914

Note: The Working Class Movement Library's website explains: 'As labelled on the banner, the two trees represent "knowledge" and "truth". Fruit trees and fields of corn represent abundance and plenty under socialism, while the poppy with its ability to grow in disturbed soil signifies beauty emerging from disturbance. [Bradford councillor Fred Liles] made the banner before the flower was adopted as a symbol of remembrance. The rising sun in the background is a common occurrence in visual political communication, and represents the possibilities of a better life beyond the present one.'

Source: Working Class Movement Library, https://www.wcml.org.uk/our-collections/creativity-and-culture/leisure/socialist-sunday-schools/banner-of-the-bradford-socialist-sunday-school/

Figure 5.9: The first four revisions of official UK life expectancy projections, 2012–20

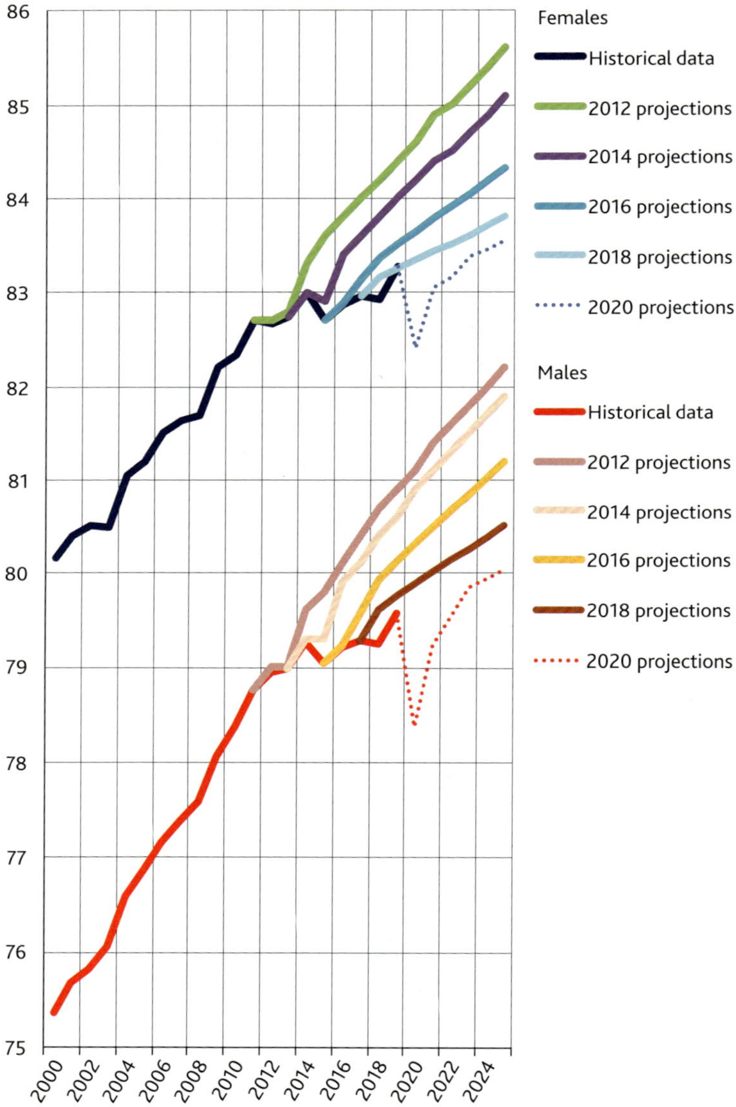

Note: This figure has been added to the original chapter to show just how much greater the effect of austerity from around 2012 onwards was than the pandemic on reducing life expectancy in the UK. By the end of 2020, the pandemic had had a similar effect to two years' worth of austerity.

Source: Lucinda Hiam and Danny Dorling (2022) 'The end of great expectations?' *BMJ*, 377, e071329, https://www.bmj.com/content/377/bmj-2022-071329

Figure 6.5: The sunlit uplands, a view near one of Rishi Sunak's many homes

Source: Photo taken by Jamie Davies, CC0, Unsplash, Hikes & Walks in the Yorkshire Dales, https://www.outdooractive.com/en/hikes/yorkshire-dales/hikes-walks-in-the-yorkshire-dales/210612045/

Figure 6.7: The spires, homes, windows and walls – Oxford, by Isabella Lill, 2020

Source: 'Oxford' by Isabella Lill – who kindly gave permission for her artwork to be reproduced here.

Figure 6.11: City Council suggestions for where those working in Oxford might live, 2019

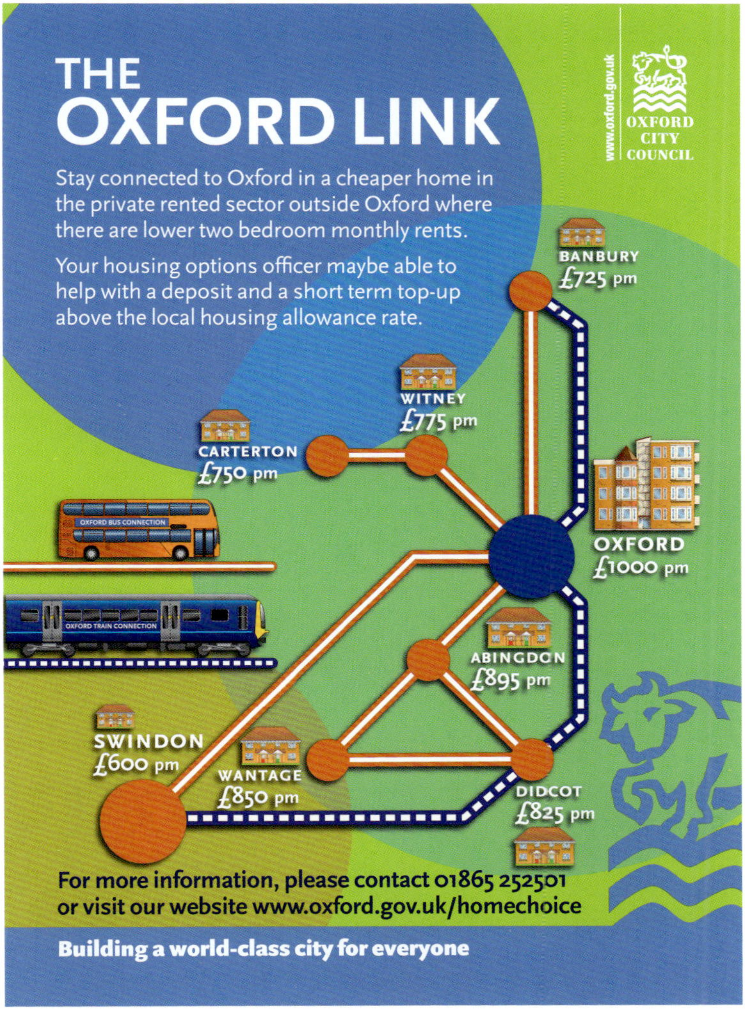

Source: Oxford City Council leaflet published in 2019, reproduced here: https://commongroundoxford.wordpress.com/2020/08/06/oxford-university-stones/

Figure 6.12: The rivers, canal, roads, lakes and buildings of Oxford, 1939–45 and 2013

Note: Areas in dark grey are urban cover based on the Dudley Stamp pre-war survey (data collected between 1939–1945). Areas in pale grey are current urban cover based on satellite imagery collected by the European Union in 2013.

Source: Dudley Stamp's survey of 1939–1945 and EU 2013 data, merged by eco-systems.org.uk

Figure 6.13: Finland topped UN's World Happiness Report again: a Helsinki view

Source: Photo Credit: Kostiolavi/Pixabay

In the UK, prices fell from a high average price of £184,000 in late 2007, to a low of just under £150,000 in early 2009. They did not return to their previous high until mid-2014. Nevertheless, this was a faster 'recovery' than in 1989. More importantly, the cause of the falls in 2008 was viewed as both external and unlikely to be repeated because – so it was said – the world would 'learn the lessons' of the banking crash.

Why do house prices matter politically? It may be coincidental, but the ending of both 18 years of Conservative rule (1979–97) and 13 years of New Labour rule (1997–2010) happened in the aftermath, or midst of, house price falls (Figure 3.16).

The current UK Conservative government, and the previous coalition that they led, have so far been in power for 'only' 11 years (2010–21). Their time in office might come to an end without a fall in house prices; or there could be a fall in house prices and their rule might not end there.

Nevertheless, if there was a drop (which would probably be described as a crash if it was anything but minimal) the

Figure 3.16: Nationwide Building Society UK house price series 1973–2021 (£s, nominal scale)

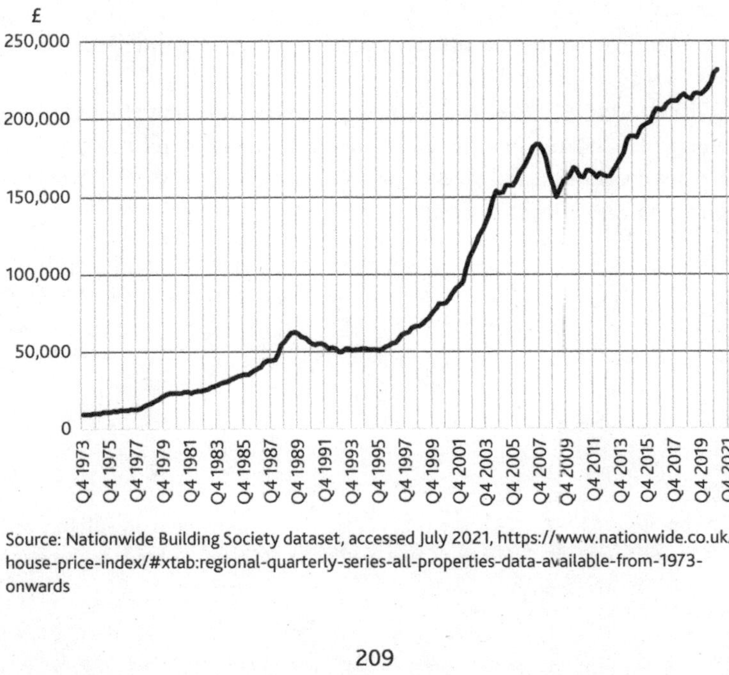

Source: Nationwide Building Society dataset, accessed July 2021, https://www.nationwide.co.uk/house-price-index/#xtab:regional-quarterly-series-all-properties-data-available-from-1973-onwards

Conservatives would be in trouble.[4] It might also be foolhardy to ignore the impact of even a slight fall, given how important house prices are to many people's sense of how well-off they are – and to their sense of well-being.

It is no coincidence that support for the Conservative Party is highest in areas where house prices are high and where a high proportion of people own their home or have a mortgage.

For a large and growing number of people, of course, increasingly high prices are the bane of their lives, forcing them to rent privately well into middle age and preventing them from being able to save because rents are so exorbitant.

High house price differentials across the UK also hinder geographical mobility, which in turn hinders social mobility. As I write in 2021, we seem to have forgotten that house prices can fall, and they can fall without an external international trigger. But many people shrug off the idea of house prices dropping even slightly in the UK.

After all (they might say) a global pandemic came and prices did not fall; so if even COVID-19 can't dent the rise in the cost of buying a UK home, perhaps nothing can.

But at some point (and we can't know when) house prices will eventually stop rising and start falling in real terms. For the UK this could be far in the future. Scenarios can be modelled where they do not fall for decades.

Alternatively, it could happen a few months from now. Eventually, house prices always do drop after reaching a peak. Furthermore, that fall need not be short-lived or slight; it could be substantial and enduring.

---

[4] Tim Bale (2021) 'Great expectations: the challenges ahead for the Conservative Party', *UK in a Changing Europe*, 8 February, https://ukandeu.ac.uk/the-challenges-ahead-for-the-conservative-party/

How do governments keep house prices high?

Rising house prices have been seen as politically advantageous by all governments since the 1980s.[5] Homeowners have seen it as evidence of both good national economic management and of their own individual success.

In contrast, in periods when house prices were falling – 1989–93 and 2008–11 – public confidence in government was far lower. John Major never really regained public confidence despite winning the 1992 general election; and the coalition government that won in 2010 used the memory of the falls from 2008 onwards to successfully paint the Labour Party as economically incompetent.

We should not underestimate how important it has been for UK governments to keep house prices high and, if possible, rising; or at least to try to steady and reverse any fall. The New Labour government did this in 2009–10 by diverting £1 billion from what had been their regional economic programmes to support the housing market as part of their 'new growth strategy'.

This included the HomeBuy Direct scheme – loans of up to 30 per cent on new-build homes, interest-free for the first five years, for first-time buyers.[6] Since then, various versions of the Help to Buy scheme have been used to prop up prices at the bottom of the market if they ever appear to be in danger of falling.

The Help to Buy schemes we have seen since 2009 have not been intended to make housing costs cheaper for 'the many'. To lower housing costs requires, among much else, two things to happen in the rental sectors.

---

5 Ben Ansell (2019) 'Has Brexit changed the relationship between elections and house prices?', *UK in a Changing Europe*, 20 November, https://ukandeu.ac.uk/has-brexit-changed-the-relationship-between-elections-and-house-prices/

6 Staff Reporter (2009) 'HomeBuy Direct – shared equity scheme launched', *Mortgage Finance Gazette*, 1 January, https://www.mortgagefinancegazette.com/market-news/homebuy-direct-shared-equity-scheme-launched-3-01-01-2009/

First, ensuring enough good-quality social housing is available to prevent private sector rents rising rapidly: inadequate social housing provision ensures a limited rental supply. This then encourages people with access to a lot of money to buy up family homes and rent them profitably on the private rental market – thereby preventing families from buying those homes.

Second, renting in the private sector must be made secure enough that families do not feel compelled to buy for fear of being evicted from their home should their landlord want to sell or raise the rent. If this has the effect of deterring people from becoming private landlords, then that would also help increase affordability for those who want to buy the home they live in.

When in opposition in 2015, 2017 and 2019, the Labour Party talked about some of these options. In particular, Labour suggested introducing better rent regulations. But they have not yet dared to suggest that house prices are too high – and when they were in power, they did nothing to help renters.

In contrast to Labour, the Conservatives do not even seriously discuss making renting less precarious and expensive. Instead, they prefer to talk about how schemes such as 'shared ownership' might allow someone to get part of a foot on the lowest rung of a ladder. When it comes to action, apart from the huge financial commitment of introducing Help to Buy schemes, their main focus has been tinkering in order to raise prices further.

In recent years, stamp duty cuts have increased UK house prices by reducing the costs to buyers – encouraging sellers to increase their asking prices. But what might they do if the current very high prices lead to a loss of confidence in the market and a slump in buying?

When the 2008 crash hit, the New Labour government introduced the Mortgage Rescue Scheme (MRS) for homeowners with a mortgage who were unable to sell but also unable to keep up mortgage payments due to changed personal circumstances.

Mortgagees could ask for help in reducing their repayments to their bank or building society. However, if those repayments were considered by government to be unsustainable, then a housing association would be permitted to purchase and rent back the property to the borrower on a three-year assured shorthold tenancy at 80 per cent of the market rent (or purchase with shared ownership if there was some equity in the property).

In 2008 the government also introduced Homeowners Mortgage Support (HMS), whereby the state would underwrite up to 80 per cent of the losses of a bank or building society that showed some leniency to a mortgage holder unable to pay their full mortgage due to a fall in income.

At the time, the belief was that MRS could be taken up by up to 6,000 borrowers, while a lender-led assessment estimated that HMS could directly support up to 42,000 borrowers.[7]

In the event, the numbers of families resorting to these schemes was much lower, although it is thought that their existence helped deter banks and building societies from repossessing properties at the rates seen after the 1989 crash.

Thus it was New Labour, just before they left office, that first instigated policies to try to ensure that when house prices did fall, they did not fall far. This included pledging government funds to underwrite potential private sector banking losses in the event of any price fall, and so encourage banks to keep on lending.

The intention of New Labour's 2008 and 2009 housing policies may have been partly to help families that might otherwise have found themselves homeless, but it was not only that. It also set a precedent for the UK government to intervene significantly in the private housing market to ensure that prices did not fall, or only ever fell by a small amount.

The first Help to Buy housing loans were issued by the coalition government in 2013. The previous schemes, HomeBuy Direct, MRS and HMS together helped only a modest number of families (around 15,000 across the three schemes).

In contrast, a huge number of people, living in 280,000 households, had had their purchase of a home underwritten with Help to Buy by summer 2020. In 2021 a new scheme was introduced whereby the government would lend up to

[7] Steve Wilcox, Alison Wallace, Glen Bramley, James Morgan, Filip Sosenko and Janet Ford (2010) *Evaluation of the Mortgage Rescue Scheme and Homeowners Mortgage Support (interim report)*, Department for Communities and Local Government, July, https://assets.publishing.service.gov.uk/government/uploads/system/uploads/attachment_data/file/6339/1648140.pdf

£25 billion directly to homebuyers – the expectation being that this whole sum would be loaned by 2023.[8]

However, even before the UK government began to spend that £25 billion, prices began to rise even more quickly than before. So, too, did sales, rising to nearly 140,000 a month by late spring 2021.[9] COVID-19 has, of course, had its own impact on the housing market. It is often said that the pandemic has increased the demand for larger properties in more rural areas. However, this is questionable.

Instead, the sad reality is that the pandemic may have resulted in more such properties coming onto the market than usual and so altering the mix of those that were sold very recently. The large majority of people who died in the pandemic were elderly, leading to an unusually large number of properties being put on the market when their occupants died.

This in turn altered the balance of what was being bought and sold during late 2020 and early 2021, changing the mix of housing transactions. That then resulted in prices appearing to rise faster as the reported prices were not 'mix-adjusted'.

And that, in turn, boosted confidence among sellers to ask higher and higher prices. The headlines in June 2021 simply suggested a 'race for space', not how the space became available (see Table 4).

Who loses when prices tumble?

So, to come back to the question this chapter began with: who really suffers when house prices fall?

Landlords suffer as the value of their assets falls. New first-time buyers benefit, if buying after the fall, which should help some tenants. That in turn should reduce the demand to rent, reducing

---

[8] Shane Hickey (2021) 'Will the new help-to-buy scheme get first-timers on the property ladder?', *The Guardian*, 24 January, https://www.theguardian.com/money/2021/jan/24/will-the-new-help-to-buy-scheme-get-first-timers-on-the-property-ladder

[9] Valentina Romei (2021) 'Why haven't house prices collapsed?', *The Financial Times*, 11 May, https://www.ft.com/content/9fdd1157-55f5-41b7-ae9c-24f68c62a194

Table 4: The housing news on Tuesday, 1 June 2021

Financial Times (Valentina Romei):

'UK house prices rise at fastest rate since 2014':

Growth in May surpasses expectations driven by stamp duty holiday and demand for larger properties. The average house price grew by 10.9 per cent compared with May last year...

(https://www.ft.com/content/bcc6fbef-7a37-4400-a421-6fc88f7ceb7f)

Telegraph (Rachel Mortimer):

'UK house prices spike 11pc despite looming tax rise':

Surging value will continue even when stamp duty increases, experts say as properties jump at fastest pace for seven years. House prices rose 10.9pc in the 12 months to May with double-digit increases expected to continue well into the summer...

(https://www.telegraph.co.uk/property/house-prices/uk-house-prices-growth-hits-11pc/)

Daily Mail / This is Money (Ed Magnus):

'House prices will boom before crashing in 2026: We speak to the man who forecast the last two slumps, but will his 18-year property cycle be right again?'

(https://www.thisismoney.co.uk/money/mortgageshome/article-9601221/The-18-year-property-cycle-tips-house-price-boom-crash-2026.html)

BBC (unnamed journalist):

'House prices jump 10.9% as "race for space" intensifies...':

England, Northern Ireland and Wales extended relief to the end of June. After that in England and Northern Ireland, the nil rate band will be set at £250,000 – double its standard £125,000 level – until the end of September.

(https://www.bbc.co.uk/news/business-57313700)

The Guardian (unnamed journalist):

But Guy Harrington, CEO of residential lender Glenhawk, predicts that the pace of growth will slow, especially if a third wave of Covid-19 cases hits the UK. 'The disconnect between the UK housing market and economic reality appears as great as ever. Government stimulus has created a false sense of consumer confidence.'

(https://www.theguardian.com/business/live/2021/jun/01/uk-house-price-growth-factories-supply-chain-inflation-ftse-stock-market-business-live)

Sky News (Ed Clowes):

'House prices soar 10.9% to seven-year high in "race for space"':

A buying frenzy in the wake of the pandemic has driven house prices to a near-seven year high, amid warnings activity could stall.

(https://news.sky.com/story/house-prices-soar-10-9-to-record-high-in-race-for-space-12321986)

(continued)

Table 4: The housing news on Tuesday, 1 June 2021 (continued)

Bloomberg (David Goodman and Marc Daniel Davies):

> 'It is shifting housing preferences which is continuing to drive activity, with people reassessing their needs in the wake of the pandemic,' said Robert Gardner, chief economist for Nationwide. 'Given that only around 5% of the housing stock typically changes hands in a given year, it only requires a relatively small proportion of people to follow through on this to have a material impact.'

(https://www.bloomberg.com/news/articles/2021-06-01/u-k-house-prices-post-double-digit-growth-as-boom-gathers-pace)

The Independent (Ben Chapman):

'UK house prices 10.9% higher in May than a year earlier on average':

> Anna Clare Harper, CEO of asset manager SPI Capital, said: 'Some will see 10.9% annual growth in the year to May as a boom, to be followed shortly by a bust, but what tends to happen in the housing market is different from other purchases and investments.'

(https://www.independent.co.uk/news/business/uk-house-prices-latest-nationwide-index-b1857318.html)

Estate Agent Today (Graham Norwood):

'Tidal Wave: some house prices up as much as 48 per cent in a year'

(https://www.estateagenttoday.co.uk/breaking-news/2021/5/tidal-wave-seaside-house-prices-up-as-much-as-48-per-cent-in-a-year?source=newsticker)

The Express (Emily Hodgkin):

'Property boom: The town where house prices have risen 48 percent in a year':

> House prices have surged in St Mawes in the South West by 48 percent. The area, in Cornwall, has seen average prices jump to over half a million pounds. The average house prices have jumped from £339,912 to £501,638.

(https://www.express.co.uk/life-style/property/1443605/house-prices-property-news-boom-seaside-homes)

Stoke-on-Trent Live (Hayley Parker):

'House prices across Stoke-on-Trent and Staffordshire sky rocket through lockdown'

> Across the UK, house values have been rising at their fastest pace since August 2008, and Stafford has seen prices rocket by the most locally in the past year.

(https://www.stokesentinel.co.uk/news/stoke-on-trent-news/house-prices-across-stoke-trent-5471933)

---

rents a little. Homebuyers who have just begun a mortgage lose out, as they might end up with negative equity. The government also loses out, as it has underwritten so many loans. Homebuyers who own outright or who have paid off a significant part of their mortgage do not suffer directly; but those looking to inherit from them might.

In April 2020, the Institute for Fiscal Studies produced a report estimating the expected variation in lifetime inherited income of households (Figure 3.17).

Those born in the 1980s into the best-off fifth of households can expect to boost their total household lifetime income by 30 per cent from inheritances, mainly from parents and grandparents. These anticipated inheritances are larger than for previous generations and are mainly the result of housing gains. It is hardly surprising that so many people are obsessed by house prices, given what this figure shows.

But just as governments appear to be giving people money when house prices rise, so it will appear that money has been

Figure 3.17: Median inheritance as a percentage of lifetime net income (excluding inheritance)

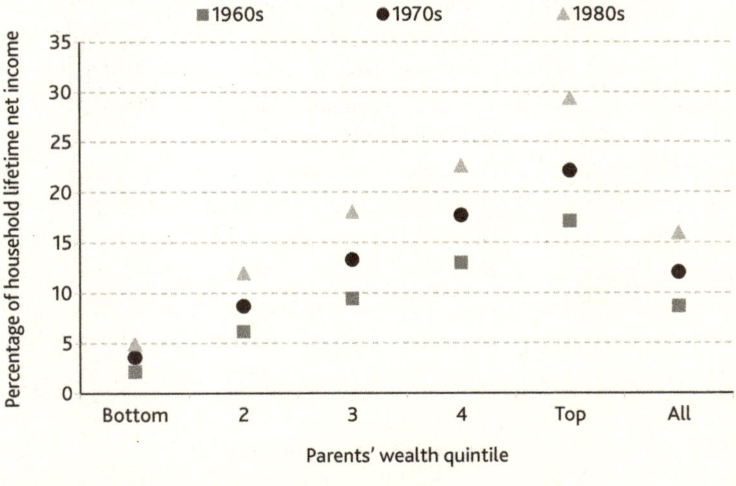

Note: Shown by parental wealth quintile and decade of birth.

Source: Pascale Bourquin, Robert Joyce and David Sturrock (2021) 'Inheritances and inequality over the life cycle: what will they mean for younger generations?', *IFS Report R188*, Institute for Fiscal Studies, 26 April, https://www.ifs.org.uk/publications/15407

taken away if prices are allowed to fall to the detriment of those expected inheritances. It is very hard to predict what the wider reaction to a fall in prices might be because, until recently, inheritances from housing were so much smaller.

Many people born in the 1960s are yet to inherit. Those born in earlier decades on average inherited far less as a proportion of their lifetime income. The implication is that the future effect on political sentiment of any house price falls could be much higher than in the past because many more people are now banking on housing holding or increasing its value.

Politicians are very much alive to these issues. Government ministers and MPs often own more than one home, partly because of the necessity to have a base in London. A high proportion are also landlords. They will not be unaware of the importance of housing for their own and their children's plans. So, while they may talk of wanting to make housing more affordable, they may also realise that doing so could be politically and personally disastrous for them and their children.

Politicians cannot say that they are content with the status quo, so they most often talk about house building as the solution to the affordability crisis. However, as long as the social distribution of home ownership remains so uneven; as long as an ever-growing proportion of property is owned by landlords and by people who have second homes; and as long as a significant and growing proportion of property is at least partially unoccupied, then it does not matter how much more is built.

Prices do not fall when more housing is built – especially when they are propped up by so much government policy to prevent them from falling. All of this raises the stakes, making housing more and more unaffordable to the majority who have to live somewhere. Increasingly this is in their parents' homes, because now younger adults can only afford to leave the family nest later in life.

The political implications of house price falls

When house prices in the UK eventually fall, we are likely to ascribe it to a particular event, such as a fall in demand from the young adult population as a result of migration patterns altered by Brexit;[10] or a change in demand away from city locations as a result of COVID-19.

Whatever the reason, we should remember that governments were actively forcing prices higher and higher in the first place. So, when the fall comes, remember it was always going to happen, and the trigger of the moment will not be crucial but coincidental. But what will happen politically when the fall happens?

In the 1992 general election, the Conservative vote fell more in areas where homebuyers were experiencing negative equity than anywhere else.[11] This was not enough to ensure that the Conservative Party lost that election. But the damage done to the confidence of Conservative voters contributed to some degree to the huge defeat the party suffered in 1997.

UK governments, and most obviously Conservative governments, try to prop up house prices because they are scared of the political implications of allowing them to fall. For ordinary people 'the economy' means jobs, wages, the consumer price index and especially house prices. In the 2019 general election, 86 per cent of Conservative seats had above-average home ownership, compared to 82 per cent of Liberal Democrat seats and only 26 per cent of Labour seats.[12]

It is likely that there will come a moment when prices will fall no matter what a government does. In September 1989 it was the ending of the MIRAS tax loophole for couples. But it could be anything that does it. For example, any government increasing social protection for tenants of private landlords risks introducing the measure that triggers this fall – which might partly explain why the current government does not implement better rights for tenants.

---

10 Jonathan Portes (2016) 'Brexit, migration, and the UK economy', *UK in a Changing Europe*, 24 November, https://ukandeu.ac.uk/brexit-migration-and-the-uk-economy/

11 Charles Pattie, Danny Dorling and Ron Johnston (1995) 'A debt-owning democracy: the political impact of housing market recession at the British general election of 1992', *Urban Studies*, 32, 8, pp. 1293–315, https://www.dannydorling.org/?page_id=1664

12 Cassie Barton (2020) 'GE2019: How did demographics affect the result?', House of Commons Library, 21 February, https://commonslibrary.parliament.uk/ge2019-how-did-demographics-affect-the-result/

Another possible trigger could be the effect of Brexit reducing affluent inward migration, having other harmful economic consequences and reducing housing demand. Once prices start to drop, confidence in the market can fall even faster. People might hold off from buying a house. Banks may become very wary of lending to landlords to buy more property and begin to worry about their balance sheets. At the extreme, a fire sale may begin. That occurred in Japan in the early 1990s. In 2005 house prices in some parts of Tokyo were still only half what they had been in 1991.[13]

What will happen next? Even if price falls are only small, people's dreams could be dashed. Affluent couples who dream of buying a home may find that sellers are not willing to accept a new, lower, market value. Tenants who dream that their child can remain in the same school and neighbourhood may find their landlord evicting them in order to reduce their property portfolio.

But the largest disappointment will be for people who thought that the property their parents owned, or that they had only recently bought, would be worth a given sum.

We have only a few examples of falling prices in the past, and each scenario is unique. But the difference next time will be that the dashing of hopes for inheritance gains will be far greater than in the past.

One recent commentator suggested that interest rate rises in future might slow price rises, concluding: 'Maybe rates will rise slightly over that time, but not by enough to trigger a housing crash. That cannot be allowed to happen: the economy and Tory politics say so.'[14] However, this view assumes that the market can be managed.

At times the market has a mind of its own.

---

[13] Martin Fackler (2005) 'Take it from Japan: bubbles hurt', *The New York Times*, 25 December, https://www.nytimes.com/2005/12/25/business/yourmoney/take-it-from-japan-bubbles-hurt.html

[14] Phillip Inman (2021) 'With house prices through the roof, young buyers' hopes go out the window', *The Guardian*, 3 July, https://www.theguardian.com/business/2021/jul/03/house-prices-through-roof-young-buyers-hopes-out-the-window

Conclusion

Social divisions in the UK are most clearly defined by housing. Countries in Europe with much more equal income distributions tend to have far better housing policies and better housing outcomes.[15] In an odd way, it may not be the banking crash of 2008, or Brexit, or COVID-19, that will have the most enduring impact on Britain this century. It may yet be the house price falls to come.

What else could drastically reduce our regional economic divides, which are also among the widest in Europe?[16] The current government's 'levelling up' agenda is little more than a cosmetic exercise with hints of pork-barrel politics.[17]

Finally, consider again the graph this article began with, but now redrawn using a logarithmic scale (Figure 3.18). That scale ensures that equal percentage changes are represented equally on the vertical axis of the graph. The peaks and troughs are identical to the graph shown in Figure 3.16, of course, but the slope of the price curve is different from that previous graph. On a log scale, a doubling of prices appears as an identical increase regardless of the actual prices. Looked at in this way, rises in housing prices have been slowing down over the entire 1973–2021 period.

The graph in Figure 3.18 is steepest in the late 1970s, when general inflation was also very high, and then again in the 10 years from 1980 to 1990, when prices increased by 150 per cent over that decade. It took the 15 years to 2005 for prices to increase by 150 per cent again. In the 16 years between 2005 and 2021, prices have 'only' risen by 50 per cent, from £153,000 to £232,000.

15 Paula Surridge (2021) 'Economic inequality: new common purpose or same old story?', *UK in a Changing Europe*, 2 March, https://ukandeu.ac.uk/economic-inequality-new-common-purpose-or-same-old-story/

16 Michael Kenny and Thomas Kelsey (2021) 'Levelling up Britain's towns', *UK in a Changing Europe*, 29 May, https://ukandeu.ac.uk/long-read/levelling-up-britains-towns/

17 Mikey Smith (2021) 'Shameless Tories hand 83% of £610m boost to towns with only Conservative MPs', *The Mirror*, 8 June, https://www.mirror.co.uk/news/politics/shameless-tories-hand-83–610m-24269389

Figure 3.18: Nationwide Building Society UK house price series 1973–2021 (£s, log scale)

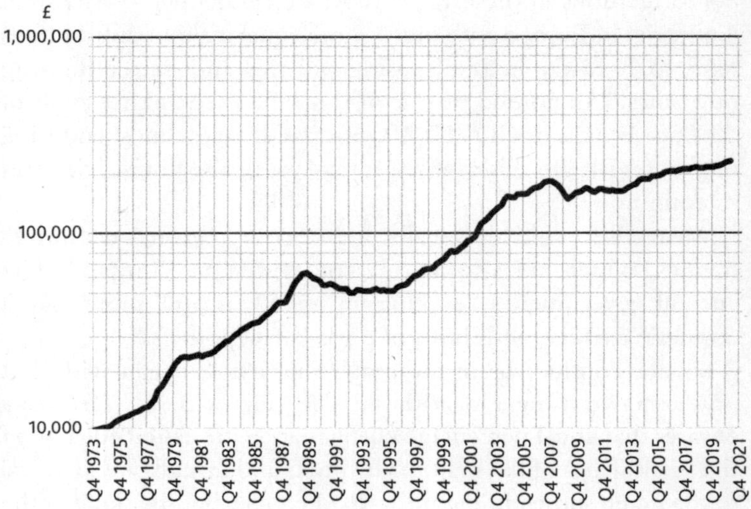

Source: Nationwide Building Society dataset, accessed July 2021, https://www.nationwide.co.uk/house-price-index/#xtab:regional-quarterly-series-all-properties-data-available-from-1973-onwards

What does Figure 3.18 portend? When house prices next stutter, or fall, or crash, the political implications may be even greater than they were in the years before the 1997 election and in the years before the 2010 election.

What may well be different next time is that they then never recover fully, and possibly (at some point) might even not keep up with general inflation. Who would then buy property as a speculative short- or medium-term investment, rather than as a home? What different kind of country might the UK become? Perhaps a better one.

CHAPTER 3.6

A letter from Helsinki[1]

I arrived in Helsinki in early summer 2022 to attend Europe's largest conference on social housing. At the airport I overheard American tourists complaining that so many shops were shut. It was a Sunday evening. The tourists didn't understand that Finland has the best work–life balance in Europe. I wondered why people who had just embarked from a plane immediately wanted to go shopping. Perhaps it was just what they had become used to.

I listened to hundreds of social housing planners, architects and housing managers, people from across the continent of Europe, talking to each other in a language most of them rarely use on a daily basis – English. There were only a few people from the UK there, and I kept quiet on all the tours I attended.

Providing housing of high quality, at affordable rents, is a distant memory in the UK. Just before I travelled to Finland the UK government had announced that it intended to introduce the right-to-buy for housing association tenants. It wasn't that I was ashamed of being British. I was just tired of trying to explain what was happening to the place I called home.

I went on a field trip to see the new residential district built on a former industrial harbour very near Helsinki city centre where tens of thousands of people now live in mixed developments under a plethora of schemes including a planned social housing block for retired rock musicians, complete with soundproofed music rooms. A passing tenant whispered to me that it is not quite the Utopia my hosts were describing – a place where everyone gets on with everyone else. I nodded, but I wondered if he knew

1 First published in *Public Sector Focus*, July/August 2022, pp. 12–15.

what conditions would be like for him if he lived in the US, or the UK.

All is not perfect in Finland. The queues to access the best social housing are many thousands of people long. However, almost no one sleeps on the streets, even in the twenty-plus degree heat of a Helsinki summer. In the evenings I tried to spot people who are street homeless – and I failed.

A heatwave was building up strength further south. I counted myself lucky not to be sweltering in it while I traipsed around block after block of new, carefully designed dwellings. An architect talked of how many of her colleagues competed to design one particular block. University students showed me their state-built and state-managed studio flats, each complete with kitchen. Hardly any students rent in the private sector. In Finland almost three out of every five university students have their own public-sector-provided apartment and choose not to share.

I learn that in Norway new housing for students is based on a dozen or even more having rooms in a large, shared house or apartment with a big communal kitchen – to reduce loneliness. Young Finns appear to place a greater value on having their own space. Perhaps it is to shelter a little from some of the conformity. But will other Finns at some point begin to resent the mostly middle-class university students having such homes? Students coming from overseas are allocated this housing first, as they are seen as being most in need. Can you imagine any of this in Britain? Extremely high-quality housing provided and managed well on the basis of need with foreigners at the front of some queues?

Back home in England, another of the prime minister's ethics advisors had just resigned. I asked if any Finnish government minister had transgressed a single regulation during the pandemic. My hosts scratched their heads, debated among themselves and finally replied 'no'. I asked them why it took them so long to agree, and they said they were also debating whether any ministers had done things they were allowed to do but should not have done if they were to set a good example. I laugh. I tell them about the government-chartered plane that had recently been prevented from leaving Britain to fly refugees in harnesses to Rwanda. They did not know about it. Why should they? Britain is an ever more alien place to them, a land where atrocities are now so frequent that they are no longer news on the European mainland.

Attending more talks, I heard details of the huge differences across Europe in terms of what is currently possible when it comes to housing people adequately. One common theme was that the cost of construction materials has risen so high and so quickly that new social housing building is being placed on hold almost everywhere. Only the most affluent, more egalitarian countries might secure the dwindling supply of girders, wiring and piping this year. The Norwegian government is now looking into spending far more than it usually does to ensure that building public housing there continues with little interruption.

I spoke only at the very end of the conference. I tried to be tactful. After all who am I – given where I come from – to offer useful insights? I told the audience about my country which, by the time I was born, had managed to house a narrow majority of its young adults during their childhood in social housing of ever-growing quality – a higher proportion than in Finland today. It was a country with lower wealth and income gaps than those seen in Finland today. It was a country that led the world in increasing the social mix of children in its schools. It was a country whose health service ranked above all others. That Britain is just a distant memory now.

I asked what would happen if the cost of building construction remains so high in Europe due to the aftermath of the pandemic and the new war in Europe. When they can no longer so readily build and provide for their poorest, will the most affluent and equitable countries in Europe learn to better share what they already have? Or will they say that everyone has to tighten their belts equally in straitened times, which means those with the least will be affected the most, and justified resentment will grow?

Less than 50 years ago planners, architects, educational researchers and ministers of health from across Europe came to the UK to see how social housing, schooling and hospitals could be best provided. We in Britain had a social contract that appeared strong, but when the prices of construction material and oil rose with inflation in the 1970s, the contract then began to be broken. The breaking started in the mid-1970s – and never ended.

I show my audience graphs of how the number of children growing up with a private landlord skyrocketed not in the 1980s, but in the 2000s. I say, it is not so much the conservative you have to fear – you understand them. It is when your own side becomes complacent and corrupted that you are in most trouble. Beware when social democrats believe they have achieved so much and done so well that asking for even greater equality (of 'outcome') would be asking for 'too much'.

I tell my audience that the most common way people under age 65 die in my home city of Oxford is to die homeless, and that it has been this way for over two decades now. I congratulate the delegates because children born in almost all their countries now have lower infant mortality than in the UK, and the Finns recently achieved the lowest rate ever recorded in history, which of course has as much to do with their housing, social and education policies as with their healthcare. I thanked my hosts for having invited me. And ended by telling them that at least they have the example of the UK to warn them of what happens when you stop caring enough; we didn't have such a useful example in the 1970s. We didn't know how bad it could become and how so much could be lost.

Shown in Figure 3.19 is one graph that sums up where we are. It is the basic graph of income inequality that compares all OECD countries. The graph reveals that Finland is exceptional, but no longer unusual. Shaded in red, it is now not quite as equitable as Denmark, Belgium or Norway, and only a fraction more equal than Austria, Sweden and Poland. Increasingly, more and more of Europe is becoming like Finland. Germany and France are not far behind – shaded purple and black on the graph. Spain and Italy, shaded green and yellow, are on the slightly less egalitarian side of the centre of the distribution. The UK is on the edge. In all of Europe only Bulgaria is more unequal. We have to look to America, or perhaps more plausibly to nearby Turkey, or at the very extreme towards South Africa, to see where the UK is heading.

You might think that it would be impossible for the UK's inequalities to increase. But we broke away from what is normal and possible when we broke out of the EU. We are now even more economically unequal than Israel. We are now firmly in the

Figure 3.19: The ranking of rich countries by their levels of income inequality in 2022

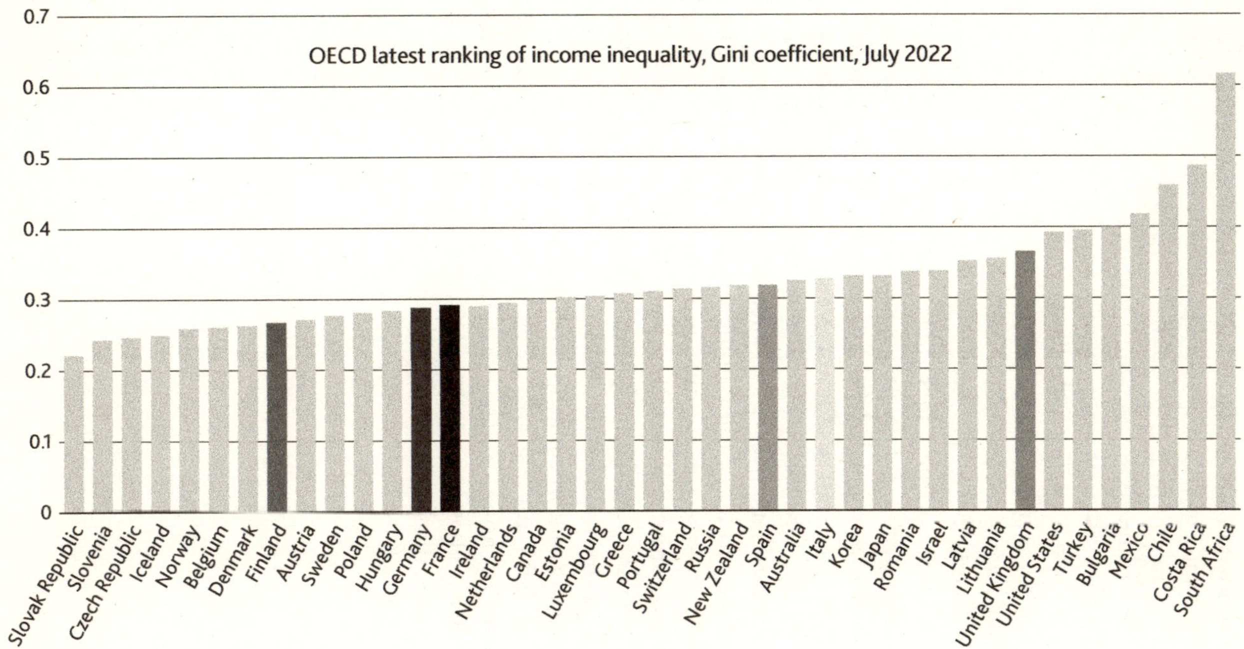

Source: OECD income inequality database, https://data.oecd.org/inequality/income-inequality.htm

see colour version in plate section

group of OECD countries where populations live parallel lives and politicians talk freely and without much criticism about the poor needing to take ever more personal responsibility. Politicians in these most unequal of countries enact laws in the name of freedom to make it easier for a few to exploit others. We have become the place on our continent to travel to if you want to see what a broken society looks like.

I try to imagine what Europe's largest conference on social housing would look like if it were ever held in the UK. Where would the field trips go? Would university students happily stand at the doors of their incredibly expensive privately provided accommodation and say how lucky they were to be living there and accruing so much debt? Would some of the incredibly well-paid chief executives of housing associations say what a brilliant model the UK has, with so much housing being charitable? Would representatives of our plethora of homelessness charities extol the virtues of the countless opportunities to work in the homelessness sector, as homelessness here is so high? Would the delegates from the mainland walk out of the conference? Or perhaps they would quietly take note of what happens when the public sector has been shrunk so far and is so deformed – not just in housing, but in education, health and care too.

I'm glad I saw Helsinki again. In the past it was an unusual beacon of hope. Today what happens there is increasingly the norm elsewhere in Europe. The Nordic model is slowly becoming the normal model.

CHAPTER 3.7

Liz Truss and autumn 2022[1]

The UK currently has the second-highest income inequality of any OECD country in Europe. Only Bulgaria is more unequal.[2] The economic announcements made on Friday, 23 September 2022 by Liz Truss's government may well ensure that the UK moves up to the unenviable top spot. This has implications for health because unequal countries tend to have worse health outcomes (Figure 3.20). Although there is debate about the causal mechanisms, the observed relationship is well known. In international comparisons, it is strongest for the youngest age groups who tend to be most affected by the most recent changes (Figure 3.21). Note that the areas of the circles in both figures are proportional to the populations of the countries and states in the 2010s.

The changes announced on Friday included a tightening of the rules on Universal Credit 'which will see benefit payments reduced if people do not fulfil job search commitments'.[3] This will make many already poor families poorer still.

---

[1] Originally published as: 'The "mini-budget" will make the UK the most unequal country in Europe', *British Medical Journal*, 26 September 2022, p. 378. Figure 3.20 and Figure 3.21 have been added from the sources given.

[2] OECD Income inequality database, https://data.oecd.org/inequality/income-inequality.htm

[3] Dulcie Lee (2022) 'As it happened: pound falls as chancellor cuts income tax and stamp duty', *BBC News*, 23 September, https://www.bbc.co.uk/news/live/uk-politics-62994747

Figure 3.20: Take of the 1 per cent in 1983 and later versus life expectancy in 2015, in 19 countries and all US states

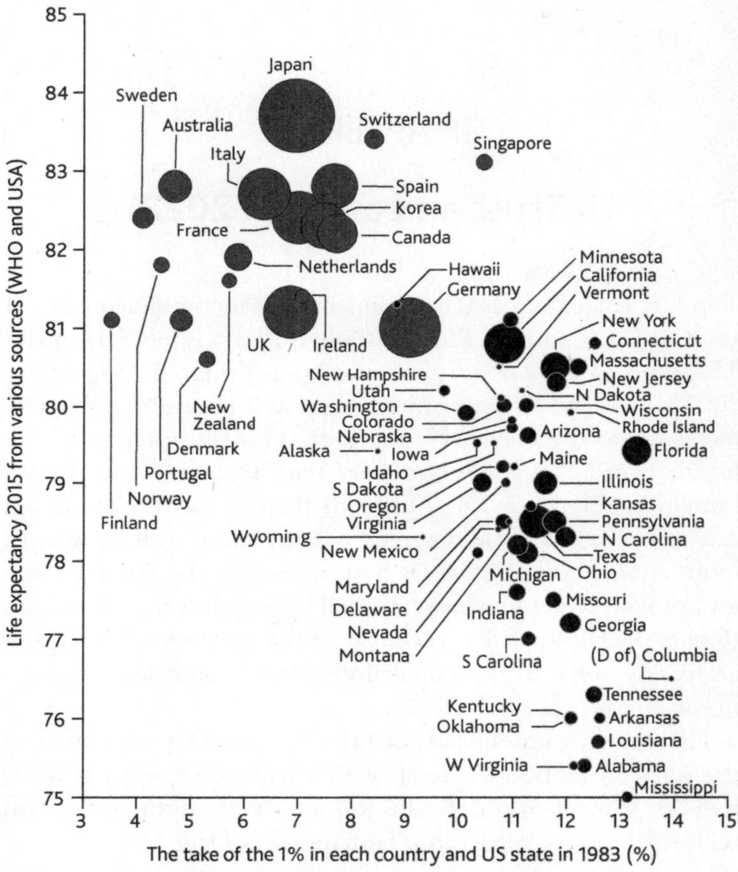

Source: Danny Dorling (2017) *Do we need economic inequality?*, Cambridge: Polity; see interactive figure at http://www.dannydorling.org/books/economicinequality/figures-and-tables/figure-5-2.html

Even before the announcements were made, the introduction of even more punitive policies meant benefit sanctions were rising rapidly (as mentioned in Chapter 1.5). The number of people sanctioned rose above 100,000 in May 2022; three times

Figure 3.21: Inequality and infant mortality, 19 affluent countries and all US states

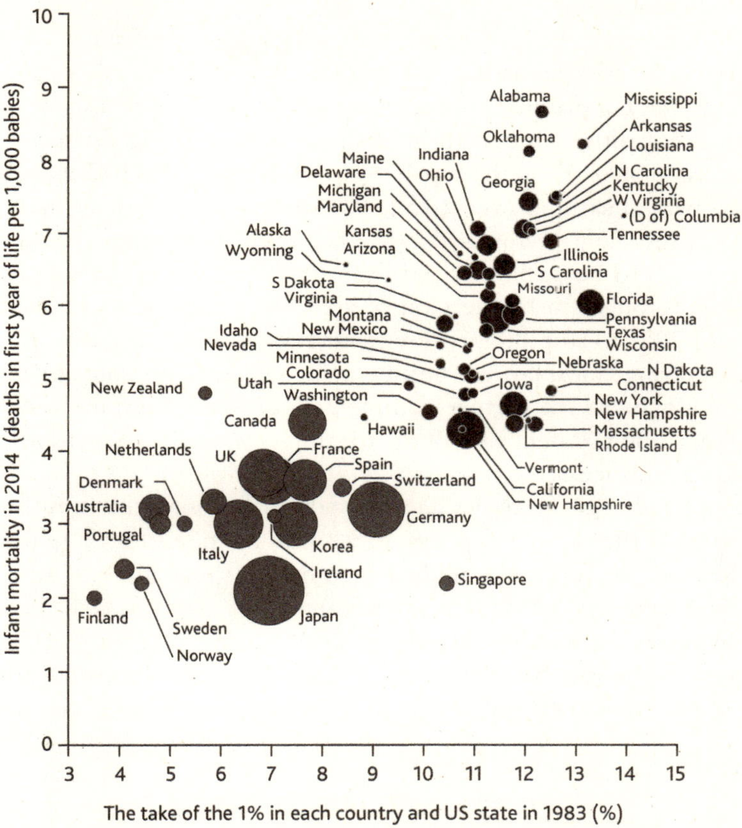

Source: Figure 5.1 in Danny Dorling (2017) *Do we need economic inequality?*, Cambridge: Polity, 2017, https://www.dannydorling.org/books/economicinequality/interactive-charts/figure-5-1.html

higher than the pre-pandemic peak in October 2019.[4] Before the changes, it had been projected that 593,000 people would be sanctioned in the financial year ending March 2023. Now even more will have been sanctioned, with almost certainly more again

4 David Webster (2022) 'Briefing: Benefit Sanctions Statistics', *Child Poverty Action Group*, 24 August 2022, https://cpag.org.uk/policy-and-campaigns/briefing/david-webster-university-glasgow-briefings-benefit-sanctions

when the figures for 2023/24 are released.[5] Those on the lowest household incomes will suffer the most. That is always the case with sanctions.[6]

Almost all the other measures announced on Friday were intended to benefit the richest. The cap on bankers' bonuses was lifted; a planned corporation tax rise was scrapped to allow those wealthy enough to hold shares to take larger dividends; outside of Scotland the top 45 per cent tax rate (that had applied to people earning over £150,000 a year) was abolished; stamp duty thresholds were raised so that the minority of people wealthy enough to buy a home paid less in tax; and the obscure IR35 rules brought in by the Conservative Party themselves in 2017 and 2021 to stop disguised remuneration will be repealed. This last change most favours already highly rewarded consultants. An employment tax partner commented: 'Today's announcement could help open the door to those wishing to promote tax avoidance'.[7]

The changes were designed to increase incomes the most for those at the top of pay scales, to increase them less for those just beneath the top, and to reduce incomes for those at the bottom. The basic rate of tax was lowered to 19 per cent, which most increases the incomes of people earning £50,270 a year, at the very top of the basic rate band. These changes will not benefit any of the 43 per cent of UK adults who pay no income tax,[8] or

5 Stuart Adam, Isaac Delestre, Carl Emmerson, Paul Johnson, Robert Joyce, Isabel Stockton, Tom Waters, Xiaowei Xu, and Ben Zaranko (2022) 'Mini budget response', *Institute for Fiscal Studies*, 23 September, https://ifs.org.uk/articles/mini-budget-response

6 BBC Political Thinking (2022) 'Jeremy Corbyn: Tory economic plan is irresponsible', *BBC News*, 24 September, https://www.bbc.co.uk/news/uk-politics-63011119

7 Jean-Baptiste Andrieux (2022) 'Government repeals reforms to the IR35 rules', *Money Marketing*, 23 September, https://www.moneymarketing.co.uk/news/government-repeals-reforms-to-the-ir35-rules/

8 Tony Shanks (2019) 'Is everybody paying income tax?', *Tax Rebate Services*, 12 August, https://www.taxrebateservices.co.uk/is-everybody-paying-income-tax/

the 24 per cent of UK households where no one in the household receives enough income to pay income tax.[9]

It is the indirect effects of the announcements, however, that may have a much greater impact on making the poor poorer. The pound fell to a 37-year low as the announcements were being made.[10] Three days later, it had fallen to its lowest ever value against the dollar and other currencies. This will increase the cost of importing the basic foodstuffs, clothes and other essentials that make up a much higher proportion of spending among households on lower incomes. Furthermore, the tax cuts were unfunded, requiring the government to increase borrowing, which makes interest rate rises more likely – increasing the costs of mortgages, and therefore also rents.

The changes will also widen policy differences within the UK. In Scotland the top tax rate will not be scrapped. The rate there was already higher than in England.[11] Scotland is becoming more progressive, England more regressive. The Scottish government has recently announced that 'emergency legislation will be introduced to bring in a freeze on rent increases and ban evictions in the private and social rented sector in response to the cost of living'.[12] So rents in Scotland, unlike in England, may well not rise as a result of today's announcements.

We can only know the direct effects of these policy changes. We cannot know their unintended consequences, up to, and possibly even including, the shattering of market sentiment, further increasing government borrowing costs. Decreasing

---

9 Office for National Statistics (2020) 'Proportion of UK households paying no income tax and direct taxes, financial year ending 2019', *ONS People, population and community*, 4 November, https://www.ons.gov.uk/peoplepopulationandcommunity/personalandhouseholdfinances/incomeandwealth/adhocs/12451proportionofukhouseholdspayingnoincometaxanddirecttaxesfinancialyearending2019

10 Noor Nanji (2022) 'Pound sinks as investors question huge tax cuts', *BBC News*, 23 September, https://www.bbc.co.uk/news/business-63009173

11 Scottish Government (2022) 'Income Tax in Scotland', https://www.gov.uk/scottish-income-tax, accessed 23 September.

12 SAL (2022) 'Immediate freeze on rent increases plus eviction ban', *Scottish Landlords Association Website*, 6 September, https://scottishlandlords.com/news-and-campaigns/news/immediate-rent-freeze-and-eviction-ban/

stamp duty might not actually strengthen the housing market, but instead cause people to question how safe the housing market is. There are many scenarios where the actions taken do not have the intended consequences. However, in the short term, a few people at the very top are about to become richer – and even more politically powerful because they are richer. The large majority of us, in contrast, will be worse off due to the rise in unsupported borrowing, the coming cuts in public services to reduce that borrowing, or simply because our incomes are stagnating as prices continue to rise.

CHAPTER 3.8

Labour and levelling up[1]

In 2022, when discussing what might be achieved by the Conservative government's 'levelling up' initiative, political scientist Peter John quoted the words spoken by Prime Minister Boris Johnson in July 2021, a year before he was forced to resign from office:

> Johnson elaborated by focusing attention on his belief that potential and talent was spread evenly across the country. He said emphatically: "We don't want to level down. I don't believe … that there is any basic difference in the potential of babies born across this country. Everyone knows that talent and energy and enthusiasm and flair are evenly spread across the UK…it is opportunity that is not …". He also added that such a condition was causing a massive waste of human resource as too many were failing to fulfil their latent ambitions. However, he purposefully did not link inequality in the UK to poor outcomes rather he stuck with the standard Conservative trope – improving opportunity.[2]

---

1 First published as: 'Growth which makes everyone, not just a few, better off', in Graeme Atherton and Marc Le Chevallier (eds) *How can Labour level up?*, Ealing: University of West London, Centre for Inequality and Levelling Up, Chapter 12, 12 July 2022, https://www.uwl.ac.uk/research/research-centres-and-groups/centre-inequality-and-levelling-ceilup. Figure 3.22 has been added here for entertainment purposes.

2 Peter John, 'Levelling up with the meritocracy: Balancing equality with opportunity', in Graeme Atherton and Caitlin Webb (eds), *Levelling up:*

Johnson had moved some distance from his 'top cornflake' days,[3] but he, and many like him, still seemed to believe that some people had greater latent potential or ambitions than others, even if he was now willing to concede that this distribution might be geographically more spread out than he had once believed (Figure 3.22). In his belief in inherent differences among humans being of great consequence, Johnson was far from alone. The British Labour Party embedded eugenic beliefs in both the original fundamental Clause IV of its constitution, and in the Blair-era rewrite that contained similar prejudices. The key text simply changed from 'workers by hand or by brain' (two types) to 'to create for each of us the means to realise our true potential' (a continuity of types with differing potentials).

Figure 3.22: Boris Johnson displaying his 'top cornflake' thinking-deeply face

Source: *New Internationalist*, 2 December 2013, reproduced under a Creative Commons Licence, https://newint.org/blog/2013/12/02/boris-johnson-elite

What is it and can it work?, Ealing: University of West London, Centre for Inequality and Levelling Up, January 2022, p. 10, https://www.uwl.ac.uk/research/research-centres-and-groups/centre-inequality-and-levelling-ceilup

3 Michael White (2013) 'Boris the clever cornflake gets his IQ in a twist', *The Guardian*, 28 November, https://www.theguardian.com/politics/2013/nov/28/boris-johnson-iq-intelligence-gordon-gekko

A belief that chaps, and it was mainly chaps they were worrying about then, were born with differing potentials served the British Empire well. Some were born to lead, others to follow. In between, a few had the potential to rise up a little in the ranks. Order was maintained and 170-odd current members of the United Nations were invaded or otherwise controlled, as another prime minister, Gordon Brown, pointed out. Interestingly, none of the 22 not invaded are among the long list of countries that Johnson insulted while Foreign Secretary.[4]

But why does any of this matter when it comes to levelling up? It matters because there is no Empire 2.0 coming. Because Britain is not going to level up by securing more overseas students forever, or by turning its banks into even riskier types of casinos; the kind that would not be allowed to operate in the EU. Britain will not level up by introducing freeports or enticing car battery companies to come here. Britain will not level up by spending paltry sums and building a few ill-thought-out edifices for sitting MPs to be photographed next to in the hope that it might benefit them in the next general election. None of it will work. None of it is showing any signs of working.

More level, and today far more prosperous, countries do not hold to British beliefs of inherent differences to anything like the same extent. Elsewhere, in the actual sunlit (and more level) uplands, people think their children should go to the same schools, together. They believe that no one should be very badly paid and that it is repulsive to be too greedy. We once thought that too, from 1918 to 1978. But becoming level back then had been easier because of the final spoils of empire. It will be harder now.

The British have an excuse for reverting to such odd ideas of inequality being good, and ability being concentrated far more within some than within others: that is Britain's history. When controlling the largest empire the world has ever seen, it helps not to see those you control as being like you. When

4 Frank Jacobs (2016) 'A world map of Boris Johnson insults: Among many others, Britain's new Foreign Secretary has managed to offend the previous, current and future presidents of the U.S.', *Strange Maps*, 17 July, https://bigthink.com/strange-maps/a-world-map-of-boris-johnson-insults/

you no longer have that empire to control, such thinking can be your greatest weakness; you begin to hurt your own fellow countrymen and women as you treat them more and more like vassals, or as your great-grandfathers used to treat 'the natives'. For those at the top, the rules are for the little people – people who can be given scraps.

Labour need to stop thinking the same way. From 1945 to 1970, Labour used the receipts of empire-attained advantage to level across. They convinced the Conservatives to copy suit. But when almost all of the last of the colonies gained their independence, the Conservatives shifted back to promoting inequality, and Labour from 1997 to 2010 followed suit. Inequality never fell in any single one of the 13 years that New Labour were in power, making it easier for the Conservatives to come up with their duplicitous 'levelling up' slogan.

In this context, the words of Keir Starmer, spoken in February 2023, sound hollow. He wanted: 'A collective ambition, a partnership – to secure the highest sustained growth in the G7. With good jobs, productivity growth in every part of the country, growth which makes everyone, not just a few, better off.'[5] If Labour continue to mimic the Conservatives, or try to claim they can be better at being 'true Conservatives', they will be ridiculed.

[Editorial note: I had to say one phrase more than any other in 2023: that 'growth' is not coming to save us. It looks now as if this will need repeating throughout 2024 and maybe for a few years yet to come.] People no longer believe that economic growth will be their salvation. They have heard those promises too many times. Johnson's 2022 promise that if we stayed close to his chosen path then soon 'we will be the most prosperous in Europe' was almost identical to one given by George Osborne seven years earlier,[6] the only difference being that Osborne had promised that the UK would soon be the richest of all larger nations in the

---

5 Keir Starmer (2023) 'Growth is the answer', Starmer's speech on Labour's plan for the economy, *Labour List*, 27 February, https://labourlist.org/2023/02/growth-is-the-answer-starmers-speech-on-labours-plan-for-the-economy/

6 Danny Dorling (2022) 'Let them eat growth?', *Tribune MPs Blog*, 29 September, https://www.dannydorling.org/?p=9467; and included as Chapter 1.5 in this volume.

world. The change over time in these promises is that they have been watered down from over one hundred 'larger' countries in the world (Osborne), to less than three dozen in 'Europe' (Johnson), to just seven mature, slow-growing economies – 'the G7' (Starmer).

Neither Labour nor the Conservatives can level up – but that is not what levelling is. Levelling is to make something more equal or similar, to create a flat and even surface. You do not level by piling on money you do not have to ignite a potential that is not there. You level by making flat that which is most egregious. You level the tax avoiders and evaders, the non-doms, the elite private schools that wish to retain the perks of registering as charities, the people who charge the heating bill for their swimming pools to expenses, and those who employ a household of personal servants.

When we last levelled we began at the top and we knocked it down. We did this in a polite British way. The country houses were 'donated' to the National Trust. We did it because we had to. And now we have to do it again. Only a fool would try to level the ground without first knocking down the outcrops that prevent it being level. It takes time to level properly, but it is the poor who benefit first and most quickly. Eventually even the rich do too; they are just often the last to realise it. No child should grow up surrounded by servants and told they have potential far above others around them. It does them no favours in the long run.

SECTION 4

Eugenics and the fear of too many people

Eugenics and population control

Eugenics is a set of beliefs and actions that a few people argue will improve the genetic quality of our human population. Eugenics has been, and continues to be, used to grow, defend and spread racist and fascist ideology. It existed long before the publication in 1859 of Charles Darwin's *Origin of Species* (with its full title 'On the Origin of Species by Means of Natural Selection, or the Preservation of Favoured Races in the Struggle for Life').

The high priests of ancient Greece practised this dark art of suggesting that selection of different human types was possible. Some claimed that children could be divided into those who had a natural inclination to become 'golden' and others who were destined to remain forever in the lower orders, and possibly their offspring too. Inevitably, the proponents of eugenics believe that they themselves are especially gifted, and those who cannot understand their arguments must simply be made of duller metals. Eugenics seeps into otherwise sound arguments with remarkable ease, like an almost invisible evil mist.

As a social movement, eugenics became most popular when we were most economically unequal worldwide, around a century ago (Figure 4.1). It was the dominant global theory of the affluent world at that time, largely accepted as a given, but simultaneously an only recently revealed, or rediscovered, truth. Almost all of the most socially progressive European writers succumbed to its alluring message. Eugenicists told themselves that they were special people, and they should seek to ensure that in future a high proportion of people should be special like them, with fewer dullards – but that there would always be dullards too.

A century ago, the political left across Europe and the Americas associated eugenics with progress. For them, the key question was how kindly we could set about altering future human gene pools. The self-appointed 'progressives' sought to do this by encouraging the very wide use of contraception in people and groups judged

Figure 4.1: Logo of the Second International Congress of Eugenics, 1921

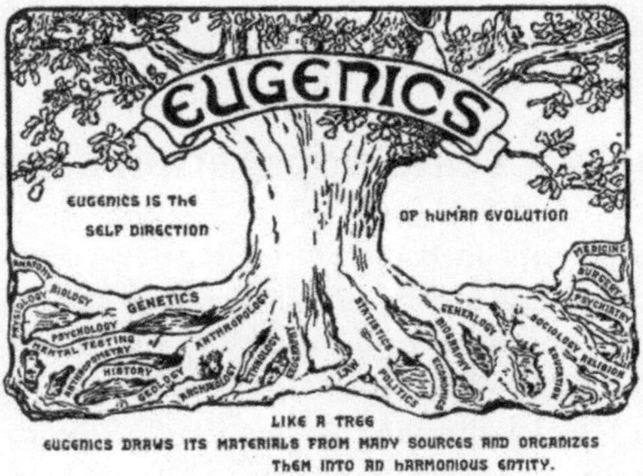

Source: Harry Laughlin (1923) *The Second International Exhibition of Eugenics held from 22 September to 22 October 1921, in connection with the Second International Congress of Eugenics in the American Museum of Natural History*, New York: William & Wilkins Co., https://commons.wikimedia.org/wiki/File:Eugenics_congress_logo.png

to be inferior, and discouraging it from being used too widely among those judged to be superior – including themselves.

However, resistance to eugenics has a history as long as eugenics itself. When told well, the tale of the four children of the Passover mealtime story, Haggadah, is an ancient story about inherent equality. It can be read as an early resistance story to counter eugenicists.[1] Whenever one group in history has become politically, economically and socially dominant, they have found eugenicists' tales alluring: telling them that they were born to be at the top. In modern versions British politicians, once at the very top of power and including many still alive today, have referred to the advantages they believe are inherent within themselves using phrases such as benefitting from their own 'god-given genes'. However, even when the eugenicists of the British empire were at their most dominant, lone voices still spoke out, including one noteworthy geographer who tried to explain to his peers that: 'Not all anthropologists concur in the assumption that there is any

[1] Ruben Brisbe (2016) 'Race and the Four Children of the Passover Haggadah', *The Educator's Room*, 21 April, https://theeducatorsroom.com/race-four-children-passover-haggadah/

inherent superiority in the White race.'[2] Today, in Britain, despite ongoing and relentlessly persistent calls to segregate children by supposed ability, campaigns promoting comprehensive education have gained renewed strength.[3]

The taste for eugenics lives on in Britain much more than elsewhere in Europe. It could be seen in New Labour policies driven by the belief that different children had different potential. 'Potential' was the phrase used in the new version of Clause IV of the party's constitution, replacing a similar notion of 'by hand or by brain'. State finance for higher, university-level, education was disingenuously characterised as giving an unfair advantage to those with greater potential, and Tony Blair's government duly introduced university tuition fees. When the right wing of the Labour Party regained control after 2019, the 2017 and 2019 manifesto promises to abolish tuition fees were abandoned.[4] Despite it being very clear how little educational ability is influenced by genetics, as had become very widely accepted by the 1960s and 1970s, it has become necessary to demonstrate it once again, as eugenics has crept back in, showing its face more often now in our times of peak injustice.

Table 5 shows that by age 18 a majority of British children who stay on at school have gained the equivalent of three C grades at A level. The only group of children for whom this is not the case are those who score in the lowest quarter by ability at age 8 and

---

[2] George Chisholm (1927) World Unity, *Geographical Review*, 17, 2, pp. 287-300, https://www.jstor.org/stable/208230 p. 291.

[3] I am one of the patrons of that campaign: 'Comprehensive Future welcomes John Bercow and Danny Dorling as patrons', Comprehensive Future (2021), https://comprehensivefuture.org.uk/comprehensive-future-welcomes-john-bercow-and-danny-dorling-as-patrons/ and see: https://comprehensivefuture.org.uk/our-patrons/

[4] Labour dropped their commitment to end tuition fees in England, despite it being one of Keir Starmer's ten leadership pledges. The Greens and Liberal Democrats retained that pledge. For detail on how fees can be unwound in future and a fair way of tapering the ending see: Danny Dorling and Michael Davies (2018) *Jubilee 2022: Writing off the student debt*, London: Progressive Economy Forum, 30 October, and Michael Davies and Danny Dorling (2019) *Jubilee 2022: Defending free tuition*, London: Progressive Economy Forum, 4 July.

who attended state schools. Of all children in the fourth (top) quartile of ability at age 8 who attended a state school around the year 2010, some 16.45 per cent were awarded AAA or above at A level. In comparison, of the children who scored in the second quarter at age 8 (below average), but who attended a private school, 17.65 per cent were awarded the same A level grades or higher at around age 18; a higher proportion. The table explains why those young people in Britain educated at a state school and attending a university that requires AAB grades or above will meet so many more students there, with the same grades, who showed less 'spark' at age 8 but who went to a different type of school that had the resources to give them more attention and where they felt greater pressure to perform and jump through the hoops. No other European country divides its children to such a great degree, so this natural experiment in determining just how much a child's future is inherently determined is only possible now in England, and those parts of Scotland which still retain this kind of an educational divide.

In Britain, we divide up our children very early in life and set them on different trajectories, not just dividing between private and state schools, but also within schools by setting and streaming

Table 5: Children awarded A level grades or equivalent by 'ability' and school type, Avon (%)

'Ability' quartile	State school pupils				Private school pupils			
	Q1	Q2	Q3	Q4	Q1	Q2	Q3	Q4
At least CCC	45.80	62.30	74.27	86.27	70.58	88.24	89.25	96.64
BBB or above	16.61	31.79	43.31	63.54	38.23	60.30	73.12	89.94
AAB or above	6.93	16.34	24.18	43.36	11.76	55.89	58.07	75.41
AAA or above	1.15	2.86	5.83	16.45	2.94	17.65	17.21	38.54
AAA+ or more	0.14	0.69	1.74	8.00	0.00	1.47	7.53	13.40

Note: All children have been divided first into the type of school they attend, and then into four equal-sized groups by quartiles of ability at age 8, as estimated according to a cognitive ability assessment made using the short form of the Wechsler Intelligence Scale for Children (WISC) at an ALSPAC direct assessment visit.

Source: Analysis of 1,768 children with an expected date of delivery (birth) between April 1991 and December 1992 who were resident in the (former) Avon Health Authority area in South West England. See: Tim Morris, Danny Dorling, and George Davey Smith (2016) 'How well can we predict educational outcomes? Examining the roles of cognitive ability and social position in educational attainment', *Contemporary Social Science*, 11, 2/3, pp. 154–68, Figure 4, https://www.tandfonline.com/doi/full/10.1080/21582041.2016.1138502

so often. It is now almost ubiquitous (nowhere else in Europe does so to the same extent). This decreases the chances of all of our children enjoying school. They cannot choose to be with others they might most wish to be, to learn alongside those they would like to learn with. They have to be always competing, much more so than on the continent. They fare worse educationally overall as a result (Figure 3.11, on page 194). Factors such as whether they enjoy school end up being just as important as any aptitude they might have and, in some cases, what type of school they attend.[5]

This section begins with an essay on how easy it is not to recognise how important circumstances are, and to believe instead that children have great inherent differences in ability, long after eugenics began to be seriously discredited (Chapter 4.1). It is not hard to link these beliefs to those on the political right of Britain who were so keen on Brexit because of their enduring view that the British are special,[6] and to show how this contrasts with the general decline of racism (Chapter 4.2), before turning to what has happened most recently to school buildings in the UK as we – hopefully – approach, or even as I write pass, peak injustice (see the Introduction to this book and Chapter 4.3 in this section). In the autumn of 2023, some 174 state schools could not fully open, and some could not open at all, because it was found that at any time their ageing concrete roofs might collapse on the pupils.[7] This risk had been known about for years, but the children's safety had not been deemed particularly valuable.

The final third of this section concentrates on the concerns that are still often expressed about there being 'too many people', in the world, and occasionally even in the UK (Chapter 4.4). This section then ends with some alternative projections to those

---

5 Tim Morris, Danny Dorling, Neil Davies and George Davey Smith (2021) 'Associations between school enjoyment at age 6 and later educational achievement: evidence from a UK cohort study', npj (Nature Partner Journals) *Science of Learning*, 6, 18, pp. 1–9, https://doi.org/10.1038/s41539-021-00092-w

6 Danny Dorling (2018) 'Brexit and Britain's Radical Right', *Political Insight*, 9, 4, pp. 16–18.

7 Sophie Huskisson (2023) 'More schools gripped by RAAC crisis as Tories bulk order temporary classrooms', *The Mirror*, 19 September, https://www.mirror.co.uk/news/politics/school-raac-list-updated-more-30974131

published by the United Nations, suggesting that soon we may be sharing the world with far fewer people than we thought (Chapter 4.5). Too few children, not too many, and with luck none being seen as being born into some chosen race or ability group. All children have their quirks, but only a dullard would believe now that they can be ordered along some 'normal' curve. The current and continuing global fall in how many children are born each year might well be what helps us slowly rid ourselves of eugenicist bigotry. We will have to start to value the young, rather than telling so many of them that they are inherently inferior.

A century ago, eugenicists were very concerned that the 'white races' were not breeding enough.[8] Others, however, contested the racism behind the belief that White children, and especially middle-class White children, were more able, and that the world would quickly degenerate if the 'lesser races' were allowed to propagate, and to 'interbreed'.[9] Today, our concern may soon be that no one is having enough children, but we should be able to easily cope with a faster than expected slowdown in population – once we learn to value each other more. Population growth slowdown is only frightening if you think you will need many others to serve you in future, or to fight in your armies, or to purchase your companies' products.

There is little difference between claims that some people and groups are inherently much more able than others, and that the British have a special destiny outside of Europe, and the eugenicism and racism of past decades – it is all part of a continuum. You could even order these things along a 'normal' curve of bigotry. However, apart from the mavericks, racism is falling; and crucially, globally, population growth rates peaked long ago and within our children's lifetimes total population is peaking. Very soon we may be confronted with too few people. This change, in just a century, is remarkable and ongoing. We may be a long way past a peak of stupidity, again globally, even if

[8] William Beveridge (1915) 'The fall of fertility among European races', *Economica*, March, 13, pp. 10–27, https://www.jstor.org/stable/2548006

[9] Iris Wigger (2002) '"Against the laws of civilisation": race, gender and nation in the international racist campaign against the "Black Shame"', *Berkeley Journal of Sociology*, 46, pp. 113–31, https://www.jstor.org/stable/41035570

we are not yet free of the outcomes of that stupidity, which range (when we zoom in from the global to the local) from Britain's extreme school segregation, to Brexit, to having to tolerate some of the world's dullest 'public intellectuals', while trying to be kind and not use the words 'slow', 'thick' or 'dim'. Because even the eugenicists have it within them to learn to be better.

CHAPTER 4.1

The blank slate[1]

Just a few days before his well-documented fall from grace – and in response to an academic article Sally Tomlinson and I had published a year earlier[2] – the Conservative government advisor[3] Toby Young posted this tweet:

> **Toby Young** @toadmeister • 24 Dec 2017
>
> Wow! Didn't know about the Danny Dorling paper.
>
> Incredible how robust the myth of the Blank Slate is![4]

---

1 Adapted for this book from a chapter that was originally published in slightly shorter form as 'The blank slate: Toby Young and social mobility', in Tom Kibasi and Carys Roberts (eds) *Move on up? Social mobility, opportunity and equality in the 21st century*, London: IPPR, December 2018, pp. 69–79, https://www.ippr.org/research/publications/move-on-up (text here as submitted on 23 October 2018).

2 Danny Dorling and Sally Tomlinson (2016) 'The creation of inequality: myths of potential and ability', *Journal of Critical Education Policy*, 14, 3, pp. 56–79, http://www.jceps.com/archives/3204

3 Member of the Board of the Office for Students, 2 January 2018 to 9 January 2018.

4 1 reply, 0 retweets, 3 likes, originally at: https://twitter.com/toadmeister/status/944958537809186818

Three people liked it. A few days later Toby was spending his Christmas holidays desperately deleting thousands of his tweets,[5] but he left this one up, maybe for posterity.[6]

The blank slate is the idea that children are all born alike. They are slates just waiting to be written upon and what they go on to do is almost entirely a product of how they are brought up, rather than their inherent nature. The blank slate idea actually has a lot of truth in it; humans are born remarkably similar, and plastic, like the material that was originally compressed to form slate. We differ in our genes, but that does not produce some normal curve of ability – why should it?

A few people have some genetic advantage that means they find the idea of rotating objects in their minds, imaginary numbers and integration, or switching between different types of scale on graphs and maps easy, routine, and intuitive – but those people always have some other disadvantage and find some other more common aspect of life harder than most, sometimes much harder. If there were some advantageous set of genes to have, with no (or little) downside, almost all of us would have them by now. We are no longer a quickly evolving new species.

There is no master race among us, no chosen people, no group who are remarkably able because of who their parents were, their caste or tribe; although women do tend to outperform men at

---

5 Ashley Cowburn (2018) 'Toby Young deletes thousands of tweets amid row over his universities regulator appointment: it comes after Boris Johnson defended Mr Young's role on the board of the new universities regulator, describing him as the "ideal man for the job"', *The Independent*, 3 January, https://www.independent.co.uk/news/uk/politics/toby-young-twitter-delete-tweets-universities-regulator-appointment-ofs-office-for-students-a8139841.html

6 It was later deleted as well, and only a few of his tweets from this era have been preserved via the Wayback Machine website, including this from 3 January 2018 as he scrambled to try to defend his new appointment, the day after it was announced: 'Let me assure the people that work in England's universities that I have enormous respect for everything you do. It's because of your hard-work and professionalism that our universities are among the best in the world', https://web.archive.org/web/20180103200550/https://twitter.com/toadmeister/

school on average whenever and wherever the playing field is made more equal.

Sometimes a set of humans go through a traumatic experience, and many are killed; mostly it is only the quick-witted and/or the richer who get out. For millions, centuries of slavery, in which no one was anything but impoverished, more quickly killed off weaker babies among the slaves and the weaker children on the plantations. But that does not make the group as a whole today stronger. Even a dozen generations of slavery is not enough to do that, and then we mix again, and whatever traits these terrible events might have selected for is mixed out. Thankfully too few infants now die, almost everywhere in the world, for natural selection to be a consideration.

Even if a little of the quirks of mental ability are inherited, we now know that:

> molecular genetics suggests that a myriad of Mendelian influences of individually tiny effect contribute to the heritability of intelligence … shuffling of such tiny Mendelian effects could, [American biologist Raymond] Pearl said, 'be relied on, I think, to produce in the future, as it has in the past, Shakespeares, Lincolns, and Pasteurs, from socially and economically humble origins' … the eugenicist inability to see that 'the economic element is perhaps the most significant biologically' was 'stupid'.[7]

In Toby Young's case what propelled him to be someone you may know is the economic element: his parents were very well off. That mattered much more for Toby's future than his mother and father being able. But few people like to think they are where they are because of economic advantage. They like to think they are realising their potential.

[7] From a discussion initially about 'Fuck off and die' in George Davey Smith (2012) 'Epigenesis for epidemiologists: does evo-devo have implications for population health research and practice?', *International Journal of Epidemiology*, 41, 1, pp. 236–47, https://academic.oup.com/ije/article/41/1/236/652408

Toby's argument is that children are born with greatly varying potentials, due to their differing genetic endowments. He suggests that only a few can go on to be great. Accordingly, the Toby Young idea of social mobility is that education should be used to identify those few who have the potential to be hugely able, and who have within them the genes for great cleverness. This short article is about why Toby and those who agree with Toby are wrong.

All slates are, of course, different. Blank slates, like newborn babies, may look very similar, but within them the grain always varies slightly. Of course, some babies are male and others female, some are more brown and others more pink, but they are all human babies, and few people today would try to argue that these different varieties have greatly differing potentials. No two slates are ever exactly identical. The shale they are made from varies. Cut two slates from the very same piece of rock and they will look identical, like identical twins; but even then, the way they have been cut and how they are later transported will alter them.

Toby didn't mention my co-author, Sally, but it might have helped him to know that she knows a thing or two about potential and meritocracy. Sally Tomlinson was a very good friend of Toby's father, Lord Michael Young. She was a council member of ACE, the Advisory Centre for Education, one of the many organisations Michael started. She was chair of ACE in 1993 and a member of Michael's Education Extra – a Learning from Experience Trust from 1992 to 1999.

Sally often talked with Michael about how one's children turn out. Michael wrote the 1945 Labour Party manifesto 'Let us Face the Future'. In *The Guardian* edition of 29 June 2001, Michael, under the headline 'Down with meritocracy', explained:

> I have been sadly disappointed by my 1958 book, *The rise of the meritocracy*. I coined a word which has gone into general circulation, especially in the USA and most recently found a prominent place in the speeches of Mr Blair. The book was a satire, meant to be a warning … it is good sense to appoint people to jobs on their merit. It is the opposite when those

> judged to have merit of a particular kind harden into a new social class without room for others.[8]

Michael continued:

> a social revolution has been accomplished by harnessing schools and universities to the task of sieving people according to education's narrow band of values … in the new social environment the rich and powerful have been doing mighty well for themselves… General inequality has become more grievous with every year that passes and without a bleat from the party who once spoke up so trenchantly for greater equality.

Michael died in 2002. Were he alive today [Editorial note: These words were written and first published in 2018; they may not apply so well in 2024.] he would see that the Labour Party does not just bleat, but now loudly proclaims the case for greater equality, and not just of opportunity, but of respect, rights and understanding.

In that 2016 article, Sally Tomlinson and I explained how the idea of great inherent differences among us dates back to Plato and his belief in golden children.[9] Plato thought that others, those unlike him, were silver, iron or brass children, destined to be farmers and craftsmen, not philosophers – and that you should 'breed according to your kind'. We know now that Plato's theories were wrong.

In the article which Toby disliked so much, Sally and I explained how the differences in the average levels of mathematics ability among nation-states could not be explained by genes but had to be due to their differing societies and educational systems. We went on to show that young adults in the US, the UK and Ireland were worst among the citizens of affluent countries at problem-

---

8 Michael Young (2001) 'Down with meritocracy', *The Guardian*, 29 June, https://www.theguardian.com/politics/2001/jun/29/comment

9 The article has now been greatly expanded into a book: Danny Dorling and Sally Tomlinson (2019) *Rule Britannia: Brexit and the end of empire*, London: Biteback, published 15 January.

solving, whereas those in Sweden, Finland, South Korea and Japan did best. We plotted the home postcodes of students who secured a place at the University of Oxford and suggested these were not the home locations of the special 'golden children', but far better reflected the wealth of the families they grew up in. We explained that geneticists know that 'genes only matter greatly when everything else matters hardly at all', and that in 2015 they calculated that 'raw parent-child correlations in education may reflect one-sixth genetic transmission and five-sixths social inheritance'.[10] We showed how people like Dominic Cummings believed the very opposite but had been misled. We went on to say a lot more than that, but we suspect Toby read little of it before he tweeted.[11]

Only within the past decade have we had access to genome-wide studies. These suggest that our inherent variation in nerdiness explains only up to 3.4 per cent of the differences between people in terms of mathematical ability.[12] In 2010 this research revealed that for measured ability in English for children aged 11–14, the genome-wide association is similarly very small, or as the researchers themselves stated: 'Put another way, these differences approximate to a tenth of that seen across the sexes for performance in English at this age'. We know that nowadays girls tend to be much better than boys, on average, at these particular ages. Children who have what appeared to be a special genetic

---

10 Dalton Conley, Benjamin Domingue, David Cesarini, Christopher Dawes, Cornelius Rietveld and Jason Boardman (2015) 'Is the effect of parental education on off-spring biased or moderated by genotype?', *Sociological Science*, 2: pp. 82–105, p. 82, https://www.sociologicalscience.com/download/volume-2/february/SocSci_v2_82to105.pdf

11 To mimic Dr Seuss's epic tale, *The Cat in the Hat*, 'Sally and I did not know what to say. Should we tell Toby, the things that we now know today?'. As the good Doctor said, it is fun to have fun. But you have to know how. Toby sometimes teases, he may think he pleases, but he is the antithesis of funny.

12 Sophia Docherty, Oliver Davis, Yulia Kovas et al (2010) 'A genome-wide association study identifies multiple loci associated with mathematical ability and disability', *Genes Brain and Behaviour*, 9, pp. 234–47, https://www.ncbi.nlm.nih.gov/pmc/articles/PMC2855870/

advantage in English had, on average, only a very small greater natural affinity.[13]

We now know that the idea of using an exam at age 11 to try to identify children with such tiny additional traits for nerdiness is futile. The inherent differences between our children are just too narrow, never mind all the other disadvantages that come from separating children from each other at such an early age into separate schools by 'ability' and labelling a few as clever and most as stupid.

If you are older than I am, or were unlucky enough to have grown up in an English county that preserved the 11-plus and were forced to take that test, at least you now know that if you failed the test, it tells us almost nothing about your ability. If you passed it, in the vast majority of cases it was because you were coached, or it was due to your upbringing and social advantages. The testers did not actually discover something special in you. Ignore the IQ score you were given as a child. It is no great measurement of achievement, and neither should you treat it as a curse.

Attempting to unlock the hidden potential in children is a futile exercise, as almost all children have great potential. And almost all of us are very capable of being stupid. Toby has gone out of his way to help demonstrate this over the course of his long series of careers.

There are no golden children.

Social mobility cannot be about allowing those with the potential to do best to rise to the top, because that group, the golden children, do not exist. Social mobility, if it is to serve any useful purpose, has to be about allowing people not to be constrained by circumstance and not to be obliged to follow in the footsteps of their parents. Who would want to constrain the child of a banker to being a banker? How cruel would that be?

That's a joke, of course. But in a society with low social mobility, those in the wealthiest brackets may find their options are almost as limited as those for people from the poorest backgrounds.

---

[13] For a much longer explanation see: Danny Dorling (2015) 'G is for Genes', *International Journal of Epidemiology*, 44, 1, pp. 374–8. https://academic.oup.com/ije/article/44/1/374/655644

The limitations come in their choice of what they might do in future, who they might meet, marry or otherwise pair up with, what jobs they might take and which neighbourhoods they might live in. The wealthy and the poor are also much more likely to fear and misunderstand each other in such societies, compared with those who have had the good fortune to grow up in more economically equitable and hence more socially mobile societies.

Education matters. Germany's education system actually serves to reduce social mobility a little in what is otherwise a much more equitable country. In contrast, at least as of the year 2008 when the data used in Figure 4.2 was collected, the comprehensive education school system that covered most of the UK slightly reduced the otherwise very high levels of social immobility that come with living in a country as economically unequal as the UK. The UK has the widest income inequalities of any large

Figure 4.2: Social and educational mobility and income inequality, early 2000s

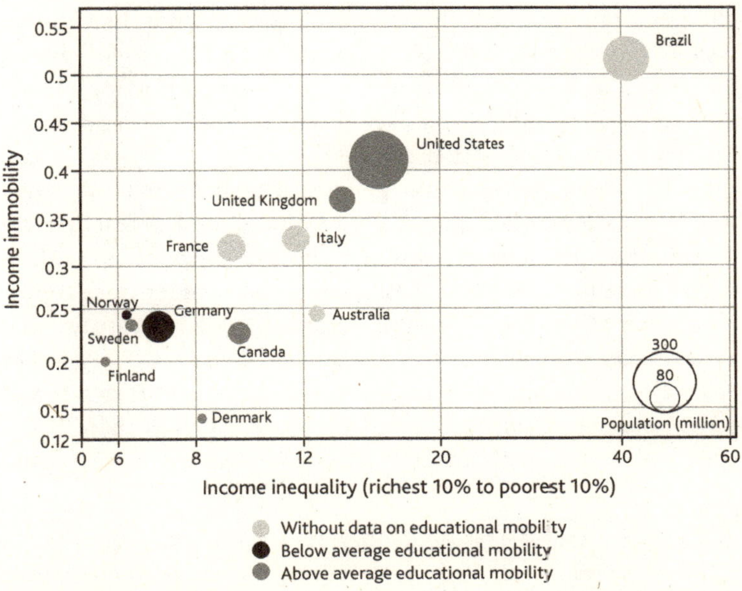

Source: Danny Dorling and Benjamin Hennig (2010) 'Angles, Saxons, Inequality, and Educational Mobility in England and Germany', *Social Europe Journal*, contribution to online debate, https://www.dannydorling.org/?page_id=598

country in Europe – on a par with Russia (whose land mass is mainly not in Europe).

When it comes to determining levels of social mobility, economic inequality matters far more than education. In countries with very wide income inequalities, most parents at the top try desperately to ensure that their children will not drop out of their wealth bracket. This is entirely understandable. Most will do everything they can to ensure that their children will not be trying to get by on two or three times less than they had. In doing this, they cut off the rungs of ladders that others might have climbed.

The unfair advantage

Genetic information is very useful. It can be used to discover that in the UK, regardless of any inherent cognitive ability, higher-performing children from disadvantaged backgrounds but with a greater inclination to learn are disproportionately less likely to attain good grades at examinations, compared to children from more socially advantaged backgrounds. In addition, systems operate to add to this inequality, as children in fee-paying secondary schools outperform their state secondary school counterparts regardless of ability (both the small amount that is inherent and all that is later attained).[14]

Furthermore, we can use genetic information to discover that it does not make sense to try to judge which teachers are doing better than others through the use of so-called 'value-added measures'. We find that genetic endowment does appear to contribute a small amount to value-added measures that additionally control for background characteristics. In other words, we find that some children may be more receptive, and easier to teach, than others. Furthermore, we find that 'value-added measures built from teacher rated ability have higher

[14] Tim Morris, Danny Dorling and George Davey Smith (2016) 'How well can we predict educational outcomes? Examining the roles of cognitive ability and social position in educational attainment', *Contemporary Social Science*, 11, 2/3, pp. 154–68, https://www.tandfonline.com/doi/full/10.1080/21582041.2016.1138502; and see Table 5 on page 246 of this volume.

heritability than those built from exam scores'.[15] In other words, the genes of children can be used to predict what teachers think of their ability much more than any actual ability each child has. As yet we do not know why this is. It could be that teachers are biased towards thinking that children who look a certain way, or who are more subservient and less cheeky, or a myriad of other possibilities – are cleverer. At present we just know it is this way.

Everything is affected by our genes. If all else is made equal, then genes become all that matters. For instance, in a world without tobacco, genes would be key to determining who dies of lung cancer. When it comes to who benefits from potentially good or bad teaching, it is hardly surprising that some children soak up conventional classroom teaching and some are more resistant to such an environment; in a system with less conventional ways of teaching, other groups of children might prosper better. Some children are more compliant, so trying to measure added value has problems that can only be revealed by genome-wide analysis. We in the UK would do much better to teach more like they do in Finland, and try to measure both pupils and teachers less. The measurements can be greatly biased.

In a summary of this very recent work, two of its authors explained that 'our results demonstrate that some value-added measures may not be robust to genetic differences between students, particularly when calculated from teacher-reported ability'.[16] You can think of this (if it helps) as the 'pretty nose' effect – one of the huge number of possible ways in which genes

---

15 Tim Morris, Neil Davies, Danny Dorling, Rebecca Richmond and George Davey Smith (2018) 'Examining the genetic influences on educational attainment and the validity of value-added measures of progress', *British Educational Research Journal*, 44, 5, pp. 727–47, first published: 3 January 2018, as a Biorxiv pre-print: https://www.biorxiv.org/content/early/2018/01/03/233635 and later on 9 September 2018 as the near identical journal paper: https://bera-journals.onlinelibrary.wiley.com/doi/full/10.1002/berj.3466

16 Tim Morris and Neil Davies (2018) 'Do value-added measures of school and teacher performance reflect genetic differences between students?', *The BERA Blog*, 10 September, https://www.bera.ac.uk/blog/do-value-added-measures-of-school-and-teacher-performance-reflect-genetic-differences-between-students

may interact with valued-added measures. Imagine if teachers believed that a child with a prettier nose – nose shape being genetically influenced – is more able. We know from a huge amount of research that White teachers often underestimate the ability of Black pupils when asked to assess them, with these pupils almost always doing better in examinations (on average) than predicted. Given what this finding tells us, it suggests there must be a huge number of other far less obvious implicit biases at play in our society, too, affecting everything from who receives attention first when two students put up their hands at the same time, to the outcomes of all job interviews.

Children are not blank slates, but they are so close to being so when it comes to their capacity to learn and be influenced that we would do well to treat them as such. Ironically the most recent study to help reveal this is one in which Toby Young himself was an author. In an article published on 23 March 2018, he and his colleagues said: 'We found substantial mean genetic differences between students of different school types: students in non-selective schools had lower EduYears GPS compared to those in grammar (d=0.41) and private schools (d=0.37).'[17]

In other words, they were saying they had discovered that children who attended private schools in England were simply genetically more able, advantaged from birth in a way that could not be modified. What Toby and his colleagues appeared not to have realised was that the key qualification for attending a private school is that your parents are wealthy enough to pay the fees.

Some private schools have entrance tests, but an equal (and in many ways opposite) number do not. Those private schools largely exist to take the children of the affluent who fail such tests. Whatever the 'EduYear genome-wide polygenic score (GPS)' Toby and his colleagues were measuring was, it was not about being especially quick or clever. It is possible it might be

---

[17] Emily Smith-Woolley, Jean-Baptiste Pingault, Saskia Selzam, Kaili Rimfeld, Eva Krapohl, Sophie von Stumm, Kathryn Asbury, Philip Dale, Toby Young, Rebecca Allen, Yulia Kovas and Robert Plomin (2018) 'Differences in exam performance between pupils attending selective and non-selective schools mirror the genetic differences between them', *Nature Partner Journals: Science of Learning*, 3, pp. 1–7, https://www.nature.com/articles/s41539-018-0019-8

associated with being acquisitive. The one thing the parents of these children tended to have in common was that they had acquired greater wealth and income than most people.

The most interesting part of Toby Young and his colleagues' 2018 paper can be found in the supplementary material which is available online.[18] Here, the authors report that they found no genetic disadvantage associated with attending a secondary modern school in those counties of England that still have such schools. In other words, whatever they found, it is not about any genes to do with being worse at passing the 11-plus.

None of this would matter much if one of the authors of the supplementary material was not Tim Leunig, the former Chief Scientific Advisor at the Department for Education during Michael Gove's tenure, and current Scientific Advisor in the Department of the Environment, which Gove now leads. Interestingly, Tim did not appear among the authors of the main article alongside Toby – but they had been working together on the data. It would be interesting to know why Tim was an author of the supplementary material on this article, but not the article itself. I have never seen that happen before with an academic article. It is not good practice. But hopefully it indicates that Tim Leunig, who is a very astute civil servant, may have had doubts as to the usefulness of going down this particular road of agreeing with Toby Young's ideas about genes.[19]

---

[18] Supplementary Online Material: Emily Smith-Woolley, Jean-Baptiste Pingault, Saskia Selzam, Kaili Rimfeld, Eva Krapohl, Sophie von Stumm, Kathryn Asbury, Philip Dale, Toby Young, Rebecca Allen, Tim Leunig, Yulia Kovas and Robert Plomin, 'Differences in exam performance between pupils attending selective and nonselective schools mirror the genetic differences between them', *Nature Partner Journals: Science of Learning*, 3, pp. 1–7, Available at: https://www.nature.com/articles/s41539-018-0019-8#Sec22

[19] [Editorial note: Tim Leunig recently left the civil service: Staff Reporter (2023) 'Third senior advisor announces DfE departure', *Education Executive*, 16 May, https://edexec.co.uk/third-senior-advisor-announces-dfe-departure/, and, famously, clashed with Michael Gove, his then boss: 'Dr Leunig's outspokenness is matched by fearlessness. When Mr Gove first proposed a new, highly traditional, history curriculum for schools, Dr Leunig emailed him to say: "You will, personally, be mocked if you go ahead with this, and rightly so"' (Glen Owen (2020) 'How senior economic adviser

Looks (and prejudice) matter

Genome-wide analysis has largely rendered research on twins obsolete. It suggests that the findings of twin studies tend to magnify the small actual differences in personality between us that can be attributed to our genes by as much as a factor of ten.[20] However, in 2013 an article was published that studied twins in a different way. It included twins who were brought up assuming they were identical, but later (genetically) found not to be (they were dizygotic, or DZ), and the opposite, twins thought to be not identical, but who technically were (they were monozygotic, or MZ).

Those incorrectly thought to be identical started with very similar birth weights and ended with very similar heights and weights. What was interesting was that the assessment of their academic ability, using the US cumulative high school grade point average, was equally highly correlated as that for twins correctly thought to be identical.

What twin studies often actually reveal is that similar-looking children have similar outcomes in life, especially if they are born at the same time and place (as all twins are). They do not reveal that some people are genetically superior to others in overall ability, but rather that we live in societies that have strong prejudices about how people are treated, based simply on looks and first impressions, and on characteristics such as being more extrovert or more impatient. This article was groundbreaking because,

---

Dr Tim Leunig is a brainbox with wheezes on everything from third class carriages to paddling pools', *Daily Mail*, 29 February). But telling his boss he is wrong is more astute than claiming that the inhabitants of an entire city are economically doomed: Liam Thorpe (2020) '"Barmy" boffin who told people to abandon Liverpool is now top government advisor: Senior Treasury aide Tim Leunig once said money would be better spent on Plasma TVs rather than regenerating Liverpool', *Liverpool Echo*, 4 March, https://www.liverpoolecho.co.uk/news/liverpool-news/boffin-who-told-people-abandon-17856289]

[20] Danny Dorling (2019) 'Review of Robert Plomin: *Blueprint – How DNA makes us who we are*', *Times Higher Education*, 10 January, https://www.timeshighereducation.com/books/blueprint-how-dna-makes-us-who-we-are-robert-plomin-allen-lane

as its authors said, 'we are the first to apply the misclassified twins approach to a recent sample with accurate genetic zygosity information for all twins'.[21]

Until the recent arrival of genome-wide analysis, it was possible to argue that there were gold, silver, iron and brass children and that they needed to be identified and separately educated. Social mobility was seen as the process of identifying golden children born to brass parents and propelling them upwards. Now we know this to be deeply flawed rubbish. We are all slates of one kind or another. We are born blank, able to be moulded into a very wide variety of forms. Growing up in a society where this truth is not widely understood is a terrible misfortune. It is time we rectified this particular error. We should thank Toby for his help.[22]

Finally, we should remember that because of Britain's unique history and remarkable class divides, a strong eugenic streak runs through every political party, including the Labour Party. The original Clause IV of the Labour Party, mentioned briefly in the introduction to this section, drafted in 1917 and accepted in 1918, began with the words: 'To secure for the workers by hand or by brain the full fruits of their industry …'. It thus included a eugenic distinction between two types of worker, which was hardly surprising since Sidney Webb, its author, was a eugenicist, as were so many leading thinkers of that time. That tradition remained when Tony Blair instituted a new Clause IV in 1995, with its promise 'to create for each of us the means to realise our true potential'. We now know just how little those true potentials vary, and thus that a concern about variance in potential is unfounded. When that clause comes to be rewritten again, whenever that

---

21 Dalton Conley, Emily Rauscher, Christopher Dawes, Patrik Magnusson and Mark Siegal (2013) 'Heritability and the equal environment assumption: evidence from multiple samples of misclassified twins', *Behaviour Genetics*, 43, 5, pp. 415–26, http://link.springer.com/article/10.1007/s10519-013-9602-1

22 I don't wish to be mean to Toby. I believe he has the potential within him to come round to another way of thinking. I'll end by writing (in my own words), following the style of Dr Seuss in *Oh! The Places You'll Go!*: 'You have brains in your head… And you know what you know. And YOU are the one who'll decide where to go.'

is, it will be rewritten in the light of all that we now know, and all that we are about to learn, about the incredible potential in almost all of us to be so much better than we currently are, when set free from today's constraints and prejudices. The implications for social mobility, for patrician politics, for elite universities, and for society as a whole are profound. We now know that there are not just a few among us who have within them the potential to be truly great, to be great leaders, steering society with their great minds. If we aimed for a society that allows the greatest number to contribute and participate, that would be true social mobility, for the many – and not social mobility merely for a few.

CHAPTER 4.2

When racism stopped being normal[1]

How can you tell when the times are changing, and great progress is being made? How can you tell when instead we appear to be going back in time, or 'going back to '79', as the lyrics of a tribute song to the recent Conservative government suggested?[2] Often it feels as if most of the great steps forward were taken a long time ago. However, it was probably the case that people did not realise that they were achieving as much as they were. The same may be true today.

Anxieties and social conflicts fuel the belief that Britain is becoming a less tolerant society. In some of the most unequal rich countries, such as the UK and the US, state benefit levels

---

1 Originally published in 2019 as 'When racism stopped being normal, but no one noticed: generational value change' in Philip Cowley and Robert Ford (eds) *More Sex, Lies, and the Ballot Box*, London: Biteback, ch 30, pp. 177–81. This chapter, in turn, is based on two articles from 2013: 'Tolerance, inequality and the recession' (Sheffield Political Economy Research Institute Blog, 2013) and 'It is necessarily so' (Significance, 2013), both of which use data from the US. For a proper introduction you should read Scott Blinder, Robert Ford and Elisabeth Ivarsflaten, 'The better angels of our nature: how the antiprejudice norm affects policy and party preferences in Great Britain and Germany', *American Journal of Political Science*, 2013, 57, 4, pp. 841–57. The US data has been updated using work by Frank Newport ('In U.S., 87% approve of Black-White marriage, vs. 4% in 1958'), Art Swift ('Americans' worries about race relations at record high') and Lawrence Bobo et al ('The real record on racial attitudes'). Ten years later, following the start of Black Lives Matter, the shift continues.

2 Not the Wu-Tang Clan's single 'Triumph', but a remake of Captain SKA's 2011 'Slipping back in time'.

are now so low compared to average wages that people will do almost any job, or more than one job, to avoid having to claim the dole. The government complains that 'locals' won't do the jobs immigrants will still take. The environment is nasty, and fears over immigration keep rising up the list of most important issues at each election.

In this environment you might expect people to become increasingly intolerant of the people from different groups who could be taking 'their' jobs. But the following graph (Figure 4.3) challenges that assumption. It shows the slow but steady decline in opposition to mixed-race marriages, a good indicator of racial prejudice. A generation ago, in 1983, a majority of White British respondents expressed discomfort with the idea of having in-laws of a different race. By 2013, this figure had fallen to less than a quarter.

What the graph shows is that some things change slowly and steadily in a way that is almost impervious to immediate events. This is because much of this slow shift is produced by generational change. Older voters, whose views were shaped by growing up in an almost all-White Britain prior to larger-scale immigration, are very strongly opposed to interracial marriage – in 2013, over 40 per cent of those born before 1940 disapproved of it. Opposition is much lower among their children, born in the

Figure 4.3: Adults objecting to having an Asian or West Indian in-law, UK 1983–2013 (%)

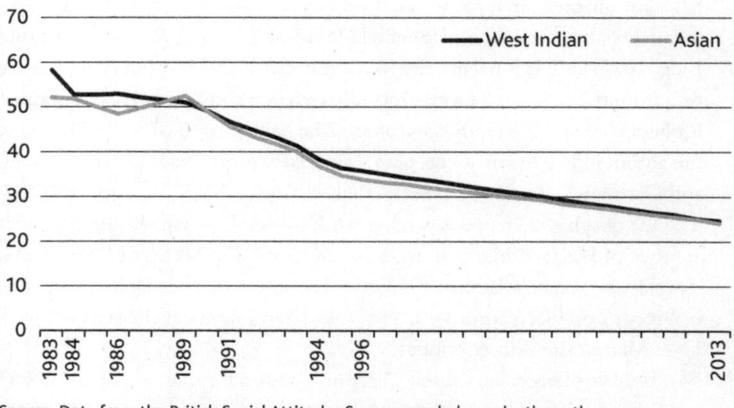

Source: Data from the British Social Attitudes Survey, graph drawn by the author

1960s, and vanishes almost entirely among their grandchildren: less than one in ten of those born in the 1990s express any discomfort about having an in-law of a different race.

Figure 4.3 shows that people can become radically more tolerant, even in times of rising inequality and social conflict. Hostility to minorities fell during the early 1990s, despite a recession and mass unemployment, and fell in the 2000s despite the rise in BNP/UKIP voting and widespread public anxiety about immigration. It is possible that the brief hiatus in the rise in tolerance in the mid-1980s was related to mass unemployment and rapidly growing economic inequalities, or a birth cohort effect, but what is most important about it is its brevity.

Your parents could well be among those who objected to mixed-race marriages. But if they were growing up in the Britain of the 1940s then they were normal. Among younger people today, few worry about whether folk get married or not, or to whom – male or female, Black or White. But not long ago it was as normal to be a bigot as not.

Exactly the same has been seen in the US. In the late 1950s in the US, 24 Americans disapproved of mixed-race marriage for every one who approved. By the late 1960s, that ratio had plummeted to 4 : 1. By 2012 the approval ratio had reached 6 : 1. In 1990, 65 per cent of Whites in the US opposed a Black–White marriage and 40 per cent opposed an Asian–White or Hispanic–White marriage. By 2008, that had dropped to 25 per cent of US Whites opposing a Black–White union in their immediate family, and by 2013 to just 16 per cent. Then, between 2013 and 2017, the proportion of Americans who said they worried a great deal about race relations rose very rapidly from 17 per cent to 42 per cent, as Trump campaigned for and won the presidency. But as yet we have no evidence of any fall in approval rates for mixed marriage.

Times may seem bad again now, but have a little sympathy for your parents. Just look at what was common in the time of *their* parents, who grew up in a generation of British imperial rule, fascists ruling half of Europe and blackshirts marching in the streets in London. And now think about how generations to come might view your generation. Look at how quickly attitudes are still changing. In a generation's time your views on whether we should worry about how few young men go to university or the sanctity of national borders or the theory that the very wealthy create jobs by investing their wealth may well be seen as sad evidence of the ignorance of our times. There will certainly be views that are widespread today that will come to be seen as misguided in the near future.

Looking at past trends in changing attitudes helps us to see how much views that appear to be very fixed can change over the course of lifetimes and between generations. Politics often appears to be in a desperate mess. Progress is slow. Many things are getting worse. But we tend to concentrate on the bad news and on the most powerful, immediate crises. That is how we improve our political lives. We complain and agitate about what matters to us right now, even as other things continue to change and often improve. In the future, we may well look back at the years just before and after the 2008 economic crash and say: 'That was when the tide of social change began to accelerate.'

If the analysis of the figures presented here is right, especially in terms of recent US trends on public opinion, the tide may be changing not just in relation to the tolerance of mixed-race marriages and what that implies for the diminishing of racism, but perhaps also in many other areas that currently do not look encouraging in contemporary data.

CHAPTER 4.3

About our schools[1]

We often don't truly value something until we have lost it. In the short term, children losing access to schools in the UK in 2020 because of the COVID-19 pandemic suddenly brought home not just what schools do as physical locations for teaching, but also what they do in the round. Schools are about far more than education. They are places where we become socialised into our society, where we learn to respect others, and in some cases, to look up to or down on others. They don't just teach skills. Schools help us form our attitudes, beliefs and prejudices.

At certain times and in certain schools, we are told that others are our betters, often other people not at our school. We learn to behave and to be disciplined, so that later in our lives our apparent superiors will find that we are respectful and compliant; that we know our place. This still occurs in England today. The idea that different children are of different rank and worth is still endlessly stamped into young minds in ways that do not often occur so forcefully elsewhere in Europe.[2]

---

1 Originally published as the foreword to Tim Brighouse and Mick Waters (2022) *About our schools: Improving on previous best*, Carmarthen: Crown House Publishing, https://www.crownhouse.co.uk/about-our-schools. [Editorial note: Tim died in 2023 at age 83. He fought for better education, including where I went to school. Two decades earlier it was written: 'He works with people rather than against them. He gives teachers a great sense of belonging rather than making them feel they are victims of policies': Wendy Berliner (2002) 'A great crusade', *The Guardian*, 9 April, https://www.theguardian.com/society/2002/apr/09/localgovernment.education]

2 [Editorial note: As Frankie Boyle observed on 22 January 2024, 'The underlying reason people send their children to private school in Britain is

When classrooms emptied during 2020–21, it quickly became clear which schools had the resources to teach online, and which had to hand out paper worksheets instead. In a crisis, the huge advantage of private schools' very low pupil–teacher ratios became glaringly obvious. For those for whom school was a sanctuary from indifference or harm at home, no longer being able to go to school was devastating. In a very small number of cases it will have been deadly. If we have learned anything from the pandemic, we now know that schools should be the last public institutions to close and the first to reopen.

Tim Brighouse and Mick Waters, the authors of *About Our Schools: Improving on Previous Best* [of which this chapter was originally the foreword], had school closures foremost in their minds, because they began writing in earnest in early 2021 when it became clear that, yet again, schools would be closed for many months. State schools were only kept open physically for the children of 'key' workers and those identified as being in special need. It turned out that everyone who worked in a school was a key worker – something that had barely been acknowledged before. It also turned out that the politics of education was not quite as clearly divided between good and bad as we might have thought. You will be reading these words many months or even years after it was accepted that the new coronavirus is endemic and a zero-Covid strategy is impossible. However, it was a right-wing government that tried to keep the schools open and the left-wing unions (championing zero-Covid fantasy) that demanded they close.

In hindsight it is much easier to see what the right course of action would have been, having now had time to contemplate and seen how other countries kept their schools almost entirely open during the pandemic. Perhaps we could have done the same over a much longer period during which we could all take stock of what we were losing without our schools even being closed – the decades during which funding per head was cut for 13 out of 14 children, that is, for all those who attended a state school in England. Note that it is a much higher proportion than 93 per

something it's considered impolite to mention: they want your kids to end up working for theirs', https://x.com/frankieboyle/status/174941470343 5035129?s=20] cent in most parts of the UK and a much lower proportion among the children of the people who get to determine education policy. Furthermore, a growing division had been sown within the state system, with schools forced to compete for pupils, to attract and retain staff (not least teachers) and to pay for the upkeep of their buildings. [Editorial note: Contrast all this with the dreams of what might have been possible in 1914, and what was achieved in the six decades that followed the creation of a banner such as the one shown in Figure 4.4.]

Figure 4.4: Banner of the East Bradford Socialist Sunday School, Fred Liles, 1914

see colour version in plate section

Note: The Working Class Movement Library's website explains: 'As labelled on the banner, the two trees represent "knowledge" and "truth". Fruit trees and fields of corn represent abundance and plenty under socialism, while the poppy with its ability to grow in disturbed soil signifies beauty emerging from disturbance. [Bradford councillor Fred Liles] made the banner before the flower was adopted as a symbol of remembrance. The rising sun in the background is a common occurrence in visual political communication, and represents the possibilities of a better life beyond the present one.'

Source: Working Class Movement Library, https://www.wcml.org.uk/our-collections/creativity-and-culture/leisure/socialist-sunday-schools/banner-of-the-bradford-socialist-sunday-school/

Tim Brighouse and Mick Waters' book takes up the story in 1976, the year that marked the end of optimism and trust in teaching and saw the dial adjusted to a new belief in the power of markets, centralisation and managerialism. The authors confess that their hope that the previous system would have thrived was 'probably misplaced'. It is worth noting that in 1976 the UK was one of the most equitable large countries in Europe, second only to Sweden in terms of income equality. By that measure, Germany, Italy, Spain and France all had more socially fractured societies in that year. In contrast, in the decades that followed – when markets, centralisation and managerialism were allowed to take over much of life in Britain – the UK's economic inequality would become by far the greatest of any Western European country. It was not just education that fractured after 1976. Health, housing, employment and the distribution of material assets (including wealth) and other determinants of life chances also all saw developments that worsened lives and increased division.

Economic inequality matters in education. In the 1980s, a large number of places in private schools were sponsored under the government's Assisted Places Scheme for (those deemed to be) the academically able children of parents who would not otherwise have been able to afford the fees. The scheme also ensured that private schools would not have to close.

As incomes were more equal at the start of the 1980s, there weren't enough adults being paid so much more than others that they could afford to educate their children privately. This meant that the commercial future of private schools was at stake. Private education only prospers in places where there is high income inequality. However, by the time Tony Blair abolished the Assisted Places Scheme in 1997, income inequalities in England had grown to such an extent that there were now enough children with parents who were so well paid that the surviving private schools could be filled without the need for a direct government subsidy. (The indirect subsidies that enabled tax avoidance were maintained.) It is also important to note that in no single year during the period since 1997 (which included all the New Labour years as well as the decade of austerity) did income inequality fall by any measurable amount.

It is perhaps unsurprising that during the same period there have been many changes in education, but few progressive movements. In fact, there has been no progressive government in the UK since the early and mid-1970s. Most recently, under New Labour and then the coalition and Conservative governments that followed, we have witnessed the almost wholesale privatisation of universities.

One of the ways we hold on to hope is the belief, at times not entirely unfounded, that after many decades of banging your head against a wall and going in the wrong direction, a group of people – in this case, those interested in education in Britain – realise that a change of tack is required. At this point we need to know what to do next, having learnt what did not work in England between 1976 and today. Although the overriding ethos of markets and competition was not conducive to progress, many individuals and some organisations, most schools and millions of children and their parents, all struggled over those long years to improve many things. For example, we should not forget that these were years in which schools became dramatically less violent places, a significant part of which was banning teachers from beating pupils. Not everything was rosy in 1976.

There are so many wonderful suggestions of how much better we could be as educators in the book for which this is the foreword. One I particularly like is that 'we should treat pupils not as they (sometimes infuriatingly) are but as they might become'. Recently I met a teacher who works at a school that I attended almost four decades ago. She told me she thought that none of her pupils would ever write a book. It was an 'average school': avoided by most of the wealthiest parents in the city and aspired to by many of the parents who live in poorer parts just outside its catchment area. I had some sympathy with her exasperation, but I had also been a child at that school, and I failed at English at age 16. I knew that did not mark me for life. I read my first word in 1976 – very late, at age 8. I had good teachers, but I found reading hard. In the end, my mum taught me to read; my teachers barely improved on what she had achieved, although they tried, and they taught me enough of maths and geography and science that I ended up writing many books. Had they only seen how I wrote when I was at school, no one would have believed I was capable of writing these words you are reading here.

We have all followed our own individual educational paths and each of these will have shaped both us and our views on education. Very probably, Margaret Thatcher, the Education Secretary from 1970 to 1974, would not have believed so strongly in her own superiority had she not been sent to a grammar school by her father or been awarded a place at an elitist university. Tony Blair, who came to power with the mantra 'education, education, education', and his one-time education advisor Andrew Adonis, might well have had very different views on what a good education consisted of had they been differently educated too. They might have been taught how every 'young person can walk more than a few steps with genius' [as this book explains]. And we could add that the geniuses among us tend not to seem quite so clever when you spend a long time hanging around with them.

So many of the people who have steered the course of the ship of English education in recent decades, from policy wonks to prime ministers, appear to believe that they, personally, have truly realised their own great potential, which has somehow been allowed to burst forth, such that now their amazing ideas should be implemented. Such pomposity!

Examples of pomposity and inability abound in English education. For all the hours of senior management teams brainstorming risk assessments, no one foresaw what might happen during a pandemic. Or think of how ridiculous it is that 1,579 pupils are permanently excluded from English schools each year for each of the five individual children excluded a year in Scotland – meaning that almost 8,000 children a year are excluded in England; and it may be higher now – we have no really reliable data on this, as we do not care very much. And then try to imagine how that feels for each and every one of those children, for the rest of their lives.

Education, at its best, frees you from being told to believe that you are *the natural inferior* of others. At its worst, it leaves you with the impression that you are *naturally superior to* others. Education in England is in a terrible mess. If you don't believe me, try describing what happens in your town, city or village to someone from elsewhere in Western Europe. Tell them how different children are selected to go to different schools. Tell them about the languages and arts that we no longer even try to teach. Tell them what ensues when our children are asked a maths or science question that is not directly connected to one of the answers that they and their teachers have guessed would be on the exam paper. And ask them what happens where they live – in any of the Western European countries that did not travel the post-1976 road we took in England.

CHAPTER 4.4

The birth of Baby Eight Billion[1]

The news of the eight-billionth person joining our species last week was a joyous affair, with the UN secretary general, António Guterres, declaring it 'an occasion to celebrate'.[2] In contrast, when the global population hit four, five, six and seven billion, in 1975, 1987, 1999 and 2011 respectively,[3] there was widespread dismay,[4] although it did abate a little with each milestone. The doubling of our numbers in 47 years did not bring about the famines and other disasters widely predicted in the 1960s.[5]

As Poonam Muttreja, the executive director of the Population Foundation of India, explained, we welcomed the new child

---

1 Originally published as: 'Don't panic about the birth of Baby 8 Billion: before he's 65 our numbers will be in reverse', *The Observer*, 20 November 2022, https://www.theguardian.com/commentisfree/2022/nov/20/dont-panic-about-birth-baby-8-million-before-hes-65-numbers-will-be-in-reverse.

2 António Guterres (2022) 'UN Secretary General's statement as the world population hits 8 billion', *Africa Renewal*, 14 November, https://www.un.org/africarenewal/magazine/november-2022/un-secretary-general%E2%80%99s-statement-world-population-hits-8-billion

3 United Nations (2022) 'Our growing population', *UN Global Issues*, November, https://www.un.org/en/global-issues/population

4 Often echoing earlier fears: George Getze (1967) 'Dire famine forecast', *The Salt Lake Tribune*, Salt Lake City, Utah, 17 November, p. 9, https://www.newspapers.com/clip/36287902/dire-famine-forecast/

5 Staff Reporter (1970) 'Dr Ehrlich, outspoken ecologist, to speak', *Redlands Daily Facts*, Redlands, California, 6 October, p. 3, https://www.newspapers.com/clip/36289639/dr-erlich/

whose birth marked this event and we are no longer afraid.[6] We have learned that most of our population growth is not due to births but to most of us living much longer, as the Swedish physician and statistician Hans Rosling so brilliantly explained.[7] When sadly he died in 2017,[8] aged just 68, global average life expectancy was 72.

Collectively we are ageing, but life expectancy growth peaked in 1981.[9] Then, people lived, on average, five years longer than in 1971 (61 years rather than 56). However, the rate of increase has been slowing globally for four decades.

Births peaked in 1990, with an echo 24 years later.[10] The UN now predicts that there will never again be as many children born in a year as were born in 1990. Globally, there were 8.5 million fewer births in 2022 than in 1990, despite there being far more potential parents. Worries about population growth in countries such as Tanzania are about people living longer, something we should not be concerned about.[11] The average woman in Tanzania in 2020 was a mother to four children, 9 per cent down on a decade earlier. UN projections are for that fall to accelerate to 15 per cent a decade, to an average of 2.3 children in 2080.

---

[6] BBC Newshour (2022) 'Earth now home to eight billion people', *BBC World Service*, 15 November 1pm, https://www.bbc.co.uk/sounds/play/w172yfc9phmvg9g

[7] Gapminder Foundation (2015) 'DON'T PANIC – Hans Rosling showing the facts about population', *YouTube*, https://www.youtube.com/watch?v=FACK2knC08E

[8] Karen McVeigh (2017) 'Hans Rosling, statistician and development champion, dies aged 68', *The Guardian*, 8 February, https://www.theguardian.com/global-development/2017/feb/07/hans-rosling-obituary

[9] UN (2022) *World population prospects 2022*, UN Department of Economic and Social Affairs, Population Division, https://population.un.org/wpp/

[10] Danny Dorling (2020) *Slowdown: The end of the great acceleration – and why it's good for the planet, the economy, and our lives*, Yale: Yale University Press, Figure 63, https://www.dannydorling.org/books/SLOWDOWN/Illustrations.html#img63

[11] Caroline Kimeu (2022) 'What Tanzania tells us about Africa's population explosion as the world hits 8bn people', *The Guardian*, 15 November, https://www.theguardian.com/global-development/2022/nov/15/focus-turns-to-africa-as-world-population-reaches-8bn

One abiding myth is that extra people will inevitably add to carbon pollution. It is a story sold like snake oil to the mathematically illiterate. 'Everyone has a carbon footprint', the tale begins. Thus, any increase in people must increase carbon pollution. But the same could be said for shoes: the corollary myth would be that if there are more people in the world, there will inevitably be more footwear. But most of us do not behave like Imelda Marcos when it comes to shoes.[12] In 2021, 22 billion pairs of shoes were produced worldwide, 9 per cent fewer than in 2019.[13] Similarly, our concerns over food, healthcare, education and housing should not be about our numbers, but instead about our inequality, greed and waste. These are the real problems of our time.

We are ill prepared for the population slowdown. We have been taught to fear an invasion of migrants. But it will be through migration that the coming slowdown is tempered. In Europe from 1946 to 1961, more than twelve million children were born each year. Fewer than seven million are born a year now and falling. In many parts of Europe, one-child families are now the norm.[14] That is only a problem if you fear migrants.

A few people still suggest that some countries are not doing enough to reduce their populations.[15] But those Cassandras are dwindling even faster than global fertility rates (Figure 4.5). Like the Trojan priestess, they fear that no one will believe their warnings. Unlike her, they do not have the gift of prophecy – none of us does. However, to date, births are falling fastest where

---

[12] Therese Reyes (2019) 'What ever happened to Imelda Marcos' 3,000 pairs of shoes?', *Vice*, 14 November, https://www.vice.com/en/article/59n8ab/what-ever-happened-imelda-marcos-3000-pairs-shoes-philippines

[13] P. Smith (2022) 'Quantity of footwear produced worldwide from 2015 to 2021 (in billion pairs)', *Statista*, 12 October, https://www.statista.com/statistics/1044823/global-footwear-production-quantity/

[14] Danny Dorling and Annika Koljonen (2020) *Finntopia: What we can learn from the world's happiest country*, Newcastle: Agenda, Figure 8.2, https://www.dannydorling.org/finntopia/figures_files/page0-1035-full.html

[15] John Vidal (2022) 'It should not be controversial to say a population of 8 billion will have a grave impact on the climate', *The Guardian*, 15 November, https://www.theguardian.com/commentisfree/2022/nov/15/population-8-billion-climate

Figure 4.5: The global population has doubled in the past 47 years

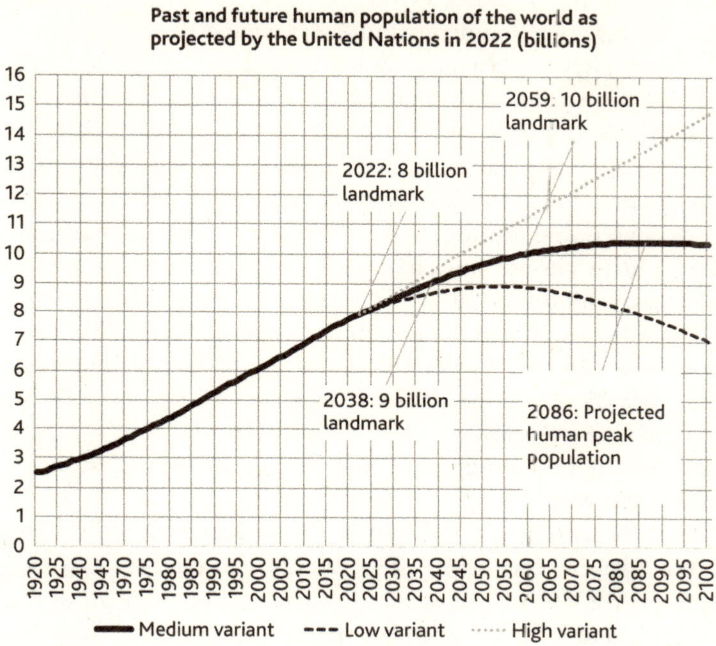

Source: UN (2022) *World Population Prospects 2022*, UN Department of Economic and Social Affairs, Population Division, https://population.un.org/wpp/

they are most common. They fall even when governments try to encourage more births.[16]

To hold up birth rates, as researchers writing in the *BMJ* explained, 'countries with smaller, older populations need to realise the full social and economic potential of all citizens, including migrants and their families'.[17] They cautioned that attempts to limit access to abortion, contraception and sexual education, in Poland in 2021 and the US in 2022, are not just misguided, dangerous and distressing, but futile.

---

[16] BBC (2020) 'Russia's Putin seeks to stimulate birth rate', *BBC News*, 15 January, https://www.bbc.co.uk/news/world-europe-51120165

[17] Stuart Gietel-Basten, Anna Rotkirch and Tomáš Sobotka (2022) 'Changing the perspective on low birth rates: why simplistic solutions won't work', *BMJ*, 15 November, https://doi.org/10.1136/bmj-2022-072670

Our worldwide population explosion began in the 19th century, largely due to the actions of a few men forcing people off the land in their own countries and invading and destabilising more stable societies worldwide.[18] When Europeans settled in colonies around the world, and imposed free trade in goods (including opium) on countries such as China, they caused such chaos that the very slow population growth of the preceding millennia was transformed into a worldwide population explosion. The global slowdown is due to the actions of billions of women demanding the right to choose how many children they have or whether they have children at all.

We will have to wait longer for the next milestone. With good fortune, I will be 70 when the global population is projected to reach 9 billion in 2038. Perhaps, by then, we will have learned to mark the occasion by celebrating the birthday of an elderly person, rather than suggesting that we reached the milestone due to an extra birth.[19]

Most of us old folk will not be around to see the 10 billion number reached in 2059.[20] That 10 billion year could be much later than 2059, or not at all. Successive UN projections have overestimated future population growth because they have repeatedly underestimated the rapidity of the fall in births. However, almost all children today will live long enough to be alive in the year, currently projected to be 2086, when for the first time in the recent history of our species the number of humans on Earth falls overall.

---

[18] Adam Clark Estes (2012) 'The British have invaded 90 percent of the countries on earth', *The Atlantic*, 5 November, https://www.theatlantic.com/international/archive/2012/11/british-have-invaded-90-percent-countries-earth/321789/

[19] Danny Dorling and Stuart Gietel-Basten (2017) *Why demography matters*, Cambridge: Polity, https://www.dannydorling.org/books/demography/

[20] Danny Dorling (2013) *Population 10 billion*, London: Constable, https://www.dannydorling.org/books/10billion/

No longer rising in our numbers will be as momentous as we imagine colonising another planet[21] or discovering a new continent[22] to be. And it is infinitely more likely.

[Editorial note: On 11 July 2024, the United Nations published the biennial update of its World Population Prospects (UNWPP) projections. Table 6 shows that the maximum was now predicted to be 140 million people lower, and to come in 2084, two years earlier than previously projected.

It was now estimated there would be over 150 million *fewer* people alive in future by the year 2090 than had been the case the day before. Because we were having fewer children.]

Table 6: UN projections for future global population

	UNWPP, 1 July projection (millions)		
Year	**2024-based**	**2022-based**	**Difference (millions)**
2080	10,283	10,415	–132
2081	10,286	10,420	–134
2082	10,288	10,424	–136
2083	10,289	10,427	–138
2084	**10,289**	10,429	–140
2085	10,288	10,431	–142
2086	10,287	**10,431**	–144
2087	10,284	10,430	–146
2088	10,281	10,429	–148
2089	10,277	10,427	–150
2090	10,272	10,424	–152

Source: https://population.un.org/wpp/Download/Standard/MostUsed/

21 Esteban Pardo (2022) 'World population to decrease from 2064, researchers say: a less populated world might hinder Elon Musk's plans to colonize Mars', *Deutsche Welle*, 2 February, https://www.dw.com/en/elon-musks-dreams-of-mars-colonization-could-be-hindered-by-depopulation/a-60624894

22 Karl Marx and Friedrich Engels (1848) *Manifesto of the Communist Party, Chapter I. Bourgeois and Proletarians*, https://www.marxists.org/archive/marx/works/1848/communist-manifesto/ch01.htm

CHAPTER 4.5

History repeating[1]

The world population is expected to peak in the summer of 2086. But do the official United Nations estimates give enough consideration to human behaviour? As the Propellerheads put it so well in their 1997 hit song 'History Repeating' featuring Shirley Bassey: '… I've seen it before … and I'll see it again … [we're all] Just little bits of history repeating.'[2]

In June 2011, I wrote a blog post[3] for *Significance* magazine. I explained that in May 2011 the United Nations (UN) Population Division had released the 2010 edition of its world population estimates and projections. It was then thought that humans would number 10.1 billion within the next 90 years and 9.3 billion by 2050. I pointed out at the time how crude their methodology was. But it had to be simple when so many countries needed to agree with it and not be offended by estimates that might greatly differ from their own.

The UN press release came with both a health warning and a handy explanation of how they estimated a particular type of confidence limit:

---

1 Originally published as: Danny Dorling (2023) 'World population projections: Just little bits of history repeating?', *Significance Magazine*, 20, 4, pp. 22–7, https://academic.oup.com/jrssig/article/20/4/22/7233203

2 Propellerheads feat. Miss Shirley Bassey (1997) 'History Repeating', written by Alex Gifford, from the album Decksandrumsandrockandroll, https://www.youtube.com/watch?v=yzLT6_TQmq8

3 Danny Dorling (2011) 'We're all … just little bits of history repeating (Part 1 – History, and Part 2 – The Future)', *Significance Magazine Website*, 13 and 14 June, http://bit.ly/44021R5 and http://bit.ly/3JgeY18

> Small variations in fertility can produce major differences in the size of populations over the long run. The high projection variant, whose fertility is just half a child above that in the medium variant, produces a world population of 10.6 billion in 2050 and 15.8 billion in 2100. The low variant, whose fertility remains half a child below that of the medium, produces a population that reaches 8.1 billion in 2050 and declines towards the second half of this century to reach 6.2 billion in 2100.

I questioned why the medium variant projection had suddenly been raised. The reason appeared to be a mini baby boom during the first decade of the 21st century. Figure 4.6 shows the medium variant projection in millions of people (left-hand axis, thick curve). It also shows the first derivative of that trend – the rate

Figure 4.6: UN world population estimates and projections published in 2011

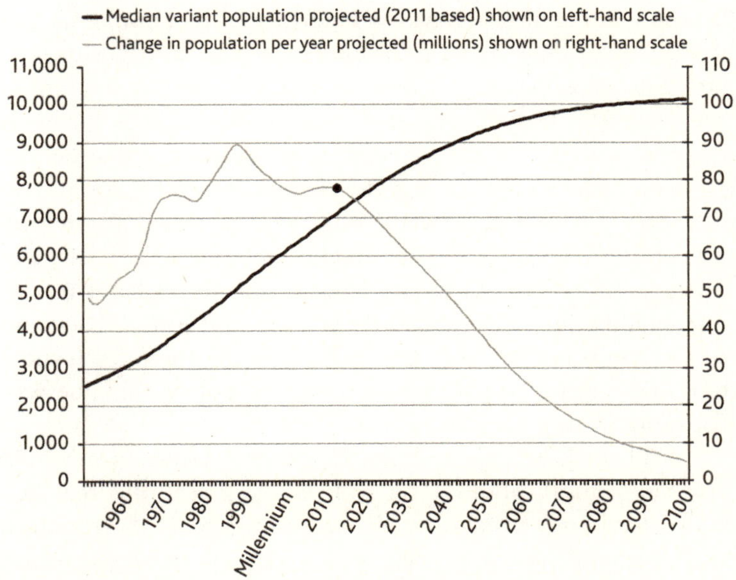

Note: World population estimates and projections (left-hand axis, thick curve) and annual population change (right-hand axis, thin curve), UN 2011 medium variant scenario (millions).

Source: UN 2011 medium variant scenario, https://population.un.org/wpp/

of change in population, which for a global population is simply the births in one year less deaths in that year (right-hand axis, thin curve). A black dot on the thin curve marks the end of the previously unexpected mini baby boom in 2011.

I suggested that demography might be a complex science, but it is also an art. The sophisticated way to make projections is to calculate life tables and tables of fertility rates by age, and then to carefully project them forward year on year, and to do this for each country, maybe even trying to take into account international migration trends and their impacts. You then add up the results and publish your global projection. There are also far more sophisticated ways of estimating error than projecting that each couple has half a child more or half a child less; although the half-a-child measure does at least have colourful echoes of the judgement of Solomon, and an implication that choices might have to be made.

Turning to the art of demography, I suggested that demographers might consider the past trend and look at the change each year, and then the change in the change, to see if there was a pattern. Figure 4.7 shows the change in the change that the UN Population Division reports. This is of both estimates of what has occurred and projections into the future, all in one thick line. It is the second derivative of population, the rate of change of the rate of change of our numbers. It is births in one year, less births the year before, plus deaths the year before, less the deaths this year. It is the degree to which population numbers are accelerating, when 'change in change' is above zero, or the degree to which they are decelerating, when the 'change in change' is below zero. [Editorial note: If you are not familiar with language like this, and very likely you are not, just go back and re-read any paragraph that you find confusing carefully. If these things were intuitive and easy then more people would question global population projections.]

In 2011 the UN suggested that the greatest deceleration would only be, at most, about 1 million people a year and that this would flatten out towards no change in change by the century's end. I asked the question: what if the future is as spiky as the past? I suggested demographers should look at the trend in Figure 4.7 of what we think occurred before 2011 and compare that to what is projected to come after.

Figure 4.7: UN and alternative change-in-change estimates and projections published in 2011

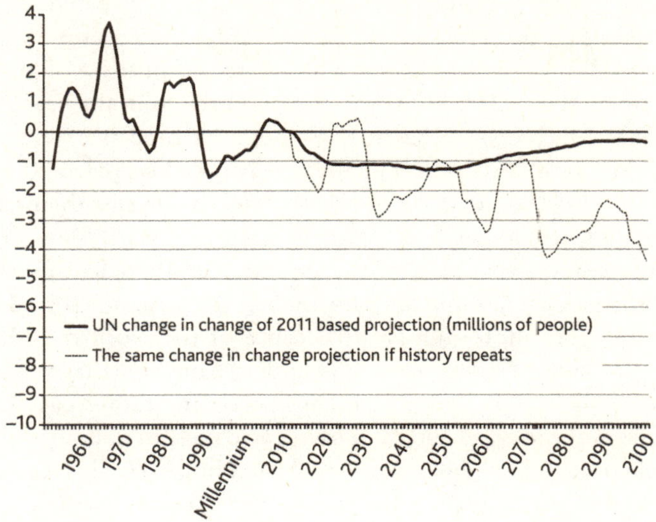

Note: World population estimates and projections, annual change in population change (millions): UN projection (thick line) and alternative scenario (thin dotted line).

Source: UN 2011 medium variant scenario, https://population.un.org/wpp/

The projection the UN was making was very smooth compared to the precedent. I debated over whether change in change is just too hard to project and, if so, whether the UN demographers had been sensible to suggest an asymptotic turn towards stability [Editorial note: 'asymptotic' meaning gradually to approach the asymptote of an exact and forever 'two child' norm]. Then I pointed out that we knew something about what we were trying to predict here. I said: 'These are people, but they are being treated as if they were drops of water flowing in and out of a bathtub.'

It was clear in 2011 that the length of time between the most recent peak in Figure 4.7 (2006) and the one before it (1986) had been 20 years, and the one before that (1966) had also been 20 years. I suggested it mattered that these were people, not baboons or fruit flies or water running in and out of the tub. I suggested that the peaks and troughs in the rate of change of the rate of change represented mini baby booms, the echoes of past larger booms and busts, and then I asked, what if those peaks and troughs were to repeat? That is what the faint dotted line in Figure 4.7 illustrated. It was a projection based simply on repeating, from 2012 onwards, the last 42 years of peaks and troughs. It is just what you get with, literally, a little bit of history repeating. Why 42? Because that takes us back from the year 2011 to 1969 and best matches the last point in time we were in a similar point in this cycle. The peaks may have been each 20 years apart: 1966, 1986 and 2006; but the last two cycles themselves appear to average nearer 21 years in length.

I suggested that many of the children of 1986 had recently become parents (around and shortly before the year 2010). They in turn, were more numerous because of the worldwide baby boom of 1966. And so we should expect a further smaller boom around 2026, 2046 and on, perhaps becoming more spaced out in time as the average length of each cycle increases because more people have their children later in life, and hopefully also damping down as compared to the strict repetition shown by the dotted line in Figure 4.7.

Back in 2011 it was clear that the introduction of a little bit of variation has a huge impact on how population changes in future. That is shown in Figure 4.8, with the dot again marking where we were in 2011. The trends from 1950 to 2011 are identical, but under this alternative scenario, births decline just a fraction more rapidly because, between the booms of the past, there were troughs which we currently ignore as we project forward from a time of boom. That potential error has great cumulative effects.

As Figure 4.8 shows, if the change in change repeats the most recent little bit of history we have enjoyed, then a human population maximum is reached in 2060 at 9.3 billion, but by 2100 there would be just 7.4 billion of us. We would be back down to total human numbers last seen around the year 2016.

Many might hope that the falls were not as abrupt as those shown in Figure 4.8. You only have to continue that rate of decline onwards another 38 years and we would all be extinct. A fall to fewer than 7.4 billion humans by the year 2100 may appear rapid, but it is a slower fall than the UN Population Division's own low variant projection, which was for the world's

Figure 4.8: Alternative world population estimates and projections published in 2011

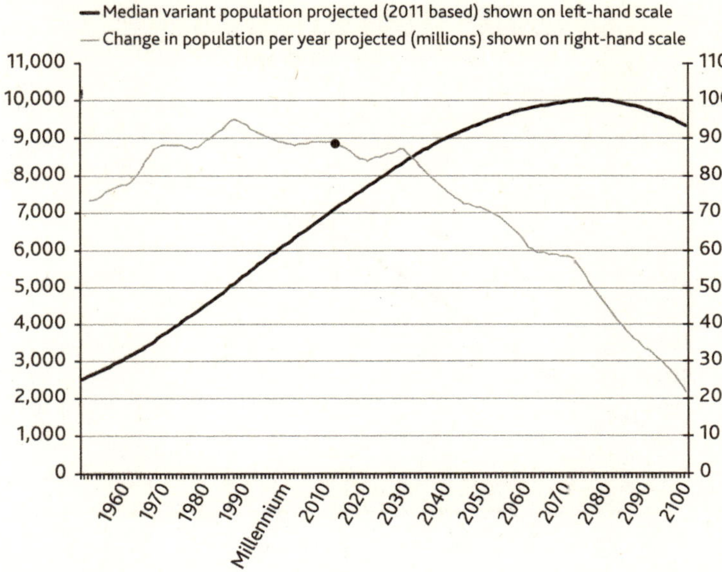

Note: An alternative scenario of world population estimates, projections and annual population change (millions) based on the idea of a little bit of history repeating. Published by the author in 2011. Change per year in millions per year is shown on the right hand axis and drawn as a thin line on the graph.

Source: UN 2011 medium variant scenario, https://population.un.org/wpp/

population to fall to 6.2 billion by 2100. It is remarkable that the UN endorsed projections that varied by some 9.6 billion people (15.8 to 6.2) in just the 89 years after 2011; and as my story explains later, we still really do not know what will happen.

The UN was born out of a world war with the mission to stop history repeating – above all else, to try to prevent the repetition of war and the harm another world war would cause in affluent countries. World war tends to result in baby booms, as did the partition of India and the revolution in China, which were both, in effect, wars involving many millions. If you are looking for the origins of the mini baby booms then look back to those events of the 1940s, and earlier.

So, what have we learnt in the last dozen years? Figure 4.9 shows Figure 4.6 updated to include the most recent 2022 UN

Figure 4.9: UN world population estimates and projections published in 2011 and 2022

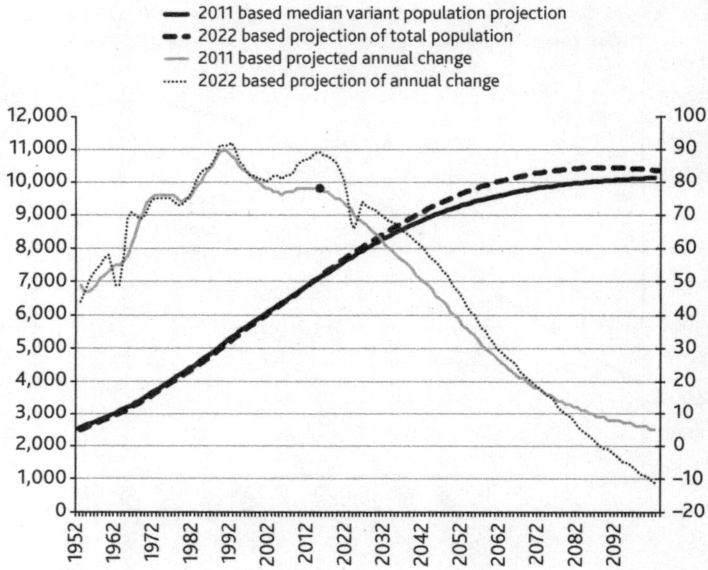

Note: Two sets of official world population estimates and projections – also showing projected and past annual population change (all numbers in millions). The first of these is the UN 2011 median variant scenario (thick black line). The second is the UN 2022 based scenario (thick dashed line). The scale for change per year in millions is shown on the right-hand axis and drawn as two thin lines, in grey (the UN 2011-based estimates) and dotted (the UN 2022-based estimates).

Source: UN 2011 and 2022 medium variant scenarios, https://population.un.org/wpp/

projections.[4] The main projection is now for population to grow a little higher, as shown by the thick dashed line, but peaking at 10.4 billion people in the summer of 2086 and then falling slowly. This does not cause great concern today because between 2011 and 2022 the UN predicted even higher growth and then revised its estimates down, so people are now surprised that the population is projected to fall by the end of the century.

The thin dotted line in Figure 4.9 shows how the change in population is now thought to be different from that believed to

[4] United Nations (2022) *World Population Prospects 2022*, UN Department of Economic and Social Affairs, Population Division, New York, https://population.un.org/wpp/Download/Standard/MostUsed/

be the case in 2011. Note that it is not just the future, but also the past, that has been revised. The global projections are now higher in the short term because there were more babies born around 2010 than the demographers in 2011 knew (and a few fewer people dying than they thought). The sudden drop in the thin dotted line around 2020–22 is the UN estimate of 8 or 9 million more deaths a year due to the pandemic in these years, and about 3 million fewer births a year during these years. But after that, the projections are for a rapid return to normal, albeit higher population growth than was projected in 2011 in the next four decades; but then much lower growth and actual decline. So, how has the picture changed in a dozen years? Figure 4.10 shows the 'change in change' each year as originally drawn in 2011 (in black thick and thin lines), and as updated (in dashed and dotted lines). The dashed line shows that we were far too certain about the past, in the past. [Editorial note: The first spike in the dashed line in Figure 4.10 shows the great famine of China that is now included in UN data, a fall and then recovery. The second great spike is the COVID-19 pandemic, which did not have as big an effect on global population.]

It turns out that the past had been even more variable than the UN had been reporting. Nowadays, the great famine of China (1959–61) can be included, whereas the UN had to pretend a dozen years ago that it had not happened, and the baby boom that followed that famine also had to be ignored. Between 2011 and 2022 it was quietly accepted that this story could be included in the global demographic record – China now much more openly accepts that there was a great famine.

What is interesting about the 2022 revision is that the UN projections for change in change are now always lower, from 2043 onwards, than they were a dozen years ago. But what is more interesting is how my alternative scenario changes. Here that scenario is started just before 2020, as if the pandemic had not occurred (otherwise the effects of the COVID-19 pandemic would be repeated in future, every 42 years, in the new alternative scenario). The same periodicity is used as before and so the thin dotted line in Figure 4.10 repeats every 42 years, just as the higher continuous thin black line did. Why still choose 42? As explained before, it is roughly two generations in length, or was in 2011,

Figure 4.10: UN and alternative change-in-change estimates and projections, 2011 and 2022

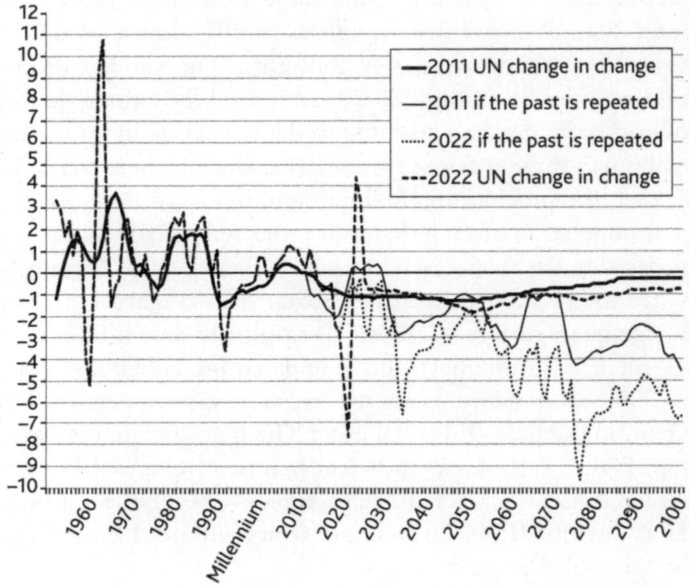

Note: The revised alternative scenario of world population estimates, projections and annual population change (millions) based on the idea of a little bit of history repeating. The original UN 2011 world population estimates of change in change are shown as a thick black line. The first alternative scenario published in 2011 is drawn as a thin black line. In dashed and dotted styles are the same two lines, but based on the UN 2022 data instead. The thick dashed black line is the UN estimates of change in change published in 2022. The dotted thin line is the most recent alternative scenario of what happens now with a little bit of the (recently revised) history repeating.

Source: UN 2011 and 2022 medium variant scenarios, https://population.un.org/wpp/

and I am tempted to stick to it for now, partly because 42 is the number that Douglas Adams once explained was the answer to life, the universe and everything. More seriously, as we have fewer and fewer children in future globally, we may not continue to have them later and later in our lives. We may want to meet our great-grandchildren. What is key is that the slight drop in the thick dashed black line in Figure 4.10 has a huge effect overall, as is shown in Figure 4.11.

The thick continuous black line in Figure 4.11 peaks in the year 2060, a little ahead of what the UN demographers now say will be the peak year. When I made that prediction in 2011 it turned out to be more accurate than the one the UN was making. At the time I was predicting that its projection would soon bend down towards mine (it did). However, as the thick dashed black line in Figure 4.11 shows, using exactly the same method and exactly the same time intervals, I would now end up predicting global population to peak in 2050, ten years earlier than I did before, at 9.1 billion.

Back in 2011, I had suggested it would reach 9.3 billion in 2060. That may not be bad news – the planet could happily fit a few more people on it, if they behave well – and behave better than a few of their parents and grandparents have done in burning so much fossil fuel. However, worryingly, this little-bit-of-history-repeating method suggests that if history carries

Figure 4.11: Alternative world population estimates and projections published in 2011 and 2022

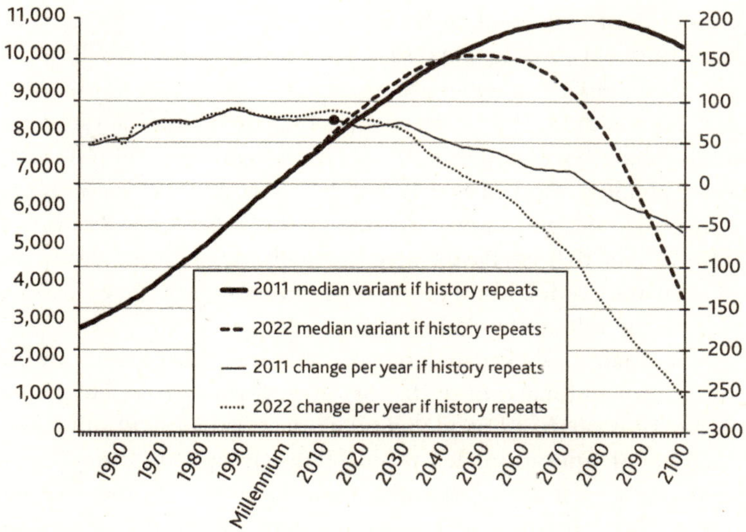

Note: The implications of the revised alternative scenario of a little bit of history repeating. In black, the thick line shows the original 2011 based alternative scenario for our total numbers each year. The thin black line is annual population change under that original alternative scenario. All numbers are in millions and the scale for annual rates of change is shown on the right-hand side. In a thick black dashed line is the new 2022-based alternative world population projection based on the updated alternative scenario, and the thin dotted black line is the annual change that updated scenario suggests.

Source: UN 2011 and 2022 medium variant scenarios, https://population.un.org/wpp/

on repeating as we know it has done most recently (prior to the pandemic) then soon the global human population will fall to below 9 billion in 2060, below 8 billion in 2075, below 7 billion in 2082, and rapidly down and down to below 4 billion in 2097. That would be extremely unlikely. It is the kind of scenario predicted in P.D. James's 1992 novel *The Children of Men*.

History will not carry on repeating, but it may yet repeat for at least one more cycle, a couple of generations. All the signs currently suggest that the peak in global human numbers will occur earlier than the UN currently predicts. Fertility is already lower now in 2023 than they predicted in 2022 – the pandemic did not result in a baby boom. Mortality is higher – the pandemic has not gone away, mortality remains higher than expected, and there are reasons to believe it will continue to be higher than we thought in the past.[5] But those two things are not what will matter most in future.

What matters most is security: social security. If people feel secure, then they tend to have fewer children. If there are not large or never-ending wars, they tend to have fewer children. If adequate pension schemes are maintained, they tend not to have as many children. If they do not see their own children die, they tend to have fewer children. If they live longer, they tend to have fewer children. And all of that could be disrupted by war, famine, economic collapse, disease, or any of the other variants on the 'four horses' that we have feared so much, throughout almost all of human recorded history – resulting in more, not fewer, people despite the initial population falls.

The effects of climate change, medical innovations, food availability and many other factors may all play a role. However, as yet we really have no idea how climate change will influence patterns of migration, let alone births or deaths. Instead, we speculate a great deal. Migrants often have fewer children if they move to an area where that is the norm. Medical innovations

---

5 George Davey Smith and Danny Dorling (2023) 'Revisiting the point-source hypothesis of the coronary heart disease epidemic in light of the COVID-19 pandemic', Poster presented at the Society of Epidemiologic Research annual meeting, Portland, Oregon USA, 14 June, https://ora.ox.ac.uk/objects/uuid:12849f9e-ffdd-40af-8b69-1250285dc2a6

may in future make it easier for people who find it hard to have children to become parents later in life. Food availability is an ancient concern in demography, although it is only in recent decades that we have come to realise that increased food security reduces our numbers as we become less afraid of the future and have fewer children.

A crucial factor is changing cultural norms, and especially the role education plays. When those around you are having fewer or no children it is much more likely that you will too. A norm of people having no, one, or (more rarely) two children – and only very occasionally more – is becoming very widely and very quickly established over an ever-increasing share of humanity. A few economists still ask how a country like the UK can enact policies to raise its total fertility rate to 2.0 as a grand societal challenge (see, for an example, a comment from the executive chair of the UK's Economic and Social Research Council, on 31 May 2023[6]). However, increasingly, social scientists have come to realise that such a medium-term aspiration is unnecessary, very unlikely to be achievable, and could well not be beneficial.

If we would like population to peak earlier and lower than 10 billion or even nine billion, we need to focus, as the UN does, on security. A very large part of that security, the most important part, is the position of women in any society. The more power women have, the faster births fall. Many years ago a survey found that the average woman in the world would like half a child less than the average man. When she can secure that, we slow down faster. Improvements in health can also increase our population numbers, as more of us are hanging around for longer. But the effect of those improvements on reducing the number of children we have is probably now greater than the increase in population numbers that lower mortality results in.

---

[6] In response to Neil Lee, writing on 31 May 2023: 'Imagine someone gives you a big pot of funding and you focus it, NESTA-style, on 3 societal challenges. What would you choose and why?', Stian Westlake replied on the same day with the suggestions: '(If we're talking UK-only, and assuming other funders exist and therefore health, climate and other popular causes are already well-funded): increasing housebuilding to 500k/year; increasing TFR to 2.0; reducing violent crime to Japanese levels'. See: https://twitter.com/stianwestlake/status/1664004520580378626

There is almost no evidence from anywhere in the world that the number of children a couple has (on average) can easily be raised to two or maintained at that level, rather than being a fraction below it; but a great deal can be done to help people who want to have an average of around 1.7–1.9 children per couple rather than averages of around 1.3 or even lower. In Japan, the debate in 2023 over what might be a decent level of state child support intensified, but so too did the discussion about the benefits of encouraging more immigration.[7] In Scotland in November 2022, the raising of the Scottish Child Payment to £25 a week per child aged 16 or under whose family receives any form of benefit is now one of the most progressive reforms in Europe to both reduce child poverty and make it a little easier to be a parent. However, greater social stability and equality tend to result in fewer births.

What, though, of the falls predicted after 2050? The UN has always had an assumption in all of its scenarios that we will, in the long term, magically move towards a world in which every potential couple on the planet will have, on average, two children. That implies that actual couples will mostly have more than two, because an increasing number of people do not have any children, or just one, and many are not in couples of any kind today. Increasing numbers of people are now single for the majority of their lives.

I suspect that the UN scenario is overly optimistic, and we will not see a return to a two-child average anywhere soon in all of those countries where it has fallen below that. They are where most people in the world now live. Pro-natalist policies may raise average numbers of children in some places from say, 1.4 to 1.6 children per couple. Immigration could be encouraged to prevent population decline, but only while there are still places with rapidly growing populations.

At the extreme, the population of South Korea is now more than halving each generation as the average number of children per potential couple there is well below 1. But whereas the UN projection may be too optimistic, mine is almost certainly far too

---

7 Kentaro Iwamoto (2023) 'Japan readies "last hope" measures to stop falling births: Experts say next 10 years are critical as Kishida eyes "children first" society', *Nikkei*, 14 February, s.nikkei.com/3CBNa3O

pessimistic – or it is modelling a future that will (optimistically!) be far more politically, socially and economically stable than what we might well experience. This is because the 42 years from 1978 to 2020 were a more stable period of human history than any previous 42 years seen for many centuries. The previous 42 years included world war (1936–78), as did the 42 years before then (1894–1936). The 42 years before then included the great famine of India and a myriad other horrors that we now understand were largely products of colonialism and imperialism (1852–94). I could go back to the effects of the beginning of the Atlantic slave trade, the destruction of almost every stable social human system on earth following European settlement, and the earlier effects of the enclosure of land within Europe; but hopefully most people now realise that our global numbers first exploded because of our actions and that they will stabilise and fall faster depending on how we collectively behave.

For my projections to come true, hundreds of millions of young people would have to decide right now, and in the next few years to come, that they were not going to become parents. That is unlikely. But we should perhaps begin to worry more about why fewer people are having children. One good way to worry is to look at the thick dashed black line in Figure 4.11. Becoming a parent should not be a financial strain. It should not mean you are much more likely to live in poverty. Note that in 2023 a majority of parents in the UK with three children now go hungry at times.[8]

What happens to us depends far more on our behaviour than our numbers, and our behaviour depends greatly on what we understand. This is why it matters whether our recent past suggests there are trends in our collective behaviour we are still not aware of. Too many people worry that there are too many people. A tiny proportion (less than 10 per cent of us) are responsible for almost all the pollution on the planet. A large number of us need to begin to realise that it is the choices being made today – by the potential parents of the elderly of 2100 – that will actually decide all this.

---

[8] Mike Brewer, Emily Fry, and Lalitha Try (2023) *The Living Standards Outlook 2023*, London: Resolution Foundation, https://www.resolutionfoundation.org/app/uploads/2023/01/Living-Standards-Outlook-2023.pdf

SECTION 5

How austerity undermined our public health

Counting the cost of austerity

Austerity increases poverty. Poverty damages health. Austerity increases poverty most quickly when applied to the already poor. Austerity, when applied to health and social services, accelerates the increase in poor health and early death. In January 2023, one in five people in Britain were living in poverty, 13.4 million whose life choices were bleak or non-existent, including 3.9 million children.[1] Many reports, dozens and even hundreds of pages long, were written. One began:

> We are driven by the unshakeable belief that poverty can be solved in the UK. Honouring our history, there is a strong moral purpose to this mission: to end the poverty that blights the lives and life chances of millions of people, and to ensure dignity and esteem for everyone in the UK, addressing insecurity, exclusion and powerlessness. This is urgent work – perhaps more urgent today than at any time in our history.[2]

1 These statistics came from government data relating to the situation from April 2020 to March 2021. However, prices were rising rapidly then, and since, so the actual number by then would have been higher, as it would also have been if a less tight measure of poverty had been used instead of the official one: Hannah Westwater, Ella Glover and Isabella McCrea (2023) 'UK poverty: the facts, effects and solutions in a cost of living crisis', *The Big Issue*, 26 January, archived here: https://web.archive.org/web/20230128065707/https://www.bigissue.com/news/social-justice/uk-poverty-the-facts-figures-effects-solutions-cost-living-crisis/

2 Carla Cebula, Aleks Collingwood, Rachelle Earwaker, Joseph Elliott, Peter Matejic, Isabel Taylor and Andrew Wenham (2023) *UK Poverty 2023: The essential guide to understanding poverty in the UK*, York: Joseph Rowntree Foundation.

What use is this fabled story of 'urgent work', presenting a rose-tinted view of our chequered history and our chequered morality? What use are these appeals to try to ensure dignity and esteem, when we have come to accept great injustice as normal? To no longer respect people as we once did? The Joseph Rowntree Foundation which published that report was set up in 1904, with the intention of extinguishing itself by helping to eradicate poverty (it was supposed to no longer exist as a Foundation by today but to have completed its work within a century). Well over a century – six score years – on, its report writers struggle to realise that it is the acceptance of inequality that maintains and increases poverty. That Foundation has become part of the establishment furniture, as has the Liberal Party that its founder supported, and the Labour Party that took on the progressive mantle from the Liberals long after Joseph Rowntree's death.

When injustice is at a peak, none of the mainstream political parties oppose it. That is how it came to be at that peak – by being accepted as inevitable.

In spring 2023, writing in support of Sir Keir Starmer, one English commentator tried to dismiss a characterisation of the Labour Party as now being: 'a middle-class party that so hankers after Conservative acceptance it has only a weak progressive spine'.[3] However, by the summer of 2023, a former prime minister (Gordon Brown) was helping to demonstrate just how weak Labour's spine had become by attacking the mechanism being used to deliver money to end child poverty in Scotland, accusing it of 'wasting more than £700 million'.[4] Brown claimed that: 'Whatever benefits the Scottish Government decide can be

---

3 Will Hutton (2023) 'Ignore the detractors – Keir Starmer is a radical who can transform the country', *The Guardian*, 26 March, https://www.theguardian.com/commentisfree/2023/mar/26/ignore-detractors-keir-starmer-radical-transform-country

4 Editorial (2023) 'Gordon Brown accuses SNP ministers of wasting money on separate social security agency: the former prime minister said Social Security Scotland was set up "for status reasons"', *The Scotsman*, 23 August, https://www.scotsman.com/news/politics/gordon-brown-accuses-snp-ministers-of-wasting-money-on-separate-social-security-agency-4266575

paid through the Department for Work and Pensions',[5] but he had never helped instigate such payments at these effective levels when he had been chancellor or prime minister. He too had become part of the inequality furniture – part of what maintained injustice. Brown co-authored a book in the autumn of 2023 which read like a tribute to those who keep the UK and the US so very unequal.[6]

Thankfully, a few days later, Scottish Labour backed down and announced that they would not scrap Scotland's welfare agency if they won the next Holyrood election. This announcement was made despite Gordon Brown's criticism of it: the Labour Party in Scotland had more spine than Gordon Brown.[7] The SNP had forced Labour to move, ever so slightly, away from arguing against the Scottish Child Payments and how they are delivered. In the long term, it is payments such as these that have the most effect on people's future health – and it was Gordon Brown not trying to reduce income or wealth inequality when he was in office that resulted in a Britain where not only the future of its children, but their height, was stunted. It was when Brown had been in power that the rise in children's height in the UK began to slow, and then fall. The Conservative–Liberal Democrat coalition that Brown let in (by not negotiating well enough with the Liberal Democrats) then accelerated the downwards trend. Children's height is affected by many things, but not least whether their mothers were living in poverty when they were in the womb. New Labour did too little to help, and that failure is today written in the stunted height of our children. Those born after 2005, aged

[5] Ross Hunter (2023) 'Gordon Brown calls Social Security Scotland a "waste of money"', *The National*, 24 August, https://www.thenational.scot/news/23743827.gordon-brown-calls-social-security-scotland-waste-money/

[6] Danny Dorling (2023) '*Permacrisis: A plan to fix a fractured world* – review', *LSE Review of Books*, 28 November, https://blogs.lse.ac.uk/lsereviewofbooks/2023/11/28/book-review-permacrisis-a-plan-to-fix-a-fractured-world-gordon-brown-mohamed-el-erian-michael-spence/

[7] Editorial (2023) 'Scottish Labour will not scrap £715m Social Security Scotland agency branded "wasteful" by Gordon Brown', *The Scotsman*, 28 August, https://www.scotsman.com/news/politics/scottish-labour-will-not-scrap-ps715m-social-security-scotland-agency-branded-wasteful-by-gordon-brown-4270547

five in 2010, were shorter than their older siblings had been at the same age. The fall occurred during Brown's term of office in the UK, and after he had been chancellor for many years; it began a little later in the United States (Figure 5.1).

Gordon Brown was among the more progressive of Labour politicians in the New Labour era, but the financial architecture he put in place as chancellor, and the ethos he espoused, made it easy for the incoming coalition government of 2010 to swiftly unwind the few good measures that had been introduced and to rapidly expand on the poor ones: tripling student fees, further privatising the health services, and undermining what little progress had been achieved on reducing inequality and poverty. So few of the more determined-to-reduce-inequality-and-injustice Labour MPs were allowed to become ministers in the 1997–2010 administrations that Brown could be painted as being

Figure 5.1: The average height of five-year-old boys in four affluent states, 1990–2020

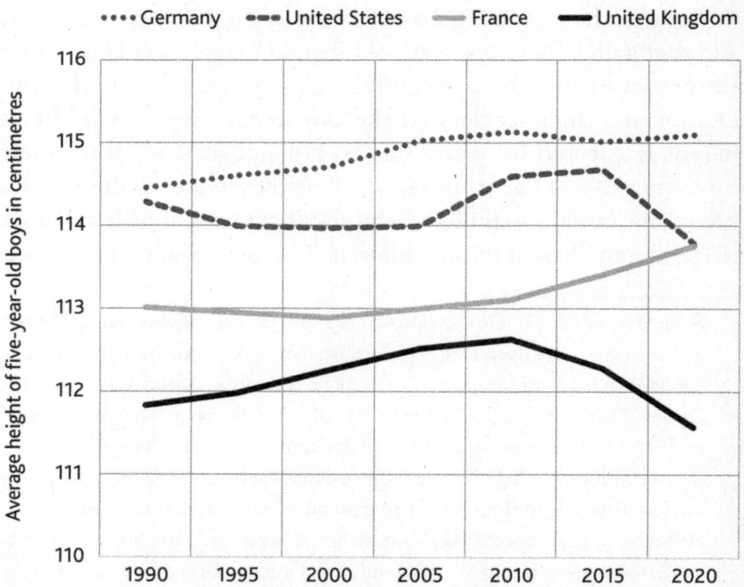

Source: Drawn from data in Press Association (2023) 'British children shorter than other five-year-olds in Europe', *ITV News*, 21 June, https://www.itv.com/news/2023-06-21/british-children-shorter-than-other-five-year-olds-in-europe

more progressive than most. Poverty hardly fell at all when Brown was in power; and inequality rose.

Fast forward through 13 years of coalition and Conservative rule, and poverty was rising again. In March 2023 the official statistics were updated: now 22 per cent of all Britain's people were reported to have been living in poverty in 2021–22, as compared to 20 per cent in 2020–21. The headline figure was now 14.4 million, up by 1.0 million. That total now included 4.2 million children, up by 350,000 children. Dreams of eliminating child poverty became vague memories of a good intention. Labour had only ever managed to move a minority of poor children ever so slightly over this statistical line in a way so flimsy that it could quickly be undone. It had been Gordon Brown who had been instrumental in 2001 in creating the Department for Work and Pensions (DWP) by merging the Department of Social Security with the Employment Service and various policy groups of the Department for Education and Employment; this was all done alongside the slightly sinister implicit message 'work is good for you'. In 2006, David Freud, who became a peer, was brought in to increase its emphasis on implementing US-style welfare-to-work programmes. Gordon Brown holidayed each summer in the US, partly to learn about social policy there. It is a great pity he could not foresee that children there would become stunted too. If only he had gone instead on holiday to mainland Europe and looked there for policy ideas, not to the United States.

Freud stayed on in his government advisor role after 2010 and became the Minister of State for Welfare Reform under both David Cameron and Theresa May, all the way through to 2016. For him, there was no change in policy between 2006 and 2016. He was succeeded in political office by another aristocrat (all Lords are aristocrats), the 8th Baron Henley, who in turn was succeeded in 2017 by Baroness Buscombe; and then she was replaced in her role, in turn, in 2019 by Baroness Stedman-Scott as the next Parliamentary Under-secretary of State for Work and Pensions, who was replaced in turn again in 2023 by James Younger, 5th Viscount Younger of Leckie, the aristocrat who still held that post through to at least May 2024, as I write. Incidentally, James's father was George Younger, 4th Viscount

Younger of Leckie, who had held two offices of state (in total for an entire decade) within Margaret Thatcher's 1979–89 cabinets. Sometimes you wonder whether British people understand that they are still ruled by overlords whose main qualification is their birthright. They should wonder what was really meant when, in 2023, the DWP's summary of the latest statistics concluded: 'It should be noted that none of the changes in these measures were statistically significant.'[8] The DWP did not explain that this was because they had cut the sample they take each year until it became so small, and unreliable, that even increases like this are not 'statistically significant' – it was the DWP that had made it so, at its masters' and mistresses' bidding.

Few people today understand what the UK child poverty statistics mean or how they are calculated, including, I believe, all the Parliamentary Under-Secretaries of State for Work and Pensions I have ever met or studied. This general ignorance results in many better-off people not giving much of a damn. After all, what on earth can these statistics mean if even the politicians and journalists can't understand them? On 23 March 2023 when the latest numbers were released – the first semi-reliable numbers to be released in two years – the headline in *The Times* read 'How can 29 per cent of British children live in poverty?'.[9] At least the article explained that 'Relative poverty is defined as any household living on less than 60 per cent of the national figure for median income after housing costs are taken into account.' But it did not explain equalisation or how income is measured.

The Times did explain that:

> About 350,000 more children were pulled into relative poverty last year after the government's decision to

[8] DWP (2023) *Households Below Average Income: an analysis of the UK income distribution: FYE 1995 to FYE 2022*, Department for Work and Pensions, 24 August, https://www.gov.uk/government/statistics/households-below-average-income-for-financial-years-ending-1995-to-2022/households-below-average-income-an-analysis-of-the-uk-income-distribution-fye-1995-to-fye-2022

[9] James Beale (2023) 'How can 29% of British children live in poverty?', *The Times*, 23 March, https://www.thetimes.co.uk/article/how-can-29-of-british-children-live-in-poverty-0mq9gnbr9

> cut the weekly £20 universal credit increase that was introduced during the pandemic. However, experts warned that the child poverty rate could climb higher, as the cut came in October.

The Times' writer meant October 2021, 18 months previously. The 'latest' figures are always quite out of date; the 60 per cent cut-off line is very arbitrary, and its worth is also falling in terms of the food you can buy on that line; and there is mounting evidence that the poorest households of all are increasingly excluded from the DWP survey.

The situation is getting worse and the reality is almost certainly worse than the statistics.

Charities expressed disbelief: 'The statistics also reveal that more than one in four (28%) of children in Wales live in poverty',[10] said Oxfam. Perhaps even more shocking is that 25 per cent of children now live in poverty in southeast England (defined as excluding London). That is more in the most affluent part of England than in all of Scotland (which, obviously, includes Glasgow), where the figure is 24 per cent – a proposition that would have been inconceivable when I began my work on poverty in the late 1980s.

Different newspapers reflected their differing ideological stances in their headlines. In Scotland, the right-wing *Daily Record*'s take was: 'Child poverty in Scotland at same "disturbing" level as when SNP first took power.'[11] *The National* was more objective: 'Child poverty rates in Scotland lower than UK-wide, data shows'.[12] Local papers published Press Association pictures, often with confusing captions and images of wistful-looking children, such

---

10 The Editor (2023) 'Welsh child poverty rate "national disgrace" says Oxfam Cymru', *Nation Cymru*, 23 March, https://nation.cymru/news/welsh-child-poverty-rate-national-disgrace-says-oxfam-cymru/

11 Paul Hutcheon (2023) 'Child poverty in Scotland at same "disturbing" level as when SNP first took power', *Daily Record*, 23 March, https://www.dailyrecord.co.uk/news/politics/child-poverty-same-disturbing-level-29530281

12 Xander Elliards (2023) 'Child poverty rates in Scotland lower than UK-wide', *The National*, 23 March, https://www.thenational.scot/news/23406974.child-poverty-rates-scotland-lower-uk-wide-data-shows/

as the one in Figure 5.2 which accompanied a story titled 'A quarter of children in Swindon living in poverty' in *The Swindon Advertiser*.[13] Not only is the ethnicity, sex and appearance of the young girl of note, designed to inspire pity among an audience that are mostly White, so is her oversized cardigan, her wistful look, the cigarette-end placed on the windowsill in front of her, and the implication by setting that she is living high up in a tower block – in fact, far higher than plausible. There are very few tower blocks in Swindon[14] and the vast majority of children who are poor there do not live in one. The image has been widely used in many publications – it is a stock photograph labelled as 'hopeless', 'depressed' and 'poor-little'.[15]

The original photo caption in *The Swindon Advertiser*, 'Child poverty in Swindon is between 13 and 25 per cent (Image: PA)', implies not really knowing nor worrying too much about the exact proportion. One number, 13, is almost half the other, 25 – but so what, as it is only a number? We mostly don't think of these numbers as people, and when we do, it is only if they are depicted as idealised 'deserving' poor children. So, how eagerly awaited were the new poverty statistics?

Political pundits and economists in the spring of 2023 placed bets on what the new poverty numbers and proportions would

---

13 Aled Thomas (2023) 'A quarter of children in Swindon living in poverty', *The Swindon Advertiser*, https://www.swindonadvertiser.co.uk/news/23405663.quarter-children-swindon-living-poverty/

14 One of these few tower blocks in Swindon has since had to be emptied of its residents because it is now so unsafe. 'During the safety works, every effort would be made to ensure the maximum amount of light is allowed into the building, but the Council would also offer to buy any leaseholder flats at the open-market rate if residents want to sell their properties. The Council would also offer to rehouse any tenants. The estimated cost of the safety work is around £5m, while the cost of rehousing tenants and buying any leasehold properties could add a further £1.8m. It is anticipated the work would be carried out over the next two years': Swindon Borough Council (2023) 'Major Swindon tower block in need of multi-million pound investment', *Swindon Local Government News*, 26 January, https://www.swindon.gov.uk/news/article/846/major_swindon_tower_block_in_need_of_multi-million_pound_investment

15 https://theconversation.com/childhood-deprivation-affects-brain-size-and-behaviour-129314

Figure 5.2: Press image, blue-eyed blonde-haired girl modelling child poverty, 2023

Source: © Viacheslav/Shutterstock (https://www.shutterstock.com/image-photo/hopeless-life-close-depressed-poor-little-336377765)

be,[16] and one gloated when he won. He said: 'To the handful of lemon-suckers who say it is in bad taste to bet on child poverty, I say that we were not betting on child poverty. We were betting on the validity of economic forecasting.'[17]

On the day in March 2023 that the (then) latest child poverty figures were released, these two grown men bought each other a drink to celebrate winning and losing their bet on the statistics with each other.[18] The drinks pictured in the tweet one of them posted[19] may well have cost more than the daily sum (£11) the

---

16 https://iea.org.uk/the-portes-snowdon-bet-5-years-on/

17 Christopher Snowdon (2023) 'Jonathan Portes – my part in his downfall', *The Spectator*, 23 March, https://www.spectator.co.uk/article/jonathan-portes-my-part-in-his-downfall/

18 https://twitter.com/cjsnowdon/status/1638962952832442369?s=20

19 The tweet was sent from the Edgar Wallace pub in London, and the photograph was captioned originally: 'It was a pleasure to buy my pal @jdportes a drink and discuss where it all went wrong (for him). Don't worry, I can afford it!', Christopher Snowdon @cjsnowdon ('Wolf sceptic. Writer/ researcher. IEA. Views my own.') Posted at 5.56 pm on 23 March 2023. The comment and picture remains on line in 2024 for anyone to view: https:// twitter.com/cjsnowdon/status/1638962952832442369

government now estimates the majority of children in the UK survive on, the sum deemed to be enough to cover their food, clothes, cleaning (including toothpaste), bus tickets, toys and everything else that their parents might spend on them other than the rent or mortgage to keep a roof over their heads. Lower-income families have less than that, at most about £7 a day if their children are growing up in poverty.

People with less triumphal outlooks tried to explain the implication of what had just been revealed: 'Child poverty rises by 350,000 to 4.2 million: 48% of children in BAME families are growing up in poverty as are 44% of children in lone-parent families.'[20] Men of the cloth demanded action: 'Bishop of Manchester calls for removal of two-child limit on Universal Credit.'[21] That limit does not exist in Scotland: children with a brother and a sister (or any number of siblings) still get support, and the additional Scottish Child payment to the two-sevenths of all children in families claiming any welfare benefits means that child poverty rates in Scotland will be very much lower when next reported.

The BBC explained that due to the rising cost of living, foodbanks were now being used by 3 per cent of all UK families, and, in a throwaway line, that: 'Other figures published by the DWP showed the number of people living in poverty in the UK has almost returned to pre-pandemic levels.'[22] There had been a brief improvement in the situation during the pandemic, although even that is disputable, as it was not the case in the first few months after the March 2020 lockdown.

Gordon Brown chipped in too, without acknowledging his part in why the situation had become so bad in the years before

---

20 Basit Mahmood (2023) 'Child poverty rises by 350,000 to 4.2 million', *Left Foot Forward*, 24 March, https://leftfootforward.org/2023/03/child-poverty-rises-by-350000-to-4-2-million/

21 Paul Britton (2023) 'Bishop of Manchester urges Government to scrap two-child limit on Universal Credit, saying it "drives" more children into poverty', *Manchester Evening News*, 24 March, https://www.manchestereveningnews.co.uk/news/greater-manchester-news/bishop-manchester-urges-government-scrap-26554657

22 Robert Cuffe (2023) 'Cost of living: Food banks used by 3% of UK families', *BBC News*, 23 March, https://www.bbc.co.uk/news/uk-65050920

2010. Child poverty never meaningfully fell when he was prime minister, or when he was chancellor (under Tony Blair). Instead, Brown pontificated that: 'As toothpaste, shampoo, nappies, toilet rolls and cleaning products are fast becoming unaffordable "luxury" items for millions, private hygiene is becoming a public health issue.' After having made it clear that the current government had been giving money to the richest, implying he would not have done that, and going on to explain where he might have been inclined to have taken a little from them or at least not have rewarded the rich as much, Brown added:

> But the real winners are rich, professional elderly people whose tax reliefs will work out costing more than £250,000 each for the 15,000 people his [Sunak's] OBR think will benefit. In contrast, a family on universal credit is now in receipt of less than half of what a 2022 report from Loughborough University showed is needed for a decent standard of living.[23]

Some think-tanks suggested the news was not so bad because:

> Unprecedented government support helped to ensure that typical disposable incomes didn't fall over the course of the pandemic, and actually rose for poor families, in marked contrast to the biggest income squeeze in a generation that Britain is currently living through, the Resolution Foundation said today (Thursday) in response to the latest Households Below Average Income (HBAI) statistics.[24]

---

[23] Gordon Brown (2023) 'Jeremy Hunt has left the UK to rot in poverty. So we must take matters into our own hands', *The Guardian*, 24 March, https://www.theguardian.com/commentisfree/2023/mar/24/jeremy-hunt-uk-poverty-hygiene-banks-gordon-brown

[24] Unnamed spokesperson (2023) 'Family incomes were protected over the course of the pandemic – but have fallen sharply since', The Resolution Foundation, 23 March, https://www.resolutionfoundation.org/press-releases/family-incomes-were-protected-over-the-course-of-the-pandemic-but-have-fallen-sharply-since/

The think-tank wonks did, however, warn that the situation was about to get much worse: 'while family incomes [an odd phrase] in general successfully navigated the pandemic they have been knocked for six by the ongoing cost-of-living crisis. As a result, typical disposable incomes are currently not forecast to surpass their pre-pandemic levels until the back end of the decade.'[25]

Who, though, was right about what had just been revealed and what it implied; and why was the language so cold and, in some cases, so callous? Why was no one pointing out that nowhere else in Europe had child poverty risen to such staggering heights? How is it possible that even now we do not understand that New Labour had failed to improve the situation? Did we simply succumb to their many claims to the contrary because we were accepting peak injustice?

The numbers came thick and fast – and were very confusing. Three days after the poverty data release, the BBC announced that the DWP had finally decided when the day would be for the date on which the poorest families in Britain would receive their next tranche of emergency cost-of-living payments: it would be some day between 25 April and 17 May.[26] Not only would they not know when they would receive this money, recipients would find it impossible to work out how much they would receive, as the payments of 'up to' £900 were to be spread out between that range of dates and spring 2024 and they would also vary greatly, depending upon 'eligibility'.

If you qualified for such a payment it might appear as a reverse direct debit, or a standard credit, or as a smart meter payment, or it could be that you would have to go to the post office to cash a voucher that you might receive or have to ask someone for.[27] To say the situation was a mess would be to underplay just how chaotic it was. Scotland had the cost-of-living crisis much more under control. Almost everyone who was eligible there had

---

[25] Adam Corlett, quoted in The Resolution Foundation's statement (n. 24).

[26] Staff Reporter (2023) 'Millions to get next cost-of-living payment from April', *BBC News*, 27 March, https://www.bbc.co.uk/news/business-65066972

[27] Kevin Peachey (2023) 'Cost-of-living payments: Who is getting them and when?', *BBC News*, 27 March, https://www.bbc.co.uk/news/business-61592496

received that payment,[28] and those throughout 2022.[29] However, the emergency payments, even for those who received everything they were entitled to, would not prevent poverty from rising because inflation for people on low incomes had been increasing faster than the rise in incomes brought about by these emergency payments. But to understand this, you would have to download the DWP spreadsheets, and other sources on inflation.[30] There was no adequate explanation of what all these very recent new statistics had revealed.

By the time you are reading this, more people will be poorer – the fact that food prices are still rising faster than benefits makes it a certainty, and, as a consequence, our public health will be worse still. For children, the effects of growing up in poverty will last a lifetime. We know all this, but the process of explaining and understanding, updating and absorbing it inevitably goes on. However, the situation is now so bad that it is hard to see it worsening much more. We had a debate for a few years, but now widely understand how austerity caused the NHS crisis (Chapter 5.1). A consensus is forming that the cuts of 2010–19 had terrible effects. We see geographical inequalities in health by occupation that are currently widening, and in some ways are wider than those experienced in Victorian times, and we wonder how recent governments' policies contributed to these

[28] Scottish Government (2023) 'Low income Cost of Living Payment', Scottish Government Website, 29 March, https://www.mygov.scot/cost-of-living-payments

[29] Levi Winchester (2022) 'Three million households not paid the £150 council tax rebate – how to claim your payment', *The Mirror*, 24 August, https://www.mirror.co.uk/money/three-million-households-not-paid-27818668

[30] Heidi Karjalainen and Peter Levell (2022) 'Inflation for poorest households likely to increase even faster than for the richest, and could hit 14% in October', Institute for Fiscal Studies, 25 May, https://ifs.org.uk/news/inflation-poorest-households-likely-increase-even-faster-richest-and-could-hit-14-october. See also ONS (2022) 'Inflation and cost of living for household groups, UK: October 2022', 16 November, https://www.ons.gov.uk/economy/inflationandpriceindices/articles/inflationandthecostoflivingforhouseholdgroups/october2022

trends also.[31] We had a Brexit vote in a period of declining health and when immigration was painted as our greatest problem, but health soon surpassed immigration as a greater concern once the new pandemic began in earnest (Chapter 5.2). But the pandemic did not lead to as many people dying younger than was expected as austerity did. We now know why life expectancy in England and Wales was 'stalling' in 2014[32] and that the stalling and then falling was no short-term blip.[33]

We have asked several times 'How many were dead by Christmas?'; not just in a pandemic made worse by poverty and austerity, but in the years before it (Chapter 5.3). We know now to blame the decimation of the NHS for routine operations having to be cancelled so many times across the whole NHS in the years before the pandemic began, and why it is just as bad, if not worse, today (Chapter 5.4). No one is shocked to find that, in terms of public health, the UK continues to fall down the global ranks (Chapter 5.5).[34] And we talk of the UK's future as a set of countries if we continue down this road any longer, with scepticism, as a 'museum future' (Chapter 5.6).

In December 2023, the United Nations released the news that child poverty had grown faster in the UK than in any other nation that they monitored (Figure 5.3). But by then no one was shocked any more. Of course, almost all news is like this on the ascent towards a new, even higher peak of injustice.

---

[31] Mark Green, Danny Dorling and Richard Mitchell (2018) 'Updating Edwin Chadwick's seminal work on geographical inequalities by occupation', *Social Science & Medicine*, 197: pp. 59–62.

[32] Lu Hiam, Dominic Harrison, Martin McKee and Danny Dorling (2018) 'Why is life expectancy in England and Wales "stalling"?', *Journal of Epidemiology and Community Health*, DOI: 10.1136/jech-2017-210401, 20 February, http://jech.bmj.com/content/early/2018/02/20/jech-2017-210401

[33] Lu Hiam and Danny Dorling (2024) 'The rise and fall of Britain's golden cohort: how the remarkable generation of 1925–1934 had their lives cut short by austerity', *Oxford University Research Archive* (ORA). Record page: https://ora.ox.ac.uk/objects/uuid:69c8d4b7-e28f-4250-b04d-d52d80da39db, and published in the *Review of Social Economy*.

[34] Lucinda Hiam, Martin McKee, Danny Dorling and Jonathan Minton (2022) 'Slowing down or returning to normal? Life expectancy improvements in Britain compared to five large European countries before the COVID-19 pandemic', *British Medical Bulletin*, 25 December.

Figure 5.3: The United Nations International Children's Emergency Fund 2023 Report

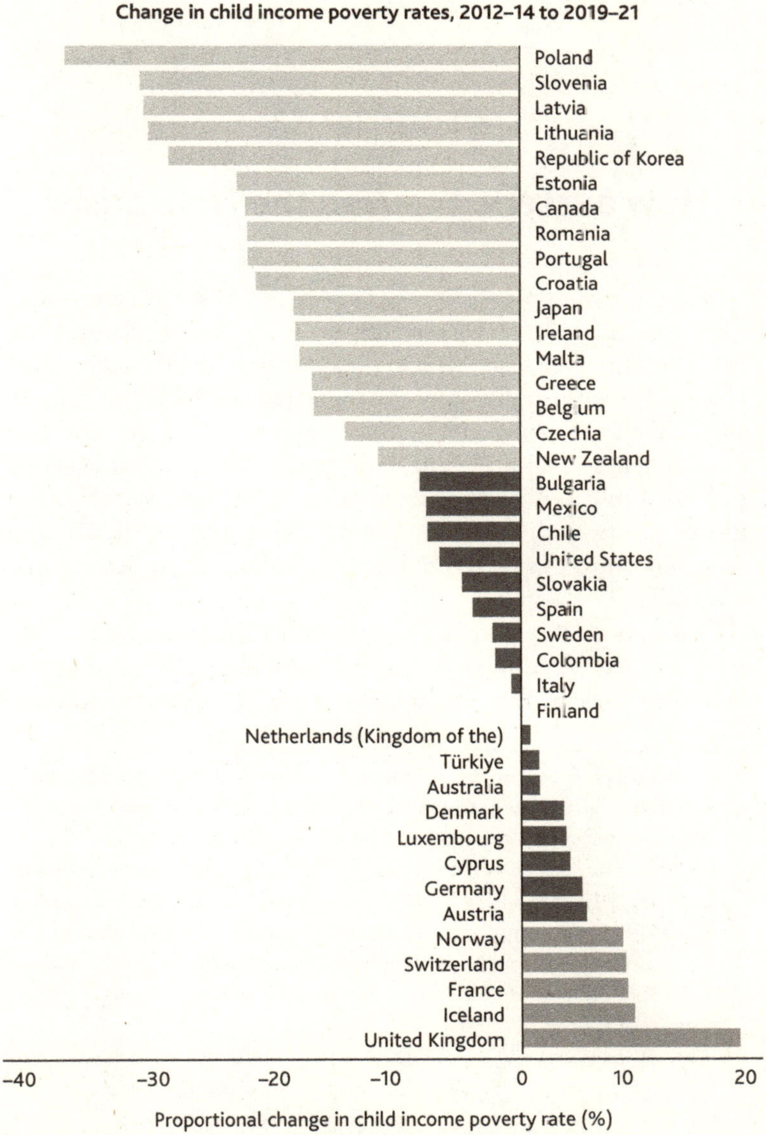

Source: UNICEF (2023) Innocenti Report Card 18: Child poverty in the midst of wealth, *UNICEF Global Office of Research and Foresight*, Florence, December, https://www.unicef.org/globalinsight/media/3291/file/UNICEF-Innocenti-Report-Card-18-Child-Poverty-Amidst-Wealth-2023.pdf

CHAPTER 5.1

How austerity caused the NHS crisis[1]

When the coalition government introduced its Health and Social Care Act in 2010, health secretary Andrew Lansley claimed the NHS would never again need to undergo such huge organisational change. But even at the time, one respected commentator warned that – far from being a final fix – the act 'could become this government's "poll tax"'.[2] In the event, it has been a slow-burn poll tax. Only now, ten years after it came into law, are we seeing its full effects, with publications from *The Times*[3] to *The Morning Star*[4] reporting that 'A&E delays are "killing up to 500 people a week"'.

This figure – 5 per cent above the normal number of people who die each week, though that baseline is also rising – can surely be traced back to the Act, which ushered in a greater wave of

---

1. Originally published in 2023 in a slightly different form in *Open Democracy*, 4 January, https://www.opendemocracy.net/en/nhs-a-and-e-delays-austerity-emergency-care-hospitals-hunt-hancock-lansley/

2. Nicholas Timmins (2012) 'Never again? The story of the Health and Social Care Act 2012: A modern drama in five uncompleted acts (by command of Her Majesty's Government)', London: The Institute for Government and the King's Fund, 12 July, https://www.kingsfund.org.uk/sites/default/files/field/field_publication_file/never-again-story-health-social-care-nicholas-timmins-jul12.pdf

3. Rhys Blakely and Henry Zeffman (2023) 'A&E delays "killing up to 500 people a week"', *The Times*, 2 January, https://www.thetimes.co.uk/article/a-e-delays-killing-up-to-500-people-a-week-g5kpxdpd6

4. Matt Trinder (2023) 'A&E delays causing 500 deaths a week', *The Morning Star*, 2 January, https://morningstaronline.co.uk/article/b/ae-delays-causing-500-deaths-a-week

privatisation than ever before. It compelled NHS management to behave as if they were in the private sector, competing to win business. At the time, the damage caused was little noticed because government cuts in the first round of austerity targeted local authorities and adult social care. The first group of people whose life expectancy fell[5] were elderly women who most often lived on their own. It was in 2014 that this connection became apparent.

Back then, the government was still confident, with the Department for Health and Social Care rebutting any suggestion that austerity and privatisation were linked to mortality. The privatisation figures were also opaque. In 2015, halfway through Jeremy Hunt's tenure as health secretary, it was reported that ministers were misleading the public.[6] By that point, private firms were winning 40 per cent of new contracts – far higher than the 6 per cent share claimed by the government and almost identical to the 41 per cent won by NHS bodies. The first great increase in mortality was recorded in that same year, a 5 per cent rise that the government tried to attribute to influenza.[7] The problem with that explanation was that the stalling and falls in life expectancy were not seen to the same extent anywhere else in Europe.[8]

---

5 Danny Dorling (2014) 'Why are old people in Britain dying before their time? Mortality rates for elderly people are rising across the country. Initially, the authorities blamed merely cold weather', *The New Statesman*, 13 February, https://www.newstatesman.com/politics/2014/02/why-are-old-people-britain-dying-their-time

6 Denis Campbell (2015) 'Far more NHS contracts going to private firms than ministers admit', *The Guardian*, 25 April, https://www.theguardian.com/society/2015/apr/25/far-more-nhs-contracts-going-to-private-firms-than-ministers-admit-privatisation

7 ONS (2016) *Spike in number of deaths in 2015 driven by increased mortality in over 75s*, Office for National Statistics, 7 April, https://www.ons.gov.uk/news/news/spikeinnumberofdeathsin2015drivenbyincreasedmortalityinover75s

8 Jonathan Minton, Lucinda Hiam, Martin McKee and Danny Dorling (2023) 'Slowing down or returning to normal? Life expectancy improvements in Britain compared to five large European countries before the COVID-19 pandemic', *British Medical Bulletin*, 145, 1, pp. 6–16, https://doi.org/10.1093/bmb/ldac036

By 2019, life expectancy for women had fallen in almost a fifth[9] of all neighbourhoods and for men in over a tenth. Poorer people, both old and young, in poorer areas suffered most, with infant mortality among babies born to the poorest parents rising. Later there was a rise in deaths of pregnant women.[10] As NHS waiting lists spiralled in 2021, a tenth of all adults, most of those who could, were using private healthcare.[11] But in doing so they made waiting lists longer by jumping the queues and thus diverting resources.

By April 2022, the number of vacant beds in hospitals was at an all-time low.[12] Estimates of the damage done kept rising. Less than six months later, it was claimed that austerity since 2010 had led to a third of a million excess deaths,[13] twice as many as from the pandemic. A&E departments are now stretched to capacity, no longer able to clear patients to other beds in our hospitals.

---

9 Theo Rashid, James E Bennett, Christopher Paciorek et al (2021) 'Life expectancy and risk of death in 6791 communities in England from 2002 to 2019: high-resolution spatiotemporal analysis of civil registration data', *The Lancet Public Health*, 6, 11, E805-E816, https://www.thelancet.com/journals/lanpub/article/PIIS2468-2667(21)00205-X/fulltext

10 Emma Baines (2022) 'Increase in death among pregnant women and new mothers', *Nursing Times*, 17 November, https://www.nursingtimes.net/news/reviews-and-reports/increase-in-death-among-pregnant-women-and-new-mothers-17-11-2022/

11 Andrew Gregory (2022) 'Millions of UK patients forced to go private amid record NHS waiting lists: 10% of adults turned to private sector or independent healthcare in past year', *The Guardian*, 11 September, https://www.theguardian.com/society/2022/sep/11/millions-uk-patients-forced-private-nhs-waiting-lists

12 John Burn-Murdoch (2022) 'The answer is not found in A&E, it's found in the rest of the hospital. Specifically, in the acute shortage of available beds for emergency arrivals. Just 7% of English hospital beds are currently unoccupied, the lowest figure since records began, and far short of safe levels.' *Twitter (and The Financial Times)*, 23 August, https://twitter.com/jburnmurdoch/status/1562005484844056577

13 Danny Dorling (2022) 'Austerity led to twice as many excess UK deaths as previously thought – here's what that means for future cuts', *The Conversation*, 6 October, https://theconversation.com/austerity-led-to-twice-as-many-excess-uk-deaths-as-previously-thought-heres-what-that-means-for-future-cuts-192033

Those other beds cannot be cleared as they were before because adult social care has been repeatedly decimated, with what is left being tendered out to private companies.

All of this was foretold. In the four years after 2015, the value of one group of private sector contracts in the NHS rose by 89 per cent.[14] These figures were released just before the 2019 general election, partly in response to Matt Hancock, then the health secretary, claiming that 'there is no privatisation of the NHS on my watch'. Again, the damage was not so much through covert privatisation, but through the wider ethos being promoted. Look at the example of the United States: most of the enormous amount of money spent on healthcare there has little impact on improving health, because the ethos is wrong. It is sometimes claimed – wrongly – that the NHS has not been further privatised, because the share of its spending that went to the private sector remained roughly the same between 2012 and 2020. By 2020 that share was about 7 per cent, or just under £10 billion a year. It rose to over £12 billion during the pandemic when the government paid private hospitals to treat patients, but because overall health spending rose, the proportion remained roughly the same, at around 7 per cent.[15]

But the number of private companies involved did increase greatly, particularly in areas where there was already more private healthcare. By 2022, according to a report by one think-tank,

---

[14] Denis Campbell (2019) 'Private firms handed £15bn in NHS contracts over past five years: figures cast doubt on government's denial of creeping NHS privatisation', *The Guardian*, 29 November, https://www.theguardian.com/society/2019/nov/29/private-firms-handed-15bn-in-nhs-contracts-over-past-five-years

[15] Charlotte Wickens (2023) *Health and social care in England: Tackling the myths*, The King's Fund, 15 March, https://www.kingsfund.org.uk/publications/health-and-social-care-england-myths [Editorial note: One commentator under the article explained how The King's Fund was politically biased towards the right wing in that it criticised left-wing newspapers but not right-wing ones and pointed to this much more impartial article: Benjamin Goodair and Aaron Reeves (2022) 'Outsourcing health-care services to the private sector and treatable mortality rates in England, 2013–20: an observational study of NHS privatisation', *The Lancet*, 7, 7, pp. E638–E646, https://www.thelancet.com/journals/lanpub/article/PIIS2468-2667(22)00133-5/fulltext]

The Health Foundation,[16] private firms were delivering a quarter of all planned NHS hospital treatment in the least deprived areas of England, and 11 per cent in the most deprived areas.[17] Those shares – which have risen since 2020 – are higher than the overall 7 per cent because it is in planned hospital treatment where the private sector has most infiltrated the NHS.

The Health and Care Act of 2022 put paid to Lansley's claim that he had fixed the NHS 'once and for all'.[18] The Act reduces the NHS's obligation to tender so many services to private sector

---

16 Cathy Irving, Sean Agass, and Eleanor Stanley (2023) 'A short history of the Health Foundation', *The Health Foundation*, November, https://www.health.org.uk/publications/a-short-history-of-the-health-foundation [Editorial note: The Foundation's beginnings lie in a mutual health insurance scheme for middle-income Londoners.]

17 Sebastien Peytrignet, Jay Hughes, Ellen Coughlan, Josh Keith, Tim Gardner and Charles Tallack (2022) *Waiting for NHS hospital care: The role of the independent sector*, The Health Foundation, 28 July, https://www.health.org.uk/publications/long-reads/waiting-for-nhs-hospital-care-the-role-of-the-independent-sector

18 Anonymous Researchers (2022) *The Health and Care Act: Six key questions*, The King's Fund, 17 May, https://www.kingsfund.org.uk/publications/health-and-care-act-key-questions [Editorial note: One comment under the report summarises the reality better than the report: 'Having experienced this new "integrated system" from both a professional and a personal point of view I can only describe it as chaotic and unresponsive to the needs of patients. Social care staff and assessments of other professionals are ignored by the ICB [Integrated Care Board] once anyone becomes fully health funded. There is a massive power imbalance; commissioning teams are a law unto themselves and don't communicate with anyone. Funding is withheld without any explanation until people die or recover enough to not need 100% NHS funding. It appears to be a way for the NHS to ignore the Care Act and save money at the expense of people's lives. It has made integrated working a thing of the past.' (Mrs JR, Social worker/Carer, 2 August 2023). ICBs replaced Clinical Commissioning Groups (CCGs) in the NHS in England from 1 July 2022, all this being the legacy of the so very wicked and destructive, market-based purchaser/provider model that New Labour had supported enthusiastically after it had initially been introduced, in the early 1990s under John Major's Conservative government. For more details and some of the controversies and characters involved at the time, please see Nicholas Timmins (2015) *Is the purchaser–provider split dying?*, The King's

bidding in future and so slightly decelerates the privatisation of the NHS, but it was not designed to stop the rot, just to make the rot less obvious and fast spreading. It will not solve the service's problems, though there is hope that it could be the beginning of an actual change in ethos if it were the start of a much greater turn and more legislation were to come late in the 2020s.

The pandemic made the effects of privatisation clear: Britons now have the worst access to healthcare in Europe and some of the worst post-pandemic outcomes.[19] But the successive health secretaries who inflicted this tragedy are unrepentant.

In 2018, Lansley criticised Hunt's cuts in screening services, blaming them for delaying the detection of his bowel cancer.[20] Hunt, meanwhile, went on to become foreign secretary and then chancellor of the Exchequer. His legacy, as Open Democracy's Caroline Molloy wrote[21] in 2022, is 'one of missed targets, lengthening waits, crumbling hospitals, missed opportunities, false solutions, funding boosts that vanished under scrutiny, and blaming everyone but himself'. Hunt was replaced by Matt Hancock. Hancock is now best remembered for eating a camel penis and cow anus[22] on live TV for money.

Belligerence, bravado and buffoonery. We got here because too many of us believed the words of fools.

Fund, 22 September, https://www.kingsfund.org.uk/insight-and-analysis/blogs/purchaser-provider-split-dying]

19 John Burn-Murdoch (2022) 'Britons now have the worst access to healthcare in Europe, and it shows', *Financial Times*, 4 November, https://www.ft.com/content/de8fc348-0025-4821-9ec5-d50b4bbacc8d

20 Aubrey Allegretti (2018) 'Former health secretary Andrew Lansley blames NHS cuts for failure to diagnose his bowel cancer', *Sky News*, 3 April, https://news.sky.com/story/former-health-secretary-andrew-lansley-blames-nhs-cuts-for-failure-to-diagnose-his-bowel-cancer-11315400

21 Caroline Molloy (2022) 'Jeremy Hunt: New chancellor is the man who ruined the NHS', *Open Democracy*, 8 July, https://www.opendemocracy.net/en/jeremy-hunt-tory-leadership-boris-johnson-nhs-junior-doctors/

22 Lobby Akinnola (2022) 'With "I'm a Celeb", Matt Hancock insults bereaved families like mine', *Open Democracy*, 17 November, https://www.opendemocracy.net/en/matt-hancock-im-a-celebrity-get-me-out-of-here-covid-inquiry-insult-bereaved-families/

CHAPTER 5.2

The Brexit vote, declining health and immigration[1]

The local authority districts of England and boroughs of London can be ordered according to how many international migrants live in each area, from the lows of South Staffordshire (0.11 per cent) and Staffordshire Moorlands (0.13 per cent) up to the highs of Westminster (5.9 per cent) and the City of London (8.5 per cent). They are ordered here by the share of the local population living in each area in June 2016 who had arrived from abroad within the preceding 12 months. Almost no one came to live in those two districts of Staffordshire between June 2015 and June 2016. In contrast, one in every 17 residents in Westminster at the time of the EU referendum was a very recent arrival, as were more than one in 12 of the residents of the City of London, many of them living in the Barbican towers.

All of England can be divided into five groups of districts by the international in-migration rate of June 2016, from the districts with the least migrants (0.3 per cent on average) to those with the most (still just 2.7 per cent on average). Each group is defined to have almost exactly the same population in June 2016 (Figure 5.4). You might have thought that this rapid influx of new people would have annoyed those who had a right to vote in the EU referendum (which did not include the international migrants themselves). In fact, the very opposite occurred.

In Westminster and the City of London, less than a third of those who voted in the referendum voted to leave the EU. In

---

1 Adapted from an article originally published in 2018 *Public Sector Focus*, September/October, pp. 20–23.

Figure 5.4: England split into five areas by 2016 immigration rate (% in the year)

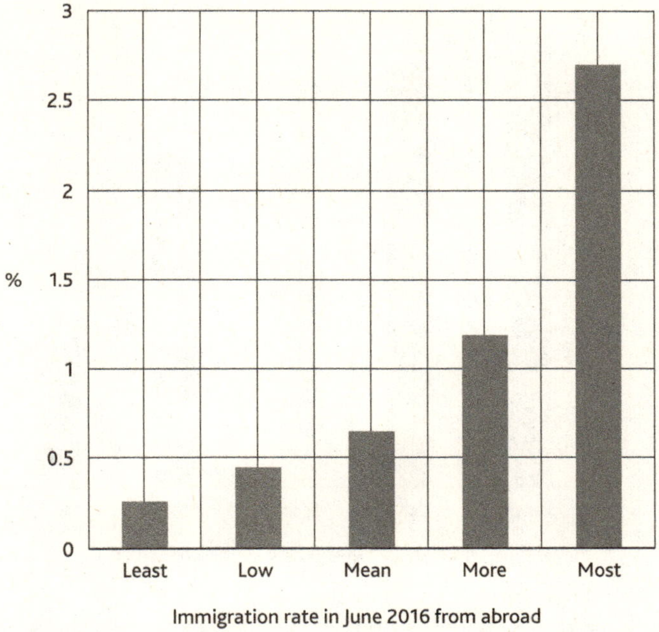

Source: ONS mid-year population estimates by local authority districts showing proportion of the population who are recent immigrants.

contrast, in both of those two Staffordshire districts with the lowest international immigration rate in all of England, some 65 per cent (almost two thirds!) of the votes cast were to leave.

Nationally, across the five groups of English districts, the fewer migrants there were, the more people voted to leave, of those who voted. In fact, it was only where there were the most migrants that a majority voted to remain (Figure 5.5).

This is, however, far from the end of the story of a very interesting anomaly. On 23 June 2016, the same day as the result of the EU referendum was announced, the official mid-year population estimates of the UK were published for the year ending June 2015 (there is always a one-year lag in this data). Those estimates revealed the most remarkable rise in mortality in that year. It was little commented upon at the time, as the result of the EU referendum was such a shock, but among the rise in

Figure 5.5: Voters who voted Leave in 2016, by 2016 immigration rate, England (%)

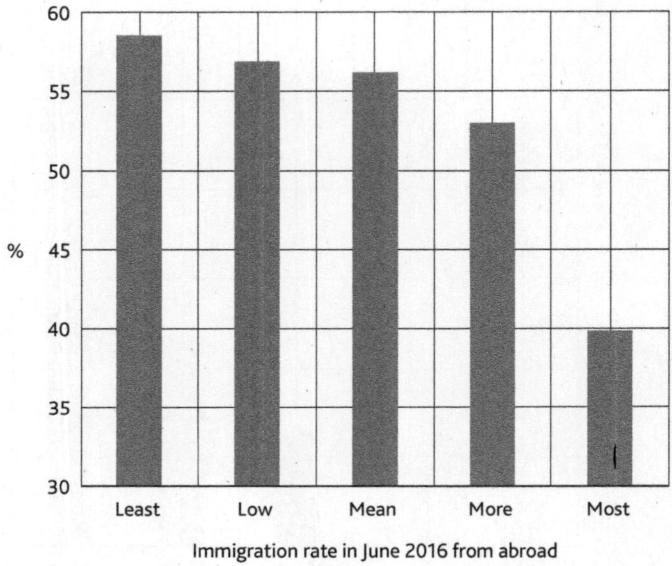

Note: Non-voters are excluded.

Source: ONS mid-year population estimates by local authority district, arranged into five groups, and the results of the 2016 referendum as published by all local authorities in England

deaths there was one anomaly. There was no rise in death rates for people aged 25–29, the age group of highest net in-migration to the UK at that time.

The 'healthy migrant effect' has been known about for a long time, but we didn't realise just how healthy these migrants were and how unhealthy those of us who were not migrants were (on average) back then. This was despite increasing numbers of people saying when surveyed that they felt more ill, because those reports were ignored. Then more people in the UK began to die earlier than before.

Between the first quarter of 2016 and the first quarter of 2018 the numbers of people dying across England rose by an average of 15.8 per cent, but by more in areas with fewer in-migrants (Figure 5.6).

Life expectancy peaked across the UK in 2014 and has been lower ever since [Editorial note: this was true until 2019, when

Figure 5.6: Increase in death rates 2016–18, by 2016 immigration rate, England (%)

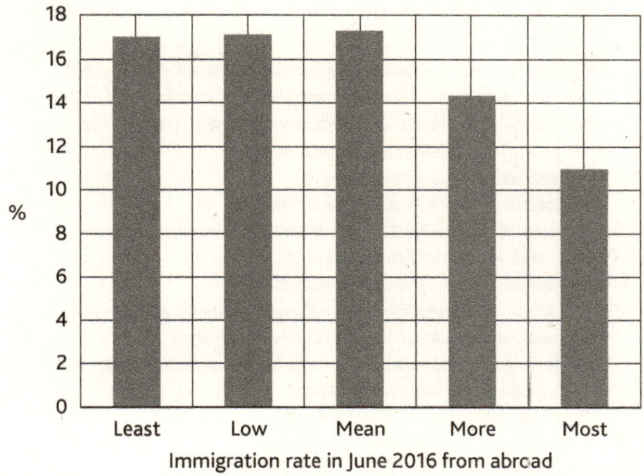

Source: ONS mid-year population estimates by local authority district, arranged into five groups. Mortality change is the number of deaths in January to June 2018 as compared to those same months in 2016, as published by ONS for all local authorities in England, not adjusted for ageing (but there was not much ageing going on, because mortality rates among the old were rising and so, as a group, they were becoming old more slowly than they would have done if more of them had lived longer – as was the case in the rest of Western Europe).

it was briefly higher than it had been in 2014], falling most years. The ONS published an analysis on 7 August 2018 that demonstrated this. One of the key graphs from the ONS analysis is shown next, in Figure 5.7, and it reveals yet another anomaly that has yet to receive much attention. It is perhaps the pattern for women that is most revealing.

All the reports on the international comparison of trends in life expectancy concentrated on the fact that women in the UK had seen the lowest rate of life expectancy improvement from 2010 to 2016 of the 20 affluent states being compared – which itself actually disguises the overall fall since 2014, as there were still some improvements in 2010–12.[2]

[2] Lucinda Hiam and Danny Dorling (2018) 'Improving life expectancy used to be the UK's forte – now it's falling behind', *The Conversation*, 16 August, https://theconversation.com/improving-life-expectancy-used-to-be-the-uks-forte-now-its-falling-behind-101573

Figure 5.7: Women's rise in life expectancy per year in weeks, 2010–16, affluent countries

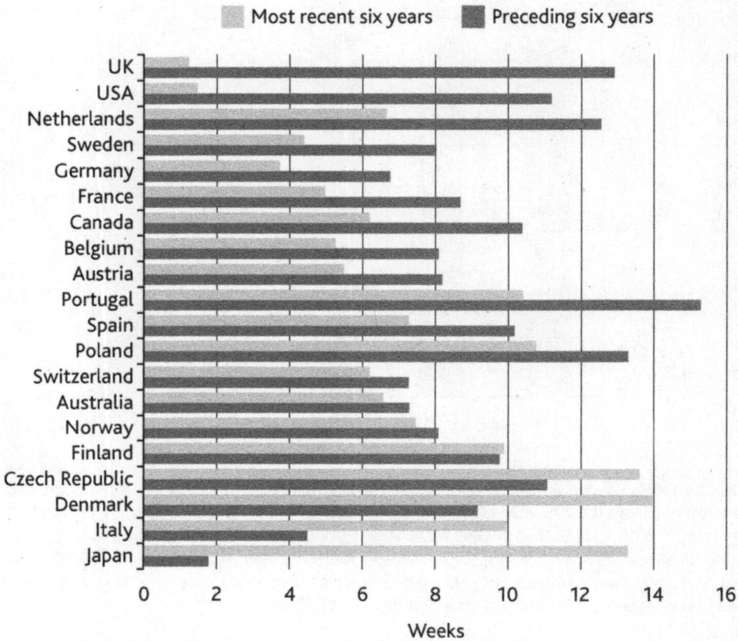

Note: The figures shown here are for women in the 2010–16 period, or the nearest period to that then released, as compared to the previous six years.

Source: Alan Evans (2016) *Changing trends in mortality: An international comparison: 2000 to 2016*, Office for National Statistics (period life expectancies selected countries globally), 7 August, https://www.ons.gov.uk/peoplepopulationandcommunity/birthsdeathsandmarriages/lifeexpectancies/articles/changingtrendsinmortalityaninternationalcomparison/2000to2016

What no one commented on was the huge rise in women's life expectancy in the UK in the six years prior to 2010: the 2004–10 period. And, given what we now know about the relationship between migration in the UK and mortality, this is, perhaps, important.

In May 2004 the EU welcomed ten new member states, almost all Central and Eastern European countries. Only the UK, Sweden and Ireland at first allowed migration from these new member states and the vast majority of those who migrated came to the UK.

In hindsight it appears that the women who migrated to the UK may have been some of the most healthy, young and well educated. This will not be the whole story; but the picture changed abruptly once migration to a wider range of Western European countries was permitted.

So, what about the men? A very similar picture is seen (Figure 5.8): rapidly improving life expectancy among men in the UK prior to 2010 (only Portugal sees a greater improvement from a lower base), and then sudden stalling after 2010, with only the United States seeing even less improvement.

Figure 5.8: Men's rise in life expectancy per year in weeks, 2010–16, affluent countries

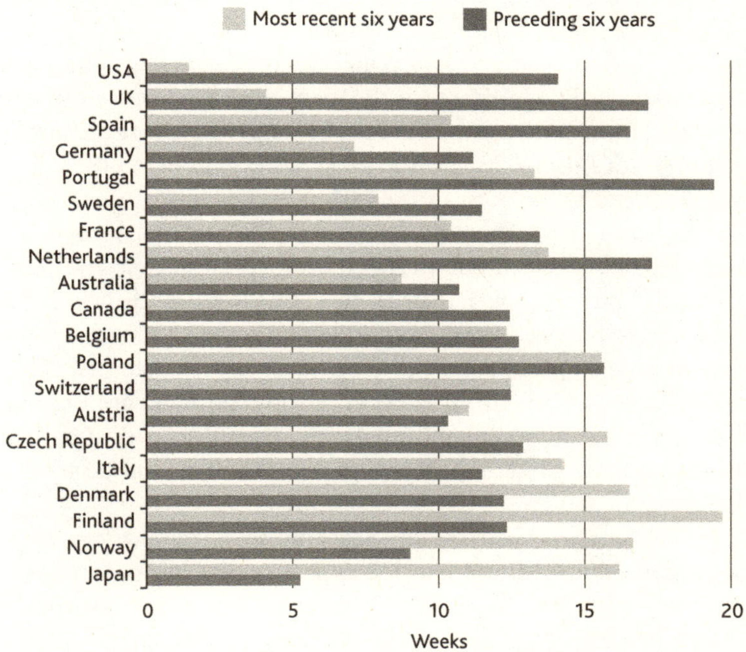

Note: The figures shown here are for men in the 2010–16 period, or the nearest period to that then released, as compared to the previous six years.

Source: Alan Evans (2016) *Changing trends in mortality: An international comparison: 2000 to 2016*, Office for National Statistics (period life expectancies selected countries globally), 7 August, https://www.ons.gov.uk/peoplepopulationandcommunity/birthsdeathsandmarriages/lifeexpectancies/articles/changingtrendsinmortalityaninternationalcomparison/2000to2016

Of course, the UK experienced huge cuts to vital public services after 2010, especially those necessary for sustaining life among people who were frailest and most in need,[3] especially the older people with Alzheimer's and dementia. Cuts to local authority budgets and the consequent repeated decimation, year on year, of adult social service visits and meals-on-wheels services, coupled with the stalling in required rises in healthcare funding and so much else very neatly matches up with the rising death rates among, at first, the most elderly women living on their own, and then not-quite-so-elderly women and the most elderly men, and then more and more of the population – almost all of them UK-born. It was not the in-migrants who were dying in rising numbers. The migrants were young and healthy, and disproportionately worked as health carers.

Infant mortality rates also rose in the UK as midwifery services were constrained. The greatest rises were seen around the time of birth when access to safe delivery services is key. The rises were statistically significant for the most recent two years and not reported from elsewhere in Europe. In some of the best organised countries of Europe, infants were half as likely to die in their first year of life as those born in the UK.

Of course, premature babies are born all across Europe. In most other European countries, more that are sick survive; and stillbirth rates are lower than in the UK. But could there be a relationship between changes in migration patterns and the recent rise in infant mortality in the UK? Here is one potential clue: up to a third of midwives working in some hospitals are EU but not UK citizens. Once all of Europe opened up to migration from the East, attracting midwives from Eastern Europe to the UK became harder.

It will be many years before we fully understand what went wrong in the UK, leading to life expectancy falling significantly for the first time from 2014 onwards and infant mortality independently also rising. I will end with an anecdote.

---

3 Mark Fransham and Danny Dorling (2018) 'Homelessness and public health', *The British Medical Journal*, 30 January, 360:k214

On Friday 21 September 2018 it was revealed by the BBC that all but one of the many maternity units in Oxfordshire had shut their doors the night before due to lack of midwifery support. That day the *Oxford Mail* newspaper reported that expectant mothers scheduled to give birth at the Cotswold Birth Centre in Chipping Norton should check Facebook to see if it was open when they went into labour.

CHAPTER 5.3

How many more will be dead by Christmas?[1]

In the week after schools went back in England and Wales, an extra 538 people died (77 a day). Over the previous five years, an average of 8,720 people had died that week in September, but this year the number surged to 9,258. How many more would be dead by Christmas?

The next week there was a lull: only 289 excess deaths. But then the universities returned, and the excess mortality count doubled. In the week ending 25 September, 574 more people had died each day. There was a drop to 319 excess deaths the following week, and then a rise to 678 (97 a day). On and on it went, week after week after week. Almost 5,000 excess deaths were recorded between the schools going back and the start of December. The year was 2015 and most people weren't paying attention.[2] No one read the numbers out.

The rise in mortality in autumn 2015 had little to do with schools or universities reopening. It wasn't due to the onset of winter. It wasn't because of a second wave of a new virus. It was business as usual. After five years of swingeing cuts to health and social services, many more people died each day than had done in the five previous years – which were themselves the depths of recession.

---

1 Originally published as the second wave of the pandemic began to rise, but not a chapter about the pandemic: 'How many more will be dead by Christmas?', *London Review of Books Blog*, 5 October 2020.

2 Anna Aslanyan (2015) 'Cold homes kill', 27 November, https://www.lrb.co.uk/blog/2015/november/cold-homes-kill

Imagine if in autumn 2015 you had been told how many people were dying each day. Would you have been fearful? Or would you have thought: 'They are mostly old, or poor; this is all very unfortunate, but I won't be in that grisly rising aggregate'? It can be hard to imagine what effect the relentless reporting of the excess deaths in autumn 2015 might have had. But imagine that the figures had been read out all year and you had already heard much higher numbers in January and February, along with front-page stories of the health service falling apart and undertakers running out of mortuary space.

The mortality surge lasted for weeks at the start of 2015. It went up suddenly. In one week in January, as the hospitals became overwhelmed, the number of excess deaths rose from 448 to 4,050, then 3,721, 3,220, 2,408, 1,719, 1,470, not dipping below 1,000 until mid-March. It rose again to 1,973 in the worst week in April, and to 1,290 in the worst week of June. Had every newspaper been reporting the weekly (never mind daily) figures in 2015, we could even have imagined five waves by the autumn. All those earlier figures were far higher than the autumn of 2015; and – so far – the excess deaths for autumn 2015 are far higher than in autumn 2020. The major difference, of course, is that five years ago there was no talk of the numbers soaring exponentially out of control (despite life expectancy stalling – Figure 5.9). The pool of potential victims appeared limited, and didn't include government ministers, newspaper editors or most of their voters and readers.

The most common listed causes of excess deaths in 2015 were Alzheimer's and dementia, but there was no biological reason these diseases should have been killing people earlier than they had before. The most important reasons were neglect, underfunding and the system becoming overwhelmed. For younger adults the causes were described as diseases of despair (drug overdose, suicide, alcoholic liver disease). Influenza played a small part, but in nearby countries with better-funded health services, far fewer people died.

If we had reported mortality in 2015 as we do today, would something have been done about a problem that was far easier to fix than a new pandemic? Might the 2015 election have turned out differently? Or would we then, as now, have been paralysed

Figure 5.9: The first four revisions of official UK life expectancy projections, 2012–20

see colour version in plate section

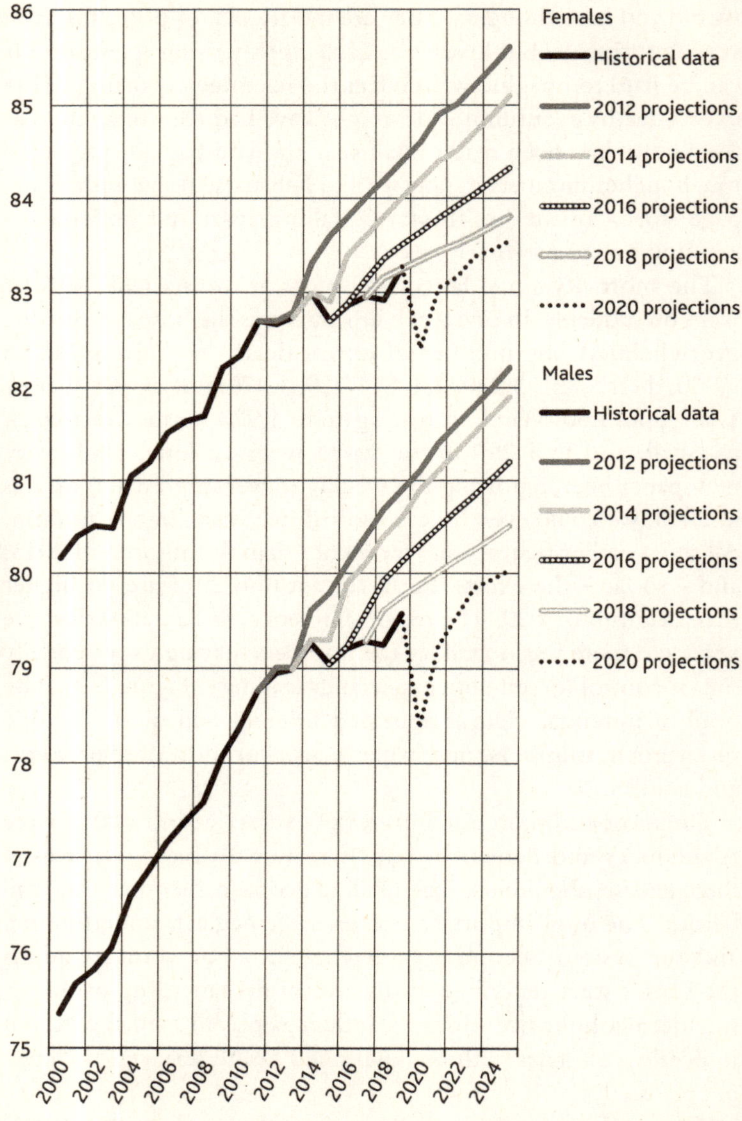

Note: This figure has been added to the original chapter to show just how much greater the effect of austerity from around 2012 onwards was than the pandemic on reducing life expectancy in the UK. By the end of 2020, the pandemic had had a similar effect to two years' worth of austerity.

Source: Lucinda Hiam and Danny Dorling (2022) 'The end of great expectations?' *BMJ*, 377, e071329, https://www.bmj.com/content/377/bmj-2022-071329

by fear? As it is, we now have not only COVID-19 to deal with, but the continued legacy of austerity, and Brexit to come, not to mention the climate crisis. The long-term solutions, once we have a vaccine, are the same ones we needed five years ago. Whether or not we will reach for them is less clear.

CHAPTER 5.4

The decimation of the NHS[1]

Geographers should be interested in what is happening to the National Health Service, because it is through making geographical comparisons with other countries that we can see that its current decimation is unnecessary. The claim that there is no alternative but to spend less can be disproved by considering how other very nearby countries manage to spend more. Furthermore, there is a geography to the cuts that have taken place in the UK that reveals which areas are prioritised and which are not. Finally, very local geographical stories, such as the two from Oxford and Glasgow told briefly here, can also help reveal what is going on.

Over a year ago, on 9 January 2020, the BBC published a news story entitled '11 charts on the problems facing the NHS'. The second of those charts is produced here as Figure 5.10 and shows how cuts in spending increases for the NHS began in earnest in the late 1970s, were briefly reversed for 13 years after 1996, but then began again after 2009. All of these changes were political choices, as the labelling of the graph makes clear, although there had been something of a political consensus between 1955 and 1978 when spending increases were usually above 4 per cent a year regardless of the political party in power in the UK.

A spending increase of 4 per cent a year does not mean an actual improvement in service, it often just means holding the line. This is especially so today when the population is ageing far faster than it was in the 1960s or 1970s. That BBC article went

[1] Originally published as: 'The decimation of the NHS', *The Geographer* (Magazine of the Royal Scottish Geographical Society), Spring 2022, pp. 6–7.

Figure 5.10: How spending on health has slowed down in the UK, 1955–2022

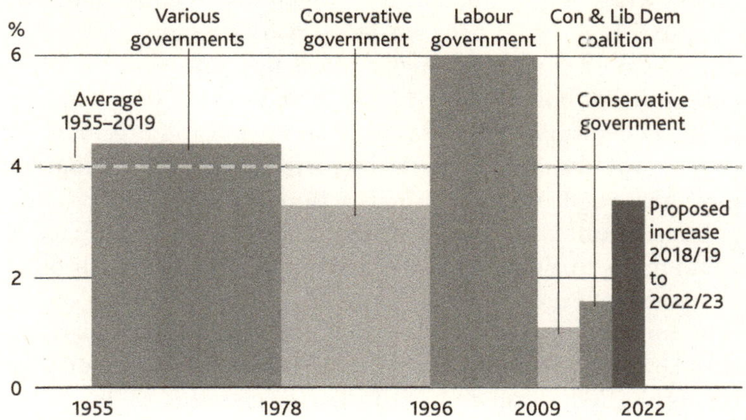

Note: Average annual increase in government spending on health, based on 2019–20 prices; projected growth is an estimate made by the Institute for Fiscal Studies for NHS England only.

Source: Nick Triggle and Ben Butcher (2020) '11 charts on the problems facing the NHS', *BBC News*, 9 January, https://www.bbc.co.uk/news/health-50290033

on to show that spending on healthcare in the UK is much lower as a proportion of GDP than it is in France and Germany, and that is even the case when private health spending is included. It also showed that there was little difference in outcomes in the different countries of the UK, almost certainly because spending across them varies so little as compared to spending across Europe. In 2017 health spending in the UK as a whole, including all the spending on private hospitals, was almost identical to the EU average. Today it will almost certainly be less than that average, not least as other countries in Europe have responded with a larger increase in emergency spending due to the pandemic. This is alongside the now usually higher increases in health spending that most other European countries are making as they bolster their health services more widely. In contrast, the UK government plans to reduce public spending overall once the pandemic has subsided, as illustrated by the submissions it has made to the International Monetary Fund on planned future public spending.

The final graph the BBC published in their series of 11 illustrates one theory as to why these choices have been made.

That graph, Figure 5.11, was entitled 'Patient satisfaction with the NHS', which was falling until 1997, then rose as public spending rose, to a high of 70 per cent being 'very or quite satisfied' in 2009, before falling again afterwards. Satisfaction with the NHS tends to track how well the NHS is able to cope, which in turn is largely determined by how well it is funded and organised.

Why would some politicians instigate changes in funding that inevitably result in a fall in satisfaction with the NHS? These politicians often say that a continuation of funding increases could not be maintained. That clearly was not the case, as other countries in Europe chose differently despite suffering similar economic shocks at particular times. Geographical comparisons are a key way to determine if the politicians are lying about what is possible, as compared to what they are choosing to do.

Of course, there is always some part of the UK that is receiving a greater increase in health funding, or less of a decrease, at any one time. Politicians tend to point to the increases to say that they are doing something substantial. It is well known that the UK government has promised '40 new hospitals' in England. What

Figure 5.11: Levels of patient satisfaction with the NHS in Great Britain, 1993–2018

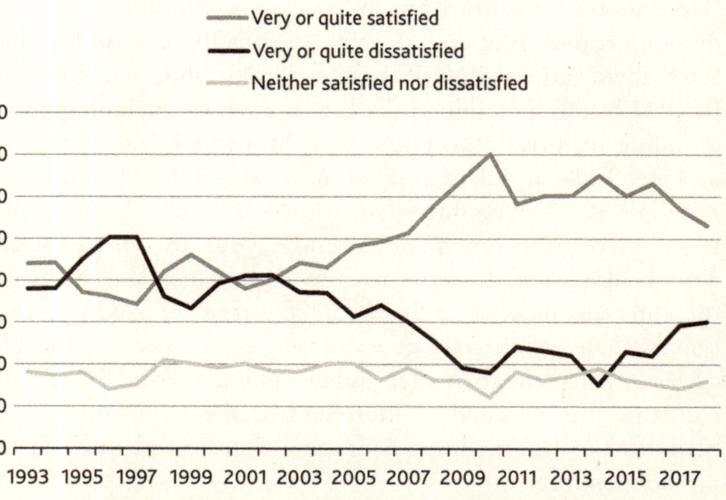

Source: British Social Attitudes Survey, in Nick Triggle and Ben Butcher (2020) '11 charts on the problems facing the NHS', *BBC News*, 9 January, https://www.bbc.co.uk/news/health-50290033

is less well known is that hardly any of these hospitals are new, and most are extensions to (or rebuilding on) existing sites. But even here there is a clear geographical pattern to what is planned, as shown in yet another graph, Figure 5.12, this time published by the BBC on 1 December 2021. The 40 planned projects are concentrated in the southwest of England; although as the BBC story that accompanied that graphic made clear, there are now doubts as to whether most of those will happen on time. More importantly, even if the planned projects were all completed they would not reverse the decimation that has been occurring more widely, or even begin to address the increase in need that comes as we age and become frailer overall. Neither would they begin to cope with the health legacy of a pandemic and a disease that is becoming endemic, resulting in greater levels of illness than before for an as-yet-unknown number of years to come.

What is going on? I grew up in the city of Oxford in England at a time when the NHS was well funded and in a city with a surfeit of public hospitals. I left the city when I was aged 18 and returned nine years ago. One of many shocks I had on returning was discovering what had happened to the old Manor Ground where Oxford United used to play. It now housed a brand new private hospital, built within walking distance of the old public hospitals so that consultants who chose to do part private work

Figure 5.12: The geographical distribution of the 40 new hospitals promised for England

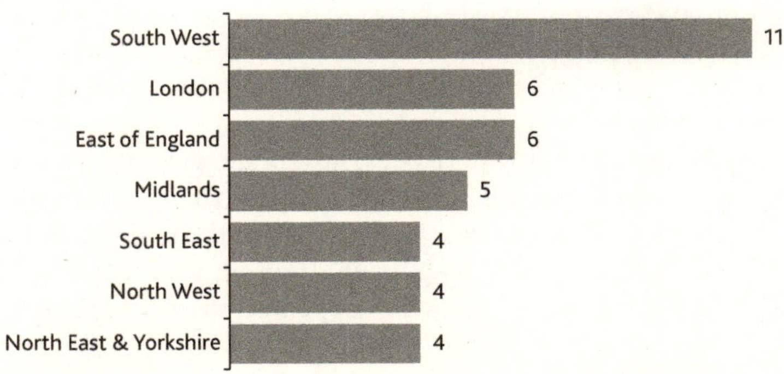

Source: Statistics from Department of Health and Social Care, 'as of 23 November 2021', via Nicholas Barrett and Daniele Palumbo (2022) 'What's happened to the 40 new hospitals pledge?', *BBC Verify*, 4 July, https://www.bbc.co.uk/news/59372348

could walk over with ease. Before the private hospital had been built, there had been much less opportunity to expand the private health sector in the city. Later I discovered that some Oxford colleges offer to fund private health insurance for their academics and other senior staff. Something dystopic was happening, however slowly and gradually. Each of us can tell a story of the dismantling of public healthcare, but few of us can see the overall orchestration underlying it.

In January 2020 it was quietly announced that a new £20 million private hospital had been opened just off the Old Govan Road in Glasgow. The Ross Hall Clinic Braehead was described as 'state-of-the-art' by the *Daily Record*.[2] Set on an industrial estate between an accountancy firm and a computer shop and opposite a new charging station for electric cars, 'The new hospital includes 17 new consulting rooms, a new MRI scanner alongside new respiratory, colposcopy and urodynamic departments. The inclusion of these key additions will mean that an extra 200 outpatients a day will be able to receive care from clinical specialists.' But, of course, only a few people will be able to afford to use these services, and others will rely on the NHS sending them there, if it is able to do so.

The pandemic could have led to a sea change in healthcare and spending on healthcare across the UK. Many private hospitals would not have survived it had they not been supported by state contracts and emergency funding to keep them solvent. We could have nationalised most of the new private facilities, at almost no cost – given that they were no longer solvent. Instead, they were supported, kept alive for when they could begin full operation again; and further private facilities were built during the pandemic.

In relation to the growth in need, healthcare spending has been decimated across the UK. One reason this is allowed to happen is because a small but growing proportion of the population can afford to bypass the ever-lengthening waiting lists; they do not have to worry about what will happen to them if and when

---

2 Alison Rennie (2022) 'New £20 million hospital opens its doors at Braehead', *The Daily Record*, 28 January, https://www.dailyrecord.co.uk/in-your-area/renfrewshire/new-20-million-hospital-opens-26077641

they fall ill. They receive an increasingly better level of service as compared to what most people can access. And the politicians who have presided over this growing social and health divide are not unaware of this. In fact, they are often lobbied by private healthcare companies or have even more direct involvement than that.

Why should British geographers care about any of this? One reason, perhaps the most trivial, is that it will affect the maps of health outcomes for many years to come – to the extent that differential health and social care is part of the reason people live shorter lives in some areas than others. A less trivial reason is that even if they are not worried about the direction their society is travelling in generally, they might worry about themselves. A recent RGS/IBG survey found that 51 per cent of students who go on to study geography at university do so because they rank 'earning a good salary' as important (while only 19 per cent said they ranked 'doing "good" through my job' as important).[3] However, only a minority, even of that 51 per cent, will ever earn enough to be able to afford private healthcare.

---

3 Steve Brace (2022) 'Geography student career concerns in rank', *Royal Geographical Society Twitter*, 29 January, https://twitter.com/SteveBraceGeog/status/1487432420215435271

CHAPTER 5.5

Falling down the global ranks[1]

In 1952, when Queen Elizabeth II came to the throne, the UK had one of the longest life expectancies (as measured from birth) in the world, ranking seventh globally behind countries including Norway, Sweden and Denmark.[2] Indeed, for many in Britain, the 1950s were a good time to be alive. The country was recovering from the devastation of the war, and Harold Macmillan, prime minister in the second half of the decade, famously told the people that they had 'never had it so good'.[3] Of course, not everyone was so lucky, with William Blake's 'dark satanic mills' still dominating many communities experiencing deep poverty. But compared with many other countries, the prospects seemed good. A survey in the city of York found that poverty had almost disappeared there by 1950, although of course it was not entirely gone.[4] However, in marked contrast to the unemployment of the 1930s, the country was actively recruiting people from the Commonwealth to fill the many job vacancies.[5]

Objectively, Macmillan's comments seemed justified. One of the best measures of the progress of nations is the health of their

---

1 Originally published as Lucinda Hiam, Danny Dorling and Martin McKee (2023) 'Falling down the global ranks: Life expectancy in the UK 1950–2021', *Journal of the Royal Society of Medicine*, 116, 3, pp. 89–92.

2 United Nations Population Division (2022) *World Population Prospects*, https://population.un.org/wpp/

3 Peter Hennessy (2007) *Having it so good: Britain in the Fifties*, London: Penguin.

4 Timothy Hatton and Roy Bailey (2000) 'Seebohm Rowntree and the postwar poverty puzzle', *Economic History Review*, 53, 3, pp. 517–43.

5 Amelia Gentleman (2019) *The Windrush betrayal: Exposing the hostile environment*, London: Faber & Faber.

people, and with life expectancy at an all-time high and, globally, higher than in many other countries, the UK was faring well. It can, of course, be unfair to compare countries without taking account of their initial circumstances. Most obviously, given a biological limit to longevity, countries that have already achieved long life expectancy have less scope to improve. However, while this may be an issue now, it was much less relevant in 1952 when life expectancy (both sexes) in the UK was only 69.5 years. The UK also benefitted from the legacy of wealth that came from possessing the largest empire the world has ever known. However, other major colonial powers, such as France, were also advantaged.

This favourable situation would not last. By the early 1960s, the UK was slipping down the global rankings in life expectancy (Figure 5.13). After particularly marked falls in the 1970s and 2010s, it had fallen to 36th place in 2020 (white dot) during the

Figure 5.13: UK ranking in international life expectancy league tables, 1950–2021

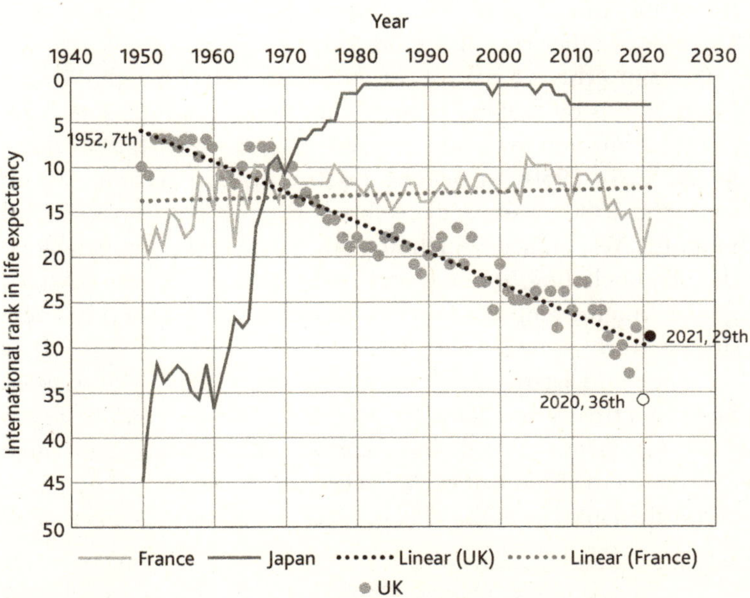

Source: United Nations Population Division (2022) *World Population Prospects*, https://population.un.org/wpp/

COVID-19 pandemic, just above the Maldives, Chile, Costa Rica and Thailand. In 2021, the UK's life expectancy rank rose seven places to 29th (black dot), possibly linked to the arrival of vaccines against COVID-19 earlier in Britain than in the countries just above it. By rolling the vaccine out first to older people, who were especially likely to die from COVID-19, this may have provided a transient advantage before other countries caught up, but this is not yet clear. However, given the current challenges faced by the UK, there is no room for complacency. While life expectancy has increased in absolute terms over recent decades, other (now much more similar) countries are experiencing larger increases. It is hard to believe that the UK is simply facing diminishing marginal returns on its investment in health, while those other countries are at a point in the curve where returns are still much higher.

Some changes would have been expected in the decades from the 1950s until the present day. The postwar period saw remarkable economic progress in some parts of the world, such as Singapore, Hong Kong, South Korea and Taiwan, giving rise to the term 'Asian Tigers'. So, is what happened in the UK simply a matter of other regions catching up?

Certainly, this is a part of the explanation, but not all. We can illustrate this by looking at two other trendlines in Figure 5.13. Japan has made remarkable progress, coming from 45th position in the early 1950s to occupy one of the top three positions since the 1980s, and regularly holds the top position in global rankings. Yet, France, which in many ways is very comparable to the UK (including, as noted previously, benefitting from having a global colonial empire), started well below the UK and has now surpassed it.

France and Japan, along with the UK, Canada, the United States, Germany and Italy, are members of the Group of Seven (G7). The G7 is a collection of countries with advanced economies that represent about half of global economic output.[6] Figure 5.14 shows the rankings of the G7 countries at each decade from 1950

---

6 The Rt Hon George Osborne (2013) *What is the G7?*, London: Her [at the time of publication] Majesty's Treasury, 9 May, https://www.gov.uk/government/news/what-is-the-g7

Figure 5.14: International life expectancy rankings, countries of the G7, 1950–2021

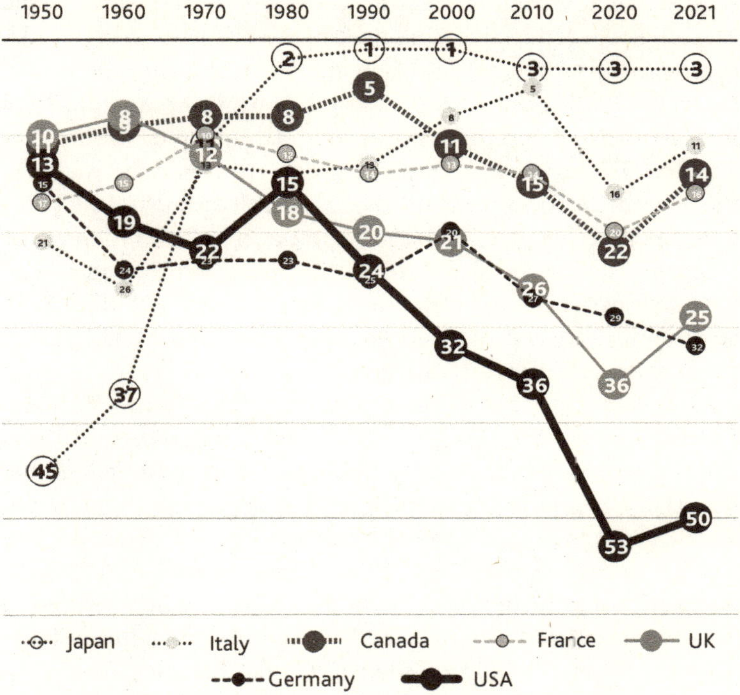

Source: United Nations Population Division (2022) *World Population Prospects*, https://population.un.org/wpp/

to 2020.[7] Along with Canada, France and Japan, Germany and Italy have now surpassed the UK. In fact, the only G7 country to do worse than the UK is the US. What has gone wrong?

7 The figure as shown here is updated to include 2021 data which have since become available (note that the data are not averages for the decade). In 2021 the UK's position improved temporarily because there were fewer deaths from the pandemic as vaccination arrived slightly earlier in the UK than elsewhere. In contrast, the position in Germany temporarily worsened, partly because it had been higher in 2020 when there was a little less transmission of the virus in Germany and much better access to ventilators. The years 2020 and 2021 were volatile for this reason and so both are included here for clarity.

As always, the first question is whether we can trust the data. Vital registration has improved immensely over this time, especially in low- and middle-income countries. However, while caution is needed in analysing the causes of deaths seven decades ago, with a few exceptions (such as in Korea during the war in the early 1950s), the countries at the top of the rankings have long-established systems for collecting demographic data.[8]

As far as we know, while these data are publicly available, the presentation, as rankings over seven decades, is new. This long-term perspective, with estimation of trends, overcomes the problem of short-term fluctuations of examining annual data. This is a particular problem in smaller countries, but even in larger ones, natural disasters or epidemics, for example, can produce quite substantial changes.

The relative decline of the UK portrayed in Figure 5.13 and Figure 5.14 is stark. Yet, it may not be a surprise to scholars from some disciplines, such as political scientists and economic historians. In the international arena, in 1962 US Secretary of State Dean Acheson's observation that the UK had 'lost an empire and has not yet found a role' drew attention to the UK's loss of international influence after Suez.[9] Since 2016, when it voted to leave the European Union, the UK has found itself increasingly isolated, despite coining the slogan 'Global Britain'. For a long time it retained considerable soft power, taking advantage of the increasingly ubiquitous English language, but squandered this in the 2010s by disinvesting in its vehicles, such as the BBC and the British Council.[10]

---

[8] Lene Mikkelsen, David Phillips, Carla AbouZahr, Philip Setel, Don de Savigny, Rafael Lozano and Alan Lopez (2015) 'A global assessment of civil registration and vital statistics systems: monitoring data quality and progress', *The Lancet*, 386, 10001, pp. 1395–1406.

[9] Dean Acheson (1962) Speech at the Military Academy, West Point. 5 December, as referenced in Douglas Brinley (2009) 'Dean Acheson and the "Special Relationship": The West Point Speech of December 1962', *The Historical Journal*, 33, 3, pp. 599–608.

[10] Preethi Amaresh (2020) 'The fall of United Kingdom as the top "Soft power-Superpower"', *Diplomatist*, 23 July, https://diplomatist.com/2020/07/23/the-fall-of-united-kingdom-as-the-top-soft-power-superpower/

Economically, while the UK came out of the Second World War in a much better position than the nations it helped to defeat, a combination of complacency and lack of vision meant that it failed to emulate Germany's Wirtschaftswunder, or 'miracle on the Rhine'[11] and similar developments elsewhere. It was ill prepared for the oil crisis of 1973, and by the end of the decade, the manufacturing industry was reduced to three-day working.[12] With its large financial sector, it was also vulnerable when the 2008 financial crisis hit, exacerbated by a misguided policy of austerity that shut off the transient initial recovery, resulting in the average UK household having lower incomes in 2012 than in France or Germany,[13] paving the way for a decade in which health and the economy stagnated.[14]

Income inequalities rose greatly in the UK during and after the 1980s and that rise also saw an increase in the variation in life expectancy among different social groups. One reason why the overall increase in life expectancy has been so sluggish in the UK is that in recent years it has fallen for poorer groups, falling slightly overall between 2014 and 2018. According to the OECD, the UK is now the second-most economically unequal country in Europe after Bulgaria.[15] Perhaps we should not be surprised to see that inequality reflected in such wide health inequalities and a declining overall position?

---

11 David Audretsch and Michael Fritsch (2003) 'Linking entrepreneurship to growth: the case of West Germany', *Industry and Innovation*, 10, 1, pp. 65–73.

12 Geoffrey Rivett (2008) '1968–1977: Rethinking the National Health Service', in G. Rivett (ed) *The History of the NHS*, London: Nuffield Trust, ch 5, and online: https://www.nuffieldtrust.org.uk/health-and-social-care-explained/the-history-of-the-nhs

13 Danny Dorling (2015) 'Income inequality in the UK: comparisons with five large Western European countries and the USA', *Applied Geography*, 61, pp. 24–34.

14 David Stuckler, Aaron Reeves, Rachel Loopstra, Marina Karanikolos and Martin McKee (2017) 'Austerity and health: the impact in the UK and Europe', *European Journal of Public Health*; 27, supplement 4, pp. 18–21; and Chapter 5.4 in this volume.

15 Danny Dorling (2022) 'The "mini-budget" will make the UK the most unequal country in Europe', *BMJ*, 378, o2318, https://www.bmj.com/content/378/bmj.o2318

Given this history, we can begin to understand why the UK has done so badly. But it poses an obvious question. What comes next? Britain's third prime minister of 2022, Rishi Sunak, inherited a country in crisis that was partly of his making as a former chancellor of the Exchequer. Commentators are asking whether large numbers of people will have to choose between heating and eating, even after some bills have been capped. Yet, despite the scale of the crisis, the UK government treaded water during the summer and autumn of 2022, with the ruling party immersed in two destructive leadership campaigns.

While politicians invoke global factors, especially the effects of the pandemic and the invasion of Ukraine, the reality is that, as in the 1950s, the country suffers from major structural and institutional weaknesses. Despite the UK being much less reliant on Russian gas than countries such as Germany, its energy prices have risen much faster, in part reflecting the ill-advised closure of storage capacity and failure to regulate the market. Although, in theory, the country was second-best prepared for a pandemic in the world, it experienced one of the highest death rates in 2020, with multiple policy failures.[16]

It is not the case that 'things can only get better'. There are many examples of once prosperous countries that experienced a long decline, such as Argentina in the 20th century.[17] Worryingly, at some point, countries can enter a vicious downward spiral, with worse health feeding into economic decline and vice versa. Meanwhile, a growing body of research is cataloguing how declining health threatens democracy itself.[18]

---

[16] Martin McKee, Kara Hanson and Kamran Abbasi (2022) 'Guided by the science? Questions for the UK's Covid-19 public inquiry', *BMJ*, 378: o2066, https://www.bmj.com/content/378/bmj.o2066

[17] Alan Taylor (2018) 'The Argentina paradox: microexplanations and macropuzzles', *Latin American Economic Review*, 27, 3, pp. 1–17, https://latinaer.springeropen.com/articles/10.1007/s40503-017-0051-8

[18] Gregori Galofré-Vilà, Martin McKee, María Gómez-León and David Stuckler (2022) 'The 1918 influenza pandemic and the rise of Italian fascism: a cross-city quantitative and historical text qualitative analysis', *American Journal of Public Health*, 112: pp. 242–7, https://doi.org/10.2105/AJPH.2021.306574; and Gregori Galofré-Vilà, Martin McKee, Jacob Bor, Christopher Meissner and David Stuckler (2021) 'A lesson from history?

The UK is at a crossroads. The cost-of-living crisis means that 'business as usual' is no longer an option. But politicians have choices, and we can only hope they make the right ones, although events in and since October 2022 have so far provided little reassurance. As they move forward, the data we present should give pause for thought.

In early 2023, both the establishment newspaper *The Times* and the left-wing *Morning Star* ran near-identical headlines: 'A&E delays are "killing up to 500 people a week"'.[19] In the short term, the government has an acute crisis to address. In the medium term, there is an economic malaise that makes it harder to address the short-term problems. At some point, it might be realised that proceeding along a particular path is slowly but surely resulting in the UK falling down the ranks. The headlines may be about what is happening now, but the causes appear to have been decades in the making.

Worsening mortality and the rise of the Nazi Party in 1930s Germany', *Public Health*, 195: pp. 18–21. And Chapter 2.2 in this volume, particularly Figure 2.9 on page 125.

19 Chapter 5.1 in this volume.

CHAPTER 5.6

Our museum future[1]

I used to be a republican, but that was before Brexit. What does Britain have that other countries of Europe will still want access to after we leave the European Union? Banking will be safer away from 'offshore London'. There are other places in the world besides Sellafield that can store spent nuclear fuel. The world's most expensive higher education is unlikely to attract so many overseas students, its declining allure mirroring that of Swiss finishing schools after their 1980s heyday.

Despite the entrepreneurial myths we tell ourselves, innovation isn't a British forte. A vacuum cleaner once constructed in Malmesbury is a fitting emblem for the land of hope and glory, if not for the reasons its inventor would have us believe. When Dyson moved its production to Malaysia, few British jobs were lost, because so few had been created here in the first place.

As the pound drops and the world's middle class grows in size, tourism is our best bet to tide us over until we learn to do something useful. And the royal family is by far our most potentially profitable earner. The town of Windsor is already booked out for the summer through Airbnb. American TV companies have reportedly paid six-figure sums to secure prime sites from which to film the royal wedding on 19 May. The birth of Prince Louis on St George's Day conveniently supplanted less happy news in the headlines.

The great skills of the British, historically, haven't been engineering and industry but exploitation and imperialism. We

---

[1] First published as: 'Our Museum Future', *London Review of Books (Blog)*, 27 April 2018.

built up our tourist attractions around ancient stone circles, small monastic universities, old London streets and the birthplace of a playwright, but without the British empire they wouldn't draw such vast crowds from around the world.

The golden square of English tourism has its corners in London, Stonehenge,[2] Stratford-upon-Avon[3] and Cambridge; at its heart is Oxford (a.k.a. Bicester Village[4]), a short train ride from both Windsor and Buckingham Palace. Everyone in the world with money has to travel here once in a lifetime. They are the Meccas and Medinas for non-believers – the places to go to give thanks for the fact that you own a plastics factory in Changchun or a software firm in Bangalore.

Some 2,640 'commoners' are to be invited to the wedding of Harry and Meghan, with golden tickets awarded to schoolchildren by regional lord lieutenants. Unlike Charlie in Roald Dahl's novel, however, none of them will be given a chocolate factory at the end of their day's holiday from poverty. In 2018, for the first time in decades, there are entire local authority districts where a majority of children are growing up in poverty.

It is time to forget selfish republican fantasies. Forget climate change and pollution: our economic plight means that we have to build that third runway at Heathrow for more tourists to land. We need to embrace our museum future. We are very good at selling the myth that all industry was invented in Britain, that England is the mother of parliaments, that we invented the modern university. We have fooled ourselves into believing it all, so it should be easy to sell to tourists.

Time to widen the pavements and get out the bunting. Build the hotels and face down the NIMBYs. Bring back red telephone

---

2 Rosemary Hill, 'Stonehenge for the solstice', *London Review of Books*, 6 July 2006, 28, 13, https://www.lrb.co.uk/the-paper/v28/n13/rosemary-hill/short-cuts

3 Michael Dobson, 'Ovid goes to Stratford', *London Review of Books*, 5 December 2013, 35, 23, https://www.lrb.co.uk/the-paper/v35/n23/michael-dobson/ovid-goes-to-stratford

4 Bicester Collection, *The possibilities are endless: From Armani to Zadig & Voltaire*, Shopping Centre, accessed April 2018, https://www.thebicestercollection.com/bicester-village/en

boxes: they don't need phones in them, just tourist information screens pointing the customer in the right direction.

If we work hard enough, we will win the global race to become the central tourist destination on planet Earth. We are in the right time zone; we speak the right language, and no other languages; we have a captive, cheap, servile labour force. We have a quaint currency with a member of the royal family on it, a souvenir in itself. And every year tourists will get more and more pounds for their dollar, euro, renminbi or rupee.

No one can take our history away from us. Just as millions flock to Rome to see the Colosseum, that site of mass murder, so we could rebuild the East India Company headquarters on Leadenhall Street. Lloyds will have abandoned the premises by then and moved to Amsterdam. Parliament will have to vacate the Palace of Westminster for good. We already have a new site for it: where HS2 will divide, just east of Birmingham.[5]

All empires crumble and an afterlife as a tourist attraction is better than what befell the Ottomans in the 1920s (Figure 5.15).[6] The worst casualties may be the youngest members of the British royal family, born into a form of slavery from which they can never escape. But perhaps, in many decades to come, when we have finally learnt to do something useful, their children or grandchildren will not face a future of forever having to smile and wave – simply because of an accident of birth or marriage, and because they are the best that we have to sell to the world.

---

[5] Christian Wolmar, 'What's the point of HS2?', *London Review of Books*, 36, 8, 17 April 2014, https://www.lrb.co.uk/the-paper/v36/n08/christian-wolmar/what-s-the-point-of-hs2

[6] Perry Anderson, 'Kemalism', *London Review of Books*, Vol. 30 No. 17, 11 September 2008, https://www.lrb.co.uk/the-paper/v30/n17/perry-anderson/kemalism

Figure 5.15: Dolmabahçe Palace in Istanbul: the 'nerve centre of the Ottoman Empire'

Note: Built between 1843 and 1856 as an alternative to Topkapi Palace, it became the largest palace in Turkey, area 45,000 m^2 (11.1 acres), 285 rooms, 46 halls, 6 hammams. Some 1.5 million people visit it each year: https://www.dolmabahcepalace-tickets.com/visit-dolmabahce-palace/

Source: Quote from: https://www.egypttoursplus.com/dolmabace-palace-in-istanbul/. Image from: https://commons.wikimedia.org/wiki/File:Istanbul_Bosphorus_Dolmabah%C3%A7e_Palace_IMG_7889_1920.jpg

SECTION 6

Hope, the elite and change

Yesterday, tomorrow – and hope

The UK's long-running crisis will not solve itself. The minor remedial actions taken by a wide variety of British governments over the past five decades have served only to briefly mitigate the worst of the most visible effects of rapidly rising – and then peak – inequality. In the 1980s there was a bitter debate about how poverty should be measured in the UK. The progressives won, but now almost no one notices when the results of the Department for Work and Pensions' annual Households Below Average Income (HBAI) analysis, based on an annual detailed survey, are released each March. This analysis has been released in the same form since the mid-1990s. Here, I summarise what could be seen within the March 2023 release, before moving on to what was revealed a year later, in March 2024. During these years there was no in-depth reporting by the British press of what the new statistics were revealing each year. Perhaps because everyone knew the situation was bad.

The 23 March 2023 data release for the HBAI survey – numbers generally referred to as the UK's 'poverty statistics' – revealed that the household incomes of individuals in the bottom quarter of the income distribution experienced *real-terms reductions* even before the cost-of-living crisis set in, up to the endpoint of the latest data collection, which was March 2022. Since then, all other households will have become poorer, too, with the poorest sinking into destitution as food prices rose more quickly than benefits.

There has been no change in overall inequality since 2011. If you exclude those in the top 1 per cent (who are never included in a representative way in the annual surveys that the progressives of the 1980s won), then peak inequality came in 2018. We reached a peak because inequality kept inching up, to achieve the most extreme excess to date in 2018 and to help demonstrate that trickle-down never actually redistributes. It took a devastating, world-economy-changing global pandemic to force the extremely rich in Britain to (perhaps temporarily) slow down the rise in what had been an ever-larger grab for themselves. They would say they were only trying to match place with the chief executive officers of the largest funds, the hedge fund managers, and a few celebrities and sport stars rising further and further away from them.

Within the past decade, the top 1 per cent were the only social group to become better off, and then only for a time – at least through to 2018.[1] Ignoring them, income inequality (measured by the Gini Coefficient) has remained unchanged since FYE (Final Year Ending) 2021, both before and after housing costs are considered. The level has remained broadly stable since FYE 2011,[2] and in fact, once you look back far enough, since at least 2002. The slight apparent drop in the pandemic years is possibly due to who is not now included in the sample. It became harder to measure poverty during the pandemic, because surveys were no longer done door-to-door, and growing numbers of potential respondents could not be contacted by phone. It is particularly because of this that the update released in March 2024 matters so much too. The next official update will be in March 2025.

Figure 6.1, taken from the 23 March 2023 HBAI report, shows that if we ignore the top 1 per cent, then *nothing changed of any significance between 2002 and 2022.* It does matter that it does not reveal how the take of the 1 per cent, and especially of the super-rich, continued to climb until 2018, with the super-rich not taking a hit until 2020. The 1 per cent and the super-rich are not included in the national statistics on everyone else; they are treated by UK statisticians as if they are a separate species. The 1 per cent are seen as not like the 'little people' who might aspire, one fine day, for better pay, or for decent pensions, or even the privilege of being able to take out a mortgage.

---

1 See the Introduction to this book for what is most likely happening now, although the present is always unsure.

2 https://www.gov.uk/government/statistics/households-below-average-income-for-financial-years-ending-1995-to-2022/households-below-average-income-an-analysis-of-the-uk-income-distribution-fye-1995-to-fye-2022

Figure 6.1: Income inequality in the UK 2002–22, before and after housing costs

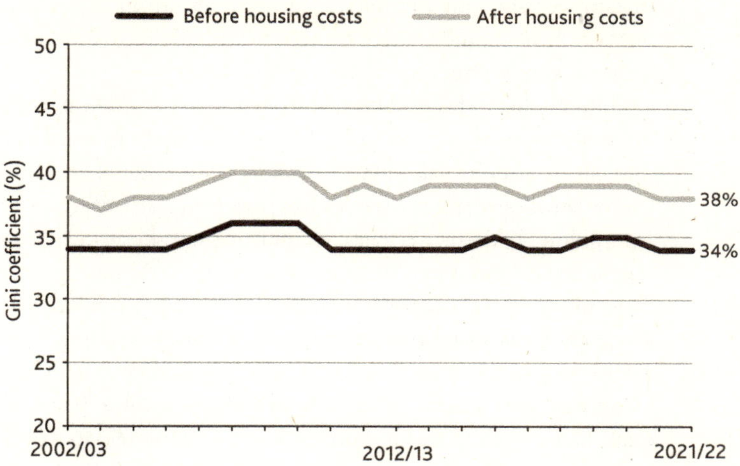

Source: DWP (2023) Household Below Average Incomes statistics, as released on 23 March 2023

When the income inequality lines are flat, injustice grows each year. The better-off can save, the worse-off fall further into debt. The rich, as they grow older, order their groceries online; and increasingly, their children eat food cooked by others, and delivered by courier.

Below, in the following long enumerated list, I have set out some of the numbers showing what changed between when the pandemic began and when we were first able to collect survey data again. Numbers such as those gathered in the HBAI survey may well not be enough, but they can help when it is suggested that the problems of inequality and poverty are not serious enough to require more than a little tinkering. Here are 21 facts about what has happened recently.

What changed between 2019–20 and 2021–22, and beyond?

1. By March 2022 there were 14.4 million children in the UK, some 500,000 (3.6 per cent) more than in 2019–20, as during those two years fewer were turning 18 than were born, and also because of net migration. Deaths of children also fell during the

pandemic. One reason was that there were fewer car crashes. Deaths on the roads have increased again since March 2022.[3] In Britain we value our children far lower in monetary terms than they do in more progressive more equal countries which have safer roads and cities for walking and cycling.

2. Children living in lone-parent families rose to 3.4 million, from 3.1 million just two years earlier. More families than usual had split up. An additional 300,000 children were living in lone-parent families where the parent had no work; a rise from 1.1 to 1.4 million children, a 27 per cent increase in just two years. No one seized on this when the statistics were first released because these numbers were, as always, hidden in the spreadsheets, and it is at the peak of injustice that apathy is usually greatest.
3. There was an increase of 200,000 in the number of children living with two parents where one of them was not in work. In total, half a million more children had at least one parent not in work in 2021–22, as compared to 2019–20. This deepened poverty further.
4. There was a large and rapid change in the average number of siblings. According to the estimates released in March 2023, there were 400,000 fewer children living with no brothers or sisters, and 800,000 with two or more siblings (three or more children in the household). This was a big change – it may have partly been due to increased error in the sample due to the pandemic; and to fewer first-time mothers filling in the survey. But in March 2024, when the very latest HBAI figures were released, we learnt that a huge change had *actually* occurred during and after the pandemic within British society. Families were becoming more overcrowded, as rising food prices left less in the budget for soaring rents. Because of this they could often less afford not to be so crowded together, and fewer new households were being formed.
5. Some 500,000 *fewer* children in 2022 lived in a household where *no one was disabled* than had done in early 2020. During the same time, the number of children living in a family where

[3] For one example of just one city, see: Danny Dorling (2023) 'The souls of the people of Oxford', Oxford Magazine, Noughth Week, Michaelmas Term, 10 October, https://www.dannydorling.org/?page_id=9883

someone received disability benefits had increased in just two years from 0.9 million to 1.5 million. This was because disability had increased, partly due to long COVID, but there were many other reasons too, not least new households forming more slowly. This 600,000 increase is a huge and very rapid change, which by March 2024 was confirmed not to be a one-off statistical artefact.

6. More children were described as being of mixed ethnicity than two years previously (300,000 instead of 200,000). This might reflect changes in social attitudes as much as other factors (people being happier to say 'mixed'). No other obvious shifts had occurred by ethnicity in the population as surveyed by the Department for Work and Pensions. There may have been increased in-migration of mixed ethnicity families; or we were continuing, on average, to become less racist.[4]
7. An extra 300,000 children were living in social housing by 2021–22, and some 200,000 more in a home with a mortgage. So, most of the increase in numbers was in children in social housing. The number of children in private renting was unchanged, but as the total number of children was rising this suggests a fall in the proportion of those living in privately rented homes during the pandemic. Little extra social housing was built in these years, so it is extremely likely that there is now more overcrowding of children within UK homes, especially in social housing, as compared to a year earlier.
8. The median child in the UK in 2019–20 (the child compared to whom half of all other children were in families with less money to live on and half had more) lived in a family with £390 a week left after housing costs to spend on everything they needed for the entire family. That has now risen to £400 a week although, because of inflation the real-terms value has fallen. However, the best-off 10 per cent of children now live in families with *at least* £850 to spend a week after housing costs. Two years ago, that was around £870 a week, so there may have been a small contraction in incomes at the top. However, as yet, we have not seen this happen among the top 1 per cent (as we know from other tax-based data sources).

[4] See Chapter 4.2 in this volume.

9. The number of children *without* access to outdoor space or other facilities to play safely outdoors fell sharply from 6 per cent to 4 per cent, so by a third in these two years. Perhaps the pandemic led to parents discovering spaces and facilities they did not know of before, and/or other spaces had been opened up or made accessible by local authorities better controlling local car traffic? Children began to find places to play again. There is always some good news in these statistics. In the future we hope the majority will be good – we will then know we have passed a peak.
10. The number of families with enough bedrooms for every child aged 10 years or over and of a different sex remained the same, at 80 per cent, meaning a fifth of UK children did not have a suitable bedroom to sleep in. Many more children will not have had a bedroom of their own, but would have been sharing their bedroom with parents, uncles and aunts, or with siblings of the same sex or mixed, but all aged under 10 years old (which is deemed suitable). The situation did worsen slightly for the majority of children in poorer families, with overcrowding in bedrooms increasing between FYE 2019–20 and FYE 2021–22.
11. The number of children living in families able to afford celebrations on special occasions, such as birthdays, remained the same at 97 per cent. However, the proportion of children living in the poorest families whose parents said they did not need to celebrate such events tripled from 1 per cent to 3 per cent (that is still very low). A celebration that can be had for almost no cost is still a celebration, so this does not mean that all other poorer children received birthday presents, just that their birthdays were celebrated. Some may have only got a card, some nothing – other than 'a celebration'.
12. The number of children whose parents could afford to buy them leisure equipment such as a bicycle fell from 90 per cent of children to 88 per cent. However, 9 per cent of the parents of the poorest two-sevenths of children now said they did not need such things (up from 5 per cent in 2019–20), as did 7 per cent of the parents of the next-poorest two sevenths (up from 5 per cent). This would suggest that people were beginning to adapt to long-term poverty and had reduced their expectations of what it was normal to be able to have.

13. The number of children who had at least one week's holiday away from home with family fell from 66 per cent to 62 per cent. The number of parents saying their children would like such a holiday but could not afford one rose from 30 per cent to 31 per cent. However, there was a big jump – from 4 per cent to 7 per cent in just two years – in parents saying their children didn't need holidays, or that they didn't see having a single holiday a year as a realistic aspiration. That jump was largest for the poorest children, 11 per cent of whose parents said in 2021–22 that a single week-long annual holiday was no longer something that was needed, as compared to the 5 per cent who had said so two years earlier.
14. Being able to afford for children to pursue a hobby or leisure activity fell from 79 per cent of all UK children to 75 per cent. The number of parents saying such things were not needed rose from 16 per cent to 18 per cent. Here the falls were not highest for those who already were able to do the least. Perhaps the parents of the best-off children discovered that they did not need to be engaged in quite so many 'activities' each week as they had been doing before the pandemic?
15. Parents able to afford for their children to have friends round for tea or a snack once a fortnight fell from 69 per cent to 62 per cent. A third (exactly 33 per cent) of children now had parents saying such a thing was an extravagance, as compared to just 27 per cent two years earlier. The fall in the possibility of inviting friends round and offering them a snack was greatest for the poorest children, unsurprisingly. There is statistical error associated with all these estimates, but the overall direction of injustice up to March 2022 was clear.
16. There was a large drop in the proportion of children whose parents said they could pay for them to go on a school trip at least once a term, from 90 per cent in 2019–20 to 80 per cent in 2021–22. Those who responded their children 'don't need such a thing' jumped from 19 per cent to 24 per cent. Again, the change was greatest for the poorest children, with a drop to only 69 per cent having parents able to afford it two years into the pandemic, as compared to 82 per cent in 2019–20. It is likely that many schools now offer far fewer trips than they did before the pandemic. The cost of hiring a coach has increased, and school budgets have been cut too.

17. Parents able to take their children to a playgroup at least once a week fell from 73 per cent to 68 per cent; again, the greatest rise was in parents saying it was no longer necessary, up from 24 per cent to 28 per cent. And again, the change was greatest for the parents of the majority of the poorest (four out of every seven children) who had seen their lives change the most, down from 65 per cent to 69 per cent (for those four separate sevenths) being able to do this in the year before the pandemic to just 59 per cent to 60 per cent two years after the pandemic had begun.
18. For the proportion of children whose parents were able to afford for them to attend organised activities once a week, the drop was from 73 per cent in 2019–20 to 68 per cent in the spring of 2022. Those no longer wishing their children to do so (whether they could afford to or not) had jumped from 19 per cent to 24 per cent. And again, the largest drops were for the four out of every seven children whose parents had the least, with fewer attending scouts, guides, dance classes, football or any other organised activity. In detail, this fell from those things being a possibility and affordable for 61 per cent for the poorest two out of seven, and 70 per cent for the next two out of seven, to 56 per cent and 60 per cent, respectively. It might also have been the case that less was now being offered, but the question in the HBAI survey was not about availability but whether you could afford it if it was available.
19. Living in a family able to afford to eat fresh fruit and/or vegetables every day actually rose from 94 per cent to 95 per cent of children in the statistics release in March 2023, and fewer parents said they did not wish their children to eat such things (a drop from 4 per cent to 3 per cent). However, that slight 1 per cent rise was for children living in the median family by income: that is, the one where four out of seven families are poorer than theirs and just two are better off. It is not easy to measure small changes, but you can take all these numbers in the round as being representative. Some will slightly overestimate falls and rises, others underestimate them as this is all based on a sample survey. These statistics then did worsen again the year after.
20. The median household by income is now actually a better-than-average household for families with children. We don't know about actual food consumption; it is very likely that more parents

say they can afford fresh fruit and vegetables than actually can, as people don't want to appear to be bad parents. Items such as these are now frequently entirely absent from supermarket shelves in poorer areas, or are prohibitively expensive if they are stocked. Meanwhile, upmarket supermarkets will deliver anywhere, at a cost.

21. On the final measure in the HBAI government survey, 99 per cent of parents reported at the start of this period that their children had a warm winter coat. It has since fallen slightly, to 98 per cent for the poorest out of every seven children, and it is quite possible that if inflation remains high, in future this number will fall significantly. As always, it is up to each parent to define what they think a warm coat is, and they are not asked if the coat actually still fits the child – just if they have one.

*

Reducing countless complex lives to statistics such as these can seem bleak and uncaring. This is the problem with statistics. But the picture is made bleaker by the fact that none of the scant media coverage of the poverty and inequality figures released on 23 March 2023 appeared to be based on more than the briefest of looks at the data. Perhaps journalists thought readers were sick of details such as these, or perhaps they struggled to open and understand the complex, and extremely hard to find, spreadsheets on the government website.

This is what else we learnt in the spring of 2023, with just a few hints of what came next included. There follow nine more facts for you, each relating to the adults living with their children. Please note that the situation I describe below is what was occurring immediately before everything became even worse again. We often forget bad news today in the UK because worse news follows it a year later.

In March 2024 we learnt from the official report not only that the average family had become absolutely poorer again in the year ending March 2023, but income inequalities between families were also rising. This resulted in a huge and rapid increase in poverty, possibly the most rapid ever recorded in the UK. For example, we were told that: 'Eighty-three percent of children in the UK population lived in a food-secure household in FYE 2023, compared to 88% last year.'[5] In other words, 17 per cent were going hungry several times a month as compared to 12 per cent the year before. If that rise – of five percentage points in a single year – were to continue even for just another few years, it would mean that the UK would become a failed state, many of its children facing rates of hunger not seen in Europe since the Second World War. So, please be aware as you continue to confront the impact of the latest statistics as described in what follows, that the situation will have since deteriorated even further and at an even faster rate.

1. The same proportion of parents of children in the UK said that they do not have enough money to decorate their homes (5 per cent) as did in 2019–20, but practically none of the best-off parents now said they could not afford it (it had been 1 per cent before the pandemic hit). The better-off had saved a little money over this period, but perhaps had also learnt a little about necessity.
2. On affording a holiday away from home one week a year (not spent with relatives), this had dropped from 59 per cent to 56 per cent of parents who said they could afford it. This is worse than for children, as increasingly only one parent accompanies children on holiday, so the rise in parents having no holiday is faster than the rise in children having none. It is a little like mothers going without food before their children have to go without. One parent carries on working.
3. Home contents insurance uptake has hardly altered. However, the proportion of parents of the poorest two children out of seven who said it was something they no longer considered needing rose from 25 per cent to 27 per cent. In contrast, only 4 per cent of the best-off children's parents said this (down from 6 per cent). Many UK families had already given up insuring

[5] DWP (2024) *National statistics: Households Below Average Income: an analysis of the UK income distribution: FYE 1995 to FYE 2023*, 21 March, https://www.gov.uk/government/statistics/households-below-average-income-for-financial-years-ending-1995-to-2023/households-below-average-income-an-analysis-of-the-uk-income-distribution-fye-1995-to-fye-2023#children-in-low-income-households

their possessions before 2019. Even though the rationale for insuring was rising, because it would cost more in future, due to inflation, to replace items lost in a fire or flood, or due to theft, many people, and especially parents, simply could not afford to insure against these risks any more.

4. On being able to make savings of £10 a month or more, the proportion did increase from 64 per cent to 66 per cent of parents in the UK being able to do this by 2021–22. However, it fell as a possibility for the parents of the majority of UK children, and rose only for the best-off minority. We know from many other sources that the better-off were able to save more during the pandemic, but it is only from these statistics that we can confirm the obvious: that those families that didn't ever eat out, travel or go to the cinema anyway due to the expense saved nothing as a result of the lockdown restrictions.
5. On being able to replace worn-out furniture, there was little overall change in the affected number of adults, rather than children. However, for the parents of the poorest two-sevenths of all children, the situation had improved a little; and interestingly, even (perhaps) encouragingly, increasing numbers of better-off parents said that they didn't need to replace their furniture. Again, maybe some were beginning to learn to make do and mend, and for the very best-off, not to want their furniture to always look new, as so desperately (and expensively) as they had wanted before the pandemic. Was more being given to charity warehouses rather than being thrown away, as people began to think a little more of others? It is very hard to know when you are at a peak and sentiment is changing. We had just lived through the worst years of a pandemic: was this helping to shift people's views for the better? Or were they just not worrying about keeping up appearances when no one was allowed round for dinner parties?
6. When it came to the usually more urgent need to replace broken electrical goods such as a phone or computer, there was a rise among the parents of the poorest children who said they no longer needed to do this, from 12 per cent to 18 per cent in two years. Either their electrical goods were not breaking as often, or they had fewer of them and had learnt to do without. But it is increasingly hard to survive without a phone or computer

in a world in which the pandemic made these items even more essential than they had been in 2019. At least now we better understand that such things are necessities today, not luxuries.

7. On money to spend on themselves each week, there was a slight fall in those parents who said they could, from 71 per cent to 70 per cent, and more of the UK's poorer parents said they didn't need to spend anything on themselves (up from 3 per cent to 5 per cent in two years). Imagine saying that you need nothing for yourself – no drink in a pub, no new clothes, no cigarettes – nothing, ever. It is a way to get by. The rich sometimes talk about de-growth as a desirable environmental outcome. The poor in the UK have been practising it recently. What all these numbers show is that a few have far too much and the many have not enough.
8. On being able to keep the house warm, this *had* risen by one percentage point, to 93 per cent of children's families. However, that was before fuel prices rose sharply. Before that rise, only 9 per cent of the parents of the poorest two out of seven children said they could *not* afford to keep their house warm in 2021–22, as compared to 13 per cent in 2019–20. That 9 per cent figure jumped to 23 per cent by 2022–23 when the very latest figures were released. This was almost certainly the fastest rise ever recorded in poorer children having to live through a winter in the UK without proper heating.[6]
9. Finally, on keeping up to date with bills – this had also hardly changed over these two years from just before the pandemic began to after we had experienced it for one year. The statistics actually became slightly better for the poorest parents, who were using more and more of what money they still had, and in some cases also relying on the temporary uplift in Universal Credit, to buy food and pay bills. They may well have done this instead of spending money on the other small things that add joy to life

[6] Table 4.8db_AHC cell C31 in the datafile 'Children-hbai-detailed-breakdown-2022-23-tables', which can be found within the UK government's incredibly complex website that almost no one can navigate to find any of these numbers. Note that you have to download the 4.1MB zip file from here: https://www.gov.uk/government/statistics/households-below-average-income-for-financial-years-ending-1995-to-2023

– a second-hand bike at Christmas, going to swimming classes, or having one short, inexpensive holiday a year. You begin to learn to live without.

★

We now know so much, but care so little.

A century ago, when inequality last peaked, we were only just beginning to have significant information about the lives of people in Britain. Social surveys revealed rural poverty, poverty among mothers, how many people were living on a pound a week, and what that meant. There were poor law commissions and increasingly frequent and heated debates in Parliament. There was a new generation of researchers and politicians who in many cases had both studied under and worked for the Victorian anti-poverty pioneers. When we look back, we often see that their reports are full of tables and numbers. This was not just because that was the style of the age, but because to them, the numbers were more real. They saw the people begging and wasting away on the streets, and smelt the sewage, but numbers were a more compelling and authoritative way to capture what they saw. We are smelling the sewage and seeing the wasting away again, but we are still ignoring the numbers – and thus there were almost no news reports about what the March 2023 statistics revealed.

By spring 2022 (as reported in spring 2023), some 4.2 million children lived in households with incomes below 60 per cent of the UK median after housing costs. That is not an easy sentence to understand, or an easy statistic to absorb. In short it means that a huge number of families with children were living below what had become the accepted poverty line. They were scraping a living, and these households were the homes of exactly that many millions of children. However, the story of just one child growing up in poverty, being hungry and cold and having their health and learning harmed as a response, is a tragedy. Turn that number into millions and you can no longer easily imagine this multitude. A million is one thousand children, sitting in a line, with another thousand lined up parallel to each one. You can try to imagine a field as far as you can see of these children. Give each a square metre to sit in and your field is a kilometre square in area. There are four whole fields and another fifth of a field of children in poverty in the UK now. But does this mean that those children not in the 4.2 million were doing well? That there are fields of other much less impoverished children? What about the next million and the next?

Because the shape of the income distribution is always humped to the left and stretches out far and increasingly thinly to the right, that 4.2 million figure is highly deceptive. It does not neatly cut off a distinct group of one set of babies, toddlers, rising fives, boisterous primary school children and more sullen teenagers from their non-poor equivalents. As Figure 6.2 shows, using data from just a couple of years earlier, the median household received about £30,000 a year. Sixty per cent of that is £18,000 a year; the figure shows that roughly two-tenths of all individuals in the UK lived in such households in 2020, but it doesn't show that these households contained far more than two-tenths of all children. It does show that just as many households had only a few thousand pounds a year more to live on than this. A thousand pounds a year is £20 a week. Another 4.2 million children were living in households with at least £20, or as much as £40–£160 a week – or, to put it another way, up to as much as roughly £20 a day more than the poorest 4.2 million. Thus, we could say, that 8.4 million children lived in poor households, or very similar households with as much as £20 a day more than the best-off of the 4.2 million. You would be hard placed to tell one group from the other in practice. If you are typical of readers likely to read this book, all these children would look poor.

The incomes of the vast bulk of families just above the UK poverty line are always very close to those of the majority of those children's families who are just below the line. It is frustrating to see phrases like 'a third of children living in poverty' being given so much emphasis in media coverage of the HBAI report, given how many more children there were living just a few pounds over any notional poverty line.

The 2022 and 2023 releases by ONS did not include a graph such as that shown in Figure 6.2, but the release of 2021 did and in the report that accompanied that graph, ONS explain: 'Growth in income of the poorest fifth of people did not keep pace with inflation, which led to the median income of the

Figure 6.2: Distribution of UK household disposable income, financial year ending 2020

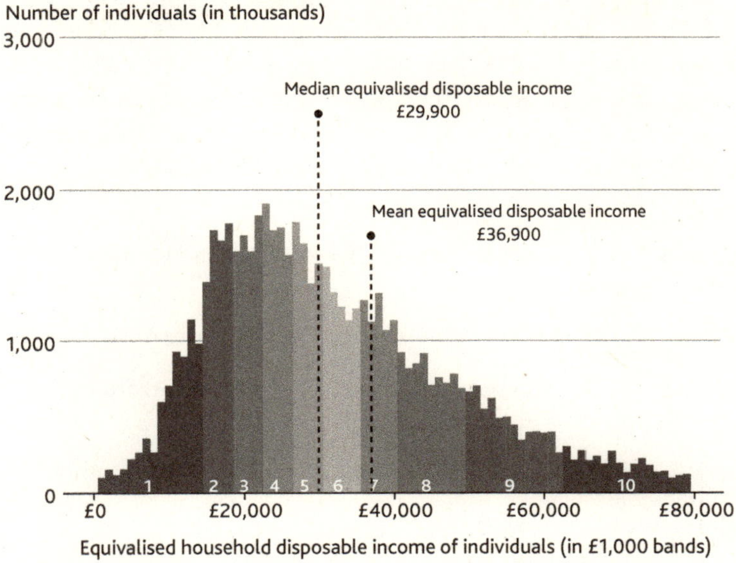

Source: Jeena O'Neill (2021) Average household income, UK: financial year 2020: Final estimates of average household income in the UK, with analysis of how these measures have changed over time, accounting for inflation and household composition, ONS, 21 January, https://www.ons.gov.uk/peoplepopulationandcommunity/personalandhouseholdfinances/incomeandwealth/bulletins/householddisposableincomeandinequality/financialyear2020

poorest fifth falling by an average of 1.5% per year between FYE 2017 and FYE 2020.'[7] Many more than a fifth of all children live in that poorest fifth of households. The best-off fifth, in contrast, experienced incomes rising above inflation in those years. By 2020–21, 800,000 children lived in families that had used a foodbank in the preceding 12 months (5.5 per cent), and 200,000

[7] Source: Jeena O'Neill (2021) 'Average household income, UK: financial year 2020: Final estimates of average household income in the UK, with analysis of how these measures have changed over time, accounting for inflation and household composition', *ONS*, 21 January, https://www.ons.gov.uk/peoplepopulationandcommunity/personalandhouseholdfinances/incomeandwealth/bulletins/householddisposableincomeandinequality/financialyear2020

in the preceding 30 days. And some 2.9 million children lived in families that frequently did not have enough food, or, as the DWP preferred to put it in their March 2023 report, they were 'individuals living in food insecure households'. However, not everywhere in the UK had children been facing this worsening trend over so many decades since the series began in 1994. Figure 6.3 shows that in Scotland child poverty had fallen in the first years of the millennium and was broadly stable now.

Figure 6.3: Child poverty in Scotland 1994–2022, before and after housing costs

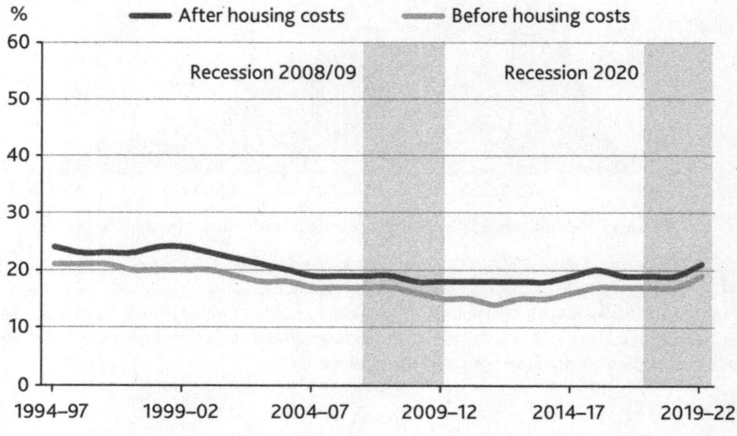

Source: Scottish Government (2023) *Poverty levels broadly stable*, Official Government Report, 23 March, https://www.gov.scot/news/poverty-levels-broadly-stable/

How Scotland is starting to address child poverty

On 23 March 2023, Scotland's government issued a statement on the latest UK-wide HBAI data release, saying:

> The latest poverty statistics, covering the period to March 2022, show little recent change in poverty levels for children, working-age adults and pensioners. Two out of the four child poverty measures in the Child Poverty (Scotland) Act (relative and absolute poverty) are broadly stable. Persistent poverty is gradually

> increasing, and the material deprivation measure continues to be affected by the pandemic.[8]

In contrast the Westminster government in London chose not to spin it in this way. Scottish social security officials were being more truthful. They could afford to be, because in Scotland so much more was being done about the scourge.

Scotland provides a lot more data than England,[9] and child poverty has not risen as much there as in England. In fact, it has been largely stable since 2010, and was falling before then (Figure 6.3). The figures we now see in Scotland are statistics that the English can only look at with envy. No region in England – not even the most prosperous southeast – has rates of child poverty as low as those now seen in Scotland, and in Scotland they are falling faster. The situation in Scotland is still bad (Figure 6.4), but it is not as bad as anywhere in England.

The reason the poverty figures for Scotland are better than those in England is partly because Scotland does not penalise the third, fourth and further children of households in receipt of any kind of benefits. Importantly, 'Some 24% of Scottish children live in poverty, which is lower than 29% UK-wide, new figures show',[10] but most important of all is what is explained next:

> the figures cover the period from April 2019 to March 2022, meaning they pre-date the full roll-out of the Scottish Child Payment, which was increased to £20 a week from April 2022 and £25 weekly from November that same year. … The Child Poverty Action Group said that the Scottish Child Payment should now be pushing young people's poverty rates down, and said that with further investment the target of reducing child poverty to less than 18% by 2024 'is still within reach'. … The CPAG further pointed to UK Government figures, also published

[8] https://www.gov.scot/news/poverty-levels-broadly-stable/

[9] https://www.gov.scot/collections/poverty-and-income-inequality-statistics/

[10] https://www.thenational.scot/news/23406974.child-poverty-rates-scotland-lower-uk-wide-data-shows/

Figure 6.4: Child poverty in Scotland, by type of household and family, 2019–22

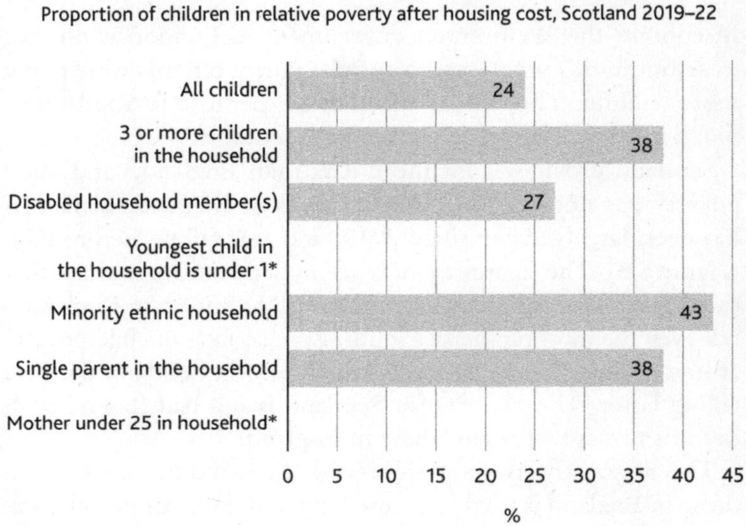

Note: * Although the labels for these two categories appeared in the source graphic, data were missing.

Source: Scottish Government (2023) *Poverty and income inequality statistics*, Official Government Report, Figure 9, accessed 23 March, https://www.gov.scot/collections/poverty-and-income-inequality-statistics/

on Thursday, which show that child poverty rates UK-wide (29%) are higher than in Scotland alone (24%). The UK Government figures also show that a further 350,000 children were put into poverty in 2021/2022, which the CPAG said was 'largely' due to the Tories' £20 cut to Universal Credit. John Dickie, CPAG director in Scotland, said: 'In a rich country these scandalous levels of child poverty are utterly unacceptable and a stark reminder how vital the Scottish Government's focus on child poverty is. The next first minister must not just sustain but increase the crucial investment being made in the Scottish Child Payment.'

This news report continued:

> The CPAG has also published research to coincide with the poverty figures, which estimates child poverty costs the UK £39.5 billion a year in lost tax and earnings, unemployment benefit, and additional public services spending. Dickie said: 'It's children that pay the highest possible price for poverty – they pay with their health, their well-being and their life chances. Our research shows the country also pays a heavy financial price. The human cost for the children in today's figures is incalculable. The economic fallout for all of us is vast. But if the political will is there, child poverty can be fixed.'

The news report went on to cover reaction to the figures from other charities:

> Jamie Livingstone, the head of Oxfam Scotland, said: 'This disturbing data shows that the pandemic and cost of living crisis have dealt a devastating double blow to those on the lowest incomes. The UK Government must act, but the next first minister must do so too. They should acknowledge that tackling poverty requires greater action to narrow the yawning gap between rich and poor and use all of the powers at their disposal to do more than just tweak tax: instead, they should introduce bold, progressive taxation, including targeting wealth. Only then will they end the deep injustice of poverty for good and build a fairer future for all of us.'
>
> … Action for Children accused UK ministers of knowing what works, given the action taken during the pandemic, but 'choosing not to do it', and said help has been 'snatched away' from families. The organisation's director of policy and campaigns, Imran Hussain, said: 'It's astonishing that, despite the pandemic, the cost-of-living crisis and the prospect

> of rising child poverty for years to come, the [UK] Government is not targeting help for children in low-income families. There is so much more this Government can do in these tough times to stop those with the least from suffering the most.'
>
> Save the Children UK described the latest figures as 'grim' and said that, coming a day after other figures revealed a surprise jump in inflation to 10.4 per cent the previous month, they 'prove families are still very much in the depths of a crisis'. Becca Lyon, head of child poverty at the charity, said: 'Families need a proper benefits system that protects them from hardship, and means children can grow up without having to know what the inside of a food bank looks like.'

The Scottish Child Payment would mean that a family with three children aged 16 or under in receipt of benefits will be £4,000 a year better off.

The Scottish Child Payment was announced by the Scottish Government in mid-2019. The payment was first introduced for eligible families with children aged under six. Applications opened in November 2020 and the first payments were made in February 2021, too early to affect the figures given earlier. The initial payment was £10 per week, per child. This was doubled to £20 in April 2021, and then, on 14 November 2022, the Scottish Child Payment was rolled out to families with children under 16 years old and the payment increased for a third time. to £25 per week, per child. The payment is given to families on low incomes and in receipt of certain means-tested benefits such as income-based Jobseeker's Allowance or Employment and Support Allowance (disability), Universal Credit, and certain legacy benefits. UK-wide, this is roughly two out of every seven children, with similar proportions likely in Scotland.

The effect, for children in Scotland, and *only for them*, is to have reduced inequality to one of the lowest levels in Europe – moving the Gini coefficient for children from 0.33 to 0.25, by my calculations, and meaning that no child in Scotland need go cold or hungry by the winter of 2023–24. It has helped begin to turn a tide which has been running only one way for over 50 years.

The change began in Scotland in late 2022; not everything in the UK is going in the wrong direction.

So how can people whose talent is reading the footnotes in obscure government reports help bring about change? The UK's prime minister could help by using what he knows all too well about the rich (Chapter 6.1). Academics can help by becoming kinder and not continuing to try to defend the indefensible (Chapter 6.2). The ancient institutions of England can help by growing up at last and acknowledging that they have been a large part of the problem for a very long time (Chapter 6.3); if only a few more of the people in them, especially younger people, do, it could have a great multiplier effect. Economists can help by recognising their discipline's complicity in injustice (Chapter 6.4). Examples from other countries are especially useful (Chapter 6.5). And even if you think you have no special skill, or talent, or energy left; you can help by not being arrogant and trying to put others down because you feel so clever (Chapter 6.6).

There is no messiah coming to lead us to some sunlit place. There is no rapturous revolution around the corner, and that never has been on offer. But there is hope that we can end injustice, and it is growing. Stop saying you cannot see any way in which things will improve. Open your eyes. It has been happening within the UK in Scotland, it has been happening elsewhere in Europe for decades. It is just that, at the peak of injustice and in the fog of confusion, you cannot easily see the road ahead that goes back down. You think this mountain will never end. The route down is signposted 'hope'.

CHAPTER 6.1

What would it take to persuade Rishi Sunak to join the Patriotic Millionaires?[1]

The Patriotic Millionaires is a group that began in the United States and launched a chapter in the UK in the very early 2020s. Its stated mission is 'to leverage the voice of wealth to build a better Britain by changing the system to end extreme wealth and make those with it make their fair and proper contribution'.[2] In 2023 I was asked what it might take to persuade the Prime Minister to join the group and why it might be good if he did, given his skill set.

I suspect the Patriotic Millionaires would agree to Britain's Prime Minister joining, were he to ask. He is, after all, both a patriot, and a multi-millionaire (Figure 6.5). I believe that he could understand their arguments for a restructuring of our tax systems in such a way that they and their wealthy peers pay a greater share of their income in taxes, should he wish to. However, he would have to discard some of the beliefs he has picked up over the years, possibly from as early as his school days. That is difficult for anyone to do. Rishi Sunak has written three books that could help us understand where he is coming from: *A Portrait of Modern Britain* (2014), *A New Era for Retail Bonds* (2017) and *The Free Ports Opportunity: How Brexit Could Boost Trade, Manufacturing and the North* (2018). He would have to rethink a lot of what he wrote about, and believed at the time,

---

1 Originally published as answers to a series of questions on the Ask Me Anything blog, *Fair Comment*, The Fairness Foundation, 24 April 2023.

2 https://patrioticmillionaires.uk/

Figure 6.5: The sunlit uplands, a view near one of Rishi Sunak's many homes

Source: Photo taken by Jamie Davies, CC0, Unsplash, Hikes & Walks in the Yorkshire Dales, https://www.outdooractive.com/en/hikes/yorkshire-dales/hikes-walks-in-the-yorkshire-dales/210612045/

see colour version in plate section

to be persuaded to join a group of wealthy people working to end the injustice of high inequality.

The countries of the UK have changed greatly since Sunak wrote those three books. In 2023, a majority of children in larger families in Britain were going hungry every month.[3] Sunak may begin to realise that something has gone badly wrong, and that the promises that we would one day reach the sunlit uplands – the promises that his Conservative Party have given every year since 2010 – were false. He may be persuaded by the evidence and do the maths.

Ultimately, it is down to his moral compass. Does he aspire to be the kind of Conservative prime minister, like Benjamin Disraeli or Harold Macmillan, who is remembered for moving towards a one-nation conservatism, in outcome and not just in rhetoric? Or would he be satisfied with being like the majority of Conservative prime ministers, who today exist as mere footnotes, or if mentioned by name today, are greeted with derision? Sunak's one great skill, by virtue of his real work experience, is that he is far more qualified than any previous prime minister to understand what would be required to tax the wealth and income of the rich properly and how to prevent them using loopholes to evade such action. Why waste such a talent?

What role do you think land value taxation could play in helping to resolve the housing crisis, especially the problem of ever-increasing house prices?

Even in a society without land taxes, house prices never continue to increase for ever. The best long-term data series that demonstrates this is from the Netherlands (Figure 6.6). However, without land taxation (and other forms of wealth regulation), a society is doomed to keep repeating the spiralling booms and crashes of the past. The Dutch in previous centuries demonstrated what a free market achieves and how inefficient it is where housing is concerned. Countries such as Austria that

---

[3] Mike Brewer, Emily Fry and Lalitha Try (2023) *The Living Standards Outlook 2023*, The Resolution Foundation, January, https://www.resolutionfoundation.org/app/uploads/2023/01/Living-Standards-Outlook-2023.pdf

Figure 6.6: The Herengracht Index (the Dutch house-price index of Amsterdam), 1620s to 1970s

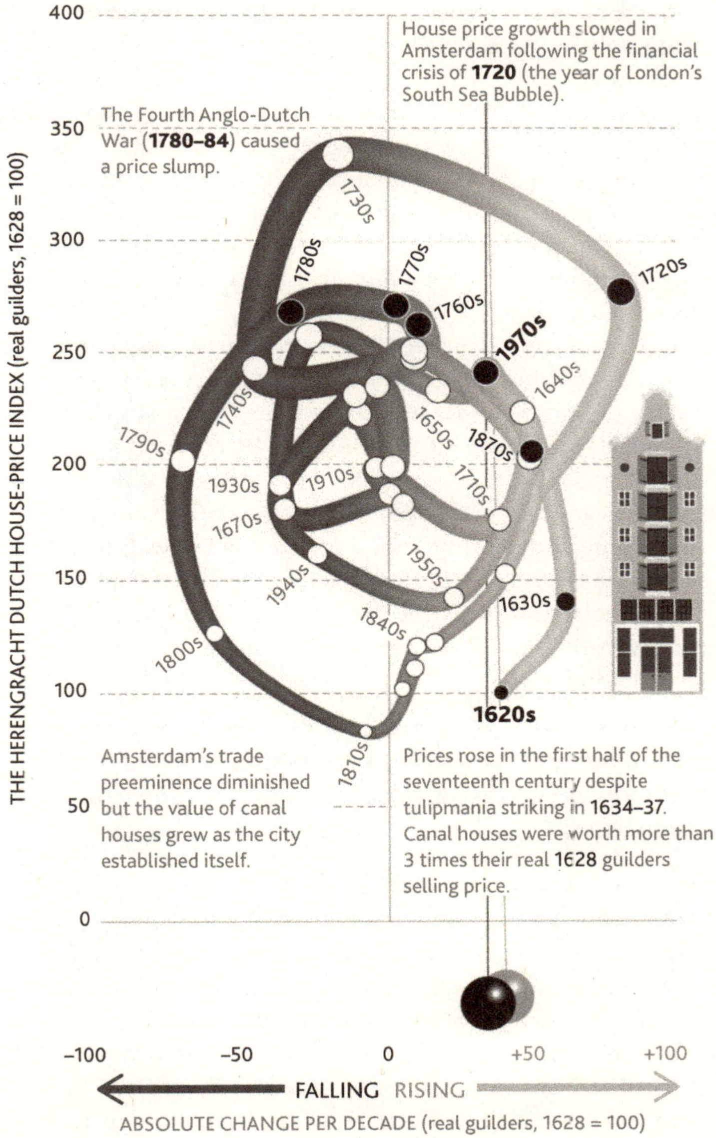

Source: Artwork by Kirsty McClure, original: https://www.dannydorling.org/books/SLOWDOWN/

better regulate their housing have better-housed populations. The United States, one of the most deregulated, has some of the worst housing outcomes in the rich world. Seventy years ago, the UK was the envy of the world because of what its housing policies were achieving; because of how well regulated its housing was.

Land taxation can be a part of that solution. One great advantage of land is that you cannot hide it. Again, Rishi Sunak's superpower, his special skills, could be harnessed to address this problem. He has greater experience than any other member of Parliament concerning the ownership of multiple valuable homes and other assets, including owning a very large property in North Yorkshire.

It may sound ridiculous to suggest that Sunak might apply his skills in this area; but perhaps one reason why Conservative Party members did not vote for him to be their leader was that some of them realised that he knows, should it be required, how what may have to be done can be done. He may not like the idea, but people can learn and begin to question their instincts. It was mostly Conservative prime ministers that held power during the period from 1920 to 1970, the period when Britain last became so very much more equal. They may not have liked it, but in various ways they aided this outcome, because there was no other acceptable option.

Would a land value tax not lead to increased food prices if most farmers own their land? Or should it only apply to residential land?

A land value tax should apply to all land. Once you begin to introduce loopholes, people will start to claim that the gardens of their Mayfair mansions are farms or sites of 're-wilding'. The value of agricultural land without development permission tends to be very low in comparison to other land, so the tax would be very low too. The price of our food has little to do with British farmers. It did not rise by a fifth in the past 12 months because we had bad harvests in Britain. However, elsewhere in Europe, other countries successfully control the prices people have to pay for food there. The Greeks even do this for the food sold on their beaches and in other public places.[4] If people ever tell you that something is not possible, first look to see what is happening elsewhere in Europe and then ask: 'If it is possible there, why is it not possible here?'

How can the law be changed so that the wealthy are subject to it in exactly the same way as people with less wealth?

That would best be done if someone who knew the wealthy well was involved in drafting the law. Similar things have been achieved in many impressive ways in the past. For instance, when the National Health Service was created, doctors were initially offered the salaries that they had been reporting to the tax authorities. When they complained that they could not live on so little, they were offered a bit more. However, the health minister, Nye Bevan, did not publicly shame them. Instead, he said that he had 'stuffed their mouths with gold', which may have made them feel more respected.

Wealth taxes can be enforced simply by changing the law to state that you do not own an item, land or shares *that you do not pay the proper tax on*. People are very keen to pay stamp duty on houses because otherwise they do not own their home. One of the most effective ways of changing the law, so that the wealthy pay their taxes, is to do what is done in some Nordic countries, where the tax that everyone pays is published annually and anyone may view the records. You can easily discover if your neighbour with three very large cars outside their property is declaring very little income. Wealth tax dodgers do tend to make annoying neighbours, and even the possibility of being investigated tends to encourage the wealthy to come clean.

Imagine that any of your friends, neighbours, work colleagues, ex-partners, annoyed siblings, or other rivals were tempted to point out to the authorities that you appear to be stealing from other people (evading tax). It may be impossible to imagine such openness ever coming to Britain; but have you ever stopped to

---

4 Consumers' Association 'The Quality of Life' (2023) *Fixed prices in canteens in Greece*, https://www.ekpizo.gr/siteBackup/en/our_work/consumer-rights/fixed-prices-canteens

wonder what the sunlit uplands actually are? Sunlight is the best disinfectant; ultimately, it is transparency that ensures that the wealthy are subject to laws, such as on taxation, as much as the rest of us.

There are many other ways in which the wealthy can abuse the law: malicious prosecutions for libel and slander are two examples. In the end, the wealthy are treated much more like other people when they are less wealthy. In Britain they became dramatically less wealthy one hundred years ago. In the decades that followed, most became unable to afford servants. Hardly anyone ever complained that they, or their children, could not become servants.

Would you ban private schools to achieve social justice?

No, because it is not necessary. Finland, one of the countries with the best state education systems in the world, still has a few private schools. It does not have many, because it makes very little sense for a parent to send their child to one. But it is a useful check on the state system to allow private schools to continue so that you can monitor the numbers going, and then know if you have a problem in the state sector if that number rises.

There are some British private schools whose geographical positions serve to prevent good networks of state schools being established: where, in the middle of all the state secondary schools in an area, there is a school that would be an ideal hub state school, but instead is fee-paying. Often that school was originally established as a public school, supposedly for the poor (which later became called private schools, although the poshest of them kept the name 'public'). So only in those circumstances of geographical necessity, which are very rare, would I suggest nationalisation (for example, in the case of the city of Oxford, which has a huge number of private schools within it, a single one, Magdalen College School, occupies a geographical site that it would be useful to share for the greater good, if the state schools of the city were to be better integrated and education divides were to be levelled).

London's Borough of Kensington and Chelsea may be the most affected by the phenomenon of an over-abundance of private schools. A majority of its children attend private schools, which makes it difficult to establish a geographically well-connected network of state schools – schools between which teachers and pupils can travel for subjects that not enough pupils in any one school are studying, for example.

Tax breaks and other concessions for private schools should be removed. They cannot be thought of as charities if the word 'charity' is to mean anything in future.

Furthermore, I would worry about boarding schools. When I was young, I was told about the problems in boarding schools. Now I am old, I am still told very similar stories. However, parents are increasingly choosing not to send their children to such schools. This is an issue of social justice even if it is about justice for the children of the extremely wealthy. If you are interested in fairness, you cannot just be concerned with the poor. The children of the very rich can suffer too, sometimes in ways that are less likely to happen to poorer children.

Is it fair for society to allow people to live in poverty? If not, should everyone be forced to work to the extent that they are able to?

No, it is neither fair, or necessary, and certainly not inevitable to allow people to live in poverty. But work is not the route out of poverty. Britain has far more people in work than almost any other nation in Europe as a proportion of its adult and child population. Britain also now has some of the worst levels of poverty in Europe. It was revealed in 2022 that the poorest fifth of families in Britain were poorer than that same group in some Eastern European countries.[5]

In early 2023, the head of economics at Bloomberg suggested that this might have worsened, with the poorest fifth of UK families now being poorer than the poorest in a *majority* of Eastern

[5] John Burn-Murdoch (2022) 'Britain and the US are poor societies with some very rich people', *The Financial Times*, 16 September, https://www.ft.com/content/ef265420-45e8-497b-b308-c951baa68945

European countries.[6] In no other Western European country are so many people now so very poor, and in no other do people work so hard, for such long hours, and for so many years of their lives, for such low pay, retiring so late in life – and dying so early.

Work does not set you free; but it can be rewarding if you have freedom at work and freedom to choose to work – or not to work. In the future, we will need far more people not to be in paid work for so many hours of their week. This is the future that John Maynard Keynes talked about in 1930 when discussing the economic possibilities for our grandchildren.[7] The opposite to what Keynes imagined occurred, but the result of working harder was not riches. In future if we are to consume and produce less, we need fewer people trying to get us to consume and produce more.

The city I live in, Oxford, produces more cars than it has ever done, but there is now the lowest number of people working in its car factories since shortly after car manufacturing began here. Although one electric Mini a minute rolls off the production line, it has largely been made by robots. In theory, that should free up leisure time. In practice, we have managed to become busier than ever.

In some ways Keynes' future is here, but what he did not predict was that it would take us more than three generations to learn how to embrace it. All of us, not just the idle rich, have to have the option to be lazy. Studies have found that, given that option, most people actually make far better use of their time than they would if forced to work. No employer that cannot attract people to work for them should be in operation.

---

6 Christiane Amanpour (2023) '"The poorest fifth of the population are now much poorer [in the UK] than most of the poorest countries in central and eastern Europe," says Stephanie Flanders', Christiane Amanpour, CNN Chief International Anchor, *Twitter*, 2 February, quoting @MyStephanomics: 'They would be better off in quite poor countries in the European Union', https://twitter.com/amanpour/status/1621219401713287174?s=20

7 John Maynard Keynes (1930) 'Economic possibilities for our grandchildren', two instalments in the *Nation and Athenaeum*, 11 and 18 October, http://www.econ.yale.edu/smith/econ116a/keynes1.pdf

What role is there for economic, social and cultural rights in the fight for social justice?

Economic, social and cultural rights are best won in societies that are more equal by income. The economic right to live in a warm, comfortable, damp-free home is best achieved where people's incomes are more equal and landlords have less power. The social right to partake in the norms of society, to be able to have a holiday away from home (and not just staying with family or friends) is almost universally achievable in such societies – and in the past it was in Britain, too. Even the cultural right to dress as you wish and be who you want to be is more easily attainable where groups of people are not viewed with suspicion because of the fear that income inequality feeds.

For example, nowhere in the rest of Europe, except for the former British colonies of Ireland and Malta, retains or enforces school uniforms for children. In Britain we think this is normal, but what of the cultural rights of children to dress as they wish?

Securing greater income equality is the trump card. It is even more effective than securing greater equality in wealth. Where income inequality is high, racism tends to fester and grow. We become used to seeing others sleeping rough on the streets; we begin to not to see them as people. We become obsessive about the life choices of others. We are less free to be who we want to be, and to be with who we want to be with.

There's been a lot of talk recently about a new 'woke elite' who don't represent the views of 'ordinary people'. What's your take on this argument?

I think it is helpful that it has been raised because it prompts the question: 'What would a society in which the woke were the elite look like?' Woke means awake. It means those who understand. The word comes from America, from the descendants of slaves. Today it describes being alert to racial prejudice and discrimination.

We are currently governed by people who say that Britain, and the past actions of its agents, can never be painted as the villainous. A villain, in the past spelt 'villein', was a feudal tenant entirely subject to the whims of the lord or manor to whom dues were paid and services rendered. This was in return for being allowed to work the land. Today the word 'villain' implies a lower-class scoundrel. In August 2022, Rishi Sunak proposed that people who suggest that any of British history might 'vilify the UK' should be referred to the Prevent counterterrorism scheme for re-education. We are not living under a woke elite – quite the opposite.

In November 2022, Jeremy Hunt, speaking as Sunak's chancellor of the Exchequer, stated, without equivocation, that 'the United Kingdom is and has always been a force for good in the world'. When Boris Johnson resigned as leader of the Conservative Party on 7 July 2022, in his resignation speech he repeated George Osborne's 2015 promise that if only we keep on doing what he wanted us to do, then soon 'we will be the most prosperous in Europe'. Osborne, however, had said 'in the world'. Although the measure of success was narrowing, both Osborne and Johnson implied that such a move would return Britain to its rightful place.

Imagine, in a fairer future, a different group governing us. A group with a better grasp of history, who know what so many people in the rest of the world understand about Britain and the role the British played in what later became their countries. That group would include a wide variety of views from a much wider variety of backgrounds than our current elite. Some of them might believe in 'no gods, no masters, no heroes, and no vanguards'. Others would have very different views. However, it is unlikely that any of them would worship the god of money, and is likely that they would not see themselves as elite, special or different. In these sunlit uplands, the phrase 'ordinary people' would be remembered as something that the old elite used to say, because they saw so many other people as beneath them – as ordinary.

CHAPTER 6.2

Kindness: rigour for British Geographers[1]

Let's face it, those of us who work in the academic discipline of Geography largely work on the subject of failure. The failure of political leaders worldwide to avert disastrous climate change. The need to prevent the continuation of the fastest species extinction the world has ever known. The social and personal repercussions of enormous global income, wealth and power inequalities. We describe all this, usually, as if it were just an interesting set of observations. Then we tell students to write an essay about it. If they cogently analyse our collective failure, we give them a high mark. Many of them can then take their university degrees and head out into banking, advertising and management and make the world an even worse place, armed with the knowledge of what they might be critiqued for by those who taught them, but never convinced them. Perhaps if we were kinder to our students when they were at university, were kinder and clearer in what we wrote and taught, more of them would use what they have learnt for good, rather than seeing their degrees as stepping stones to their allotted place in the social hierarchy.

British Geography is distinct from US or Canadian Geography. For undergraduates outside of the UK, studying Geography does not come with the association of being more likely to have come from a socially privileged position as a child. In North America and New Zealand, geography is not perceived as especially posh or easy. In the US, it is more of an unknown and hidden discipline

1 Extract of article originally published in 2019 as 'Kindness: A new kind of rigour for British Geographers', *Emotion, Space and Society*, Volume 33, 100630, November, https://doi.org/10.1016/j.emospa.2019.100630

that students discover in their third or fourth years. More North American geography 'grads' go into work in city planning or in Geographic Information Systems (GIS) than to any other job (or so anecdote has it). So, when I speak of 'our' or 'we' in this paper, I must be clear that I mean Geographers at British universities and their students. In this paper I use a capital G for Geography whenever I am talking about British Geography. I am writing for people like me, a British Geographer, and our collective failure.

It's not a weakness to admit failure, it is a strength. However, Geographers still have to contend with the peculiarly masculine legacy of exploration, colonial appropriation, and the original military function of much mapping. Today we may critique the ethos of exploring 'virgin lands', or 'Empire 2.0' thinking, and explain the derivation of the words 'Ordnance Survey', but often we carry on being like our forefathers (they were almost all men) in other ways. For instance, we tend to still be remarkably self-assured. In the 1949 Western *She wore a yellow ribbon*, John Wayne gave a young man a piece of advice: 'Never apologise, mister, it's a sign of weakness.'[2] The clip of him playing the cowboy, astride his horse and uttering these words of supposed great wisdom to a younger man epitomises the macho attitude of arrogance and brittleness that continues to pervade much of Western society, academia included, and especially Geography. Geographers are 'tough', they climb mountains, they are still explorers, they are more robust, more rigorous and more 'out there' than other academics, and thus that legacy of toughness of attitude still endures. It does so today, long after we began to deconstruct our recent past.

Geography in the UK emerged as a discipline at a time of emotional repression and the famous British stiff upper lip, where admitting your feelings was – as Wayne would say years later – 'a sign of weakness'. In this article I discuss emotion, failure and the role of kindness within contemporary British Geography. At times I may appear to be disheartened; but being trained as a Geographer I have learnt to persevere, to hide my feelings in meetings, not to say what nonsense so much of what we do still is;

---

[2] John Wayne (1949) *Never Apologize*, movie clip, https://www.youtube.com/watch?v=0hY4iqMfGU4

and not to come clean about what we could do if we cared more and held back a little less. Other British Geographers have started to speak out, but (so far) not many. Kye Askins, in describing a research project that she felt was going wrong, is unusual:

> I realised that this emotional drain had bled into my academic role, also demeaning my sense of professional value, and the idea of a Research Council grant and some 'big papers' had become seductive. The more I reflected, the more upset I was with myself: I felt that I'd let everyone down …[3]

Geography became acceptable as a British university subject in 1899, when *The Times* announced that a new school of Geography was to be established in Oxford, England. This was to ensure that there would be no future excuses of ignorance for the establishment's efficient 'conduct of the [British] Empire's affairs'. Geography was created as a discipline for 'Men who think of entering on a political or military career, or who intend in one capacity or another to take service in some part of the Empire beyond the seas, or who look forward to having dealings with foreign countries …'.[4] Geography was a discipline for young men drawn from the upper orders of society, those destined to rule over the lower orders. From the outset, a token nod to widening participation was made. *The Times* article of 1899 ends: 'There will be at least one scholarship of £60, attached to the school. There is every reason to hope that complete success will attend this new departure.'

A little history

But what is success, and what is failure? Geography departments began to proliferate not only across the UK, but around the Empire; including (but only rarely) in those former colonies that

[3] Kye Askins and Matej Blazek (2017) 'Feeling our way: academia, emotions and a politics of care', *Social and Cultural Geography*, 18, 8, pp. 1086–105.

[4] *The Times* (1899) 'The Oxford School of Geography', 29 March, Issue 35789, p. 4.

are today the US. The Department of Geography in Liverpool was founded in 1917. Today on its website, its successor, the Department of Geography and Planning, boasts that: 'Liverpool is home to the oldest Black African community in the UK.'[5] Yet nowhere does it mention that Liverpool was once one of the three key points on the triangular slave trade. This is just one of many examples of attempts to deconstruct and then reconstruct our past; while at the very same time echoes of toughness and obscuration endure. At the centenary celebrations of the Department in Liverpool, 'Vice-Chancellor Professor Janet Beer said: "Here at the University of Liverpool we have a very proud history of leading the way in Geography …".'[6] Leadership is still seen as so important in both Geography departments and universities as a whole. Whenever I hear the word 'leadership', I am reminded of the pith-helmeted Geographer leading his men and porters through the jungle.

Although Liverpool was one of the key points of the triangular slave trade, its university Geographers were educated long after that trade had ended. Today we like to pretend that all that we do is for the good, all the bad being in our past. However, no one has ever audited the undergraduate output of the discipline. Instead, we whisper to each other, isn't it amazing that so many of the banks took on so many of our students to work in London before the 2008 crash? Out loud we say that 'Geography has a critical role to play as we face global challenges that span the

---

5 University of Liverpool (2019) 'The perfect place to study Geography', University webpages, accessed 27 May, https://www.liverpool.ac.uk/geography-and-planning/geography-programmes/geography-at-liverpool/

6 The 2017 event included a three-course black-tie dinner priced at £60 a head in St George's Hall, Liverpool. The hall is associated with funding from former slave-trader families, although it was built after the formal abolition of that trade, aided by the British government's full compensation of the slavers. Details can be found here (these websites were accessed in 2019 by the author): https://web.archive.org/web/20180122004221/https://alumni.liv.ac.uk/events/a-tale-of-two-centenaries and University of Liverpool (2017) 'Centenary of Geography and Geology celebrated', University web page published on 26 September: https://www.liverpool.ac.uk/earth-ocean-and-ecological-sciences/news/articles/university-celebrates-centenary-of-geography-and-geology

social, economic and environmental'. In secret we comment on how remarkable it is that so many of us who did not stay in academia went on to work in the military (including in spying), for hedge funds, as financial consultants, and as teachers, some of which can be seen as fields where a sense of superiority and of command over others are key assets.

Pride and success have a tendency to come before a fall. In the 1970s, as the British Empire fell and its colonies won a new freedom, the fate of Geography as a frontier imperial discipline hung in the balance. A subject that trained (by then mostly) young men to wield control over foreign places could easily have been consigned to the dustbin of history. In the US, and elsewhere around the world, many departments were closed or merged into something else. In Britain, the new 1960s universities of Warwick, York and Strathclyde decided not to include Geography in their remit. However, Geography survived. Climate catastrophe, growing global inequality and the rising popularity of interdisciplinarity have helped; but Geography in the UK has in part become a soft option for those who come from upper middle-class families, where increasingly you are expected to go to university, and especially for those who were privileged (and so often have high GCSE marks) but are not actually that good at maths, or writing, or reading, or science, or imagination. And so, a century on from the founding of departments such as those in Oxford and Liverpool, it may finally be time (and kind) to talk about failure – despite the emotional costs involved.

At the start of the 1970s in England, boys from the top public schools[7] were not always expected to go to university. Some went directly into the military to be trained as officers, while others went directly into the City of London to start work at age 18. However, by the end of the 1970s parents who sent their children to such schools increasingly expected them to gain a

---

7 For readers from abroad who do not yet know, and also those from England who have not been forced to learn this yet, in England – where up is down and down is up and people drive on the left and dress to the right – public school means extremely elite, private, very expensive, often boarding away from their parents, school. One goes 'up' to university but can be 'sent down' for bad behaviour.

place at university, especially a place at a prestigious university. Geography's association with the English upper classes and upper middle classes can be traced back to that time. Knowing this helps you understand why so many went into finance (they had family connections) and why British Geography departments so often are found to have some of the narrowest and poshest social profiles when the backgrounds of students across an entire university in England are assessed. All this is changing, but if we don't admit to this legacy, we will not easily understand ourselves. Geography in Britain, from the time of my childhood onwards, began to admit an unusually high number of students from more privileged backgrounds, often from schools that were not especially kind; and often those who arrived were not seen to have succeeded by arriving at university, because almost every child at their school went on to university. They were more and more usually seen by their peers as not having done that well, and hence having had to apply to study Geography.

Talking about failure may be a sign of hope. In the summer of 2018, Tom Disney, Thom Davies and Elly Harrowell of the universities of Northumbria, Nottingham and Coventry organised a session at the Royal Geographical Society annual conference in Cardiff, on 'failure' within human Geography.[8] It was titled 'Reclaiming failure in geography: academic honesty in a neoliberal world'. This article has been written in response to that call, and because I wanted to say something both about our history and reality, and about being kind and compassionate in Geography. I want to suggest that we should think more about kindness.

Kindness in Geography

When asking a question at an academic conference, when posting on Twitter, when commenting on a piece of written work by a student, or writing a book review and making a particular point,

8 Elly Harrowell, Thom Davies and Tom Disney (2018) 'Making space for failure in geographic research', *The Professional Geographer*, 70, 2, pp. 230–38.

'is your intention to correct or connect?'[9] Refusing to accept that failure is normal and is all around us is not kind. The discipline of the stiff upper lip badly needs more kindness shown, both to others and to oneself. The need to face our failures applies to the subject as a whole, and to how Geographers choose to conduct their own work of research, teaching and administration.

When this article was first published, I was the Director of Graduate Studies in the School of Geography and the Environment at the University of Oxford. This means that I had a duty of care for roughly 150 PhD students. I got to see all the termly comments of their supervisors, the internal reviews of their work by other academics, their requests to suspend their studies due to illness, many of their applications for permission to do something not normally permitted by a particular rule, their applications for funding, for exceptional leave to delay, and all their final examination reports; including all those that said that what they had done was not good enough.

Some academics can be very brusque. It is not a great problem when they generally like the work they are commenting on; but where they don't agree with it – and especially when a student's work is actually weak – then kindness is essential and being brusque and to the point often means being brutal. As Geographers we must turn our critical gaze on our own actions and interventions, as well as assessing others. We must recognise we have a legacy of 'the strong man' despite so many younger academics now being women. In the past, hardly any older academics in Geography were women, as books on 'Great Geographers' made clear. If we Geographers can better deal with that legacy, and with our past properly, we could be so much better, so much kinder in the future. Geography could become the discipline of the future, the subject that studies the impending world in an involved and helpful way – not a distant, arrogant or all-knowing way. We could use our reputation as a weak science to our advantage, taking people with us rather than lecturing down to them. We know what we expect the climate to be like

9 Angelika Selle (2017) 'Presidents Corner: Living by the logic of love', *Blog of the Women's Federation for World Peace USA*, 14 August, https://www.wfwp.us/presidents-corner/president-s-corner-august-17

and how we could prevent it becoming that inhuman, we could talk more of what we hope society will develop towards, we could talk far more about compassion and empathy. Few people do not hope for a kinder future.

Kindness is a kind of rigour. It is hard to be kind; much harder to be kind than to always (in your own mind) be right. If Geography aimed to be 'the kind discipline', it would help to break a wider problem that academia has in spades, and the social sciences have by the bucketload: academic arrogance. As was tweeted in 2014 by an anonymous academic (who at the time of writing had over 311,000 followers): 'We're all smart. Distinguish yourself by being kind.'[10] But we are also all stupid, which is an even better reason to be kind.

Don't be nasty, not least because it is so easy to be wrong – especially if you think you are ever so clever (and I really do not mean to be unkind here). In several books I have written at length on how richer and more powerful people often 'assume they must be "phenomenally bright", when in fact any ability they may have to pass examinations is not unusual given their social advantages'.[11] Kindness is much more than the geography of care. To be kind you have to try to be less sure of your superiority, your great knowledge, and your power to discern whether others' work is very good or very bad. And you have to understand why we are also so equal, which includes all having the ability to very often be stupid in what we do. We must talk less of brilliant minds and exceptional students. Apart from anything else it reveals how unaware we are of what is now known about the human mind. Few minds are brilliant, but with dogged determination and a lot of help (and luck) you can train your mind to work in unusual ways; including to be less arrogant and more kind.

Kindness is a vital yet unseen aspect of academic work in general, and Geography in particular. It is something that all Geographers rely upon during fieldwork and data collection and in gaining access to archives, to data and to interviewees. Without

---

[10] Academics Say (2014) Tweet by 'Shit Academics Say', *Twitter*, 12.38 pm on 20 August, https://twitter.com/AcademicsSay/status/502057155437281280

[11] Danny Dorling (2018) *Peak inequality: Britain's ticking time-bomb*, Bristol: Policy Press, p. 213.

kindness, we are all surely destined to fail. However, as Professor Marie Price once explained, 'geographers seem reluctant to admit how much we rely on the kindness of strangers'.[12] Marie went on to explain that Geographers, like many academics, are also prone to overestimate their importance and insight. She explained when talking about writing up fieldwork:

> In conversations with other academics about this essay, the term 'war stories' was tossed around, usually in the context of, 'So you're going to tell your war stories!' The more I encountered the phrase, the more it bothered me.... To be honest, what I actually write will be of little interest to the immigrants themselves.

What she wrote was indeed of little interest to the immigrants she was studying, because they knew it already. Often Geographers are of the privileged few, writing almost exclusively for each other, about what they have discovered concerning other, almost always very different, peoples' lives.

[Editorial note: Here the extract ends – but the article continues and can be read online. An open access copy is here: https://www.dannydorling.org/?page_id=7437]

12 Marie Price (2001) 'The kindness of strangers', *Geographical Review*, 91, 1/2, pp. 143–50.

CHAPTER 6.3

The stones of the University of Oxford[1]

Figure 6.7: The spires, homes, windows and walls – Oxford, by Isabella Lill, 2020

see colour version in plate section

Source: 'Oxford' by Isabella Lill – who kindly gave permission for her artwork to be reproduced here.

The stones that make up the University of Oxford are dense, much denser than any normal stone. These stones are more than their base material. They are not just the Corallian Limestone first cut in Oxfordshire quarries in the 1300s and transported

---

1 First published in *Common Ground Journal*, 4, 28 July 2020, pp. 15–22, https://commongroundoxford.wordpress.com/2020/08/06/oxford-university-stones/

into the city by oxcart; they have long since metamorphosed into something far more potent. A mineral that can apparently endlessly suck in money and sweat, labour and blood, while not seeming to undergo any significant change to its outward appearance. The stone from those same quarries was used to build Eton College, Blenheim Palace and Windsor Castle,[2] flourishing there too with later rises in those institutions' riches, but not quite to the extent that the stones of the University of Oxford have changed over time from within. For a start, there were far more of them in Oxford. By 1756, the university was enormous, but what happened within was largely hidden from sight (Figure 6.8).

The University of Oxford was not built as the giant medieval cathedrals in mainland Europe were – designed to tower over the surrounding countryside and inspire awe, wonder and subservience. Instead, the university was built to be hidden away in a valley, a secret hollow between the hills, a gravel bank at the confluence of two small rivers. It was built to be defended,

Figure 6.8: The colleges of Oxford and the streets and rivers of the city around the year 1756

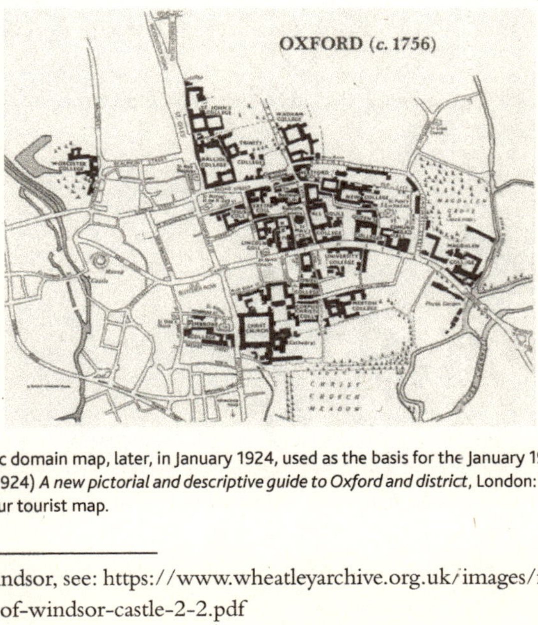

Source: Public domain map, later, in January 1924, used as the basis for the January 1924 Ward Lock & Co. (1924) *A new pictorial and descriptive guide to Oxford and district*, London: Ward, Lock & Co., a colour tourist map.

[2] For Windsor, see: https://www.wheatleyarchive.org.uk/images/files/0677-stones-of-windsor-castle-2-2.pdf

a place in which to hide away from the material world – the world outside which came later to exist to serve it and its higher purposes. Its motto: *Dominus illuminatio mea* (the Lord is my light).

Over time, the stones grew denser as the financial surplus grew greater. The local quarries were emptied out. Far away, in Wales, coal and slate mines were slowly emptied by children and adults working in the dark. Farms were bequeathed to colleges with names such as Jesus. For centuries, the farm labourers' efforts filled the colleges' coffers, and slowly all that sweat further saturated the wealth within its walls.

The culture of getting something for nothing, continuously and in perpetuity, became well established. The plantations of Ireland and later of the empire were brought into the levy of many of the colleges and became part of a global flood of tribute. The stones grew heavier; the towers rose higher and spread across the gravel bank. Tribute was brought in by horse and cart, at times containing concealed silver and gold (Figure 6.9).

In *Brideshead Revisited*, Evelyn Waugh describes 1920s Oxford as 'a city of aquatint'.[3] (Aquatint is a printing technique that produces areas of tone, rather than lines, so that colours blend more easily.) When the British Empire was at its peak, the university was populated by students whose wealth was often derived from

Figure 6.9: View of Oxford from Shotover Hill in flood-time, when the water was over the bank

Source: Painted on 10 January 1791 by John Baptist Malchair, on the old road from London to Oxford

---

3 https://archive.org/stream/in.ernet.dli.2015.201980/2015.201980.Brideshead-Revisited_djvu.txt

their family's investments in that empire (Figure 6.10). However, Oxford's intake changed as the British Empire's power waned, triggering the subsequent decrease in income equality that saw a rising proportion of state school admissions to the University. Oxford, both the city and university, began to change.

By the 1980s the tide had turned again, away from growing equality, away from a rising state school intake, and away from a diminishing Oxford influence on the nations of the UK. Oxford returned to the building-up of unequal wealth, the defence of snobbery, and the eugenic thinking that only a few had great potential.

Recently, it's become apparent that we are close to seeing the end of this trend. Between 2019 and 2020, the number of British undergraduate offer-holders from state schools rose from 60.5 per cent to 69 per cent, with the 2020 figure expected to translate into 67 per cent of places [Editorial note: it did, and now hovers around 70 per cent]. However, although these figures look promising, we must account for the fact that very few of these state school students come from normal homes when measured by income. The median child in the UK grows up in a household

Figure 6.10: State-school undergraduates admitted to the University of Oxford, 1927–2018 (%)

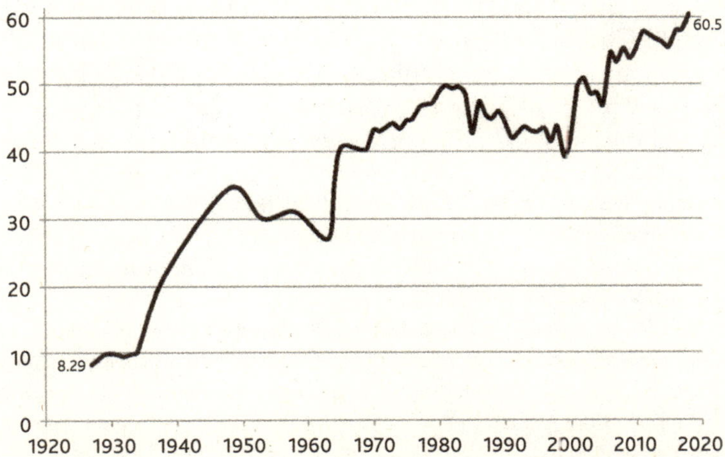

Source: Claire Hann and Danny Dorling (2019) 'A changed institution', *The Oxford Magazine*, 411, pp. 4-6, 0th Week. Michaelmas Term 2019

that survives on a total household income of £21,840 per annum after tax and before paying for housing, food, travel, clothes and all other essentials.[4]

In Britain today, a child's A-level results are mainly determined by the school they attend – not by inherent ability, or by how hard they work. A child of below-average ability (in the second quartile at age eight, to be precise) is *three times* more likely to receive AAA+ at A level if they are sent to a private school than a child of above-average ability who is sent to a state school. That child of privilege is *six times* more likely to receive AAA+ than a child of similar ability who is not wealthy. As a result, England's 'top universities' – which require such A-level results for admission – are more likely to offer places to the less able children of the rich.[5]

I, too, was a median child. As a boy in the 1970s, I would play on Shotover Hill. The trees had grown high by then and there were no clear views of the university. The city had grown up around it. More people now worked in the car factory at the foot of the hill than served at college tables, but the university continued to accumulate wealth and become progressively more cloistered. In the 1980s, the bursar of Magdalen College built a moat around his college lands to keep out teenagers like me. In his memoirs, he wrote about those locals he saw as miscreants, and also recounted his predecessor visiting a local school in Temple Cowley and pointing out a boy with the ideal servile demeanour to work in his college.[6] This boy would later become the College's head porter. By contrast, as I grew up in the city throughout the 1980s, the University of Oxford (and some of its

---

4 Danny Dorling (2018) 'Which children in Britain will have no holiday this summer?', *Oxplore Story Board*, University of Oxford, https://oxplore.org/question-detail/can-we-end-poverty#2055 and at https://www.dannydorling.org/?p=6732

5 Tim Morris, Danny Dorling and George Davey Smith (2016) 'How well can we predict educational outcomes? Examining the roles of cognitive ability and social position in educational attainment', *Contemporary Social Science* (Journal of the Academy of Social Sciences), 11, 2–3, pp. 154–68, https://www.tandfonline.com/doi/full/10.1080/21582041.2016.1138502

6 Bill Johnson (2015) *Look back in laughter*, Newbury: Threshold Press, http://www.threshold-press.co.uk/memoir/r_w_j_laughter.php

colleges more than others) gave succour to teenagers who – their egos expanded and confidence boosted – would later become prime minister after prime minister after prime minister. The stones had infected their minds. I later learned that what I saw was not new, but rather part of an unbroken chain that goes back centuries. A few months ago, I heard the word 'miscreants' yet again being used by a college fellow to describe Oxford residents.

Boris Johnson, when he was a teenager in the city, was inspired by Margaret Thatcher – the prime minister of the day. Thatcher, in turn, looked up at Winston Churchill's portrait and saw her destiny while studying in Oxford in the 1940s. Churchill, similarly, looked to the Oxford-educated prime minister of his teenage years, Robert Gascoyne-Cecil, 3rd Marquess of Salisbury, when he was in Sandhurst in the 1880s.[7] Cecil, in turn, looked to Robert Peel – the first modern Conservative (according to A.J.P. Taylor) – for inspiration while he was a teenager studying at Christ Church (Oxford) in 1847. Peel himself, as a teenager at Christ Church in 1805, had Pitt the Younger as a role model. And today, a teenager amid the stones of Oxford will be looking up at Johnson [Editorial note: or Truss, or Sunak, or Starmer] and feel the very same weight of destiny upon their shoulders – the destiny that continues the unbroken line whereby a tiny few rule over the many – and almost every prime minister was once a student at the University of Oxford [Editorial note: Starmer came up as a postgraduate].

Those who taught the generation now in power in Britain were, at the very same time, building up endowments and laying down wine for their successors – wine often still being drunk today. They were defending and deepening their justification for a place apart. It was a time when things could have changed for the better but, instead, Britain became more divided (Figure 6.11). The colleges took in more women and more children from state schools, but the aim was to co-opt and cultivate, not to diversify. The progressives of the past were now few and far between. The stones of Oxford became a petri dish for the new, more brutal,

---

7 Danny Dorling (2010) 'The Darwins and the Cecils are only empty vessels', *Environment and Planning A*, 42, pp. 1023–5, https://www.dannydorling.org/wp-content/files/dannydorling_publication_id0769.pdf

Figure 6.11: City Council suggestions for where those working in Oxford might live, 2019

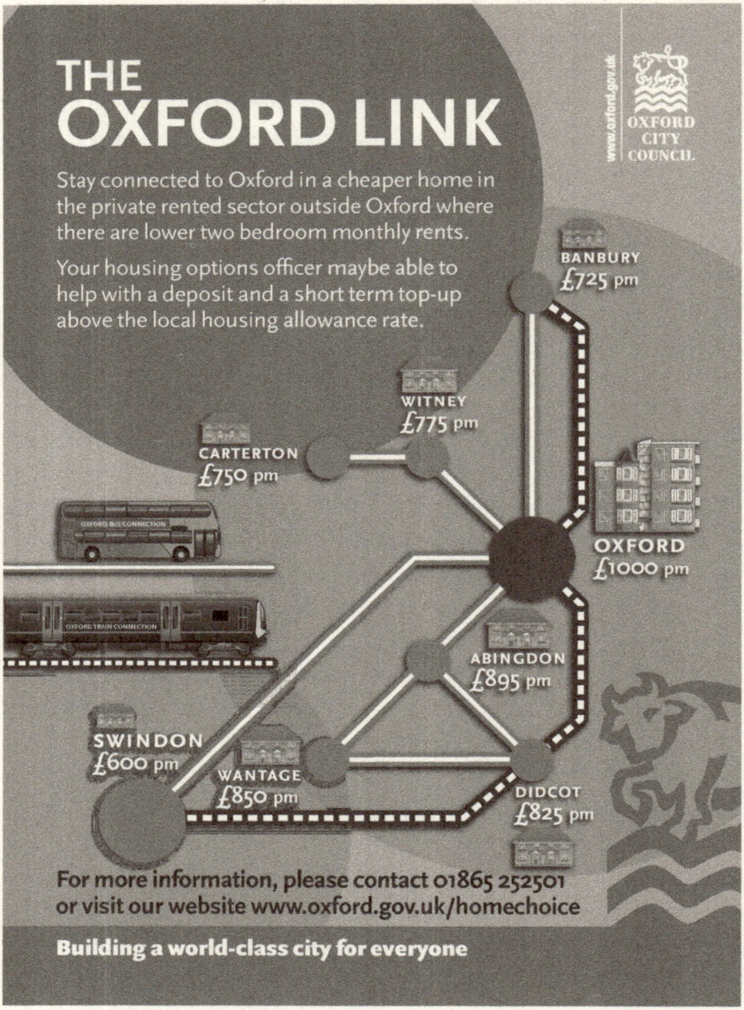

see colour version in plate section

Source: Oxford City Council leaflet published in 2019, reproduced here: https://commongroundoxford.wordpress.com/2020/08/06/oxford-university-stones/

more callous future. Today that could change again, and possibly for the better. But to change requires facing up to what you are and what you produce, and knowing what lies deep within the stones. The same stones that were mainly shaped, a very long time ago, by local people from the Quarry (Headington Quarry) to build palaces for newcomers to live and be educated in for their own good.

As inequalities in income and wealth began to rise again, the University of Oxford accepted many more millions in donations, in return for putting the name of a man on a building. In 2017, Bo Rothstein, then Professor of Government and Public Policy at the Blavatnik School of Government, resigned from the university, citing Blavatnik's donation to Donald Trump's inauguration, which he called 'incomprehensible and irresponsible'.[8] In 2019, the university accepted a £150 million donation from Stephen Schwarzman, current CEO of the Blackstone Group and former chairman and Head of Mergers and Acquisitions at Lehman Brothers. Questioning the legitimacy of the ways in which Blavatnik and Schwarzman made and continue to make their money results in threats, most recently from the latter billionaire's spokesman.[9] Today, the old men's money is used to renew the old stones.

There have been many times in the past when the city of Oxford and its people would rally against the desires of the university; however, Oxford City Council now has a leaflet that informs residents about cheaper areas outside of the city centre, while colleges continue to expand their accommodation in central Oxford. But who will come to live with and beneath the new stones, and what will they be taught? The slogan on the leaflet reads, 'Building a world-class city for everyone'. But the city of Oxford is increasingly for the select few.

The future of Oxford could be so different from what the university has planned for the city. Oxford could be the greenest city in Europe (Figure 6.12), but because of the 40,000 people

---

8 Matthew Weaver and Helena Bengtsson (2017) 'Oxford University professor quits Blavatnik school in Donald Trump protest', *The Guardian*, 29 August, https://www.theguardian.com/education/2017/aug/28/oxford-university-professor-bo-rothstein-resigns-donald-trump-protest

9 Alayna Lee, Rose Horowitch and Olivia Tucker (2019) 'Schwarzman donation to Oxford draws criticism', *Yale News*, 1 October, https://yaledailynews.com/blog/2019/10/01/schwarzman-donation-to-oxford-draws-criticism/

Figure 6.12: The rivers, canal, roads, lakes and buildings of Oxford, 1939–45 and 2013

see colour version in plate section

Note: Areas in dark grey are urban cover based on the Dudley Stamp pre-war survey (data collected between 1939–1945). Areas in pale grey are current urban cover based on satellite imagery collected by the European Union in 2013.

Source: Dudley Stamp's survey of 1939–1945 and EU 2013 data, merged by eco-systems.org.uk

who drive over its greenbelt each day, it is one of the least green (Figure 6.11). Today, as its university supports the construction of a motorway to Cambridge, the city exemplifies just how ignorant people in power can be made by money. It is so important to unearth the university's past, to show how much it has contributed to and profited from exploitation, and to illustrate how it is currently in danger of becoming the pet project of Trump's billionaires – because if we don't, we may not see a better future in our lifetimes. The Oxford–Cambridge Expressway need not be built.

A plaque occasionally appears on a college wall acknowledging the fact that a college building was financed through slavery, but that is about as far as change around here goes. The stone statue of Cecil Rhodes has not fallen; it remains the highest statue on the high street. The university will not be able to make any really significant strides in access and diversity until those in charge acknowledge the problem with putting Rhodes on a pedestal. Although the proportions of state school and ethnic minority students that Oxford admits at undergraduate level are on the rise, changes such as those which have recently come into effect at elite Scottish universities – which now admit students from lower socio-economic backgrounds with ABB grades while requiring those from higher socio-economic backgrounds to gain AAA+ – tend to still be viewed as an impossibility at Oxford.

Oxford is built on a swamp. It is built on the land between and around the rivers (Figure 6.12). The settlement was here long before the university appropriated its name, and the settlement will be here long after the collection of buildings in its centre is no longer the apex of such money and power. Our world is at peak inequality. In Oxford today, the most common way to die for young people is to die homeless. Most homeless people who recently died in Oxford went to school here; they were locals. As adults, many lived in hiding, including in tents in the undergrowth.

The University of Oxford is changing. It is waking up to its past and, slowly, some within it are writing a better version of its history. Many of the portraits on its walls are being taken down, partly to try to hide the culpability, partly in the hope of creating something better. The people of this city are beginning to imagine what a 'world-class' home for everyone who lives and works in it would actually look like. One in which people who worked in the city could also live in the city, as almost all of the car workers did when I was a child. The university could decide that there is more to having a soul than simply selling something when the price is right.

It's time to begin to lighten the stones. It's time to work out how to be good without believing that it is mutually exclusive from being rich. Dear University of Oxford; take down the statue of Rhodes and move him indoors, where he can be looked down on rather than up to. Begin to question the stories you have been told, because far too many are untrue. Work out how to finance the university from sources that do not include the most disreputable of donors, investments in the most unethical of funds, or some of the highest (postgraduate and visiting student) university fees in Europe. If another source of finance is needed to preserve the old buildings, then look to the tourists – they will come to see the stones for many decades to come. Plan for a city that is green and open, not grey and exclusive. Accept students from normal backgrounds again, from median income households and average state schools. Ask how reparations can be made for all that has been done that was wrong. There is no need to hide behind the stones anymore, unless you are ashamed of what is within.

CHAPTER 6.4

Economics and compassion[1]

Why do economists in particular, more than any other group of policy-orientated social scientists, appear to lack compassion, and what can be done to address this problem? Over the past few decades evidence has grown that people are more likely to be attracted to study Economics if they are less compassionate. They are most likely to complete their courses if they are less compassionate than those who chose to drop out of studying Economics, and then 'do something more useful instead'. Less compassionate people are more likely to go on to gain higher-level qualifications in Economics and to later both become and remain professional economists. While many people find compassion to be more intuitive, it is possible that in Economics it may need to be more explicitly taught. The example of viewing education as a public good for the greater benefit, rather than as something that is acquired for individual self-promotion, is mentioned briefly at the end of this chapter as one issue that can illustrate the need for greater compassion in economic understanding in future. However, first, Economics still needs to recognise that it has a very big problem with compassion.

Introduction

There are many studies now that show how university students of Economics find moral behaviour unusually difficult to understand,

1 Extract from a chapter published in 2019: Danny Dorling, 'Economics and compassion', in Matt Hawkins and Jennifer Nadel (eds) *How compassion can transform our politics, economy and society*, Abingdon: Routledge, Chapter 9.

and that less morally inhibited students perform better in learning the subject, or at least the subject as it is currently taught in the US and the UK. This has now been clear for more than three decades. It has become routine, at least once every ten years, to point out that economists tend to lack morals and compassion, and yet little is done to address the problem.[2]

A decade ago one of Britain's leading philosophers explained that it was well known that selfish people are more often found among 'the kind of people we find in business schools and economics departments'.[3] Many have come to the conclusion that a generation of economists will simply have to retire before this bias is properly addressed; with the discipline of Economics only progressing towards being compassionate one retirement at a time. However, if older economists appoint and promote those in their images, then the hangover may last longer.

Fifteen years ago, a few economists began to explain that their subject had veered so far from having an interest in human beings, that it had become 'so obscure that even orthodox economists are bemoaning its intellectual poverty'.[4] Then the worldwide economic crash descended, and the discipline lost most of what was left of its shine, but it proved resilient, and by 2019 had reverted to type. There are some obvious solutions. In Australia, as a subject to study before age 18, 'economics is offered mostly in private and boys' schools'.[5] However, it is as much what is

---

2 Robert Frank, Thomas Gilovich and Dennis Regan (1993) 'Does studying economics inhibit cooperation?', *Journal of Economic Perspectives*, 7, 2, pp. 159–71; Laszlo Zsolnai (2003) 'Honesty versus cooperation: a reinterpretation of the moral behavior of economics students', *American Journal of Economics and Sociology*, 62, 4, pp. 707–12; Zach Ward-Perkins and Joe Earle (2013) 'Economics students need to be taught more than neoclassical theory', *The Guardian*, 28 October, https://www.theguardian.com/commentisfree/2013/oct/28/economics-students-neoclassical-theory

3 Zygmunt Bauman (2007) *Consuming life*, Cambridge: Polity Press, p. 101.

4 Michael Kitson (2005) 'Economics for the future', *Cambridge Journal of Economics*, 29, 6, pp. 827–35, p. 827.

5 Duygu Yengin (2018) 'Secret men's business: why the public image of economics is bad news for all of us', *The Conversation*, 13 June, https://theconversation.com/secret-mens-business-why-the-public-image-of-economics-is-bad-news-for-all-of-us-98145

taught, as who it is taught to, that matters. Given a choice, an individual who was both numerate and compassionate would be likely to avoid studying Economics. At this point I should confess to one of my many biases. I am often described as an economist, especially when the commenter is more right-wing than me, but agrees with what I have to say.[6] However, I only studied Economics at school, not at university.

In 1986 I was taught the particularly Thatcherite version of economics when I took an A level in the subject. I was not an especially able student (my exam results at age 16 would have been too poor for me to have been allowed to take A levels at the local state school today) but it was not hard to get the top mark in Economics at age 18, as long as you gave the answers that the economists wanted – so I did. And then I, like the large majority who took A-level Economics at the time, did not pursue the subject any further. I went to university to study mathematics, statistics and social sciences (geography) instead. I had been put off Economics by my perception of it as being inhuman, naïve, and ridiculously simplistic – a subject then dominated in England by people with physics envy and a weird admiration for Margaret Thatcher and her advisors.

Changing the heart and soul

On May Day 1981, the traditional Labour Day, *The Sunday Times* interviewed Thatcher very early on in her career as prime minister. The interview was published two days later and ended with her saying:

> What's irritated me about the whole direction of politics in the last 30 years is that it's always been towards the collectivist society. People have forgotten about the personal society. And they say: do I count, do I matter? To which the short answer is, yes. And therefore, it isn't that I set out on economic policies;

6 Simon Jenkins (2015) 'The myth of the housing crisis', *The Spectator*, 28 February, https://www.spectator.co.uk/article/the-myth-of-the-housing-crisis/

> it's that I set out really to change the approach, and changing the economics is the means of changing that approach. If you change the approach you really are after the heart and soul of the nation. Economics are the method; the object is to change the heart and soul.

I was 13 years old, the age at which your opinions begin to crystallise into something more concrete. I didn't read newspapers, but you would have had to have been weirdly unconnected to society then not to have seen the damage being done – that the soul of much of British society was being ripped apart. The very same was happening across the Atlantic.

Ronald Reagan came to power in the US in 1980. Being a trained actor, he was better able to fake compassion. He also used fewer words than Mrs Thatcher. The phrase he is best remembered for is: 'the nine most terrifying words in the English language are, "I'm from the government and I'm here to help."'.[7] It was exactly the same message that was being given at that time to people in the UK: that there is no such thing as society; people do not care enough for society to function well; there are only individuals and their families; do not trust other people, everyone is selfish.

When they were talking of others, Reagan and Thatcher were actually describing themselves. Neither had to rely on the state in their older years, Reagan dying surrounded by his family (but not in society), Thatcher died alone in the Ritz Hotel (without even her family). One of her epitaphs was the speech of 'Coco the Scab' in the film *Brassed Off*, which begins 'So god was creating man, and his little assistant came up to him and he said "Hey we've got all these bodies left, but we're right out of brains, and we're right out of hearts ..."'.

Growing compassion in economics requires reinserting a heart and then adding more brains. Compassion was cast out and lost through the rekindling of a particular selfishness – the idea that

---

[7] Mitchell Bard (2011) 'Reagan Was Wrong: The Nine Most Terrifying Words Are, "I'm a Libertarian and the Market Will Save You"', *The Huffington Post*, 28 June, https://www.huffpost.com/entry/reagan-was-wrong-the-nine_b_628022

the poor either do not deserve more than they have or that money will eventually trickle down to them. A more collective economics is needed, the object of which should be to reduce inequality and eliminate poverty. Through that, you rebuild the heart and invite back in the soul. Without that, you are simply telling people that the best they can hope for is a soulless survival of the fittest.

As the *Los Angeles Times* explained at the time of Reagan's death: 'he understood the presidency was a pulpit, and he used it to preach. Mostly his sermons were about a simple kind of conservatism: cut taxes so investments of the wealthy would trickle down to the poor.'[8] Trickle-down was not Reagan's idea; it was one that had been dreamed up by a group of economists who told him that if he helped the rich get richer everyone else would also get richer because a fraction of their wealth would somehow trickle down. These economists did not just get into Reagan's brain, they got into many other people's minds too, including Margaret Thatcher's. She carried one of their books around in her handbag (it was not a good or helpful book). The message of these then dominant economists was that greed is good, compassion is weakness, and collective provision is the road to serfdom, a road that leads to no one being free.

The message that compassion was economic weakness spread during the 1980s, 1990s and into the new millennium. By 2007, researchers studying students in the US had photographed their brains using MRI scanners while simultaneously showing them photographs of people, including the homeless. They did this to ascertain how much a key part of their prefrontal cortex, the part which is normally active when empathy is felt, reacted upon seeing each photograph shown. The researchers were shocked to find that when university students in the US in the very early 21st century viewed photographs of people such as

[8] J. Neuman (2004) 'Former President Reagan dies at 93', *The Los Angeles Times*, 6 June, https://www.latimes.com/local/obituaries/la-reagan-story.html

the homeless and drug addicts, this stimulated no activity in the region associated with empathy at all.[9]

Scholars looking into the new MRI findings suggested that these otherwise typical US university students had come to consider their fellow citizens who were homeless and/or addicts to be less than human.[10] They thought that this learnt lack of compassion might be a new coping mechanism developed among students and encouraged within US society at this time by economists who explained that people got what they deserved. This was a mechanism that allowed them to carry on with their lives without having to think further and deeper.

The United States has far more people who have been made homeless per capita than any other nation not at war. Fortunately, hope remains for a renewal of compassion. The researchers with the MRI scanning equipment also reported finding that if a question was asked about the homeless people while the photographs were being shown, such as 'What food do you think this beggar might prefer?', then the emotional part of the cortex began to become active on the scanner. The damage that had been done to these students was thus not irreversible.[11]

It is perhaps fortunate that, as yet, no MRI scans have been made of American students of Economics being presented with images of those in need. It is likely that in a disproportionate number of cases, even when asked what kind of food the beggar might prefer, the more dedicated Economics students might answer that she would prefer the food she is willing to work harder for because true preferences can only be ascertained by behaviour, not simply asked about.[12] Many studies have found

---

[9] M. Buchanan (2007) 'Are we born prejudiced?', *New Scientist*, 14 March, https://www.newscientist.com/article/mg19325952-000-are-we-born-prejudiced/

[10] Susan George (2008) *Hijacking America: How the religious and secular right changed what Americans think*, Cambridge: Polity Press, p. 248 and the footnote on that page.

[11] Danny Dorling (2015) *Injustice: Why social inequality still persists*, Bristol: Policy Press.

[12] Laszlo Zsolnai (2003) 'Honesty versus cooperation: a reinterpretation of the moral behavior of economics students', *American Journal of Economics and Sociology*, 62, 4, pp. 707–12.

that those who take degrees in Economics in the US go on to express an even greater preference for selfish beliefs at the end of their courses than they did at the beginning. Those students become more self-interested and less compassionate as they are being taught.[13]

Economics, men and compassion

In 2005, Larry Summers, an economist and at that point president of Harvard University, claimed that part of the gender gap in academic appointments could be due to differences in innate aptitude, with women simply being less able than men.[14] Although Summers was taken to task at that time, within just four years he was appointed to advise President Barack Obama on economics. It was reported that in April 2009 he fell asleep on the job.[15]

Within a year Summers had been forced to resign. In 2013, he lost out in a competition to become chair of the Federal Reserve. Janet Yellen won, and became the first woman to hold the position. Summers' critics suggested he had 'a limited understanding of empathy, holds his friends to a lower bar, and does not know how to admit mistakes'.[16] Compassion requires empathy, not treating your own gang as special, and understanding how fallible you are yourself. Economics has not encouraged these traits.

Young economists are encouraged not to see people as people, but as personal optimising machines, each seeking to maximise

---

13 Robert Frank, Thomas Gilovich, and Dennis Regan (1993) 'Does studying economics inhibit cooperation?', *Journal of Economic Perspectives*, 7, 2, pp. 159–71.

14 Kathryn Crim (2005) 'Notes on the intelligence of women', *The Atlantic*, 18 May, https://www.theatlantic.com/magazine/archive/2005/05/notes-on-the-intelligence-of-women/304042/

15 Sheryl Gay Stolberg (2009) 'Summers caught a-snoozin', *The New York Times*, 23 April, https://thecaucus.blogs.nytimes.com/2009/04/23/summers-caught-a-snoozin

16 Matthew Clarida (2014) 'Professor Summers', *The Harvard Crimson*, 23 October, www.thecrimson.com/article/2014/10/23/larry-summers-profile/

their own utility through satisfying their desires as much as is personally possible, and (to the limit of their own ability) to manipulate others and the system in their favour. Young people who find such an approach attractive are themselves attracted into economics and to stay in economics. They then referee, and accept for publication, papers that make ridiculous claims, but claims which do not jar with their worldview, such as the well-known paper from the *Journal of Economic Perspectives*, which argued that eating junk food was beneficial because of the amount of time people saved given how much more quickly they could eat. This paper is often given as an example of what went wrong in UK and US economic thinking and planning in recent decades.[17]

Seeing other human beings as having only the basest of urges has a long history in Anglo-American economics. A key essay on urges and economics was written by Thomas Malthus in 1798. That essay led him to be appointed as the world's first paid economist when, in 1805, he became Professor of History and Political Economy at the East India Company College in Hertfordshire. He was the chief economist of colonialism. His essay, on population growth, coupled with a partial reading of some of the works of Adam Smith, led to the economic theory that to hoard and patriate wealth was 'necessary to bring the urges of sexual attraction under control … [with the warning that] wealth gave rise to temptation, temptation to indulgence, and indulgence ate up the wealth'.[18]

Both Margaret Thatcher and Ronald Reagan were influenced by economists who saw the poor as monsters driven by 'growling stomachs, clenched fists and insatiable genitalia'.[19] In language that is today seen as unfair to people who are on the autistic

---

[17] George Irvin (2008) *Super rich: The rise of inequality in Britain and the United States*, Cambridge: Polity Press, p. 127.

[18] Avner Offer (2006) *The challenge of affluence: Self-control and well-being in the United States and Britain since 1950*, Oxford: Oxford University Press, p. 53.

[19] R. Patel (2008) *Stuffed and starved: From farm to fork, the hidden battle for the world food system*, London: Portobello, p. 85, and n. 34 on p. 334, concerning Thomas Malthus, the English reaction to the French Revolution, and Malthus' fascination with 'the untamed and fecund flesh of the destitute' French revolutionaries.

spectrum, for well over a decade now there has been a growth in the heterodox side of that discipline and in a 'post-autistic economics' movement. That movement has identified the origins of the problem as being a lack of compassion, a problem that began with some, but not all, of the works of Adam Smith. Adam Smith (1723–90) influenced Thomas Malthus (1766–1834), Thomas Malthus influenced Francis Galton (1822–1911), Francis Galton influenced Karl Pearson (1857–1936), Karl Pearson influenced Joseph Schumpeter (1883–1950), and Joseph Schumpeter influenced Milton Friedman (1912–2006), who had the greatest effect on the politics of both Thatcher and Reagan. In 1947, Schumpeter claimed that what was crucial to economic success was having enough 'men of superior energy and intelligence'.[20]

Francis Galton is worthy of extra attention as a key advocate of eugenics. Galton's thinking influenced economists from across the political spectrum. From 1937 to 1945, John Maynard Keynes was director of the British Eugenics Society, now known as the Galton Institute. Much more recently one of the more radical current US economists published a book in 2008 containing a chapter entitled 'High heels and school uniforms', under a picture of two large male moose locking horns.[21] It contained some ideas about human mating that even just over a decade later seem highly dated. As one British economist, Tim Harford, explained around the same time about economists' theories on sex: 'there is not usually a queue to jump into bed with economists'.[22]

[Editorial note: Here the extract ends – but the article continues and can be read online. An open access copy can easily be found, such as: https://www.dannydorling.org/?page_id=8314]

---

20 Renee Prendergast (2006) 'Schumpeter, Hegel and the vision of development', *Cambridge Journal of Economics*, 30, 2, pp. 253–75, at p. 254, n. 1.

21 Robert Frank (2008) *The economic naturalist: Why economics explains almost everything*, London: Virgin Books, p. 101.

22 Tim Harford (2009) *Dear Undercover Economist: The very best letters from the 'Dear Economist' column*, London: Little Brown, p. 15, letter to Cecilia.

CHAPTER 6.5

Finland: how much better life can be[1]

Finland is rarely mentioned as an example by leftists and Greens who want to build a better future. Yet this little-noticed country is one of the most equal, peaceful and happiest on the planet. How did Finland come to demonstrate the benefits of investing in people – and what could its model offer the rest of the world?

Finland has become the 'by way of contrast' country, as the *British Medical Journal* described it in 2018. It is the one place that shows that something much better than the status quo is possible. That is a weighty responsibility. Of course, Finland is not Utopia, but today it offers one of the closest approximations (Figure 6.13).

In 2018, when Finland first achieved its top placing in the UN's World Happiness Report, a UK newspaper reported the news with the caveat 'even though its GDP is below that of the US and Germany'.[2] When Finland overtook Norway to take first place in the World Happiness Report, it did so with a GDP per capita that was more than a third lower than that of Norway; and it then went on to hold that top-ranked position in both 2019 and 2020.

The World Happiness Report ranks countries according to GDP, life expectancy, generosity, social support, freedom and corruption levels to evaluate the quality of their inhabitants'

---

1 With Annika Koljonen, originally published in the *New Internationalist*, January/February 2021, based on our 2020 book *Finntopia: What we can learn from the world's happiest country*, Newcastle: Agenda.

2 Sarah Boseley (2018) 'Nordic countries' "happy" reputation masks sadness of young, says report', *The Guardian*, 25 August, https://www.theguardian.com/world/2018/aug/25/nordic-countries-happy-reputation-masks-sadness-of-young-says-report

Figure 6.13: Finland topped UN's World Happiness Report again: a Helsinki view

see colour version in plate section

Source: Photo Credit: Kostiolavi/Pixabay

current lives on a ladder scale ranging from 0 for the worst possible life to 10 for the best possible life.

Finland is the country that most clearly shows how it is possible for world-beating happiness to be achievable without becoming ever richer, and while having living standards in terms of material wealth that are below those in the most affluent parts of the world, including Finland's wealthier Scandinavian neighbours.

Recent research conducted in Finland has established that 'well-being is to a significant extent conditioned by the position one occupies in the social structure and by the welfare regime one lives in'. However, that research also found that Finland is unusual in one other way, namely when it comes to the thoughts and feelings of recent migrants to the country.

In affluent countries, immigrants usually tend to be more optimistic than the natives of their new country. When the UN measured the happiness of immigrants for the first time in their 2018 report, Finland scored the highest of any country being compared. However, in general in Nordic countries, including

Finland, where people's well-being is generally so high, being of an immigrant background is an adverse factor, when all else is taken into account. It is possible that it is very hard for outsiders to fit into a society that is already so equal and cohesive.

If you turn up in London or New York, you are just one of countless immigrants. What is more, you have just arrived in a society that is deeply divided. The rich do not trust the poor, and the poor have good reason not to trust the rich. Almost everyone is an outsider in one way or another. Many, if not most, people you meet will be migrants like you, or their parents were. The same cannot be said of Finland or of other countries that top the list of most happy or most politically stable places.

The Fragile State Index (previously the 'Failed State Index') has been published annually since 2005. It ranks 178 countries across 12 indicators that attempt to summarise the key risks and vulnerabilities faced by individual nations. Currently, Finland ranks highest overall in this index, as the least fragile state in the world. It also ranks highest on many components of the index, including on low group grievance, on high (as well as socially even) economic development, on good public services and on low demographic pressures – all as compared with the other countries in the top ten shown in Figure 6.14.

At first it appears quite remarkable that as well as performing very strongly on so many other international rankings, Finland ranks highest of all 178 countries for political stability. However, international rankings are very positively correlated with each other. It is easier to be happy if your state is not fragile, your press is free and responsible, your schools are cohesive, the health of your infants is good and the health of the population as a whole is improving rapidly from what used to be quite a poor record.

Finland today is one of the few places on earth that replicates most closely the situation in which we are most content: when we are caring for each other and not competing; where we are each valued very similarly, and where no one is greatly elevated or diminished. In another affluent country that is in many ways Finland's opposite, today's UK, one in every 200 people is homeless. In Finland the proportion is at least four times lower and almost no one is sleeping on the streets.

Figure 6.14: The happiest and most stable countries in the world, 2016–19

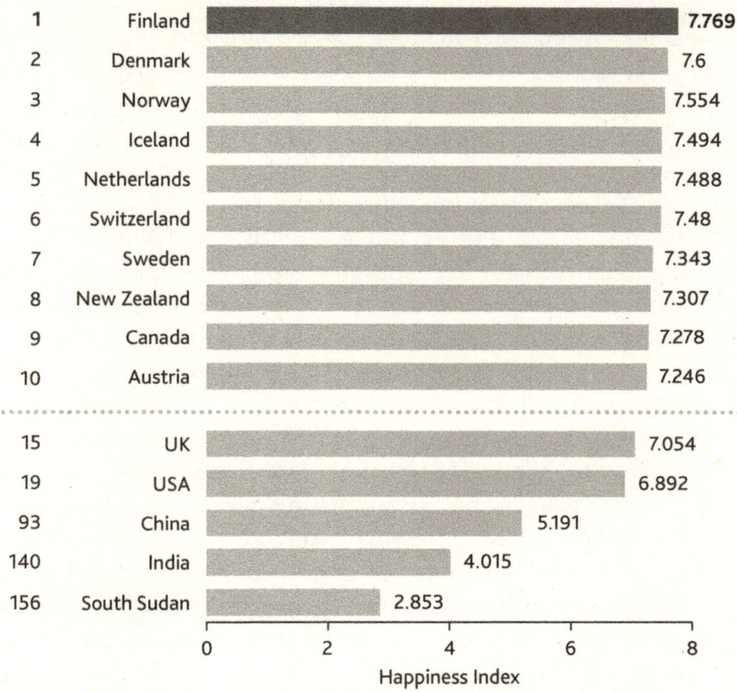

Source: Annika Koljonen and Danny Dorling (2020) *Finntopia*, Newcastle: Agenda, https://www.dannydorling.org/finntopia/figures.html

Countries that care less tend to count less carefully. Crude estimates by the UK government show that in England the number of people who were street homeless rose by 169 per cent between 2009 and 2018. In Finland over the same period, much more precise estimates revealed that long-term homelessness fell by 35 per cent, and rough sleeping was all but eradicated in Helsinki, where only one 50-bed night shelter remains. Every week on the streets of England in recent years, three people die because they have nowhere safe to sleep. The BBC reported that Finland was 'the only EU state not suffering from a housing crisis, which is the result of Finland's Housing First initiative which started in 2008'. The report continued: '… in Finland housing is seen as a right, not as a reward, as it often is in other EU countries. The Finnish system is financed by public funds and Finnish slot machines',[3] and the government is considering using new (including online) gambling taxes and licences as well. Finland is abandoning transitional and temporary housing for the homeless. Instead, they are given a normal apartment, immediately.

However, as news spreads of Finland's success across so many areas of public life, there is a risk of success fatigue setting in, of Finns resting on their laurels, and of people who would like lower taxes proclaiming that enough has already been achieved. On the other hand, success also encourages success, and Finland has a reputation to maintain. As a small nation, Finland inevitably pays a lot of attention to its rankings. Finns are aware of the country's prominent position in such measures, and the Foreign Ministry shares news of its success frequently via social media.

Its high rankings help draw attention to the value of Finnish institutions. The current government tends to speak of restoring honour to the Finnish education system (by investing once again, rather than cutting). In a more theoretical sense, happiness or achievement is always relative; you value good times more when you've had bad times. In one of his best-known works, Eino Leino, a pioneer of Finnish poetry in the late 19th and early 20th century, wrote 'he who has happiness, should hide it'. Jukka Ukkola, whose columns in the weekly newspaper *Suomen Kuvalehti* are typically satirical, quoted this line when Finland was first proclaimed the world's happiest country, and joked that because Finns can no longer hide their happiness, they should learn to market it. As with the PISA [Programme for International Student Assessment] educational rankings, he suggested, perhaps researchers will soon start arriving to ask how Finland has become so happy.

An image of the five women leading the parties that formed the coalition in Finland was widely circulated in a tweet that 'went viral' when Sanna Marin became prime minister on 10 December 2019.[4] People around the world immediately commented on

---

[3] Hannah Price (2018) *BBC Three*, 10 October, https://www.youtube.com/watch?v=yKrZIYBF7ks

[4] Original collage reported by Tuomas Nisakangas, journalist and writer including at Helsingin Sanomat, see: https://twitter.com/TNiskakangas/status/1203729511658995713

all five coalition leaders being women and four being in their early thirties. Four of the five remained in 2021; Katri Kulmuni resigned as deputy prime minister in June 2020 and as Centre Party leader in September. She was replaced in the latter role by Annika Saarikko, who is also female and in her thirties.

The good news for the rest of the world is that Finland will not always be at the top of the rankings, because its achievements are not an unobtainable extreme. In Finland, as elsewhere, there are always things that could be better. And Finland has only a fairly modest amount of natural resources, no unusual historical advantages, no innate national characteristic, no special trick or magic formula to account for its current position.

To treat each other with respect is to be human; not to do so is inhumane. All of us are capable of both. By choosing the right path more often when there was an option, Finland has shown that any nation could do as well. And by doing so well it achieves so much else as a by-product of greater equality.

Progress, it is often said, is the battle to remember in a time of forgetting, including remembering some lessons learned over a century ago. Finland's equality was not a gift given by the profits from natural resources, or the spoils of an empire. Finland does not have Sweden's larger population and legacy of imperial wealth, nor does it have the petroleum riches of Norway. It cannot use geothermal activity to smelt aluminium as in Iceland, or use its proximity to the rest of Europe to its advantage, as Denmark does. Nor did Finland have equality imposed upon it, as was the case in Japan, and to a lesser extent in Germany, after 1945.

Many of the policies fundamental to Finland's success have come out of compromise. One of the first major interventions by the state into social and health services was accomplished many decades ago, with the 1937 Maternity Grants Act, by a government made up of the Social Democratic Party and the Agrarian League (now the Centre Party) – the country's first left–right coalition in decades (and dubbed a 'red-mud coalition'). Even before this, the land reforms passed into law immediately after the bloody civil war of 1918 had enabled the rural proletariat to purchase small holdings of land. The reforms required the Social Democratic Party to drop its opposition to private ownership, and the bourgeois parties to accept that parts of larger estates would have to be sold off.

By no means did Finns quickly forget the deep divisions of the civil war, but, as author Kjell Westö explains, Finns were pragmatic and worked together despite a history of both internal conflict and oppression from outside. Policies that emerge from compromise between parties of different ideological stripes can end up being broader, stronger and more innovative than those forged by any single political party. Problematic elements of how a society is organised, such as maintaining segregation in education, can then be discarded when empirical support emerges for action, as comprehensive education reform following Finland's 1968 Basic Education Act illustrated.

Finns were no doubt influenced by what was occurring elsewhere in the world, not least the radicalism in the US, and to a lesser extent in the UK, France and Germany, in the 1960s. Finland's most significant student protests in that era, which are not widely known outside of the country, occurred in 1968 when the Old Student House in Helsinki was occupied. While it may be overstating the case to suggest that Finland had a 'summer of love', nevertheless young Finns travelled and brought home new perspectives. From the 1960s onwards, a vision of what the greater welfare state could achieve became a widely shared dream. That dream became a reality through establishing common ground and common agendas between political left and right. This alliance helped all of Finnish politics to (in fits and starts) drift leftwards.

It was also during the 1960s that Finnish activists created the anti-authoritarian November Movement, which advocated for stigmatised peoples, among them disabled people, LGBTQI+ (referred to in Finland as 'rainbow people'), prisoners, alcoholics, the mentally ill and the homeless. The movement's goal was to reduce the pressure for uniformity in society.

Viewed from a British or American standpoint, a Finnish conservative today is likely to look very much like a socialist. Finland avoided the alternative that often arises when social democrats are dominant for a time and introduce a more wishy-washy form of welfare state, ripe for easy erosion. Instead, the left in Finland in the 1960s and 1970s managed to establish in the national mindset the idea of social investments. From there, the idea of investing in people entered the normal practice of the National Coalition Party, the country's moderate right. Finland's investment in universally good schooling, health insurance and the only genuinely comprehensive safety-net housing system in Europe, was not seen as social transfers from rich to poor, but as sound macroeconomic policy. The Finns are, above all, pragmatic.

The Finnish welfare state developed through consensus; it has never been an idea owned by a single party. However, in the past few decades, parties on the right (by Finnish standards), such as the National Coalition Party, have called for greater outsourcing and privatisation. Under the banner of offering greater choice and decision-making capabilities to citizens, this would represent an ever-so-small step towards the US model for healthcare and other services and away from the aims and norms of welfare state provision.

Finland may be the pre-eminent model of the Nordic welfare state, but there are Finns who find fault with that model. They might well point out that, until very recently, Finland had been moving away from it, and, they might argue, for good reasons. The government in power in Finland until early 2019 had made changes reminiscent of the British, or in some cases the US, model. These changes included attempts to further outsource healthcare services, and levying fees for university tuition for non-EU students, unlike, say, in Germany, where university education remains essentially free for all.

Although Finland is still to a very large extent the exemplar Nordic welfare state, the foundations of those ideals have recently been under attack. This would not have happened had all been well in paradise, or if those outside of Finland had not wanted to change the direction in which it was going. In recent years right-wing think-tanks in the UK and the US have been targeting Finland, as have far-right parties and politicians who hate and fear the Nordic model. Many of those think-tanks are almost certainly largely funded by US businesses and billionaires, but they claim to present independent research and their funders hide behind a veil of anonymity.[5]

---

5 Adam Ramsay and Peter Geoghegan (2018) 'Revealed: how the UK's powerful right-wing think tanks and Conservative MPs work together',

In the not-so distant past, and still occasionally today, some far-right and extreme-right groups have lauded Scandinavia as the home of the 'White race'. The notion of the true Aryan home of the White master race is an extreme fantasy that never quite goes away. Because eugenic practices, including the sterilisation of those deemed unworthy to have children, were permitted in Sweden – right through to the 1970s – Scandinavians have partly lived up to their bit-part in this fantasy. Thankfully, however, Scandinavians and the Finns then looked out to the rest of the world. They saw the criticism of eugenics and reacted. Just as importantly, they saw how society could be arranged otherwise, especially when children are not allocated to schools based on eugenic assumptions about inherent ability.

Due in part to recent policy proposals running counter to established Finnish practice, such as the previous government's plans for privatisation, the more left-wing parties now in power have become steadily more vocal in their opposition to conservative economic policies. Their positions are far more critical than those heard from, for example, today's UK Labour Party, and are emphatically far to the left of the US Democratic Party. Today Finland is arguably the antithesis of what the world's political right admires, and the government elected in 2019 is moving Finland again in the direction of greater equality.

Inequality and tax

Improving competitiveness in global markets is currently high on the Finnish political agenda, just as it was in the post-war reconstruction era. Finland is not just aiming for international competitiveness in economic terms, but achieving it with due concern for its social values and institutions.

In a country with significantly higher taxes, but little wage stagnation and much lower income inequality than, for example, the UK, Finland's political parties rarely emphasise social transfers from the rich to the poor as their fundamental aim. Instead, they

---

Open Democracy, 31 July, https://www.opendemocracy.net/en/dark-money-investigations/revealed-how-uk-s-powerful-right-wing-think-tanks-and-conse/

focus on how health, housing, education and financial security benefit the whole community, not just the present recipients. This is easier to achieve in a parliamentary democracy where compromise and consensus are essential and there is widespread use of public services, than it is in countries where two-party systems prevail. Ideas such as transfers from the rich to the poor being beneficial to all don't sell as well in countries where people have not seen the results of such choices.

Wealth inequality has been increasing in Finland and is higher than income inequality, which, despite a small increase since 2017, has remained relatively low and stable after a rise at the end of the 1990s. Wealth inequality is probably greater than official measurements indicate, given the wealth that is hidden in tax havens, and it has become more difficult to measure accurately since the abolition of the wealth tax. But if inequality is considered from the perspective of post-tax national income, then the share of the richest 1 per cent decreased from the year 2002 (when it was 7.2 per cent) to 2016 (6.1 per cent).

Finland's high levels of happiness and contentment can be understood partly in relation to accepted social norms and expectations of what is possible in Finnish society. These norms are good, due to excellent public services and low levels of inequality, particularly in comparison to conditions prevailing today in all other countries, including most other affluent societies. We know that Finns are happy and contented with their lives, although they are often disinclined to show it. Public displays of emotion of any kind are rare. The humour is dry. This may be part historical, reflecting the former dominance of Russia and Sweden, and has now become cultural. It is also possible that both Finns' reserve and their contentment makes funding excellent public services easier, as higher taxes are more accepted.

Today employees in Finland still contribute some of the world's highest proportion of personal income in tax. In 2016, when the take in income of Finland's richest 1 per cent was less than 6 per cent of the country's total (compared with 15 per cent in the UK and 22 per cent in the US), the tax collected from personal incomes in Finland made up 13 per cent of GDP. In Chile, one of the rich world's most unequal countries, it amounts to just 1.8 per cent of GDP by OECD estimates. As the mass protests and police repression of late 2019 demonstrated, the burden of Chile's economic travails has long been falling most heavily on its badly paid, indebted and politically voiceless majority. When income is more evenly spread, overall taxation is far more effective, public services can be far better, and civil unrest is very rare.

A huge proportion of Finns, 79 per cent, say they are 'happy to pay their taxes'.[6] An astonishing 96 per cent agree that 'it's important to collect tax to maintain the welfare state'. The tax bills of everyone in Finland are public documents, although individuals earning above €100,000 ($119,000) a year can, as of 2019, opt out of their tax information being released on the list of high-income earners provided to the media (4,400 such requests were successful in 2020). Individual tax records remain public, but this list facilitates the media's commentary on income and wealth distribution. This publicity has made it harder to hide corruption and tax evasion. In an equitable country with well-run public services, tax avoidance is rightly seen as no different from shoplifting.

Trust in journalism – and critical thinking

Part of how Finland avoids success fatigue is the robustness of its press. Former UK Labour Party leader Ed Miliband has been a passionate campaigner on climate change and helped steer his political party to becoming both greener and more democratic, with every party member having the opportunity to vote for the next party leader. As a result, Britain now has a far more Finnish-style party in its Labour Party than it would have had if it were not for Miliband; but he was often subjected to personal attacks in place of criticisms of his policies. His successor, Jeremy Corbyn, was attacked even more relentlessly, and in particular during the 2019 election, where he was misrepresented and demonised by both privately owned media and the state-owned BBC.

---

6 Kate Whiting (2018) 'Finland publishes everyone's taxes on "National Jealousy Day"', *World Economic Forum Agenda*, 2 November, https://www.weforum.org/agenda/2018/11/finland-has-just-published-everyone-s-taxes-on-national-jealousy-day/

It is true that the Labour Party has recently proposed some policies that would be too left-wing for Finland. For instance, in November 2019 it proposed nationalising the largest broadband company in the UK and providing free broadband for all. However, it is more often the case that Labour's policies, including most of those when Corbyn was leader, are significantly to the right of Finnish public policy; in its 2019 election manifesto, Labour proposed raising spending on public services, but only to German levels, rather than those of Finland. You would know little of this from reading the British press.

Featured on Ed Miliband's podcast 'Reasons to be Cheerful', Vesa Häkkinen, the director of current affairs communications at Finland's Ministry for Foreign Affairs, spoke of the anti-disinformation campaign launched in Finland in 2014. The campaign encourages critical thinking and awareness to increase people's ability to spot fake news, from training election officials to reforming the education curriculum. When Miliband asked at what age Finnish children were educated about identifying disinformation, Häkkinen mentioned seeing a children's television show featuring a teddy bear that was critical of the news during its adventures. To prevent cynicism rising, a reputable press and a well-informed citizenry are both vital.

According to Reporters Without Borders, Finland scores highly in global freedom of the press; in first place in 2015 (see Figure 6.15), fourth place in 2018, and second place in 2019. Finns typically see press freedom and responsibility as a more serious matter than do citizens of other states.[7] Finland is in the minority of countries where freedom of the press is characterised as good. In 2018, Presidents Vladimir Putin and Donald Trump, arriving for a summit in Helsinki, were greeted with billboards and posters created by Finland's highest-circulation daily newspaper, *Helsingin Sanomat*, welcoming them to the 'land of free press'.

---

[7] Dominic Ponsford (2017) 'Survey finds that UK written press is (by some way) the least trusted in Europe', *The Press Gazette*, 26 May, https://pressgazette.co.uk/publishers/nationals/survey-finds-that-uk-written-press-is-by-some-way-the-least-trusted-in-europe/

Figure 6.15: Trust in journalism, 2015–16, leading countries – the net trust index rankings

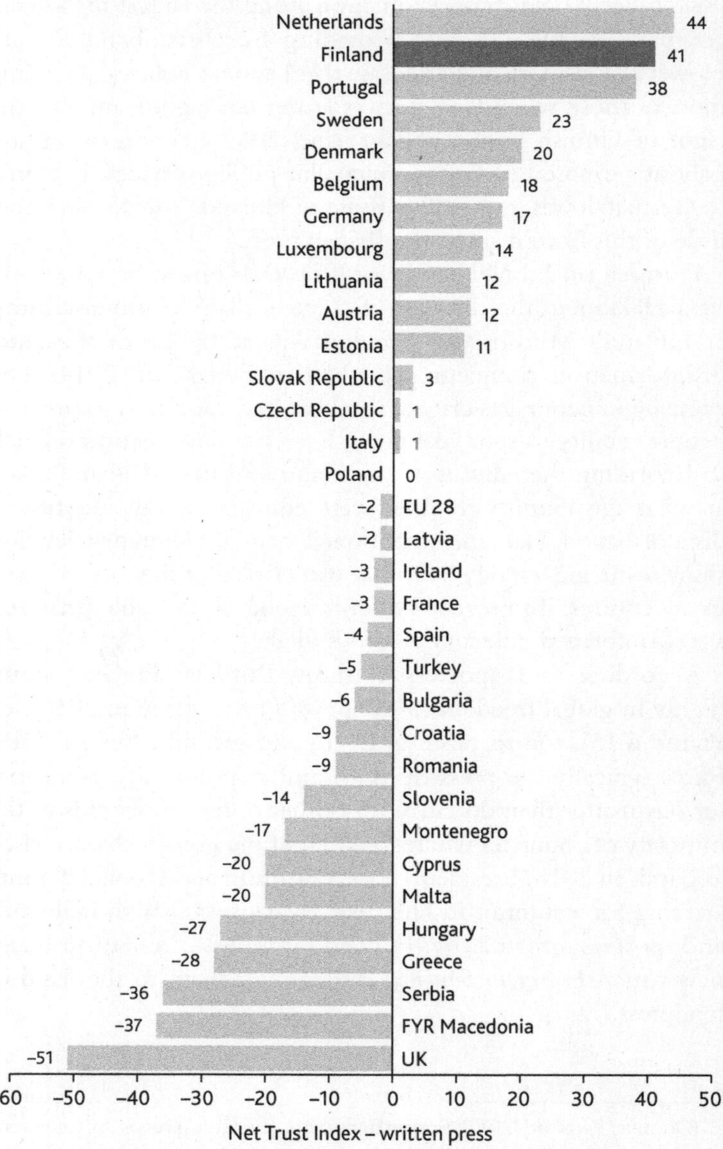

Source: Dominic Ponsford (2017) 'Survey finds that UK written press is (by some way) the least trusted in Europe', *The Press Gazette*, 26 May.

Even in Finland, though, things could be better. A concern raised by the Centre for Media Pluralism and Media Freedom's annual *Media Pluralism Monitor* is the concentration of media ownership in Finland, and the lack of government regulation of that ownership.[8] The centre's 2017 report found that the four largest companies in Finland's television-broadcasting sector together claimed a 92 per cent audience share and 72 per cent of revenues; in radio the figures were 94 per cent and 87 per cent respectively; and in the newspaper market they were 55 per cent and 71 per cent, respectively. Another concern raised by the report is the lack of proportional access to airtime by Finland's minorities.

Media ownership became even more concentrated in February 2020 when media conglomerate Sanoma acquired another major media company, Alma Media. Although concerns were raised over the decreased media pluralism, the deal was not considered a significant risk to competition in the media market by the Finnish Competition and Consumer Authority.

Universal basic income

When we think of Finland as a role model for other countries, one frequently cited idea is universal basic income (UBI). Universal basic income could represent a major shift in the welfare state model of the West. Pilot experiments have recently been run in the city of Seattle and the Canadian province of Ontario, and in 2016 the Finnish government launched a basic income experiment involving 2,000 participants. UBI is not the only proposal for reforming social security in Finland, however, and most of the country's political parties have their own models.

The first Finnish basic income trial, which ran from 2017 to 2018 and was targeted rather than universal, was initiated in response to the changing nature of work and the fact that

8 Elda Brogi, Iva Nenadic, Pier Luigi Parcu and Mario Viola de Azevedo Cunha (2018) 'Monitoring Media Pluralism in Europe: Application of the Media Pluralism Monitor 2017 in the European Union, Former Yugoslavian Republic of Macedonia, Serbia & Turkey', European University Institute: Centre for Media Pluralism and Media Freedom, https://cmpf.eui.eu/wp-content/uploads/2018/11/CMPF_MPM2017_FINAL_REPORT.pdf

a greater proportion of the population are now employed in temporary and part-time jobs. The participants, who were unemployed when they began the trial, received a basic income of €560 ($665) every month for two years regardless of any other income and whether or not they were actively seeking work. The trial aimed to assess whether the existing social security system could be simplified, and whether the alternative basic income system encouraged employability, since existing benefits diminish on starting paid employment or on receipt of other sources of income. The theory was that because basic income payments alone are not necessarily sufficient to cover all living costs (such as holidays) in the long term, UBI would not discourage recipients from finding work. One participant, journalist and writer Tuomas Muraja, responded to critics of the experiments saying:

> Concerns have been voiced about the high cost of the basic income model. But free school meals, free basic education and universal basic healthcare are expensive too… The system requires more investment to boost the minimum income level, to improve the level of financial incentives and to simplify it. Critics fear that basic income will make people lazy. However, limited evidence from several basic-income trials from around the world prove that people use basic income to improve their quality of life and not as a license to do nothing.[9]

The results published in 2019 showed that the intervention did not increase the number of people who found employment, but neither did it reduce it.[10] Some attributed this to the design of the experiment; but even with these results, Rutger Bregman argued

---

[9] Tuomas Muraja (2018) 'Universal basic income hasn't made me rich. But my life is more enriching', *The Guardian*, 7 August, https://www.theguardian.com/commentisfree/2018/aug/07/universal-basic-income-rich-finland-work-benefits

[10] Sigal Samuel (2019) 'Finland gave people free money. It didn't help them get jobs – but does that matter?' *Vox*, 9 February, https://www.vox.com/future-perfect/2019/2/9/18217566/finland-basic-income

that other outcomes of the study warranted attention – namely, that participants reported higher levels of well-being, less stress and greater overall happiness.[11]

The experiment was criticised on the basis that, in addition to including unemployed youth, the pool of participants was limited to primarily the long-term unemployed who would benefit more from services to help with health issues or outdated skills rather than from financial incentives. In addition, taxation was not taken into account, and halfway through the experiment the 'activation model' was introduced, which skewed comparisons with the control group – that is, everyone else who was unemployed.

One thing worth bearing in mind about the early results of the trial is that increasing employment need not be a major aim of UBI. If people in Europe are to consume less, and pollute less, then they need to also produce less and learn to live on lower incomes than they currently do. A basic income makes it possible to spend your time doing what you really want to do, including useful unpaid work. If you need a little more money, you can work, but it need not be high-paid work. If Finland is to remain one of the happiest countries in the world, it won't be because everyone works for as many hours as they can, for as much money as they can get.

One day ...

One day, a country will provide a basic income to everyone. Finland may not be the first to do so, but it will experiment further and remains very open to similar new ideas. Many people say that UBI is unaffordable. But how much more unaffordable is it than the practice in the UK and especially the US of keeping large numbers of people in overcrowded prisons, with plans to build more prisons and calls for more and longer sentences? A universal basic income would not be compatible with wasting money on antisocial policies such as these. It would, however, be compatible with massive reductions in carbon emissions, as those who chose to consume less would be able to. They would

[11] Rutger Bregman (2020) *Humankind: A hopeful history*, Little, Brown & Co (advance copy read pre-publication).

not have to drive to work if they chose not to work, and a basic income means exactly what it says – basic. A universal basic income is only unaffordable if you think it is necessary for some to go hungry, cold and homeless to keep many of the rest of us at the grindstone of paid employment, much of which is of little ultimate benefit to society.

One day, a country will have no need for prisons; and Finland already has very few prisoners. People find the idea of no prisons strange, because when it is suggested, they think of a future society that is just like their current society, but without jails. However, as Alice Speri, a journalist based in the Bronx in the US, explains:

> in a society that is tackling things like white supremacy, economic deprivation, toxic masculinity, and that is providing connections between people, and where communities are responsible for each other, I actually don't think it would be weird at all [not to have prisons]. You wouldn't even need the things that we now think of as elemental parts of our society, like the local jail.[12]

One day, a country will have no homeless people. Finland is very nearly that country.

One day, no one will die prematurely. This utopian vision is at least two centuries old. In Western countries it is best remembered through the words of mill owner Robert Owen, and his address to the inhabitants of New Lanark in Scotland on New Year's Day 1816:

> What ideas individuals may attach to the term 'Millennium' I know not; but I know that society may be formed so as to exist without crime, without poverty, with health greatly improved, with little, if any misery, and with intelligence and happiness increased a

[12] Alice Speri (2019) 'The criminal justice system is not broken. it's doing what it was designed to do', *The Intercept*, 9 November, https://theintercept.com/2019/11/09/criminal-justice-mass-incarceration-book/

> hundredfold; and no obstacle whatsoever intervenes at this moment except ignorance to prevent such a state of society from becoming universal.[13]

Finland is not Utopia and its people know that there is still much that could be better. However, they also know that they live under a flexible system in a pragmatic country that will permit better ways to be found and further improvements to be made. Knowing that things are going to get better, especially for the less well-off, is often more important than how the situation is today. We will always worry, but we also need to be able to hope.

Finland's recent history can give us all hope. On 20 March 2020 it was announced – for the third year in succession – that Finland was once again the happiest country in the world. The report in which this was declared included a chapter dedicated to the Nordic countries that concluded:

> There seems to be no secret sauce specific to Nordic happiness that is unavailable to others. There is rather a more general recipe for creating highly satisfied citizens: ensure that state institutions are of high quality, non-corrupt, able to deliver what they promise, and generous in taking care of citizens in various adversities.

We should learn more about how and why the Finnish recipe works in practice – because it urgently needs to be made more widely available.

---

[13] See Chapter 2.8 in this volume.

CHAPTER 6.6

Dyslexia and the problem with pride[1]

Dyslexia, for me, is a problem of pride, mine and others'. I work in academia. Many academics are understandably proud of the fact that they can write well and construct sentences carefully, and that they have mastered the rules of grammar. It is a part of their job that gives them quiet satisfaction, I think. I often receive emails that have been well crafted and display the authority with words that the sender has, and I am not complaining about that. But I know that even if I take a great deal of time over what I send, it will not have quite the same effect (or is it affect)?

I often hear people make remarks about the standard of student essays. Or about a paper they are reviewing, written by someone for whom English is not their first language, or at least does not appear to be their first language. Being able to write well and read quickly is often taken as a necessary but not sufficient basis to be a part of the humanities or social sciences at university. At the same time, often the same people are very happy to put up some numbers at a departmental meeting and say that because they are not numerate, they really do not understand them, as if only some 'geeks' can count. Self-deprecation is allowed with numeracy but not with literacy.

'When I was five I was just alive,' wrote A.A. Milne in 1927. When I was five, in 1973, I first went to school. I had a teacher who was very caring. She was so caring that she cut badges out of balsa wood for all her pupils. It must have taken her hours

---

[1] First published as Danny Dorling (2012) 'The problem with pride', RASP (*Rebelling Against Spelling Press*), 8 October, and reposted in 2019: https://www.dyslexicacademic.com/post/dyslexia-and-the-problem-with-pride

with the jigsaw. She painted each badge brightly using enamel paint that shone when it reflected the light. My badge was a red elephant and I sat on the table with the other children with elephant badges; all pinned to our shirts or jumpers. We were slow and plodding. I used to wonder what it took to where (sorry 'wear') a blue busy beaver badge and be on the table for the fastest six children. I can't remember all the animals and colours in between; but I still know several of the children on those two tables at that one small school – the slowest and the quickest.

It was when my younger brother overtook me in reading, and then my next younger brother, Ben, overtook me as well, that I began to realise I was a little bit slow. Ben was unusually quick with words. He later won prizes for poetry. I won prizes for maths. That got me through, along with a mother who, when I was eight, made me read a page of a children's book a day for every day of the summer holidays. By the end I was no longer the only child who could not read in the class. I was also lucky that I went to normal schools with a wide range of children in them. You don't stand out as much in a normal school.

I went into the wrong business really. But I like ideas, and I now like to write. The problem is that what I write is not actually what I think it is. It takes a long time and the help of quite a few others to turn it into something you can understand (it always makes sense to me). Between me writing this, and you reading it, more than one person is likely to have helpfully intervened (I have learnt to ask for a great deal of help). It also becomes easier with years and years of practice. My parents didn't tell me that they thought I had a problem with writing until 1991, after I had submitted my PhD. They had corrected seven drafts of it, which I now realise is not usual. The year I first published this short story on a very obscure website, in 2012, my PhD thesis was published as a book: *The Visualization of Spatial Social Structure*, all about how we see things and can draw pictures of things we cannot see. It is a book of many pictures and not so many words that were mine (there are a great deal of quotations in that book)!

In my family some children find words very hard. Some find them ever so easy. I watch a family member struggle and I get it. I know exactly why it makes absolutely no sense that we spell things like we do. I watch a young child I am related to read, and it is like watching magic at work. The child asks if I can check his spelling, and I cannot because already he can spell some words better than I can. He is aged six – I am in my fifties. Spellcheckers help, but you write toady instead of today and quite instead of quiet and you worry that people might think that you are being lazy and don't really care when you send them messages that are full of errors; the spellcheckers do not help that much at all.

Some people can be too proud of being able to write well and other people can worry too much about their pride in admitting that they find writing and reading very hard and extremely tiring. Being able to think in clear and imaginative ways is very different from being able to write in a clear and entertaining style. I wanted to tell that six-year-old child how proud I was that he was so good at words, but I am just as proud of the other older one, struggling through his homework, avoiding being where I was; not being labelled as the slowest. Not made to stand on a chair by a teacher in an English class at age ten because I was 'not trying hard enough'. A lot has changed; I suspect that English teacher had no idea why some children found reading and writing harder, in the late 1970s in Oxford. But that is all I remember about that one teacher. Other teachers were much kinder.

Above all else, I think I should not have to be proud at all. I should know that the next generation will be safe, whether they find using words as easy as a tightrope walker finds walking on a rope, or whether they fall off the minute they try to construct a sentence in this strange, garbled language of English where there is no reason why piece is spelt peace or board is not bored. Even if you have the letters the right way around (or round or rowned) you can still easily have the wrong word. And then they tell you every sentence needs a verb ...

We should be proud of what we do when we do something useful and what we have to say when that thing is worthwhile and what we have done when it helps, not about the way we have learnt to say it. Being proud of writing well is not dissimilar to being proud of having a cut-glass accent or of thinking that you look ever so good as you are talking. It is the content that matters over the style. The style can make the reading easier on the eye, but it is a surface thing, it is not substance.

If you can devour a novel in an evening and if, for you, words tip off the end of your fingers effortlessly, then it is hard to understand why some people find it so hard to read and write. Don't be proud of it; just count yourself lucky. And ask others not to look down on you for what you find harder, because we all have weaknesses – everyone does.

Conclusion: What ten things can we do?

The final section of this book suggested that, at the peak of injustice and in the fog of confusion, you cannot easily see the road ahead that leads back down. This mountain may seem as though it will never end, but there is a route down that is signposted 'hope', even if there is not much sign of hope in the UK today.

As I write, in early 2024, there are attempts to restore a functional government in Northern Ireland; it may come back fully into normal operation this year, it may fall apart again. That is just one of the many legacies of Brexit. I have not written much about the many other Brexit legacies in this book, but have done elsewhere, including on how the fallout of Brexit is continuing to make Scottish independence more likely and is leading to rising disillusionment in Wales.[1]

There are two other great omissions in these pages. Firstly, I have said very little about the pandemic that reached the UK in early 2020; what we learned about ourselves in terms of how we reacted to it; and how we still – even years later – don't really appreciate who was most affected (Figure 7.1).

The new disease spread in different ways as compared to past pandemics.[2] Its initial breakout was led by the better-off business people and tourists, both within China,[3] and into and across

---

1 See: Danny Dorling (2023) *Brexit: A failed project in a failing state*, London: Friedrich Ebert Stiftung, 25 October, https://www.anothereurope.org/report-brexit-a-failed-project-in-a-failing-state/

2 Danny Dorling (2020) '3 graphs that show a global slowdown in COVID-19 deaths', *The Conversation*, 7 April.

3 Qiujie Shi, Danny Dorling, Guangzhong Cao and Tao Liub (2020) 'Changes in population movement make COVID-19 spread differently from SARS',

Figure 7.1: Deaths per week by age due to the pandemic, wave 1 in England and Wales

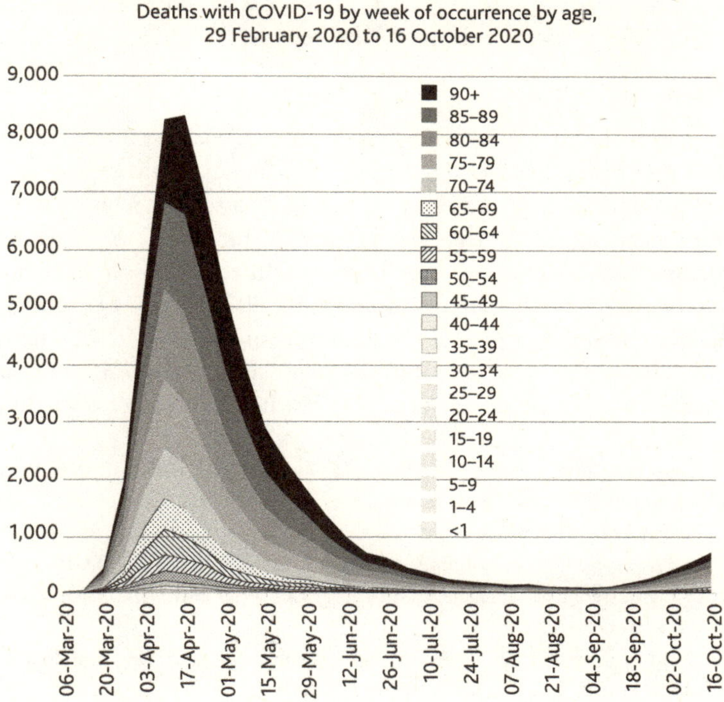

Source: Drawn by the author from data released by the Office for National Statistics; men and women combined.

Europe.[4] We knew little about the disease despite it being a variant of the common cold.[5] In the summer of 2020 we were not sure that there would be a second wave.[6] Perhaps many people

Social Science and Medicine, Vol. 255, available online 15 May, 113036, doi: 10.1016/j.socscimed.2020.113036.

4 Danny Dorling (2020) '3 graphs show where the coronavirus death rate is heading', *The Conversation*, 27 April.

5 Danny Dorling (2020) 'Why aren't death rates rising with case numbers?', *The Conversation*, 9 September.

6 Danny Dorling (2020) 'Why coronavirus death rates won't fall as quickly as they rose', *The Conversation*, 5 June.

had acquired immunity?[7] Perhaps more in the south of England had?[8] These were fractious and confused times.[9] By late 2020 we realised it was not going away, no matter what we then did, and despite vaccination coming.[10] The second wave, in early 2021, was in many places worse than the first.[11]

By 2022 it became obvious that this would be a long-running pandemic, coming back again and again but with far fewer deaths after the first two waves due both to repeat vaccination of the old and growing acquired immunity being boosted by re-infections among everyone.[12] But we also knew that the official inquiry, that continues as I write, was too limited in its scope to uncover the full extent of the injustices suffered.[13] By 2023, a fifth of children ('ghost children') were still regularly missing school.[14] Parliament had debated these ghost children a year earlier, but its attempts at intervention had been ineffective.[15] We need to learn how other

---

7 Danny Dorling, Anthony Brookes and George Davey Smith (2020) 'Why are coronavirus rates rising in some areas of England and not others?', *The Conversation*, 1 October.

8 Danny Dorling and George Davey Smith (2020) 'Why is COVID-19 more severe in the north of England? The story in four graphs', *The Conversation*, 2 December.

9 Danny Dorling (2020) 'Is the cure worse than the disease? The most divisive question of 2020', *The Conversation*, 6 October.

10 Danny Dorling (2020) 'It's not going away: We need a real, non-political debate about the best way to live with COVID or countries will fracture', *Genetic Literacy Project: Science not ideology*, 12 October, https://geneticliteracyproject.org/2021/09/10/its-not-going-away-we-need-a-real-non-political-debate-about-the-best-way-to-live-with-covid-or-countries-will-fracture/

11 Danny Dorling (2021) 'The City of Oxford and the pandemic', *The Oxford Magazine*, 432, 22 April, pp. 11–12.

12 Danny Dorling (2022) 'The never-ending pandemic', *Social Europe*, 12 April.

13 Lu Hiam and Danny Dorling (2022) 'The end of great expectations? The pandemic inquiry must account for stalling life expectancy before the pandemic', Editorial, *British Medical Journal*, 6 May.

14 Andre Rhoden-Paul (2023) 'One in five children regularly misses school, figures show', *BBC News*, 3 September, https://www.bbc.co.uk/news/uk-66701748

15 Education Committee (2022) 'Government must act on "ghost children" missing from education system', House of Commons News Article, 25 May, https://committees.parliament.uk/committee/203/education-committee/

countries made the right call in early 2020 and allowed their children quickly back to school. Working-class children suffered the most from being denied access to schools.[16]

The issues remain emotive. Across Europe people are still trying to assess what the political, economic and social effects of the ongoing pandemic are.[17] And so that work continues, now looking back to the past to see when and how this happened before, and with what possible long-term effects.[18] It would be remarkable if what the Director General of the World Health Organization described as the most traumatic event to have occurred worldwide since World War Two does not have many implications that – as yet – we cannot clearly see. But new traumas arise, with the low-level 2014–22 war between two superpowers escalating in Europe following the Russian invasion in February 2022. Now Ukraine has become the name of a war that goes on and on, and nuclear war is imagined as a possibility again. And then, no further away from the UK than the Ukraine–Russian border, the killing in Gaza quickly rose to the highest levels seen anywhere in the world in all of the first quarter of the twenty-first century.[19]

The second, far greater, omission from this book is what has quickly become widely understood, worldwide, to be the greatest

news/171073/government-must-act-on-ghost-children-missing-from-education-system/

16 Staff reporter (2020) 'Coronavirus: Denmark lets young children return to school', *BBC News*, 15 April, https://www.bbc.co.uk/news/world-europe-52291326

17 Danny Dorling (2023) 'From the pandemic to the cost-of-living crisis – what are we learning?', in Kalina Arabadjieva, Nicola Countouris, Bianca Luna Fabris and Wouter Zwysen (eds), *Transformative ideas: Ensuring a just share of progress for all*, Brussels: European Trade Union Institute (ETUI), ch 1.

18 George Davey Smith and Danny Dorling (2023) 'Revisiting the point-source hypothesis of the coronary heart disease epidemic in light of the COVID-19 pandemic', presented at the Society of Epidemiologic Research annual meeting, Portland, Oregon, US, 14 June; a record is held on the Oxford Research Archive: https://ora.ox.ac.uk/objects/uuid:12849f9e-ffdd-40af-8b69-1250285dc2a6

19 David Nieto (2024) 'Daily death rate in Gaza higher than any other major 21st century conflict', *Oxfam International*, Jerusalem, 11 January, https://www.oxfam.org/en/press-releases/daily-death-rate-gaza-higher-any-other-major-21st-century-conflict-oxfam

injustice of 2024. Its origins stretch far back before 2023, to the intifada of the 1980s which continued into the 1990s, and the intifada of the 2000s; back to the Nakba of 15 May 1948; and to Britain's Balfour Declaration of 2 November 1917, and yet further back again.[20]

With an eye on history, on 26 January 2024, the International Court of Justice gave its first ruling:

> The highest court in the world, the apex of the United Nations, has found there is a plausible risk that Palestinians' right to be protected from a genocide are under threat from Israel's actions. … For the global south, and for South Africa in particular, this is a famous victory, a moment that will be remembered for decades to come. The plight of the Palestinian people in Gaza was recounted in open court and believed.[21]

It is unlikely that you do not know why the words used by the highest court in the world mattered so much in its first judgment of 2024. I have been told, to my face, that it is an *indulgence* to worry about such things given all the problems that the UK faces.

But why should we in Britain expect our politicians to care about people in Britain if they have so little regard for international law and for the consequences of our actions on people living overseas?

As *The Guardian* reported, the judgment of the highest court in the world 'also presents a test for Israel's allies, particularly the US and the UK'.[22] What that newspaper did not go on to explain was that Israel's two greatest allies also have the worst records among rich world states for inequality and injustice where their own people are concerned. That is hardly likely to be a coincidence.

---

20 See https://en.wikipedia.org/wiki/Nakba_Day; and https://en.wikipedia.org/wiki/Balfour_Declaration

21 Patrick Wintour (2024) 'ICJ's Gaza decision shores up rules-based order and puts west to test', *The Guardian*, 26 January, https://www.theguardian.com/law/2024/jan/26/icj-gaza-decision-shores-up-rules-based-order-and-puts-west-to-test

22 Patrick Wintour (2024) (n. 21).

It is in the UK and the US that the height of their subjects' and citizens' children is now falling, and only in these two places (see Figure 5.1 on page 302). It is only in the UK and the US that life expectancy fell during the decade before the pandemic arrived. I could draw a diagram similar to Figure 7.1, but of deaths in Gaza. It would differ in that most of the deaths would be of children or very young adults, in that the weeks would become months and also in that, as yet, there is no downward trend in the curve of what the highest court in the world describes as an on-going plausible risk of genocide.[23]

In 2024, we in Britain are governed by a set of politicians who do not value human life as the majority of the people of the world and its top judges do, and given how our general elections are run, for most of us the only effective alternative choice is to vote for His Majesty's loyal opposition. From early 2020 onwards this became an opposition that expressed very similar sentiments to the 2019–24 British government. No wonder we are living with such injustice at home, if we are so willing to support such terrible injustices abroad.

What ten things could be suggested to think about when looking for a way down from the peak of the mountain of injustice? The following list begins with what is internationally recognised as the greatest current injustice today. It ends very much at home in the UK, by asking that we take a long hard look at ourselves.

1. Take international law seriously. Don't try to brush it off, suggesting that the rest of the world is wrong and the British and Americans are right. If you don't see and treat others as human, you too will begin to lose your humanity, compassion and kindness.

[23] If you compare this map – https://www.un.org/unispal/document/auto-insert-203247/ – with this diagram – https://upload.wikimedia.org/wikipedia/commons/e/ee/Bev%C3%B6lkerungspyramide_Gazastreifen_2016.png – then the cold demographic reality of why so many children were killed becomes obvious. For many years I have shown these images to children in British schools when explaining demography. It is hard to continue to do that now, but I do, because to suddenly pretend that Gaza does not exist would be an injustice.

2. We have to learn what our response to the pandemic told us about ourselves and those who govern us. This includes the reaction of many of us to Boris Johnson's complaint: 'Why are we destroying [the] economy for people who will die anyway soon?'.[24] Most, incidentally, would not have died that soon.
3. Why are we the first and only state to have fully left the European Union? Do we really know why we did it? You might want to suggest that one of the ten things we should do is work out how to start to repair the damage but, first, we need to know why we caused it.
4. What message should you take from the first section of this book, on 'The politics of hope'? I would suggest it could be that the entirely unexpected is possible, even probable. The 2017 general election showed that. Those who care are not alone. For example, Labour won an outright majority in parliament in 2024, but its Members of Parliament may not accept the austerity that its leadership tries to continue with, entirely private sector financed housebuilding programmes made possible by degrading planning regulations,[25] or bringing in enormous US corporations to run parts of the state[26] – all of which were mooted in the first week after that election victory.
5. We can eliminate the worst of child poverty within a year, should we wish to. The Scots did – see Chapter 2.8; thus, the unexpected and positive is entirely possible too.
6. Look at what other countries in Europe have achieved in reducing housing inequalities – especially as described in Chapter 3.6. Rather than being about a specific policy,

[24] Ben Quinn (2023) '"People will die anyway": Pressure on Boris Johnson over Covid messages', *The Guardian*, 30 October, https://www.theguardian.com/uk-news/2023/oct/30/boris-johnson-mad-if-he-did-not-think-whatsapps-would-become-public-civil-servant

[25] Faisal Islam and Daniel Thomas (2024) 'Reeves to bring back housebuilding targets', BBC, 8 July, https://www.bbc.co.uk/news/articles/ckkg2l1rpr4o

[26] Blackrock were among the corporations invited to attend when the Chancellor gave her first speech on 8 July 2024: see HM Treasury, Angela Rayner, Rachel Reeves and Ed Miliband (2024) 'Chancellor unveils a new era for economic growth', 8 July, https://www.gov.uk/government/news/chancellor-unveils-a-new-era-for-economic-growth

this is about having the will to act and seeing other people as human.

7. Realise just how easy it is to stoke up racism in the UK while thinking that we are ever so sophisticated and understanding, as explored in Section 4.
8. We are well on the way to destroying our National Health Service and cutting the local state back to a nightwatchman skeletal service. Patching will not be enough. We should know this. Any future government must take urgent steps to protect the NHS from further damage and to begin to restore the ethos of care over profit.[27]
9. Think about how much pride we tend to place on our past and our supposedly great institutions. It is time to recognise our past and our great institutions as not being as glorious as we so often suggest they are. We have only taken a few steps along that road so far – there is a very long way to go but we travel more quickly when we become more equal again.[28]
10. And, finally, please realise that policy proposals alone are not enough – not when you are at the terrible impasse the UK currently is at. There is a need for soul-searching and a sea-change which we have not had to properly address for a long time.

You will hear a great deal about how bad everything is in the coming months. You have heard it over the last few years, especially on hospitals, schools and housing.[29] However, what you will hear next will be worse. For example: 'It's hard to overstate the level of emergency that the housing crisis in Britain has become. … one in four voters are now affected by the housing emergency.'[30]

[27] Gavin Francis (2023) *Free for all: Why the NHS is worth saving*, London: Profile.

[28] Common Sense Policy Group featuring Kate Pickett, Richard Wilkinson, and Danny Dorling (2024) *Act now: A vision for a better future and a new contract*, Manchester: Manchester University Press.

[29] It is described in painful and personal detail in Danny Dorling (2024) *Seven children: Inequality and Britain's next generation*, London: Hurst.

[30] Polly Neate and Hannah Rich (2024) 'Housing: a system in meltdown', *Academy of Social Sciences Blog*, January, https://acss.org.uk/housing-a-system-in-meltdown/

Don't succumb to the suggestion that all of this is somehow inevitable. Many of us do not, and there are always new voices, new movements and new hopes. As was written about Dawn Foster, to whom this book is dedicated: 'She never got comfortable enough to forget that poverty is a political choice inflicted by those who don't live in it.'[31] Every injustice is the choice of a few people, made possible by the majority of us with means becoming comfortable and forgetting, and by most people having very little power, or money, or hope, at all.

So, I'll leave the last word to Dawn. In one of the final pieces she wrote shortly before she died, she explained that:

> Starmer shows little seriousness in his approach to various forms of racism. He's more concerned with winning back right-wing voters, briefing right-wing journalists, hand-wringing about excessive closeness to unions, and sacking left-wing MPs at the first opportunity. The problem is that in trying to win over right wingers, he risks completely alienating the many young left wingers who joined the party. And at the next election the party will find very few campaigners to knock on doors.[32]

When politicians fail to inspire young people and the rest of us with a vision of justice and a plan for a better tomorrow – when they focus only on winning – what will actually have been won if the winners are so soulless, so cynical, so lacking in hope, in heart or in courage?

We would not be at a peak of injustice if the circumstances were not this bad; and we will not get down from the mountain by carrying on along the same path that took us so far up it.

---

[31] Lynsey Hanley (2021) 'Remembering Dawn Foster', *Tribune Magazine*, 20 July, https://tribunemag.co.uk/2021/07/in-memory-of-dawn-foster

[32] Dawn Foster (2020) 'Keir Starmer is moving Labour even further to the right', *Jacobin*, 25 June, https://jacobin.com/2020/06/labour-party-rebecca-long-bailey-keir-starmer-police-antisemitism

Index

References to footnotes show the page number and the note number (388n6)

D

E

F

G

H

J

K

Q

R

S

T

U